The Story of the Western Wing

Wang Shifu

The Story of the Western Wing

Edited and translated with an introduction
by Stephen H. West and Wilt L. Idema

University of California Press
Berkeley   Los Angeles   London

University of California Press
Berkeley and Los Angeles, California

University of California Press, Ltd.
London, England

© 1995 by
The Regents of the University of California

Wang, Shih-fu, fl. 1295–1307
   [Hsi hsiang chi. English]
   The story of the western wing / Wang Shifu ; edited and translated
with an introduction by Stephen H. West and Wilt L. Idema.
      p. cm.
   Includes bibliographical references and index.
   ISBN 0–520–20184–1 (pbk. : alk. paper)
   I. West, Stephen H. II. Idema, W. L. (Wilt L.) III. Title.
   PL2693.H75E5 1995
   895.1'244--dc20   94–41014
                                           CIP

Contents

PREFACE

This book reprints the translation of the *Xixiang ji* and the introduction that accompanied its first publication in *The Moon and the Zither. The Story of the Western Wing* (Berkeley and Los Angeles: University of California Press, 1991). We have taken the opportunity to correct errors and infelicities found in the original. We would like to thank reviewers of *The Moon and the Zither* for pointing some of these out. Special thanks should go to Judith Boltz for her extensive comments. Practical considerations involved in producing the present book have led to the excision of Yao Dajuin's fine essay on woodblock illustration, "The Pleasure of Reading Drama: Illustrations to the Hongzhi Edition of *The Story of the Western Wing*," and the seventy accompanying plates which originally constituted Appendix III of *The Moon and the Zither*.

FOREWORD

For Chinese people of the past, of both sexes, all ages and all classes, the peak and pinnacle of romantic love was the union of the genius and the beauty, *caizi-jiaren*. The genius, *caizi*, is a young scholar; the beauty, *jiaren*, a girl in her teens, of good family and modest demeanor. The young scholar by definition is poor, quite possibly an orphan, in his early twenties, slender and pale with clear eyes and refined features. He wears a plain long gown and a close-fitting, square-cut black hat—an austere figure in contrast with the gaudily appareled rich young wastrels whose company he forswears and whose competition he despises. His companion, if any, is his bookboy, a young lad who bears the essential accoutrements of books, sword, and zither: our young scholar is virile enough to use the sword if he has to and has sufficient musical talent to provide his own spiritual sustenance through lonely evenings in the village inn or on the river boat. For he is on his way to the civil service examinations, where locked in a cell for days on end he will compose prose essays of flawless balance and impeccable erudition. The sweep of his vision of the nation's past history and current policies, the force of his logic, and the precision of his allusive style will place him first among all contestants, and his appointment to high office (and ultimate success therein) will follow as the night follows the day

But for the moment he has something else in mind, the lithe, enchanting grace of a slip of a girl he has glimpsed by chance—by chance, for she is not to be viewed by the common herd. She is no village maiden but the daughter of a gentry family, her father himself no doubt a former official of unchallenged probity and prestige. This worthy man has taken sufficient interest in her education to ensure that she has developed skills not only in needlework and allied feminine crafts but in calligraphy and painting also, and she has a pretty poetic talent that will make her a valued companion to her future husband and his guests. Meanwhile her delicate beauty blushes unseen, cloistered as she is in the rear courtyard of a high-walled mansion and closely guarded by a staff of nannies and maidservants, gatekeepers and gardeners and grooms.

Innumerable stories and plays celebrate the course of true love between these two. In mood and tone these entertainments run the gamut from awed adulation to cynical satire, from comedy to pathos, from the attenuated ideal to the earthy and erotic. Much ingenuity attends the first meeting, that initial skirmish with the guardianship of the virgin's treasure. Some unforeseen chance must bring heroine into the range of hero's vision. One possibility is indicated by the phrase "over the wall from horseback," which describes a situation in a ballad by the great Tang poet Bo Juyi and eventually provides the title for a superb Yuan dynasty romantic comedy by Bai Pu. The heroine of another play floats into the hero's astonished and delighted vision on a garden swing, as he stands gaping in the street outside. But more usually the young lady must somehow be extracted from her domestic prison for the encounter to occur. So, a journey is in progress or the company of ladies takes advantage of a festival to visit a local temple or (as in the combined circumstances of the present play) the temple is the place of temporary residence for the ladies during the journey so that occasion arises for repeated meetings (the monks having been suitably bribed to facilitate the process).

Once the two have set eyes on each other, passionate longings are swift to grow The effect is the more marked in the man, who (heretofore too conscious of his career to give thought at all to the opposite sex) falls seriously ill of love-sickness. It is this pining more than anything else that establishes his credentials as a lover and that convinces the young lady of the sincerity of his devotion. But since maiden modesty prevents her doing much in return, an intermediary is needed, and there enters into our story that joyous mainstay of the romantic plot, the clever (if cheeky) maidservant-confidante. When our heroine first appears on the stage (after announcing her presence via a first line of aria sung fortissimo from the wings), this pert miss follows a mincing step or two behind her. Whether standing patiently in attendance at the side or engaging in some spirited exchange, her elfin appeal is nicely calculated to offset the tranquil beauty of her young mistress. Indeed, the costumes and conventions of the classical theater have developed the perfect balance between heroine and helper. The young lady is all demure and shrinking yet stately loveliness, concave flowing line of long gown over floor-length skirt, eyes downcast, movements a rippling shimmer accentuated by the "water sleeves" of white silk that can droop to the floor in despair or be flung like a banner behind her head in an anguished gesture of defiance. The maid on the other hand contrasts sharply in every detail with this kind of dignified grace. The maid is quick; she is agility personified in her silk jacket and trousers of some bright hue, rose or green or bright blue, selected to enliven but at the same time to intensify the more subtle elegance of the young mistress's robes. While the heroine sings, the maid stands in a respectful, attentive pose, hands clasped together and resting on her hip. But as occasion demands she can whirl round the stage, spring acrobatically at an attacker, or skilfully box the ears of an impudent serving lad. She is the sprightly complement to the young lady's serenity; vigor rather than virtue is her trademark. Little wonder that more than one play has been taken over in the end by the irresistible personality of the clever maid: in the case of *The Story of the Western Wing*, the customary modern performance is actually known by this character's name, Hongniang.

What I have been describing is of course the scene in the classical-style theater as we may see it today But our *Western Wing* is in fact a very old play indeed. Its antecedents go back to prose fiction of the Tang period and thence to Song dynasty balladry The thirteenth-century Yuan period, when Kubilai Khan's Mongols ruled China, was in respect to the theater a sort of Elizabethan age, when plays were written that not only were fully mature but in the opinion of many have never since been surpassed in quality. *The Story of the Western Wing* is preeminent even among Yuan plays. It is a giant in length as well as in poetic stature, consisting of no less than twenty acts and comprising a sequence of five normal-length plays. It is a work of consummate literary and dramaturgical skill, and given the perennial Chinese passion for theatergoing and the seven centuries that have elapsed since it was written, there is a strong likelihood that it has delighted more people than any other play in human history

The second great era of the Chinese drama was the late Ming–early Qing, a period whose outside limits we could set at roughly 1550 to 1700. Our surviving texts of *The Western Wing* come mostly from this period. Tastes, by the time these texts were established by the Ming and Qing editors, had changed, and although there had surely been advances in elegance and decorum, there can be no doubt that much of the original vigor, the bawdy fun and grittiness of the Yuan dynasty work was smoothed out and polished away.

Stephen West and Wilt Idema are literary scholars of formidable powers who share a passion for reconstructing, as faithfully as can be done, the closest possible approach to the play of the early time, before late Ming editors, nineteenth-century actor-managers, or twentieth-century rewriters or translators had prettified or bowdlerized its text and modified its performance to suit the latter-day proprieties of scholar-and-beauty romance. It is the great virtue of their translation that it follows with scrupulous exactness the edition of 1498, a year close to the midcareer mark of the Ming dynasty Those long processes of adaptation of popular works to suit the tastes and reflect the concerns of the scholar-official class of the day, which characterized so much activity in fiction and drama throughout the whole second half of the dynasty, had at this time barely begun. There runs through this early version of the play, for example, an undercurrent of sexual innuendo, so constant and so germane to the text that West and Idema have felt the need for a list of some thirty items to aid our comprehension of the "allegory of love" presented here; much of this stream of innuendo has either receded or has been diluted by flowery euphemism in the mid-seventeenth-century version by which, through the serviceable but rather windy translation of S. I. Hsiung, the play has been known to some readers of English under the title *The Romance of the Western Chamber.*

But this restoration of a vividness that persuades us we are coming closer to the Yuan original is only one virtue of the work of West and Idema. At the beginning of chapter 5 of the extensive historical and critical study that prefaces their new version of the play, they express their conviction that "a translation, like an original work of literature, should allow the reader to discover the text for himself." They have followed this apparently modest but in fact excruciatingly demanding precept with unflinching honesty. The careful gradation of their English style between the often crude dialogue and certain poetic flights in climactic arias; the generous notes informed by a wealth of period detail; the exhaustive critical study of the play (including a searching elucidation of dominant patterns of imagery), which is only a part of a most comprehensive introduction—all of these features and more plunge us deeply into the vanished culture of the Yuan stage and into the debt of two of its most distinguished interpreters.

December 1989   Cyril Birch

TABLE OF DYNASTIES

SHANG CA. 1460–1045 B.C.

ZHOU 1045–256 B.C.

    Western Zhou 1111–771 B.C.   Eastern Zhou 770–256 B.C.

    Spring and Autumn 722–481 B.C.   Warring States 480–221 B.C.

QIN 221–207 B.C.

HAN 202 B.C.– A.D 220

    Western Han 202 B.C.–A.D. 9 Eastern Han 25–220

THREE KINGDOMS 220–80

    Wei 220–65 Wu 222–80 Shu-Han 221–63

WESTERN JIN 266–316

EASTERN JIN 317–420

NORTHERN AND SOUTHERN DYNASTIES 386–589

   Northern 386–581

      Northern Wei 386–534 Eastern Wei 534–50   Northern Qi 550–77

      Western Wei 535–57   Northern Zhou 557–81

   Southern 420–589

      Song 420–79   Qi 479–502   Liang 502–57   Chen 557–89

SUI 581–618

TANG 618–907

FIVE DYNASTIES 907–60

    Later Liang 907–23   Later Tang 923–36   Later Jin 936–47

    Later Han 947–50   Later Zhou 951–60

SONG 960–1279

    Northern Song 960–1127   Southern Song 1127–1279

LIAO 916–1125

JIN 1115–1234

YUAN 1260–1368

MING 1368–1644

QING 1644–1911

Dramatis Personæ

This is a list of role types, names, and designations by which the characters of the play are alternately denoted in the Hongzhi edition of *The Story of the Western Wing* We have not attempted to systematize the designations of the text, but have followed it as closely as possible.

NAME	OTHER DESIGNATIONS	ROLE TYPE
Student Zhang	Zhang Gong, Zhang Junrui	Male Lead
Oriole	Cui Yingying	Female Lead
Crimson	Hongniang	Extra Female Lead
Zheng Heng		Extra Male Lead
Old Lady	Madame Cui	Extra Female Lead
Benevolent Perception	Bald One	Extra
Dharma Wit	(Dressed as Bald One)	Clown
Dharma Source	Bald One	Extra
Du Que	White Horse General	Extra Male Lead
Sun Biao	Flying Tiger General	Clown
Happy		Child
Lute Boy		Lute Boy

INTRODUCTION

1

The Status of Wang Shifu's *Story of the Western Wing* in Chinese Literature

Since its opening performance, *The Story of the Western Wing* (*Xixiang ji*) by Wang Shifu (ca. 1250–1300) has been China's most popular love comedy It has been continually performed to the present day, both in its original shape and in numerous later adaptations for other forms of theater and prosimetric literature. At the same time *The Story of the Western Wing* has been highly popular as reading matter, going through more than a hundred editions between 1600 and 1900. The play dramatizes the tale of a young couple, the brilliant student Zhang Gong and the beautiful maiden Cui Yingying (Oriole), who fall passionately in love at first sight. An account of their repeatedly thwarted desire to be happily united in wedlock, *The Story of the Western Wing* was eagerly devoured by innumerable young men and women in the patriarchal society of traditional China who easily recognized themselves in the protagonists of the play The play consequently came to acquire the notorious status of a lover's bible. For this reason many champions of morality decried Wang Shifu's master-work as "a book that teaches lechery" (*huiyin zhi shu*) and damned the author to a life in hell, an opprobrium that only further increased the appeal of his work.[1]

Both the popularity of *The Story of the Western Wing* and the ambivalent attitude toward it in premodern society are clearly demonstrated in that other lover's bible, the eighteenth-century novel *The Dream of the Red Chamber* (*Honglou meng*) by Cao Xueqin (1715–63). The main plot of the novel concerns the manifold and complicated relations between the young Jia Baoyu and two female cousins, the sentimental but sickly Lin Daiyu (with whom Baoyu is in love) and the practical and sturdy Xue Baochai (whom he will eventually marry). When, in chapter 23, Lin Daiyu surprises Jia Baoyu reading *The Story of the Western Wing*, he first tries to hide the title from her, but his attempts are unconvincing:

> "Don't try to fool *me*!" said Daiyu. "You would have done much better to let me look at it in the first place, instead of hiding it so guiltily "
>
> "In your case, coz, I have nothing to be afraid of," said Baoyu; "but if I do let you look, you must promise not to tell anyone. It's marvelous stuff. Once you start reading it, you'll even stop wanting to eat!"
>
> He handed the book to her, and Daiyu put down her things and looked. The more she read, the more she liked it, and before very long she had read

several acts. She felt the power of the words and their lingering fragrance. Long after she had finished reading, when she had laid down the book and was sitting there rapt and silent, the lines continued to ring on in her head.

"Well," said Baoyu, "is it good?"

Daiyu smiled and nodded.[2]

As soon as Baoyu starts to tease her with a quotation from *The Story of the Western Wing*, however, she calls it a "horrid play" and threatens to denounce him to his parents for reading it. On another occasion, when Jia Baoyu again offends her by quoting from Wang's work, she calls it a "crude, disgusting book." Nevertheless, she continues to compare herself to Oriole and is caught quoting from the play herself by Xue Baochai, who sternly rebukes her—but first confesses she herself had read plays while still in her grandfather's household.

> "My grandfather was a bibliophile, so the house we lived in was full of books. We were a big family in those days. All my boy cousins and girl cousins on my father's side lived with us in the same house. All of us younger people hated serious books but liked reading poetry and plays. The boys had got lots and lots of plays: *The Western Chamber* [i.e., *The Story of the Western Wing*], *The Lute-player*, *A Hundred Yuan Plays*—just about everything you could think of. *They* used to read them behind *our* backs, and we girls used to read them behind theirs.
>
> "As for girls like you and me: spinning and sewing are *our* proper business. What do we need to be able to read for? But since we *can* read, let us confine ourselves to good, improving books; let us avoid like the plague those pernicious works of fiction, which so undermine the character that in the end it is past reclaiming."[3]

At a later occasion Xue Baochai even feigns total ignorance of the contents of *The Story of the Western Wing* and another romantic play, only to be berated in turn as overly "stuffy" by yet another character in the novel:

> "There can't be a man, woman or child who isn't familiar with them [i.e., the places mentioned in those plays]. And even if one knows them from the *books*, it can hardly be said that to have read a few lyrics from *The Western Chamber* or *The Soul's Return* is tantamount to reading pornography."[4]

Whether or not *The Story of the Western Wing* was fit reading for impressionable adolescents, performances of scenes from a later adaptation of the play are presented before the collected household in other chapters of the novel.[5] Actually, *The Dream of the Red Chamber* itself might never have been written if *The Story of the Western Wing* had not already established in vernacular literature the images of the talented student, the beautiful maiden, the stern parent, and the witty girl servant.

The controversy surrounding *The Story of the Western Wing* goes back at least to the beginning of the fifteenth century Defending contemporary music and its texts, the prolific playwright Zhu Youdun (1379–1439) notes in one of his prefaces that *The Story of the Western Wing* was considered by many to be a "light and mocking," "irreverent" work.[6] In another preface he shows that he does not subscribe to the opinion popular among the literati and lists Wang Shifu among the "eminent and outstanding   men of letters and talented poets of recent times."[7] The earliest completely preserved edition of *The Story of the Western Wing*, the Hongzhi edition of 1498, on which we have based this translation, includes in its prefatory materials both songs in praise of the author and songs to assure us that after his death he was punished for writing this play by having his tongue pulled out in hell.[8]

The Story of the Western Wing was written by Wang Shifu as a *zaju*, or, more correctly, a cycle of five *zaju* plays. *Zaju*, or comedy, was the dramatic genre that dominated the stage in northern China from the middle of the thirteenth century until well into the fifteenth century.[9] We have no information on performances of individual plays for the Yuan dynasty, but it would appear that *The Story of the Western Wing* quickly achieved great success, apparently in large measure because of its stage popularity This notoriety is attested to by numerous references to the story and its main characters in many contemporary plays and songs. *The Story of the Western Wing* also quickly engendered imitations and parodies: Zheng Dehui's *Formidable Maidservant* (*Zou Meixiang*), for example, and the anonymous *Story of the Eastern Wall* (*Dongqiang ji*). If Wang Shifu as a playwright never attained the reputation of his contemporary Guan Hanqing, the most versatile practitioner of *zaju* and reputed originator of the genre, his *Story of the Western Wing* outshone all other works in the genre because of its format and quality, and it quickly established itself as *the* preeminent *zaju*. Early in the fifteenth century the playwright Jia Zhongming (1343–after 1422) could write: "Of all new comedies / And old musical plays, / *The Story of the Western Wing* takes first place all over the world!"[10] His contemporary Zhu Youdun informs us through a stray remark in one of his many *zaju* that the role of Oriole was played by a *huadan*, or "flowery female lead," a role type that usually portrayed courtesans and comparably risqué characters.[11] This categorization of our heroine may also lie behind her characterization in Li Kaixian's (1502–68) *Noontime Dream in a Garden Grove* (*Yuanlin wumeng*), a little skit that pitches Oriole in a shouting match against the courtesan Li Wa, famous for her destruction and rehabilitation of the student Zheng Yuanhe.[12] To judge from the anonymous sixteenth-century novel *Jin Ping Mei*,[13] which is ostensibly set in the early twelfth century but describes living conditions in northern China at the time of its composition, acts from Wang Shifu's drama were still being performed at that time.

If we know but little about the performance of our play during the heyday of *zaju* in the theater, we know that it was the last play of its genre to remain in the repertoire as *zaju* retreated from the stage during the final decades of the Ming dynasty Shen Defu (1578–1642) records as a rarity that in 1604 a certain Ma Siniang from present-day Nanjing visited Suzhou with a group of fifteen or sixteen girls, who performed a complete version of Wang's *Story of the Western Wing* Shen Defu especially praises a certain Qiaosun, who was very ugly but whose singing "stopped the clouds." He concludes by noting that the group had long since disbanded.[14]

The *Story of the Western Wing* continued to be played in other forms, however. *Zaju* had employed music that originated in northern China; but contemporaneous with the rise of *zaju* (or even slightly earlier), another dramatic genre that employed native southern tunes appeared in China south of the river Huai. This genre was originally known as *xiwen* (play-scripts) but eventually came to be known in the Yuan as *chuanqi* (musical plays). From a very early date *The Story of the Western Wing* was adapted for this genre. Usually, the adaptation from *zaju* to *chuanqi* requires considerable expansion of the plot since *zaju* are very short, allowing for only four suites of songs that are all assigned to a single performer, while *chuanqi* require sprawling narratives and provide songs for each actor and actress in the cast.

In the case of *The Story of the Western Wing* no such drastic rewriting is called for because of the exceptional length of this five-*zaju* cycle—roughly that of the average *chuanqi*. There are extant today fragments of a (probably) fourteenth-century southern adaptation of *The Story of the Western Wing* and two later full-fledged *chuanqi* adaptations. One of these was originally done by the virtually unknown Cui Shipei and later revised by the equally unknown Li Rihua, both active in the early sixteenth century The other was done by the sixteenth-century Suzhou playwright Lu Cai.[15] When *chuanqi* came to be replaced on the stage by varieties of regional drama, *The Story of the Western Wing* was again adapted for these forms. Since the main distinction between the many varieties of regional drama is based on the type of music employed, the story itself usually suffers only minor alterations, even if in some local versions the role of Oriole's witty and resourceful maidservant Crimson (Hongniang) becomes so prominent that the play is named after her. In many cases *The Story of the Western Wing* or its variation *Crimson* has remained in the regional repertoire until the present day [16] No less a luminary of modern literature than Guo Moruo (1892–1978) hailed the play's stylistic and linguistic qualities in the wake of the Literary Revolution of 1917 and the May Fourth Movement of 1919, movements that were aimed at overthrowing traditional Confucian society and its ideology and at the replacement of the classical language with contemporary vernacular idiom as the major medium of written communication. In the preface to his own revised version of the play Guo calls it not a "book that teaches lechery" but a "song of triumph, a monument to the victory of living human nature over dead morality "[17] Some of the most prominent dramatists of twentieth-century China, Tian Han for instance, have provided the public with stage versions for the modern theater by fitting the action into a two-and-a-half hour time span (often by omitting the fifth play of the cycle). In the People's Republic of China *The Story of the Western*

Wing was among the earlier plays to be revived following the Cultural Revolution, when all traditional pieces had been banned from the stage. In the autumn of 1983 in Beijing one of us had the good luck to see a performance of a northern *kunqu* version of *The Story of the Western Wing* by the contemporary critic and playwright Ma Shaopo.

When northern *zaju* ceased to be performed onstage in the course of the late sixteenth century, *The Story of the Western Wing* not only continued to be played in other forms of theater but also staged a spectacular comeback as closet drama. From the final four or five decades of the Ming dynasty alone nearly forty different editions of Wang Shifu's masterwork have been preserved, and from the succeeding Qing dynasty another sixty or so editions are known. No other work of vernacular literature can boast a comparable number of editions.[18] In 1980 a few fragments of a very early printed edition of *The Story of the Western Wing* came to light. These fragments preserve the text of the final segment of the fourth act of the first play and the opening lines of the second play. The character of their layout suggests that the fragments may derive from an edition printed in either the final years of the Yuan or the early decades of the Ming dynasty. In contrast to other preserved Yuan dynasty printings of *zaju*,[19] which include only arias and the barest of stage directions and prompt lines from the dialogue, this edition of *The Story of the Western Wing* includes full stage directions and dialogue as well as full-page illustrations. The fragments suggest that the text was not accompanied by any explanatory annotations.[20] The tradition of annotating *The Story of the Western Wing* was well established by the beginning of the fifteenth century, as shown by Zhu Youdun, who, in a set of poems called *Smart* (*Fengliu*), ridicules the "smart student"

> He discusses essays on the dancing stage,
> He takes his exams in the flowery lanes.
> Bundling up his tuition money, he blows his cash
> And annotates *The Story of the Western Wing*[21]

The Hongzhi edition of 1498 carries such explanatory annotations, which indeed testify to the low level of erudition of their anonymous compiler or compilers.

The Hongzhi edition of Wang Shifu's work is preserved only in a single copy, unknown to the scholarly world until the late 1940s, when it was acquired by Yanjing University, from which it passed into the holdings of the Beijing University library This very handsome edition was produced by a commercial publishing firm, the Yue family of Jintai, Beijing.[22] The upper register of each page of the main text is graced by a continuous set of illustrations that occupy two-fifths of each page. These illustrations are of a fine quality, especially when compared to those in other Ming editions, and by themselves provide an interesting interpretative commentary on the text.[23] It is clear from the publisher's advertisement that the illustrations are meant to provide visual clues to famous scenes onstage, but it is also clear that they represent the story itself and not any one performance.

In the main text of the play each aria is preceded by the title of its melody printed inside a black "fishtail" cartouche. The arias are distinguished from the stage directions and prose dialogue by larger-sized characters (although the person who copied the text for the woodblocks sometimes let smaller characters grow disproportionately large). Annotations are grouped together at irregular intervals throughout the text. When annotations run to length, the illustrations compensate with added woodblocks of interiors and gardens, void of people, until the action of the play begins again.

The play is printed in two large volumes; in each volume the main text is preceded by a variety of other materials, more or less (but sometimes not at all) related to the play and occasionally carrying their own illustrations. Some of these materials we have included in our translation since they may be helpful in understanding the late fifteenth-century reception of our play.[24] Although there are abundant references to a number of sixteenth-century editions, the earliest preserved independent editions date from only the final decades of the century—almost a hundred years after the publication of the Hongzhi edition. Yet various song anthologies of the mid-sixteenth century contain extensive extracts of Wang Shifu's work. *The Popular Songs of an Era of Peace* (*Yongxi yuefu*) compiled by Guo Xun (1475–1542) contains all twenty-one suites of songs from *The Story of the Western Wing*,[25] and *The Brocade Sachet of Breeze and Moonlight* (*Fengyue jinnang*) compiled by a certain Xu Wenzhao and printed in 1553 contains sizable excerpts, including the dialogue.[26] The number of editions increases dramatically in the middle of the Wanli reign period (1573–1619). These editions vary greatly in both scholarship and artistic execution. Whereas some recensions appear to be hastily touched-up versions of earlier editions, reproducing even their annotations, critical comments, and some introductory materials, others provide us with carefully prepared critical editions. An example of the latter category is the edition prepared by the playwright and drama critic Wang Jide (ca. 1560–1623) and published in 1614,[27] containing a detailed line-by-line comparison between the text of the play and Wang Shifu's immediate source, Dong Jieyuan's (fl. 1190–1208) *Story of the Western Wing in All Keys and Modes* (*Xixiang ji zhugongdiao*), a chantefable treatment of this famous love story.[28]

Many editions in the former category display a clear contamination by the editorial conventions of *chuanqi* in their presentation of *The Story of the Western Wing*. A typical example is the relatively early edition of our play produced by Liu Longtian. This edition still contains all of the prefatory materials in both volumes of the Hongzhi edition but has relegated these to an appendix; in Liu's edition, however, our original *zaju* has acquired a *jiamen*, the typical introductory scene in *chuanqi*. Moreover, the acts are designated as *chu*, the normal scene designation for *chuanqi*, and numbered consecutively, each *chu* having its own four-character heading.[29]

An edition that appeared in 1622 and deserves separate mention is the one prepared by the playwright and novelist Ling Mengchu (1580–1644), who claims that his edition is based on an earlier one published by Zhu Youdun. Although this assertion may be just a sales pitch to assure buyers of a reliable and authentic text, the edition is indeed remarkable among late Ming printings for its close similarity in places to the Hongzhi edition—a text that, in turn, appears to imitate the editorial practices employed in Zhu Youdun's private printings of his own *zaju*. So Ling Mengchu might have based his edition on a copy of the Hongzhi edition—one missing the vulnerable final leaf of the second volume that carries the publisher's colophon, that is—and he might have concluded, on the evidence of similarities in editorial convention, that this edition was indeed prepared by Zhu Youdun.[30]

All of these earlier editions were quickly eclipsed by Jin Shengtan's (1610–61) recension of 1656. Jin was a highly idiosyncratic literary critic who had the audacity to put major works in the vernacular language on a par with the hallowed masterworks of the classical tradition. Earlier, in 1641, he had produced an edition of the famous novel *Water Margin* (*Shuihu zhuan*) that was supposedly based on an "ancient edition" (*guben*) and was distinguished by an extensive critical commentary including general introductory essays, individual essays accompanying each chapter, and a detailed interlinear commentary Jin Shengtan frequently rewrote the main text in order to make it fit his own critical statements—even to the extent of completely cutting out the final third of the text. Because of the resulting literary quality of his abridged text, however, its manageable bulk, and the acumen and wit of his commentary, this edition of *Water Margin* remained the standard version of the novel until well into the present century [31]

Jin Shengtan's edition of *The Story of the Western Wing* adheres to basically the same format as his earlier venture into vernacular criticism. The main text is preceded by two prefaces and two general essays, each act is preceded by its own critical introduction, and the body of the text itself is accompanied by an extensive interlinear commentary Again, the wording of the text occasionally has been changed to fit the commentary Because metrical requirements keep most of the songs inviolate, the prose dialogue suffers all the more. One of Jin Shengtan's major concerns is to safeguard Oriole from any accusation of indecency He attempts this by proving that she remains chaste under all circumstances—even when she gives herself to the student Zhang Gong (in Jin's opinion she simply enacts the promise of marriage her mother has retracted). Accordingly, he makes many small changes throughout the text, once more supposedly on the authority of an otherwise unspecified "ancient edition", in the process the text is thoroughly bowdlerized.[32] As in the case of his edition of *Water Margin*, Jin Shengtan's textual changes may well have enhanced the readability of the text and increased its general acceptability by downplaying its morally offensive aspects. The breadth and wit of his com-mentary, moreover, remain an attraction to readers even to the present day

During the nearly three centuries of the Qing dynasty, Jin Shengtan's recension enjoyed popularity equal to that of his edition of *Water Margin* and likewise virtually eclipsed all earlier editions; Western-language translations of *The Story of the Western Wing* have heretofore all been based on the Jin Shengtan edition. Jin firmly subscribes to the view that Wang Shifu authored only the first four plays of *The Story of the Western Wing*, an opinion quite common during the sixteenth century and later,[33] and he consequently includes the fifth play of the cycle only as a sequel. As a result, some Western-language renditions do not translate the fifth play at all. In the wake of the Literary Revolution and the May Fourth Movement, Jin Shengtan was often hailed as an early champion of vernacular literature. Although in the People's Republic he was initially criticized with vehemence for his editorial changes, which were seen to detract from the "progressive" tendency of *Water Margin* and *The Story of the Western Wing*, during the last decade his editions have been more positively evaluated.[34]

A final Qing dynasty edition of *The Story of the Western Wing* that merits mention was published in the early years of this century by the well-known bibliophile Liu Shiheng (1875–1926). In editing the main text of Wang Shifu's work, Liu Shiheng relies heavily on Ling Mengchu's edition, thereby making it once again generally available. Liu's edition also includes a comprehensive selection of source materials (including Dong Jieyuan's *Story of the Western Wing in All Keys and Modes*), an extensive compilation of critical comments, and the two preserved *chuanqi* adaptations. The complete set of materials has recently been reissued under the title *Nuanhongshi shi huike Xixiang ji*.[35]

Wang Shifu's *Story of the Western Wing* has exerted a tremendous influence on Chinese vernacular literature. *Zaju* parodies and imitations surfaced as early as the end of the fourteenth century, and echoes of its arias can be detected in many *zaju* of the fourteenth and fifteenth centuries; the characterization of the student Zhang, Oriole, and her maidservant Crimson have often contributed to shaping similar roles in those plays. After *The Story of the Western Wing* had been adapted as a *chuanqi*, sequels and "inversions" (*fan'an*) also appeared in that genre. In one such sequel of Ming date, Oriole, having married, becomes extremely jealous of Crimson and has to atone for her sin in hell. In one inversion the author outdoes even Jin Shengtan in his defense of Oriole's reputation, preserving her virginity until the marriage ceremony by having Crimson stand in for her in the student's study at night. In another inversion Oriole has no affair with Zhang Gong but dutifully marries her original fiancé Zheng Heng.[36] None of the sequels or inversions, however, ever succeeded in subverting the established image of Zhang Gong and Oriole as ideally matched but (initially) star-crossed lovers. This *caizi* (talented scholar) and his beloved *jiaren* (beautiful maiden)—he, brilliantly gifted and handsome, fully confident of his eventual success in the examinations but easily upset by setbacks in love; she, exceedingly beautiful and appreciative of literary talent—have provided the model for countless young couples in later drama and fiction.

The Story of the Western Wing has been adapted to other genres of performing literature. In the Qing dynasty the story was retold in all the major forms of prosimetric storytelling: the *guci* (drum rhymes) and *zidi shu* (young playboys' scripts) from northern China; the *tanci* (plucking rhymes) from central China; and the *muyu shu* (wooden-fish books) from southern China.[37] These versions substantially contributed to the popularity of our love story even among those who could not read and were only rarely able to attend theatrical performances. The vitality of this tradition is testified to by the recent appearance of *The Story of the Western Wing* as a 750-page *tanci* by the Suzhou artist Yang Zhenxiong: the latest in a long line of poems, songs, ditties, and skits inspired by *The Story of the Western Wing*[38]

In view of the immense popularity of this romance, it comes as no surprise that *The Story of the Western Wing* has also come to exert a considerable influence on the visual arts. We have already pointed out that the earliest known printing of Wang Shifu's play carries full-page illustrations. The Hongzhi edition is noteworthy for its lavish illustrations that occupy the upper register of each page of the main text. The conception and execution of these woodcuts far surpass both the page-top illustrations in early fourteenth-century *pinghua* (vernacular narratives of famous episodes from Chinese history) and in late sixteenth- and early seventeenth-century printings of novels from Fujian Province.[39] Extant late Ming editions of *The Story of the Western Wing* almost all feature full-page illustrations that are either interspersed through the text or are grouped together in a separate volume at the beginning of the book. The quality of these woodcuts usually varies with the overall quality of the edition, but some editions carry illustrations that may confidently be ranked among the finest from this heyday of the blockprint in China. As a rule the illustrations are printed only in black and white, but the final decades of the Ming dynasty witnessed a remarkable flowering of the art of color printing. *The Story of the Western Wing* inspired Min Qiji's (1580–after 1661) 1640 production of a superb set of color prints depicting scenes from the tale of Zhang Gong and Oriole, a copy of which is now kept at the Museum für Ostasiatische Kunst in Köln.[40] Many of the prints are original and witty in conception and were probably created for sophisticated connoisseurs. By the middle of the seventeenth century scenes from the play had also become popular decorative motifs on porcelain—painters of porcelain often derived their models from woodblock prints.[41] The modern age has also seen the publication of a high-quality comic book version of the story and even the issue of stamps featuring scenes from the play

One of the results of the Literary Revolution of 1917 and the May Fourth Movement of 1919 was a drastic reevaluation of traditional Chinese literature. Vernacular forms of literature like the novel, the short story, and the various types of drama, which, for all their popularity among the literati used to be looked down upon by them, were now hailed by progressive young scholars and writers as forerunners of their movement to replace the classical idiom. Texts that for centuries had at best been tolerated attained the status of classical masterworks overnight. If such works moreover could be interpreted as attacks on the old morality or endorsements of the individual pursuit of happiness, their chances of a ranking of importance within the new canon rose accordingly. *The Story of the Western Wing* is everything the champions of the vernacular could have hoped for. Not only is it a superb love comedy that fully demonstrates the potentials of the vernacular idiom as a medium for literary communication, it also features as its protagonists a pair of lovers who flout traditional morality and its mainstay, parental authority. Whereas the original author of *The Story of the Western Wing* observes the lovers with ironic detachment as the helpless victims of passion, to twentieth-century Chinese readers Zhang Gong and Oriole have become victorious fighters for the right to love and choose one's own marriage partner. Guo Moruo's enthusiastic endorsement of the play would be affirmed by a new consensus. The early decades of this century witnessed a number of modern stage adaptations of our play and a remarkable resurgence of critical and scholarly interest in Wang Shifu's work. Early editions were collected and occasionally reprinted, and the first editions with modern commentary were prepared. No history of Chinese literature could appear that did not devote a sizable space to this drama.

The establishment of the People's Republic of China and the introduction of Marxism into Chinese literary criticism has only enhanced the preeminent position of *The Story of the Western Wing* (except during the period 1966–78, when practically no work of literature, traditional or modern, was considered to possess redeeming value sufficient to allow its dissemination or discussion). The still-swelling stream of articles and monographs has stressed over and over again the progressive nature (in the context of its own time) of the behavior of the student and the maiden in their daring pursuit of love. Oriole's mother, a chancellor's widow who, besieged by bandits, promises her daughter in marriage to an impecunious student but reneges as soon as the danger is over; who assents to the marriage only after she finds out that her daughter has been sleeping with the student but then requests that he absent himself for a considerable length of time; who is only too eager to believe the tale told by her daughter's original fiancé Zheng Heng that the successful student has made a better match—in the post-1949 critics' reading this widow has become the very incarnation of all the evils of the old society: class prejudice, hypocrisy, and the denial of love. The lovers are seen to incorporate the progressive ideals: love, free marriage, and a belief in individual talent and achievement.

One of the major areas of contention is the issue of Oriole's maidservant Crimson and the monk Benevolent Perception: whether they, as characters of lower-class backgrounds who enable their highborn superiors to fulfill their desires, should be evaluated as more or less progressive than their masters. Another area of contention is the question of which work is the more progressive: Dong Jieyuan's *Story of the Western Wing in All Keys and Modes*, in which the lovers elope at the end, or Wang Shifu's comedy, in which the marriage eventually takes place because of the timely arrival of Zhang Gong's friend, General Du Que—at present, the latter is overwhelmingly favored. Because these critics view the protagonists of our play as motivated by only the noblest of sentiments, they feel uncomfortable about the many passages of low and bawdy humor in *The Story of the Western Wing*; fortunately they can always exculpate Wang Shifu with the concept of "the limitations imposed on the author by his age and class."

For a long time criticism of *The Story of the Western Wing* almost always consisted of such exercises in ideological scrutiny, but in recent years other aspects of the text and its history have received more and better attention.[42] One aspect is the bibliography of *The Story of the Western Wing* Since World War II numerous early editions of our play have come to light. The most distinctive of these, beginning with the Hongzhi edition, have been photomechanically reproduced in facsimile. Some scholars, like Denda Akira in Japan and Jiang Xingyu from Shanghai, have devoted almost their entire lifetimes to researching the printing history of Wang Shifu's work.[43] A number of new annotated editions of the play were published in the 1950s: the annotations in Wu Xiaoling's edition of 1954 are concise and to the point;[44] and the notes in Wang Jisi's repeatedly revised edition of the play present us with one of the finest achievements of modern philological scholarship.[45] Because Wang Jisi bases his text of the play on the Ling Mengchu edition, his glosses are extremely useful in reading the Hongzhi edition. Since 1978 at least two new editions have been published that take into account the greatly diminished knowledge of classical literature and traditional society among younger readers in the People's Republic.[46] The usefulness of such commentaries to the Western reader should be obvious. It may also be pointed out that since 1978 at least three separate publishers have produced punctuated typeset editions of Jin Shengtan's recension of *The Story of the Western Wing*[47]

Wang Shifu's model, Dong Jieyuan's *Story of the Western Wing in All Keys and Modes*, and later adaptations of this romance have shared the attention continuously lavished on *The Story of the Western Wing* As early as 1955 the great scholar Fu Xihua edited an extensive collection of Qing dynasty prosimetric adaptations of Wang Shifu's work.[48] Several early editions of Dong Jieyuan's ballad have been reproduced in facsimile upon discovery, and at least two new annotated editions have also appeared.[49]

Wang Shifu's *Story of the Western Wing* has often been translated into Western and Eastern languages.[50] The earliest translation into a European language is the French version by the eminent sinologue Stanislas Julien, which first appeared in 1872 in the pages of the periodical *Atsume Gusa* and was reissued in 1880 in book form as *Si-siang-ki: ou, L'histoire du pavillon d'occident, comédie en seize actes*. From the very start of his career, Julien had been a student and translator of Yuan drama. In 1839 he translated Ji Junxiang's *Orphan of Zhao (Zhaoshi gu'er)* in an attempt to redress the eighteenth-century prejudices against Chinese drama that stemmed from Prémare's earlier rendition, and his translation of Li Xingdao's *Chalk Circle (Huilan ji)* indirectly influenced Bertold Brecht in his conception of *Der kaukasische Kreidekreis*. Julien's *Si-siang-ki* was the crowning achievement of a lifelong involvement with Chinese vernacular literature. Like other, earlier Western translators, Julien based himself on the Jin Shengtan edition and accordingly translated only the four "authentic" plays of the five-play cycle. Because his work was intended primarily as a crib for students, it was accompanied by extensive notes and the Chinese text of the arias.

The next Western-language translation to appear was the German rendition of all five plays by Vincenz Hundhausen in 1926, entitled *Das Westzimmer, Ein chinesisches Singspiel aus dem dreizehnten Jahrhundert*. This is a very free adaptation in the German tradition of *Nachdichtung*, or "re-creation," which allows the translator a very wide leeway in superimposing his own thoughts and fancies on the text of his choice. Nevertheless, it caused quite a scandal upon its appearance: Hundhausen was accused by one reviewer of having plagiarized Julien's translation and in response sued the reviewer for libel. One way or another many members of the German sinological community became involved in the imbroglio.[51]

In the mid-thirties two English-language versions of *The Story of the Western Wing* appeared almost simultaneously In 1936 Stanford University Press published Henry H. Hart's *The West Chamber, A Medieval Drama*. Hart limits himself to a translation of the first four plays and even omits the final act of the fourth play since "it is an anticlimax and adds nothing to the interest of the play "[52] In his preface Hart chides Hundhausen for casting his rendition of the arias into rhymed couplets, calling it "an effort which more often than not distorts the sense of the original."[53] Hart accordingly presents the arias as free verse. Ironically, Hart's version has been "poeticized" by Henry W Wells, who published an adaptation of Hart's translation in 1972 in which all prose passages have been recast into blank verse and all arias have been rhymed.[54]

Hart's rendition was preceded a year earlier by the publication of another, soon-to-become-standard translation, S. I. Hsiung's *Romance of the Western Chamber*, which includes all five plays. It was reissued as late as 1968 by Columbia University Press with a new introduction by C. T Hsia, who regrets that the translator relies on the Jin Shengtan edition rather than one of the earlier Ming editions. Although Hsia credits Hsiung with having done "a conscientious job of reproducing in English the paraphrasable meaning of his adopted text,"[55] he makes it abundantly clear that in his opinion the translator has failed to do justice to the stylistic variety of his original. We should not forget, however, that whatever the modern view may be, for their times and for the sources then available these earlier translations constitute quite creditable, even excellent, achievements.

Wang Shifu's *Story of the Western Wing* is one of those masterworks of world literature that merits a new translation with every generation, and there is a pressing need now for a new rendition since those presently available are over half a century old. Moreover, these translations, as we have seen, are based on a rather late, highly idiosyncratic, and heavily bowdlerized edition of the text. During the half century since their appearance great progress has been made in our knowledge of the colloquial language and of the staging of Yuan drama. Thanks to the labors of many Chinese and Japanese scholars, the modern student of early Chinese theater and dramatic literature can refer to a broad offering of annotated editions, specialized dictionaries, and monographs—an array of philological aids that was unheard of in the early part of the century. Early editions that were not generally available or not yet known are now easily accessible.

We have based our present translation on the Hongzhi edition of 1498, the earliest complete text available. Although this edition dates from two centuries after the probable lifetime of the author, it shows clear evidence of editorial revision when compared to Yuan editions of other plays, if only because the role type that plays Zhang Gong is alternately designated as *mo* (male role) and *sheng* (student). Nevertheless, it precedes all other complete editions by nearly a century and on close reading proves to be a fine and reliable text: whenever its readings depart from later editions, we have found, they usually make perfect sense both as theater and as literature. We have therefore decided to abide faithfully by the text of the Hongzhi edition, except in the instance of a very few orthographic mistakes. We have consistently compared this text with the Ling Mengchu edition but have made no attempt at a consistent comparison with any other late Ming editions. Our aim, as in our earlier translations, is to provide the Western reader with a rendition that is as close to the original as a literary translation will allow, warts and all. We feel this is crucial to the play as represented in this edition since one of the features of its characterization is the shifting register of language between characters, or even of a single character. Our version may seem to some to be excessively literal, but we have been guided by the belief that it is both unnecessary and undesirable to resort to well-worn English equivalents or clichés to smooth over any passages that challenge the reader to active engagement. This we have done in the belief that the modern Western public will be as capable of imaginative collaboration with the translation as the thirteenth-century audience was with the original.

Notes

[1] For a certainly not exhaustive collection of general comments from the Yuan, Ming, and Qing dynasties on Wang Shifu's *Story of the Western Wing*, see the chapter "Gejia zongping" compiled by Zhang Renhe in Wang Shifu, *Jiping jiaozhu Xixiang ji*, 207–57. For a number of highly unfavorable comments on *The Story of the Western Wing*, see, e.g., Wang Liqi, *Yuan Ming Qing sandai jinhui xiaoshuo xiqu shiliao*, 371–74.

[2] Cao Xueqin, *The Story of the Stone*, 1:464. For the Chinese text, see, e.g., Cao Xueqin, *Honglou meng bashihui jiaoben*, 1:234. For simplicity's sake we have altered the romanization in this and subsequent extracts to conform with our own.

[3] Cao Xueqin, *The Story of the Stone*, 2:333–34. For the Chinese text, see *Honglou meng bashihui jiaoben*, 2:448–49. *The Lute-player* refers to Gao Ming's (d. 1359) famous southern play *Pipa ji*, which has been translated into English by Jean Mulligan as *The Lute*. *A Hundred Yuan Plays* is an alternative designation for the *Yuanqu xuan*, an anthology of one hundred *zaju* plays from the Yuan and early Ming dynasties, compiled by Zang Jinshu (1550–1620) and published in 1615/16. This anthology, which does not include Wang Shifu's *Story of the Western Wing*, quickly established itself as the most authoritative collection of *zaju*.

[4] Cao Xueqin, *The Story of the Stone*, 2:515. For the Chinese text, see *Honglou meng bashihui jiaoben*, 2:550. *The Soul's Return* refers to *Mudanting huanhun ji* by Tang Xianzu (1550–1616). This play has been translated into English by Cyril Birch as *The Peony Pavilion*.

[5] The modern scholar Jiang Xingyu has devoted a number of articles to various aspects of the complex relationship between *The Story of the Western Wing* and *The Dream of the Red Chamber*: "Guanyu Baoyu Daiyu suo du de shiliuchu ben *Xixiang ji*," "*Xixiang ji* de zhuangtai kuijian yu *Honglou meng* di ershisan hui," and "Cao Xueqin yong xiaoshuo xingshi xie de *Xixiang ji* pipingshi." The vehement denunciations of our play as reading matter should perhaps be related to the traditional reading practice: students were trained to intone a text repeatedly and intently until they knew its words by heart and had internalized its values.

[6] Zhu Youdun, "Baihezi yong qiujing youyin." For an English translation of this preface, see Idema, *The Dramatic Oeuvre of Chu Yu-tun*, 204–5.

[7] In his preface to the play *Jimu daxian* as it appears in the original fifteenth-century woodblock edition, *Xinbian Qinghexian Jimu daxian*, 1a. Cf. Idema, *The Dramatic Oeuvre of Chu Yu-tun*, 206.

[8] See below, "Eight Satiric Songs Against *The Western Wing*," pp. 110–13.

[9] The formal characteristics of *zaju* will be discussed in chap. 4 of the introduction. In his *History of Chinese Drama*, William Dolby devotes two chapters to this genre (pp. 40–70). It is the sole subject of Chung-wen Shih's *Golden Age of Chinese Drama*, which contains an extensive bibliography In his *Chinese Theater in the Days of Kublai Khan*, James Crump devotes the major part of his extensive introduction to a reconstruction of "The Actor's Art" (pp. 67–175). The theater and theater life are documented in our *Chinese Theater 1100–1450*. A bibliography of Chinese, Japanese, and Western publications on Yuan drama is provided in He Guichu, *Yuandai xiqu lunzhu suoyin*.

[10] Zhong Sicheng, *Lugui bu*, 173. The *Lugui bu* is our earliest preserved catalog of *zaju*. It is arranged by author and provides a laconic biographical notice for each. The text went through different redactions during the second quarter of the fourteenth century. One of these drafts served as the basis for Jia Zhongming's expanded version of 1422.

[11] This is mentioned in Zhu Youdun's *zaju* entitled *Xiangnang yuan*. See his *Xinbian Liu Panchun shouzhi Xiangnang yuan*, 5a, and our *Chinese Theater 1100–1450*, 394.

[12] For a discussion and translation of this skit, see Idema, "Yüan-pen as a Minor Form of Dramatic Literature", see also the revised translation in Appendix II.

[13] For a discussion of the role of references to our play in this novel, see Carlitz, *The Rhetoric of Chin p'ing mei*, 104–5.

[14] Shen Defu, "Beici chuanshou," in his *Guqu zayan*, 212.

[15] The fragments of the *Xixiang ji xiwen* have been collected by Qian Nanyang in his *Song Yuan xiwen jiyi*, 243-49. The *chuanqi* adaptations by both Li Rihua and Lu Cai are reprinted in Liu Shiheng, *Nuanhongshi huike Xixiang ji*. For studies on these southern adaptations, see Tanaka Kenji, "Zatsugeki Seishōki no nangekika," and Cong Jingwen, *Nanbei Xixiang ji bijiao*.

[16] Tao Junqi, *Jingju jumu chutan*, 181–82; Wang Yisheng, *Yuju chuantong jumu huishi*, 239–40.

[17] Guo Moruo, *Xixiang ji*, 2.

[18] Fu Xihua, *Yuandai zaju quanmu*, 52–61; Denda Akira, *Min kan Gen zatsugeki Seishōki mokuroku*; Jiang Xingyu, *Ming kanben Xixiang ji yanjiu*; his *Zhongguo xiqushi gouchen*, 101–58; and his *Zhongguo xiqushi tanwei*, 124–261. See also Zhang Dihua, *Shanben juqu jingyan lu*, 1–20; and Zheng Qian, "*Xixiang ji* banben lu," and "*Xixiang ji* banben lu buyi."

[19] For the texts of these early plays, the "thirty Yuan editions of *zaju*," see Zheng Qian, *Jiaoding Yuankan zaju sanshizhong*, and Xu Qinjun, *Xinjiao Yuankan zaju sanshizhong*.

[20] For discussions of these late Yuan–early Ming fragments, see, e.g., Duan Miheng, "*Xinbian jiaozheng Xixiang ji* canye de faxian," which includes transcriptions and reproductions of these fragments; Jiang Xingyu, "Xin faxian de zuizao de *Xixiang ji* canye"; Zhou Xugeng, "Tan *Xinbian jiaozheng Xixiang ji* canye de jiazhi", Lu Gong, "Mingchu kanben *Xixiang ji* canye."

[21] Zhu Youdun, "Zuixiang ci ershipian," 1.6a. For a complete translation of this song (and some others from that series), see our *Chinese Theater 1100–1450*, 423–25.

[22] See the publisher's advertisement in Wang Shifu, *Xinkan qimiao quanxiang zhushi Xixiang ji*, 161b, and p. 287 in the translation.

[23] See Yao Dajuin's essay on the woodblocks in our *The Moon and the Zither: The Story of the Western Wing* (Berkeley and Los Angeles: University of California Press, 1991), pp. 437–68.

[24] The Hongzhi edition is available in photographic facsimile reproduction: Wang Shifu, *Xinkan qimiao quanxiang zhushi Xixiang ji*; in much reduced size, this edition also constitutes the first two volumes of the *Guben xiqu congkan*, 1st ser. Both reproductions have been repeatedly reprinted. See Jiang Xingyu, "Hongzhi ben *Xixiang ji* de tili yu 'Yue ke' wenti."

[25] The *Yongxi yuefu* is available in three editions dating from 1540, 1566, and 1617. The *Sibu congkan* has reproduced the latter. Because the twenty-one suites of songs were at that time the earliest available (partial) text of our play, they attracted considerable attention during the 1930s. They have been published twice (in 1933 and 1934) and have been discussed by a number of leading scholars. See, e.g., Zheng Zhenduo, "*Xixiang ji* de benlai mianmu shi zenyang de", Sun Kaidi, "Ji *Yongxi yuefu* ben *Xixiang ji* quwen xu", Tanaka Kenji, "*Seishôki* shohon no shimbyôsei", and Sui Shusen, *Yongxi yuefu quwen zuozhe kao*. The *Qunyin leixuan* of ca. 1595, a song anthology compiled by Hu Wenhuan, also includes all song suites in *The Story of the Western Wing*, but as it subsumes the second suite of the second play under the first suite of that play, it appears to derive its text from a relatively late sixteenth-century edition; see Hu Wenhuan, *Qunyin leixuan*, 3:1739–1829.

[26] The title *Fengyue jinnang* was already on record by the Yongle period (1403–24), but the one preserved printing, which survives in a single copy, dates from 1553. The contents are described in James J. Y. Liu, "The *Feng-yüeh chin-nang* " On the *Fengyue jinnang* version of *The Story of the Western Wing*, Prof. Liu writes: "The present text contains only· Part I; Part II, Acts 2 and 3; Part III, Acts 1 and 2 (incomplete); Part IV, Acts 1 and 3; Part V, Act 1. All the Inductions are omitted; so are many passages of the spoken dialogue" (p. 92). The *Fengyue jinnang* was reprinted in 1987 by the Xuesheng shuju of Taipei in the fourth series of its *Shanben xiqu congkan*.

[27] In 1927 this *Huitu xin jiaozhu guben Xixiang ji* was photomechanically reproduced in facsimile in Beijing by Fujian shushe and Donglaige shudian.

[28] The sources of our play will be discussed in more detail in chap. 3.

[29] This *Yuanben tiping Xixiang ji* has been reproduced as vols. 3 and 4 of the *Guben xiqu congkan*, 1st ser.

[30] Ling Mengchu's edition of Wang Shifu's *Story of the Western Wing* was reprinted by Liu Shiheng in his *Nuanhongshi huike Xixiang ji*.

[31] John Ching-yu Wang, *Chin Sheng-t'an*, provides a succinct but lucid survey of Jin's life and criticism.

[32] *Ibid.*, 82–104.

[33] This issue will be dealt with in chap. 2.

[34] At least three recent typeset editions of Jin Shengtan's version of the play are available: *Guanhuatang diliu caizishu Xixiang ji*, collated by Fu Xiaohang; *Guanhuatang diliu caizishu Xixiang ji*, collated by Cao Fangren; and *Jin Shengtan piben Xixiang ji*, collated by Zhang Guoguang.

[35] This twenty-volume work was reprinted from the original blocks by the Guangling guji keyinshe of Yangzhou in the 1970s.

[36] The most comprehensive Western-language survey of the many adaptations of the romance of Student Zhang and Oriole is provided by Lorraine Dong in "The Creation and Life of Cui Yingying." The Ming dynasty dramatic adaptations are discussed on pp. 513–604. See also her "Many Faces of Cui Yingying." The "jealous Oriole" is discussed on pp. 89–90; the "virtuous Oriole" is treated on pp. 90–94. Cf. Tan Zhengbi and Tan Xun, "Wang Shifu yiwai ershiqi *Xixiang* kao."

[37] For an extensive anthology of popular songs and prosimetric texts on the romance of Student Zhang and Oriole, see Fu Xihua, *Xixiang ji shuochang ji*.

[38] Yang Zhenxiong, *Xixiang ji*.

[39] See n. 23.

[40] These color woodblock prints are reproduced in facsimile in Edith Dittrich, *Hsi-hsiang chi, Chinesische Farbholzschnitte von Min Ch'i-chu, 1640*.

[41] See, e.g., Craig Clunas, "The West Chamber: A Literary Theme in Chinese Porcelain Decoration", and Hsu Wen-chin, "Fictional Scenes on Chinese Transitional Porcelain and Their Sources of Decoration," esp. pp. 10–28 and pp. 104–28 (plates 22–51).

[42] Wang Jisi, *Cong "Yingying zhuan" dao Xixiang ji*; Zhou Tian, *Xixiang ji fenxi*; Huo Songling, *Xixiang ji jianshuo*, and *Xixiang shuping*; Dai Bufan, *Lun Cui Yingying*; Duan Qiming, *Xixiang lungao*; Wu Guoqin, *Xixiang ji yishu tan*; Sun Xun, *Dong Xixiang he Wang Xixiang*; and Zhang Yanjin, *Xixiang ji jianshuo*. A survey of *Western Wing* studies published in the People's Republic of China from 1949 to 1985 may be found in Ning Zongyi, Lu Lin, and Tian Guimin, *Yuan zaju yanjiu gaishu*, 187–207. The same work provides bibliographies of Chinese studies on Wang Shifu and his *Story of the Western Wing* on pp. 410–12 (1913–49) and 467–87 (1949–85).

[43] See n. 18.

[44] Wang Shifu, *Xixiang ji*, annotated by Wu Xiaoling.

[45] Wang Shifu, *Jiping jiaozhu Xixiang ji*.

[46] Wang Shifu, *Xixiang ji xinzhu*, annotated by Zhang Yanjin and Mi Songyi, and *Xixiang ji tongsu zhushi*.

[47] See n. 34.

[48] See n. 37.

[49] See chap. 3.

[50] Wang Lina, "*Xixiang ji* de waiwen yiben he Man Meng wen yiben", and Jiang Xingyu, "*Xixiang ji* de Riwen yiben."

[51] See Haenisch's "Review of Vincenz Hundhausen, *Das Westzimmer*." Hundhausen went on to produce a *Nachdichtung* of Tang Xianzu's famous sentimental melodrama, *The Peony Pavilion*, in 1933.

[52] Wang Shifu, *The West Chamber, A Medieval Drama*, translated by Henry H. Hart, x.

[53] *Ibid.*, ix.

[54] Wang Shifu, *The West Chamber (Hsi-hsiang chi)*, rendered into English verse by Henry W. Wells, in Irwin, *Four Classical Asian Plays in Modern Translation*.

[55] C. T. Hsia, "A Critical Introduction," xxxi.

2

AUTHOR AND AUTHORSHIP

Biographical information about Wang Shifu is meager indeed. During the second quarter of the fourteenth century, when Zhong Sicheng compiled the earliest extant catalog of *zaju* authors and their works under the title *A Register of Ghosts* (*Lugui bu*), he could provide only the information that Wang Shifu was "a man from Dadu [present-day Beijing]," then the capital of the Mongol Yuan empire.[1] In the 1422 manuscript revision of and supplement to *A Register of Ghosts*, Jia Zhongming adds that Shifu is Wang's courtesy name and that his personal name is actually Dexin.[2] As a given name, Dexin was not uncommon in Yuan times, but attempts so far to identify our playwright with better known historical characters are unconvincing.[3] From Zhong Sicheng's classification of Wang Shifu as one of those "already deceased noble lords and talented poets of the former generation whose plays still circulate in the world," we may broadly date Wang Shifu's activities to the middle or second half of the thirteenth century.

A Register of Ghosts credits Wang Shifu altogether with the production of fourteen plays. Apart from *The Story of the Western Wing*, only two of these plays are complete and extant. *The Hall of Beautiful Spring* (*Lichun tang*) is Wang Shifu's only work to be included in the *Selection of Yuan Songs* (*Yuanqu xuan*), a collection of one hundred *zaju* published in 1615 and 1616 and since that time the single most influential anthology of the genre. The action of *The Hall of Beautiful Spring* is set during the reign of the Jin dynasty emperor Zhangzong (r. 1190–1208) and concerns a feud between two high officials that eventually is peacefully resolved.[4] The other play, *The Story of the Dilapidated Kiln* (*Poyao ji*), has been preserved in a manuscript copied from the library attached to the eunuch agency for theatricals at the Ming imperial court. This play dramatizes the popular legend of Lü Mengzheng's spectacular rise to fame and fortune. The historical Lü Mengzheng (946–1011) was descended from a family of officials—both his grandfather and father had held high office—and he was himself a man of high position, having passed the metropolitan examinations as "head of the list" (*zhuangyuan*) in 977. But once the Song emperors established the examination system as the most prestigious and important means of entry into the bureaucracy and seemed thereby to have achieved the institutionalization of a Confucian meritocracy, Lü Mengzheng was transformed in popular lore into the archetype of the poor student who solely on account of his literary talent and perseverance eventually succeeds in the examinations. The play is set in Luoyang, where Liu Yue'e, the daughter of a rich squire, is to select a husband by throwing an embroidered ball from a bunted loft into the crowd below.⁵ When Liu Yue'e hits Lü Mengzheng and refuses to repudiate her choice, her father throws her out of the house, forcing the new couple to live in a dilapidated kiln outside of town. Lü Mengzheng figures out a way to get a free meal every day by joining the noontime assembly of monks at Luoyang's White Horse Monastery, but the abbot of the monastery, apparently with the intention of shaming the young man for his freeloading, has the mealtime bell struck after the repast and not before, as was usual. Later, a gift from a friend enables Lü to travel to the capital to take part in the examinations. When he successfully returns to fetch his faithful wife, he learns that it was Squire Liu who had instructed the abbot to shame him and who had provided Lü's friend with the money to send him to the capital. Realizing that this was all done in order to spur him on toward greater efforts, Lü Mengzheng becomes reconciled with his father-in-law. Earlier, when shamed out of the monastery, Lü inscribed two lines of verse on the wall:

> The gathering is finished, each goes his way;
> How shameful to hear the ashram bell ring after the meal.

Upon his return, Lü finds that this piece of calligraphy, because written by the head of the list, has been protected by a gauze covering, and he completes the quatrain with the following lines:

> For ten years it was darkened by dust and grime,
> But now it is at last encaged by azure gauze.⁶

In the Hongzhi edition of *The Story of the Western Wing*, at the end of the first act of the fourth play, Zhang Gong also recites this poem, but under rather different circumstances.⁷ Neither *The Hall of Beautiful Spring* nor *The Story of the Dilapidated Kiln* has ever attracted much attention; some critics have expressed surprise at the mediocrity of these works and have even doubted Wang Shifu's authorship.

Single suites of arias are extant from two more plays by Wang Shifu. The first suite is from the first act of a play entitled *The Lotus Pavilion (Furong ting)*. The plot of this play is not known, but the arias are apparently sung by a young woman who visits a student in the study of his aunt's house at night, only to be (initially?) rebuffed. The arias exhibit a remarkably high density of references to *The Story of the Western Wing*.⁸ The other suite probably constitutes the second act of a play entitled the *The Tea-Trading Boat (Fancha chuan)*,⁹ a dramatic adaptation of the romance of the student Shuang Jian and the courtesan Su Xiaoqing. This was perhaps the most popular of all romances between the twelfth and fifteenth centuries (until supplanted by *The Story of the Western Wing*). During the twelfth century it was written up as an all-keys-and-modes (*zhugongdiao*) chantefable that was revised during the early thirteenth century, and the story is repeatedly referred to in practically any comedy on the student, courtesan, and merchant triangle. The basic outline of the romance is as follows. The student Shuang Jian falls in love with the courtesan Su Xiaoqing. After his departure for the capital in order to take part in the examinations, she is determined to remain faithful to him. But her madam tricks her into believing that Shuang Jian, following his success in the examinations, has betrayed her, whereupon she allows herself to be married off to Feng Kui, a rich but repugnant tea merchant from Jiangxi. When he takes her down south on his boat, they visit the Gold Mountain Monastery, on whose walls she inscribes a poem bemoaning her fate. Shuang Jian, newly appointed to a magistracy, passes by the same place, sees the poem, pursues Feng Kui's boat, and overtakes it. He abducts Su Xiaoqing and has her awarded to himself by the authorities in Nanchang, who are well-disposed toward him, curtly dismissing Feng Kui's claim.[10] There is no indication, however, that this second adaptation of an all-keys-and-modes to the *zaju* form by Wang Shifu had the same exceptional length as his *Story of the Western Wing*.

Of the remaining nine titles attributed to Wang, not a single aria has survived. From their titles, some of these plays were love tragedies, some featured famous characters from history; in other cases, the titles allow no inferences as to the contents of the plays. Surveying the full list, we are immediately struck by the variety of subject matter. Although deliverance plays, courtroom plays, and *zaju* with a clearly martial theme are absent, we do find works that treat love, duty, and official career, either separately or in combination. We are also struck by Wang Shifu's preference for highly popular subject matter. In a catalog of play-wrights included in his handbook of prosodic rules for *qu*-style music, *A Formulary of Correct Sounds for Great Peace* (*Taihe zhengyin pu*), Zhu Quan (1378–1448) designates five of Wang Shifu's plays as being one of "two texts" (*erben*), indicating that the same title is listed in the handbook under another playwright's name as well.[11] The tale of Lü Mengzheng, for example, was also adapted for the stage by Guan Hanqing, and the romance of Shuang Jian and Su Xiaoqing also existed in versions by Ji Junxiang and Yu Tianxi.

All these factors combined—the paucity of biographical information, the wide variety of subject matter, and the remarkable preference for popular materials—strongly suggest that Wang Shifu was one of those professional playwrights of his age who regularly provided *zaju* for the commercial stages of the capital. He was anything but a hack, however; the preserved titles testify to both his learning and his versatility His plays, especially *The Story of the Western Wing*, demonstrate not only that Wang Shifu had received a sound traditional education in the classics, the histories, the philosophers, and the major authors, but also that he was widely read in the lighter branches of literature such as tales and lyrics. His deep acquaintance with the vernacular literature of his own day is apparent. If he could pen an aria that reads as a brilliant embroidery of quotations, he could also write in a very simple and straightforward or even vulgar manner, depending on the character and the situation. But for Zhu Quan in his *Formulary of Correct Sounds for*

Great Peace, the distinctive quality of Wang Shifu's arias is the sensuality of the language. He compares his style to "a beauty amidst flowers," adding, "His disposition is brilliant and fully realizes the intent of the author of 'Encountering Sorrow', repeatedly he has fine lines, such as 'Yuhuan emerging from her bath at Huaqing hot springs' or 'Lüzhu collecting lotuses on the reaches of the river Luo.'"[12]

Apart from plays Wang Shifu also wrote *sanqu*, or nondramatic arias: two long *sanqu* suites attributed to him have survived in sixteenth-century anthologies. One of these is occasionally mined for biographical information,[13] though even if one overlooks their questionable authorship, the fictional nature of both works is quite apparent. If we do not identify the "I" in a first-person complaint of a young courtesan jilted by her lover as an autobiographical statement by Wang Shifu, neither should we accept a first-person ode to the joys of a life of retirement by a sexagenarian gentleman as self-referential. Moreover, the terminology in both suites of arias is utterly conventional.

Various attempts have been made to specify Wang Shifu's dates in more detail, although the results have been quite contradictory The modern scholar Wang Guowei, whose publications established the history of Chinese drama as an academic discipline, suggests that Wang Shifu began writing for the stage sometime before 1235. He bases this supposition on the fulsome praise for the "present emperor" in the final line of the final aria of *The Hall of Beautiful Spring* [14] Since nearly every *zaju* ends with such an encomium whatever the setting of the play, this argument carries little weight. More recently, Dai Bufan has also tried to prove that Wang Shifu lived during the Jin. His conclusion is based mainly on the intimate knowledge of Jin dynasty institutions displayed in *The Hall of Beautiful Spring* [15] But what now appears to be esoteric information may well have been common knowledge during the thirteenth century And even if the wording of the self-introduction of one Jin official replicates that of *The History of the Jin Dynasty (Jin shi)* of 1344, it may simply be because the speech was copied into the dialogue on the occasion of a later revision for the stage or publication. The commonly accepted view is that full-fledged *zaju* emerged only around the middle of the thirteenth century; but Dai Bufan sees all deviations from strict Yuan conventions of *zaju* in *The Story of the Western Wing* as further supporting evidence for his thesis of an early date, completely disregarding the issue of editorial revisions. We will see shortly that other eminent scholars, on the basis of many of these same deviations, have argued that *The Story of the Western Wing* could not have been written earlier than the end of the fourteenth century Based on circumstantial evidence at best, Dai Bufan's dating of neither Wang Shifu nor the play can yet be accepted.

In order to make his case, Dai Bufan first deals with the more influential theory of dating proposed by Wang Jisi, and here he is more successful. Wang Jisi dates Wang Shifu's activity as a dramatist to the years 1297–1307. His argument is based on two pieces of evidence. The first of these is three lines from an aria in the third act of *The Hall of Beautiful Spring* that occur verbatim in an aria to the tune "Yingwu qu" written by a certain Bai Wujiu in 1302. Wang Jisi assumes that Wang Shifu borrowed these lines from Bai. The second piece of evidence is a line from the final aria from the fourth act of the fifth play in Jin Shengtan's edition of *The Story of the Western Wing*, which might be translated, "Thanks be to the two sagely rulers who reign from behind the screen." Wang Jisi accepts Jin Shengtan's statement that his recension was based on some authentic "old edition" and that this line refers to the regency of Empress Bu'erhan during the Dade reign period (1297–1307).[16] Now, Jin Shengtan may have seen editions of *The Story of the Western Wing* that are inaccessible today, but in general his editorial changes derive from his own invention. Dai Bufan notes that the line under discussion might very well have been inserted by Jin Shengtan in reference to the regency during the early years of the Shunzhi reign period (1644–61). He also argues that it is just as likely that Bai Wujiu borrowed his (utterly conventional) lines from Wang Shifu as it is that Wang Shifu borrowed his lines from Bai. Dai Bufan continues by pointing out that if indeed Wang Shifu was active around the turn of the century, it is quite surprising that Zhong Sicheng should have so little information about him or his work.[17] If Wang Jisi's dating lacks the power to convince, we can only resign ourselves to the more general traditional dates, which place Wang Shifu's activities as a playwright between the years 1230 and 1300.

In recent years a number of eminent Chinese scholars—Chen Zhongfan, Zhou Miaozhong, and Zheng Qian, for example—have put forward the theory that whatever the dates of Wang Shifu, the presently available *Story of the Western Wing* should be seen as an anonymous work of around 1350 or later that may incorporate a single *zaju* by Wang Shifu on the same subject but that should by no account be identified with the whole five-play cycle. Their main argument is based on the exceptional length of the play. They point out that Yuan dynasty playwrights as a rule take exceptional care to reduce their plots, irrespective of the length of the original story, to a four-act format. Moreover, the only other examples of lengthy cycles of plays date from the early Ming dynasty.[18] Of these, *The Story of Jiaoniang and Feihong* (*Jiao Hong ji*) by Liu Dui has been preserved in an edition from the Xuande reign period (1426–35). In a two-*zaju* cycle it dramatizes Song Meidong's "Tale of Jiaoniang and Feihong" ("Jiao Hong zhuan"), the story of the tragic love affair between the student Shen Chun and his maternal cousin Wang Jiaoniang, whose girl servant is called Feihong. This tale of the late Song or early Yuan is itself of exceptional length for its genre and must have enjoyed a considerable popularity during the Yuan and early Ming dynasties: two more dramatic adaptations are known to us by title, one of them ascribed to Wang Shifu. According to Liu Dui's preface, *The Story of Jiaoniang and Feihong* was composed in conscious emulation of Wang Shifu's *Story of the Western Wing*.[19]

The second example of an early Ming *zaju* cycle would be a six-play cycle that adapts portions of *Journey to the West* (*Xiyou ji*). It is preserved in an edition from

the final years of the Wanli reign period (1573–1619), which ascribes its authorship to the early Yuan playwright Wu Changling. This is clearly wrong. The play
has subsequently been attributed to the early Ming playwright Yang Ne, but
recent critical opinion tends to date its composition to the end of the sixteenth
century [20] Thus, it appears that for the late Yuan and early Ming dynasties it is
barely possible to speak of a tradition of *zaju* cycles to which *The Story of the
Western Wing* should belong. It would have been just as exceptional had it been
written around 1350 or 1450 instead of around 1250.

A second argument in favor of a late Yuan–early Ming dating of *The Story of
the Western Wing* is supposedly found in the entry concerning our play in *A
Register of Ghosts*. The full title and name of the play as recorded in the manuscript
of Jia Zhongming's revision of the catalog do not correspond to those found in
any of the extant editions. It is debatable, however, how much weight should be
attached to this fact since similar discrepancies between titles and names recorded
in *A Register of Ghosts* and those in the extant texts are all too common. We may
further point out that while Zhong Sicheng does not say a word about the
exceptional length of the play here, elsewhere he notes that a play consists of six
acts. Perhaps in the case of such a popular play Zhong saw no need to stress the
obvious—that it too consists of several acts.

Further circumstantial evidence for a late fourteenth-century date for the
composition of *The Story of the Western Wing* is the length of some of the suites,
the refined and sensual style of the arias, and the frequent assignment of arias in a
single suite to more than one performer. While few scholars would deny that our
presently available *Story of the Western Wing* possibly incorporates extensive later
revisions, the theory that it was composed around 1350 or later has been generally
rejected.[21] Apart from the counterarguments cited above, it should also be
pointed out that Zhou Deqing, in his *Sounds and Rhymes of the Central Plain*
(*Zhongyuan yinyun*), a handbook of pronunciation of the northern vernacular for
the benefit of southern practitioners of *zaju* and *sanqu* (preface dated 1324),
quotes songs now found in the third act of the first play and the third and fifth acts
of the second play from *The Story of the Western Wing* [22] (*A Formulary for Correct
Sounds of Great Peace*, compiled roughly a century later, also quotes from the third
and seventeenth acts.) We further stress that all the early authorities on *zaju*—
Zhong Sicheng, Zhu Quan, Jia Zhongming—mention Wang Shifu as the author
of our play To these authorities we may add Qiu Rucheng and his 1435 preface
to Liu Dui's *Story of Jiaoning and Hongfei*. If indeed *The Story of the Western Wing*
was composed during the second half of the fourteenth century, this unanimity of
attribution by early Ming authorities would be very difficult to explain.

Yet despite this unanimity of opinion, by the early sixteenth century, when
zaju was quickly losing the stage to *chuanqi*, a completely different notion concerning the authorship of *The Story of the Western Wing* had become widespread:
it was now believed to be the work of the preeminent practitioner of the genre,
Guan Hanqing. This must have seemed a logical supposition at a time when plays
were often printed without an author's name and when sources like *A Register of*

Ghosts or *A Formulary for Correct Sounds of Great Peace* were rare or circulated only in manuscript. The first writer to refer to the "vulgar notion" (in order to refute it) that Guan Hanqing had composed *The Story of the Western Wing* was the Suzhou author Du Mu (1459–1525) in his *Poetry Talks of Nanhao (Nanhao shihua)* of 1513.[23] Instead of simply correcting this error, scholars who had access to the catalogs of Zhong Sicheng and Zhu Quan tried to reconcile common notions with documentary evidence by assigning the play's authorship to both Guan Hanqing and Wang Shifu. From a series of satirical songs about the characters in *The Story of the Western Wing* and its authors, included among the prefatory materials of the Hongzhi edition, it is clear that the editor of this recension was already acquainted with the theory of dual authorship.[24] Since many critics of the sixteenth century and later were convinced of marked stylistic differences between the first four *zaju* of the cycle and the final play, the first four were assigned to Guan Hanqing and the final one to Wang Shifu, or the other way around. This observation of stylistic differences is essential to the argument of dual authorship. But the argument soon becomes circular: whoever is convinced of dual authorship of the play will discern stylistic differences that will in turn become "irrefutable" evidence of dual authorship.

Eventually, common opinion, strongly influenced by Jin Shengtan's edition, came to ascribe authorship of the first four *zaju* of *The Story of the Western Wing* to Wang Shifu. To ascribe the final *zaju* to Guan Hanqing of course meant that according to common opinion, the weakest play in the cycle was assigned to the finer playwright. Some critics have therefore preferred to assume that the fifth *zaju* was the work of a late and anonymous hack. Jin Shengtan, especially, avoids mentioning the name of Guan Hanqing in his discussion of the authorship of the fifth *zaju*.[25]

Once it was commonly agreed that *The Story of the Western Wing* had been composed by Wang Shifu and someone else, the exact spot at which Wang Shifu had laid down his brush had to be determined. Jin Shengtan argues that the final act of the fourth *zaju* constitutes the logical conclusion to the action of the play This act takes place following the famous farewell scene in the third act, when Zhang Gong departs for the capital and takes leave of Oriole. Asleep in the room of an inn during the first night of his trip, Zhang Gong is visited in a dream by Oriole. She informs the student that she has decided to elope with him, but she is rudely torn away by soldiers. Jin Shengtan interprets this act as an expression of the author's conviction that all the preceding action and, even more broadly, all of life in general, is only a dream. Accordingly, he interprets the fifth play of the cycle, which traces the lovers' separation and their joyous reunion, as a superfluous sequel.[26] Others who view this final act of the fourth play as the work of a later hand draw on a late but widespread legend that Wang Shifu died from exhaustion after finishing the first four lines of the opening song of the third act.[27]

This supposed collaboration has been used to determine Wang Shifu's dates: since Guan Hanqing was active around the middle of the thirteenth century, Wang Shifu must have been too. Efforts to date Wang Shifu either earlier or later therefore deny the possibility of cooperation between Wang Shifu and Guan Hanqing. Nowadays the theory of dual authorship of *The Story of the Western Wing* is generally rejected, even though it was defended as recently as 1967 by no less a scholar than C. T. Hsia:

> To justify Wang Shihfu's fair name as a playwright, tradition had early maintained that he was the author of only the first four plays and that the fifth was a continuation by Guan Hanqing.   It is highly unlikely that an older man of greater fame would have wanted to complete the work of a younger contemporary. Besides, it amounts to slander to ascribe to Guan something deemed unworthy of Wang.
>
> If the traditional assumption that Wang did not write the fifth play is not entirely groundless, then it would seem reasonable to assume that some later hand, writing in the decadence of the *zaju* tradition, wrote a sequel to meet popular demand for a complete cycle of plays based on Dong's poem.[28]

Modern scholars have stressed that the same early sources that unanimously ascribe the play to Wang Shifu make no mention of cooperation of any kind.[29] Nor do any of our early sources connect Guan Hanqing to *The Story of the Western Wing* in any way, even though the list of over sixty titles ascribed to him probably contains a number of errors.[30] If modern readers find the final *zaju* of the cycle lackluster, it may tell us more about these readers' expectations than about the text; and even if the final play is not on a par with the preceding four, this does not necessarily lead us to the conclusion that all five plays could not be by the same hand. Most important, the five-play cycle as a whole constitutes a remarkably faithful and unified adaptation of its direct source, Dong Jieyuan's *Story of the Western Wing in All Keys and Modes*, which ends on the happy note of marriage.

Notes

[1] Zhong Sicheng, *Lugui bu*, 109–10. Cf. Fu Xihua, *Yuandai zaju quanmu*, 52–66; and Tan Zhengbi, *Yuanqu liudajia lüezhuan*, 119–74.

[2] Zhong Sicheng, *Lugui bu*, 173; Jia Zhongming, *Tianyige lange xieben zhengxu Lugui bu*, 7b. According to some modern scholars this was an emendation by Jia, a nonsensical string of three characters in the manuscript.

[3] Sun Kaidi's suggestion; see his *Yuanqu jia kaolüe*, 69–70. The theory that identifies our playwright as Wang Dexin, father of the high official Wang Jie (1275–1336) from Dingxing, is discussed at length and rejected by Yao Shuyi in "Yuanqu jia cuotan."

[4] For a modern typeset edition of this *zaju*, see, e.g., Zang Jinshu, *Yuanqu xuan*, 3:900–13.

[5] This is a marriage custom that appears never to have existed in China in fact but was quite popular on the stage.

[6] The manuscript copy is found in the *Mowangguan chaojiaoben gujin zaju*. This collection has been reproduced in the fourth series of the *Guben xiqu congkan*. Typeset

editions are provided in Wang Jilie, *Guben Yuan Ming zaju*, vol. 1; and in Sui Shusen, *Yuanqu xuan waibian*, 1:324–36. For a detailed study of this play, its sources, and its later adaptations, see Chiu-kuei Wang, "Lü Meng-cheng in Yüan and Ming Drama."

[7] I.e., when, after an arduous period of courtship, he finally seduces Oriole.

[8] This song suite may be most conveniently found in Zhao Jingshen, *Yuanren zaju gouchen*, 25–28.

[9] *Ibid.*, 29–34.

[10] Cf. Idema, *The Dramatic Oeuvre of Chu Yu-tun*, 115–16; Crump, *Songs from Xanadu*, 171–92.

[11] Zhu Quan, *Taihe zhengyin pu*, 3:26–27. On the issue of second texts, see Zhao Jingshen, "Yuanqu de erben."

[12] *Ibid.*, 17. The author of "Encountering Sorrow" ("Lisao") is the statesman and poet Qu Yuan (fl. 300 B.C.), who in this poem voices, in most extravagant language, his despair at being neglected by his king. Yuhuan is better known as Yang Guifei, the favorite concubine of the Tang dynasty emperor Xuanzong (r. 712–56); Lüzhu was the favorite concubine of the immensely wealthy Shi Chong (249–300). Both bewitching beauties were believed to have caused their masters' downfalls.

[13] These poems have been collected and collated by Sui Shusen in *Quan Yuan sanqu*, 1:291–96.

[14] Wang Guowei, *Qulu*, 88 (2.2b).

[15] Dai Bufan, "Wang Shifu niandai xintan." See also Jiang Xingyu's rebuttal to Dai Bufan's arguments in Jiang, "Wang Shifu *Xixiang ji* wancheng yu Jin dai shuo pouxi."

[16] Wang Jisi, "*Xixiang ji* xushuo" of 1955, reprinted in his *Yulunxuan qulun*, 33–34, and his *Cong "Yingying zhuan" dao Xixiang ji*, 38–39.

[17] Dai Bufan, "Wang Shifu niandai xintan,"63–65.

[18] Chen Zhongfan, "Guanyu *Xixiang ji* de chuangzuo niandai ji qi zuozhe," quoted in Wang Shifu, *Jiping jiaozhu Xixiang ji*, 316–17; several articles in the "Wenxue yichan" section of the *Guangming ribao* during the course of 1961; Zheng Qian, "*Xixiang ji* zuozhe xinkao," esp. pp. 1–19; and Zhou Miaozhong, "*Xixiang ji* zaju zuozhe zhiyi."

[19] For a study of the "Jiao Hong zhuan" and the plays based on it, see Itô Sôhei, "Formation of the *Chiao-hung chi*." Liu Dui's play has been photomechanically reproduced in the first series of the *Guben xiqu congkan*, and an annotated typeset edition is provided by Zhou Yibai in his *Mingren zaju xuan*, 1–84.

[20] The most accessible modern edition of this play can be found in Sui Shusen, *Yuanqu xuan waibian*, 2:633–94. See also Goldblatt, "The Hsi-yu chi Play," esp. 38–40; and Dudbridge, *The Hsi-yu chi*, 76–80.

[21] Wang Jisi has gone to great lengths to refute Chen Zhongfan's points one by one; see his "Guanyu *Xixiang ji* zuozhe de wenti" and his "Guanyu *Xixiang ji* zuozhe wenti de jinyibu tantao." See also the summary of this debate in Li Xiusheng, "Jianguo yilai Yuan zaju yanjiu zhi huigu."

[22] Zhou Deqing, *Zhongyuan yinyun*, 233.

[23] Wang Shifu, *Jiping jiaozhu Xixiang ji*, 208. Zhang Renhe conveniently collects and discusses the various pronouncements on the authorship of *The Story of the Western Wing* from the sixteenth and seventeenth centuries in his "*Xixiang ji* lunzha." For another compendium of premodern pronouncements on the authorship of the play, see Li Hanqiu and Yuan Youfen, *Guan Hanqing yanjiu ziliao*, 388–414.

[24] Guan Hanqing is mentioned as the author of our play in the second introductory suite to the first book; see our translation of this song, p. 112.

25 John Ching-yu Wang, *Chin Sheng-t'an*, 101–3.

26 *Ibid.*, 102.

27 Wang Shizhen (1526–90) refers to the two conflicting opinions concerning the cutoff point in his *Quzao*, 31. For the manner of Wang Shifu's death, see Liang Tingnan (1796–1861), *Quhua*, 291.

28 C. T Hsia, "Critical Introduction," xxii–xxiii.

29 Although they are meticulous about noting two cases in which different authors collaborated on a single *zaju* by contributing individually written acts.

30 But in the anonymous Ming dynasty anthology *Yuefu qunzhu*, Guan Hanqing is credited with the authorship of a series of sixteen *sanqu* lyrics recounting the romance of Student Zhang and Oriole; see Sui Shusen, *Quan Yuan sanqu*, 1:158–62, "Cui Zhang shiliu shi." The wording of these songs would appear to be heavily indebted to the play, so Guan's authorship is strongly doubted. Cf. Tan Zhengbi and Tan Xun, "Guan Hanqing zuo huo xuzuo *Xixiang ji* shuo suyuan."

3

THE PEDIGREE OF THE MATERIALS

Dong Jieyuan's *The Story of the Western Wing in All Keys and Modes* may be the direct source for Wang Shifu's play, but it is not its ultimate source. That is "The Tale of Oriole" ("Yingying zhuan"), a short story in the classical language by the Tang dynasty statesman and poet Yuan Zhen (779–831).[1] In contemporary literary history Yuan Zhen is remembered primarily as the bosom friend of the poet Bo Juyi (772–846). During their lifetimes they were equally renowned for their verse; but whereas the poetry of Bo Juyi has continued to this day to be extremely popular both inside and outside China, Yuan Zhen's reputation as a poet has suffered considerably His "Tale of Oriole," however, is rightly considered one of the finest examples of the Tang classical tale.[2] As a genre, the classical tale (*chuanqi*) has roots that go back centuries, though it flowered spectacularly in the final decades of the eighth century and early decades of the ninth. When Bo Juyi and Yuan Zhen were both students and aspiring young officials in the capital at Chang'an between 803 and 810, they and their friends eagerly wrote their own tales and composed long narrative poems on the subjects of others' Bo Juyi's best-known work in this connection is his "Song of Unending Sorrow" ("Changhen ge"), a poem in 120 lines on the disastrous passion of the Tang emperor Xuanzong (r. 712–56) for his favorite concubine Yang Guifei, written to accompany a tale on the same topic by his friend Chen Hong.[3] Bo Juyi's younger brother Bo Xingjian (776–826) composed "The Tale of Li Wa" ("Li Wa zhuan") about the affair of the capital courtesan and her rich student-lover (in later versions called Zheng Yuanhe), whom she first fleeces and later rescues from direst poverty Yuan Zhen turned the tale into a long narrative poem from which only a few lines survive.[4] Yuan's "Tale of Oriole" would similarly provide the material for a long poem by his close friend Li Shen (772–846).

"The Tale of Oriole" narrates the story of Student Zhang, who at the age of twenty-three and still very proudly a virgin travels from the capital and across the Yellow River to Puzhou, where he stays at the Monastery of Universal Salvation outside of town. When local troops mutiny, he uses his connections with the officers to save the monastery from looting. A distant aunt who is also staying at the monastery, a widow, expresses her thanks by spreading a banquet for him, at which she introduces him to her daughter Oriole. Student Zhang immediately falls in love with the young girl and tries to arrange a meeting through her maidservant. Oriole sends Zhang a poem inviting him to her room at night; but when he shows up, she rebukes him sternly for harboring immoral designs. A few nights later, however, she comes to his room of her own volition, and over the following months they carry on an affair (in which her mother apparently acquiesces, hoping for a marriage) that is interrupted only by Zhang's temporary return to the capital. On the eve of his final departure Zhang asks Oriole to play the zither for him, but overcome by grief, she stops in the middle of the melody In the capital, despite a very touching letter from her, Student Zhang decides to break with Oriole because, he claims, her beauty would destroy him. A year later both are married to someone else, and when he asks to see her, she refuses.

Within its genre "The Tale of Oriole" is remarkable for its absence of supernatural elements and its insistence on psychological realism. The character-ization is not without irony· the author stresses both Student Zhang's lack of experience in matters of love and sex and his total infatuation, which initially render him an easy victim to women's wiles. Despite his protestations, he slowly and never completely recovers from his obsession. In the case of Oriole, we catch only glimpses of contradictory behavior, the outcome of a continuing inner conflict between desire and shame. The resulting enigma of her personality adds greatly to the appeal of the story As early as the eleventh century it was suggested that "The Tale of Oriole" is autobiographical and that in Student Zhang we may recognize a thinly disguised alter ego of the author, Yuan Zhen. In fact Yuan Zhen's poetry strongly suggests that before marrying he had had a love affair that continued to haunt him over the years.[5]

Some modern scholars have been struck by the similarity between the sur-names of the protagonists in "The Tale of Oriole" and other tales that describe dalliances between young students and immortals. "Immortal" or, more pre-cisely, "realized one" (zhenren) is a common metaphor in vernacular literature for a courtesan. Both the alternate title of Yuan Zhen's tale, "Huizhen ji" (Story of an encounter with an immortal), and the student's utterance that Oriole was of the "class of spirit immortals" (shenxian zhi tu) have led these scholars to deduce that Oriole was actually such a courtesan.[6] Those who read the text in the traditional manner of seeking its links to history have been struck by the fact that Yuan Zhen's mother was surnamed Zheng and had a sister who was married to a certain Cui Peng—and thus could have been Oriole's mother. Once the all-keys-and-modes and the play established the character of Zheng Heng, Oriole's original fiancé, he became identified with the anonymous husband in Yuan Zhen's tale. During the early Ming dynasty it was even rumored that the grave inscription of this happily married couple had been discovered.[7] This "discovery" was interpreted by traditional positivist critics as incontrovertible proof that "The Tale of Oriole" was a malicious fabrication, and by extension, The Story of the Western Wing was also exposed as a fraud, a fiction.

Although "The Tale of Oriole" has survived by virtue of inclusion in various collections of tales, only fragments of the Li Shen ballad on which it is based are extant.[8] These four fragments are enough to prove that Li's version is not a simple recasting of the prose narrative into metrical form but a re-creation that brings many new touches to the story In "The Tale of Oriole" Student Zhang appears to arrive at the Monastery of Universal Salvation in late autumn or early winter, but in the first fragment of Li Shen's ballad, possibly the opening lines of his poem, the inception of action is clearly placed in early spring, the season of budding love, and emphasizes Oriole's longing. The second fragment provides an extensive description of the mutiny and the plunder of Puzhou, whereas "The Tale of Oriole" deals with the mutiny in only a few words. In the third fragment Li Shen furnishes the friendly officer, the White Horse General, who saves the monastery from pillage; it remains unclear whether he identifies this White Horse General with Du Que, which later happens in the all-keys-and-modes and in the play The fourth fragment recounts the exchange of poems preceding the couple's first nightly encounter and is the only fragment of the ballad to add no new details. While Dong Jieyuan takes Yuan Zhen's "Tale of Oriole" for his base, he also draws heavily on the ballad by Li Shen: all four fragments are actually quoted in *The Story of the Western Wing in All Keys and Modes*.

By the eleventh century "The Tale of Oriole," already circulating in written form, had entered the realm of oral literature. When the poet Zhao Lingzhi (1051–1134) adapted "The Tale of Oriole" as a drum song (*guzi ci*), he stated in his preface that scholars were fond of talking about this romance and that entertainers could recite it in outline.[9] He also suggested that these versions departed considerably from the original tale. In his own version he provides an extensive excerpt from Yuan Zhen's work, to which he adds twelve lyrics to the tune "Dielianhua" one lyric is placed at the opening of the tale and one at its conclusion; nine others interrupt the main narrative wherever Zhao Lingzhi sees fit. These songs add little or nothing to the narrative but rather summarize the preceding action in the highly conventional language of *ci* poetry. We may note that in his opening lyric Zhao Lingzhi too calls our attention to Oriole's love-longing. The tale proper is followed by a short discussion on the propriety of Student Zhang's and Oriole's behavior, concluded by a final lyric. The final two songs clearly censure Zhang for his lack of love and his betrayal of Oriole. In his preface Zhao Lingzhi expresses regret over the absence of a singable version of the authentic "Tale of Oriole." He may have invented the narrative *guzi ci* to remedy this, but neither the form nor the content of his drum song appears to have met with any great success—only one other and much later example of a narrative *guzi ci* survives. When Dong Jieyuan adapted "The Tale of Oriole" to the format of the all-keys-and-modes, he chose to depart radically from his source in the opening and conclusion of the story. He did not make these changes out of ignorance of the original work—he repeatedly quotes from it in his text—but out of a desire to pursue the other possibilities so clearly hinted at in Li Shen's ballad.

The genre of the all-keys-and-modes originated during the second half of the eleventh century in the north of China, in the southeastern part of modern

Shanxi Province; by the early years of the twelfth century it had spread to the capital at Kaifeng in modern Henan Province. In language and choice of subject matter the genre continued to betray its regional provenance.[10]

The all-keys-and-modes is one of the many forms of prosimetric narrative, or, to use the Chinese term, "tell-and-sing literature" (*shuochang wenxue*). In prosimetric texts the narrative is carried forward in alternating prose and verse. In the majority of forms the verse sections are written to a fixed meter of five, seven, or ten syllables per line; these lines are chanted to a melody or melodies specific to that form, while each form prescribes the musical instrument or instruments for the accompaniment. In the all-keys-and-modes these verse sections are songs written to a variety of melodies; each verse section may consist of a two-stanza song, a two-stanza song and a three-line coda, or a suite of songs in either one or two stanzas but belonging to the same mode or key and culminating in a coda. As the genre developed, both the relative number and the length of suites (*taoshu*) increased. The genre derives its name from a feature characteristic to it: two consecutive verse sections are rarely if ever in the same key or mode. Individual songs and song sets tend to end with a punch line: the earliest known performer of the genre, a certain "Professor" Kong, was famed for the wit and humor of his songs.[11] The genre as a whole manifests an outspoken proclivity for satire and ribaldry, to which it gives free rein in the love stories that are its preferred subject matter.[12]

Unfortunately, Dong Jieyuan's *Story of the Western Wing in All Keys and Modes* is the only complete example of the genre extant. Fragments of an earlier all-keys-and-modes about the life and loves of Liu Zhiyuan, founder of the Later Han dynasty, were discovered in the early years of this century,[13] and from the second half of the thirteenth century we have some fifty-odd song sets from an all-keys-and-modes about Emperor Xuanzong and Yang Guifei written by the dramatist Wang Bocheng.[14] In *The Story of the Western Wing in All Keys and Modes* and the fragments of the anonymous *All Keys and Modes of Liu Zhiyuan* (*Liu Zhiyuan zhugongdiao*), the text is divided into books (*juan*). We may assume that a book corresponds to that segment of the text that the performing artist would "tell-and-sing" on a single day Each book (except the last) leaves the audience in suspense over the outcome of the action—presumably to induce the audience to return the following day for the continuation. Within each book at least one other point of tension may be discovered, usually two-thirds through the text, which would provide the performer with a suitable occasion to pause and pass the hat. This tension reaches its highest pitch of course at the end of each book.[15]

"The Tale of Oriole," with its emphasis on psychological realism rather than spectacular action, may well appear at first sight an unlikely choice for adaptation to a genre that sets so much store by the repeated buildup of suspense. In his opening songs Dong Jieyuan warns the audience that

> This tale won't talk about sword duels and stick fights,
> Long lances and heavy horses.

He also requests their indulgence:

> You who are intelligent, please consider,
> You who are smart, please think it over.
> This is not your usual tale of hustle and bustle,
> Insipid and bland, it's hard to write up—
> One-third is female complaints and love-longing,
> One-half of it concerns the joyous game of clouds and rain.[16]

We know even less about Dong Jieyuan than we do about Wang Shifu. Zhong Sicheng, in his *Register of Ghosts*, can tell us only that he lived sometime during the reign of Emperor Zhangzong of the Jin dynasty, roughly in the years 1190–1208.[17] Jieyuan is not actually a personal name: originally the term *jieyuan* denoted the first on a list of successful candidates in the provincial examination; in Jin and Yuan times it was a widely used term of address for members of the scholar-gentry class who held no official position. In *The Story of the Western Wing*, for instance, Student Zhang is repeatedly addressed as Zhang Jieyuan. The breadth of learning displayed in *The Story of the Western Wing in All Keys and Modes* makes it quite conceivable that Dong Jieyuan too belonged to the scholar class, but we cannot exclude the possibility that he was a professional entertainer who borrowed this designation as a stage name in order to play up his erudition. He must have been a character himself, having generated enough of a legend to be the subject of two plays (now lost) that from their titles were evidently romantic comedies.

In his adaptation Dong Jieyuan expands the original material of "The Tale of Oriole." Whereas Yuan Zhen's work in English translation runs to about ten pages, Dong Jieyuan's runs to over two hundred. This is because of the more detailed narration of episodes from "The Tale of Oriole" and the addition of many new episodes, for which Dong Jieyuan often found his inspiration in other Tang tales and in popular lore. Not only does Dong Jieyuan expand the opening section of the story, he gives the tale a completely new ending. Unfortunately, it is impossible to determine to what extent Dong Jieyuan draws on earlier treatments of the romance in oral literature.

The earliest preserved edition of *The Story of the Western Wing in All Keys and Modes* was prepared by a certain Zhang Yu. In the preface dated 1557 Zhang informs us that he based his version on a manuscript and an earlier (Yuan dynasty?) edition of Dong's work.[18] The 1557 edition is divided into eight books. The content of book 1 is almost entirely new Student Zhang, newly arrived in Puzhou, visits the Monastery of Universal Salvation and joins the monk Dharma Wit on a tour of the grounds. Catching a glimpse of Oriole, he tries to rush after her and has to be forcibly restrained by the monk. Subsequently, when Zhang Gong is introduced to the abbot, he rents a room at the monastery. Walking one night, Zhang notices Oriole praying to the moon and chants a poem for her; she responds with one of her own but is then called inside. Some days later, Student

Zhang learns in a conversation with the abbot that Oriole's mother is going to have a mass said for her late husband. The student is allowed to participate in a portion of the mass, and when Oriole makes her appearance, the student, the monks, and all the congregation are befuddled by her striking beauty. Suddenly the approach of mutinying troops is reported. In "The Tale of Oriole," we must remember, Student Zhang appears unaware of the very existence of Oriole until after the mutiny; here she has become the very reason for his stay at the monastery

Book II is devoted to a description of the mutiny. After looting Puzhou, the mutinying soldiers led by Flying Tiger Sun approach the monastery. The monk Dharma Wit hastily organizes defenses, and when the troops lay siege to the monastery, he rides out to challenge their champions. Even Flying Tiger Sun is unable to defeat him. But when the soldiers launch a massive attack, Dharma Wit breaks through their lines and disappears while his poorly armed monks have to flee inside. Flying Tiger Sun now demands that Oriole be given up to him. Oriole and her mother are desperate—Oriole even considers suicide—but Student Zhang, laughing, offers his help on the condition that he not be treated "as a stranger." The widow promises to treat him "as a relative," words that the student takes as a promise of marriage to her daughter. Thereupon Zhang reads aloud a letter he has written asking for aid from his old friend Du Que, a brilliant military officer stationed nearby We have already noted that Yuan Zhen's description of the mutiny is extremely laconic where Li Shen's is lavish, so here it is certainly the ballad and not the tale that has inspired Dong Jieyuan.

Book III resumes the description of the mutiny with Zhang Gong's disclosure that Dharma Wit has left in order to deliver his letter to Du Que. Du Que, the White Horse General, arrives shortly, subdues the mutinying troops, beheads Flying Tiger Sun, and departs, having conversed briefly with Student Zhang. The next day Zhang asks the abbot to act as matchmaker. When the abbot calls on the widow, she assures him that she will invite the student for a banquet. She eventually does so, but Zhang Gong is disappointed in his hopes, for the widow keeps her promise by instructing her son Happy (Huanlang) and her daughter Oriole to greet the student as an elder brother. Zhang then bluntly asks for Oriole in marriage, only to be told that she is already engaged to her cousin Zheng Heng. Overcome by wine, Zhang Gong returns to his room in despair. Crimson visits him the following day to inquire about his condition. Zhang tells Crimson that he wants to leave, but she notices his zither and suggests that his playing might arouse Oriole's feelings. The White Horse General, we have noted, is Li Shen's addition to the original story. Though Dong Jieyuan adheres more closely to the description of the banquet as told in the tale, he changes the context and meaning of the banquet scene significantly He also transforms Crimson into an active participant in the unfolding action.

Book IV opens with an extended description of Zhang Gong playing his zither and singing a song of longing. Oriole, burning incense to the moon, is indeed aroused and comes on tiptoe to the window of his study to listen. But she sneaks away when he rushes from his room, and Zhang finds himself clasping Crimson in his arms. The next day, our student has Crimson deliver a note to her mistress. Although she feigns anger as she reads it, Oriole sends Crimson back with a note in return, which Zhang Gong interprets as an invitation to the western wing. When he arrives in her room that night, however, Oriole sends him off with a stern lecture, and our student once again returns to his room in despair. In Yuan Zhen's tale it is Oriole, not Zhang Gong, who is the expert zither player; it is her broken performance that signals the end of their affair. Dong Jieyuan reverses the situation. His inspiration may have been a line from Oriole's letter to Zhang after his arrival in the capital: "You enticed me by playing your zither," a reference to the famous tale about the poet Sima Xiangru's (179–118 B.C.) seduction of the young widow Zhuo Wenjun (summarized in chapter 5).

This story of Sima Xiangru and Zhuo Wenjun has remained popular through the ages and has provided the prototype of the "mad scholar," whose confidence in his talents and eventual success allows him to scoff at conventional morality, and the beautiful young woman, whose ability to recognize the potential for greatness in an impoverished student compels her to share his tribulations en route to glory Dong Jieyuan repeatedly compares his protagonists to Sima Xiangru and Zhuo Wenjun: the episode of Zhang's zither playing could not have been written without that poet's model. The second half of book IV again closely follows "The Tale of Oriole."

Book V presents the consummation of the affair. On his return from the western wing, Zhang Gong receives a visit from Oriole. Discovering after he awakes that their union of clouds and rain was only a dream, Zhang falls ill. The abbot calls on him, as do Oriole and her mother, who summons a physician to treat him. Realizing that she has caused the imminent death of her savior, Oriole has Crimson deliver a poem to Zhang Gong assuring him that she will visit him that night. She indeed shows up and they make love, and she returns to his room on the following night. Both Student Zhang's dream and his subsequent illness appear to be Dong Jieyuan's invention: in "The Tale of Oriole" the heroine's sudden change of heart is not explained, nor does she send any announcement before appearing in Zhang Gong's room.

In the final three books Dong Jieyuan turns the story in a completely different direction from his source, though he continues to quote from it. In book VI the widow learns of her daughter's affair. She summons Crimson to scold her but is soon persuaded by the latter that it would be folly to expose the affair and much wiser to agree to the marriage. Oriole is only too happy to consent, and with the help of Dharma Wit, Student Zhang is able to present a suitable gift to formalize the engagement. He must now leave for the capital to take part in the examinations, and the widow, the abbot, and Oriole see him off; the parting of our student and his love is long and tearful. On the first night of Zhang's trip, Oriole and Crimson join him, then are threatened by soldiers who pound on the doors of the inn in their search for the two women—again Zhang awakens to find he has been dreaming. He continues his journey while back at the monastery Oriole is consumed by longing.

Oriole's appearance at the inn is clearly inspired by the Tang dynasty tale "The Disembodied Soul" ("Lihun ji") by Chen Xuanyou (fl. 779).[19] In this tale, a certain student leaves his uncle's household when the old man goes back on a promise to give the young man his cousin in marriage. On the first night of his journey, he is joined by his cousin who has eloped. The couple lives together for five years and has two children. When they return to the uncle's, uncle and aunt are greatly surprised because for all these years their daughter has kept to her bed at home. The bride and the daughter confront one another, fusing into one woman: her soul had left her body to be with her lover.

Zhang Gong succeeds in the examinations, and in book VII he sends his servant to announce the happy news in Puzhou. Overjoyed, Oriole sends him gifts and a letter imploring him not to betray her. Zhang Gong, who had taken ill in the capital, now hastens to the monastery to fetch his bride. But Zheng Heng arrives first with the story that the new graduate Zhang has been forced to marry a minister's daughter who has hit him with her embroidered ball; upon this the widow decides to marry her daughter to her original fiancé, Zheng Heng. Zhang Gong is at a loss what to do, and at the banquet that night a tearful Oriole is positioned between her lover and her fiancé. In book VIII, Dharma Wit shares his room with Zhang Gong for the night and offers to kill the widow for him. At that moment they are joined by Oriole and Crimson. When the young couple begins to contemplate suicide, Dharma Wit suggests that they seek the help of Du Que, who has been promoted to the position of governor. The lovers, accompanied by Crimson, elope that very night. Du Que welcomes them hospitably, and when Zheng Heng appears in court the following morning to claim his bride, Du Que shames him into killing himself. Zhang Gong and Oriole happily celebrate their marriage.

Dharma Wit's offer to abduct Oriole recalls the Tang dynasty "Tale of Lady Willow" ("Liushi zhuan") by Xu Yaozuo (fl. 790).[20] In this tale Lady Willow is taken into the harem of a powerful general but is finally restored to her husband, a student, by a dashing young military officer. Zheng Heng's unsuccessful complaint to the highest local official finds a striking parallel in the final book of the *All Keys and Modes of Liu Zhiyuan*, when Liu Zhiyuan's fiendish brothers-in-law, unaware of his identity, appear before him in court and lay plaint against him. The lost all-keys-and-modes about Shuang Jian and Su Xiaoqing probably also contained a comparable scene toward the end. *The Story of the Western Wing in All Keys and Modes* does not comment on the eventual fate of Oriole's mother.

This extensive summary of *The Story of the Western Wing in All Keys and Modes* clearly shows that Dong Jieyuan, spurred on by the dictates of his genre, changes "The Tale of Oriole" almost beyond recognition from the story of a young man's recovery from infatuation into a rich and varied love comedy. At times his ironic portrayal of the protagonist Zhang Gong verges on caricature: as soon as this prime example of Chinese manhood is struck by love, he becomes a babbling fool, wax in the hands of admiring women.[21] The characterization of Oriole is well developed. She is portrayed as a passionate and intelligent but well-educated maiden, torn between her emotions and her equally strong sense of morality Her mother is shown as outwardly stern but inwardly weak and doting, a condition that causes all of her clever schemes to backfire. Crimson, who has scarcely any identity at all in Yuan Zhen's tale, now becomes, in the time-honored and apparently universal tradition of love comedy, one of the most important characters in the story· the clever servant girl, whose stratagems are essential in bringing the highborn but ineffectual lovers together. The abbot, only too eager to meddle in worldly affairs, turns out to be of little practical use. The only monk in the monastery who proves capable of daring self-sacrifice is Dharma Wit, who can barely recite a sutra. Flying Tiger Sun has some of the traits of the *miles gloriosus*, and the battle between the rebels and the provisionally armed monks is pure farce. Du Que is portrayed as the ideal official but his appearances are kept to a minimum, whereas the characterization of Zheng Heng, the suitor who relies on connections and riches instead of talent and good looks, is pure grotesquerie, developed in loving detail.[22]

The setting at each stage is carefully synchronized with the action. Our lovers meet in early spring, continue their affair through the summer, and part in autumn; Zhang returns again in spring to carry his bride off from the monastery into town.[23] Names and other details often seem designed to suggest a second level of meaning in the text, an allegorical treatment of the art of love.[24] The comic characterization, rich narrative detail, and careful construction all come to life through the language of Dong Jieyuan's songs. These vivid songs are equally capable of every function they are meant to fulfill: narration, description, dialogue, and interior monologue. Drawing freely on the idiom of earlier prosimetric literature and lyric poetry, Dong Jieyuan fully exploits the registers in vernacular poetry as his language shifts from sophisticated lyrical effusion to bawdy innuendo and coarse curses and back again.[25] Nowadays *The Story of the Western Wing in All Keys and Modes* is duly recognized as a masterwork of Chinese vernacular literature, and it is no exaggeration to state that Wang Shifu's success to a large measure is because of the degree to which his talent has allowed him to cannibalize such a remarkable source.

If Wang Shifu follows his source closely, he does not follow it slavishly The dramatic as opposed to the narrative form posits different requirements, to which are added the formal features specific to *zaju*. Even though the Chinese stage has never been hampered by an academic insistence on the unity of time, place, and action, any playwright tends to concentrate action in a limited number of more or less self-contained major scenes, and Wang Shifu is no exception to this rule. Narration and description have to be reconceived as dialogue or monologue; repetition of action is to be avoided, and flashbacks are impracticable (for dreams the traditional Chinese stage has evolved appropriate conventions). Moreover, Wang Shifu must deal with the typical *zaju* convention that within each act all the songs be assigned to a single role type. In this way, over half the text of any act may be assigned to only one of the many characters in it, and it is that character's perception of the situation and reaction to it that most vividly impresses itself on the audience. In general, Wang Shifu abides by this convention, even if he is less strict about the rule that assigns all four suites of songs within a single *zaju* to the same role type.[26]

Wang Shifu starts out by following his source very closely indeed. The first *zaju* of the cycle is a faithful adaptation of book I of Dong Jieyuan's composition, the principal differences being Wang Shifu's initial emphasis, like Li Shen's, on Oriole's receptivity to spring and his merging Zhang Gong's two visits to the abbot into a single conversation.

Wang Shifu's approach changes in the second *zaju*; he devotes only two acts to the siege of the monastery and the suppression of the mutiny The long-drawn-out battle scenes in the all-keys-and-modes have almost vanished. The most warlike scene is now the second act of the second play, which is devoted to the martial posturing of the monk Benevolent Perception (Huiming) before he sets out to deliver Student Zhang's letter to the White Horse General (it is also a satirical jab at the student). Once the siege is lifted, the play again adheres to the all-keys-and-modes up to the scene of Student Zhang's haunted dream at the roadside inn. Wang Shifu omits a number of lesser scenes (he slips up once by referring to an incident that occurs in the all-keys-and-modes but is omitted in his play) and concentrates the action of books III through VI in eleven acts. Wang Shifu's fifth and final play quickly disposes of Dong Jieyuan's books VII and VIII: the first two acts of the fifth play follow the first half of book VII; the remainder of book VII and all of book VIII are covered in the final two acts. Zheng Heng makes his first appearance in the third act. Only in the fourth act does Zhang Gong arrive at the monastery to celebrate the wedding; and since Du Que is present when Zheng Heng wants to claim Oriole, Zheng immediately backs out, allowing the ceremony to be happily celebrated.

In his *Story of the Western Wing* Wang Shifu considerably tightens up the plot of the story. With the first appearance of Oriole's mother onstage, we know that her daughter has a fiancé who is supposed to be on his way to Puzhou, and in his opening lines Zhang Gong informs us that his primary motive for coming to Puzhou is to visit Du Que. During the siege of the monastery the widow promises her daughter in marriage to anyone capable of repulsing the rebels, so that when she subsequently refuses our student as a son-in-law she commits a clear breach of promise. Her young son, Happy, is now given a role in her discovery of the affair between his sister and the student. In the play, moreover, it is not Zhang Gong who wants to leave to take part in the examinations but the widow who demands that he succeed in the examinations to secure her consent to the couple's marriage. In this way Wang Shifu has sharpened the characteriza-tion of the widow who, while still the doting parent, is now more status-conscious, stern, and devious.

She more than finds her match in Crimson, however, who benefits most from the convention to assign all songs within a single act to one performer. In her expanded role she sings in six separate acts. And while she continues to play an important part in the plot, she often also serves as an ironic commentator on the behavior of her social betters. In his characterization of Zhang Gong and Oriole, Wang Shifu basically adheres to *The Story of the Western Wing in All Keys and Modes*, but our student emerges as a somewhat more positive, if less central, character, and some of the elements of caricature that are found in Dong Jieyuan's handling are toned down—probably because they would conflict with the student's role type. The stage apparently neither allows for the ribaldry of the all-keys-and-modes nor requires the frequent fits of suicidal desperation so convenient for creating suspense. Some characters do not fare as well at the hands of Wang Shifu. Zheng Heng's role is severely diminished, and Flying Tiger Sun is almost written out of the play. Dong Jieyuan's Dharma Wit is split into two figures: his much-reduced fighting role is taken over by Benevolent Perception, and the original character of Dharma Wit is accordingly reduced. The most convenient explanation for this operation would be that in performance the martial role of Benevolent Perception requires a different type of actor, but such good stage logic has left us with two rather dull characters.[27]

Comparisons of Dong Jieyuan's and Wang Shifu's versions of *The Story of the Western Wing* so far have paid little attention to the issue of the extent to which the technical requirements of the two genres may explain the differences between these two works. Traditional critics have preferred to compare individual lines from the songs in both works in order to prove Wang Shifu's indebtedness to his lesser-known predecessor or to determine the relative literary merit of both authors.[28] Modern Marxist critics, as we have noted, have tended to compare plot and characterization in order to ascertain the ideological level of both works.[29] Dong Jieyuan's work is a masterpiece of prosimetric narrative that gives a single performer full scope to demonstrate his talents as a storyteller and singer. Without Dong Jieyuan's earlier work, Wang Shifu, if his other plays are anything to go by, probably would have been incapable of conceiving his *Story of the Western Wing* Thanks to Dong Jieyuan's composition, he succeeded in the conception and execution of a play of exceptional scale and quality If Wang Shifu borrowed heavily, he had an uncanny aptitude to pick the very best.

Notes

[1] The text of the "Yingying zhuan," also known as "Huizhen ji" (Story of an encounter with an immortal), has been preserved in chap. 488 of the huge repository of tales and anecdotes from the second to the tenth century known as the *Taiping guangji*, compiled in the late tenth century on imperial command under the direction of Li Fang (925–96); see 10:4012–17. For a critical edition of the "Yingying zhuan," see Wang Meng'ou, *Tangren xiaoshuo yanjiu*, 2:254–61. For a fine study and translation of this tale, see Hightower, "Yüan Chen and 'The Story of Ying-ying.'" This translation has been reprinted in Joseph S. M. Lau and Y W Ma, *Traditional Chinese Stories*, 139–45.

[2] Palandri, *Yüan Chen*.

[3] For a combined translation of tale and ballad, see, e.g., Elizabeth Te-chen Wang, *Ladies of the T'ang*, 107–32.

[4] For a critical edition and translation of this tale, see Dudbridge, *The Tale of Li Wa*.

[5] The identification of the male protagonist of the tale with its author was first put forward by a certain Wang (fl. 1131) and has been taken up and developed by many later scholars. For a summary and critical evaluation of these theories, see Hightower, "Yüan Chen and 'The Story of Yingying,'" 106–19, and Lorraine Dong, "The Creation and Life of Cui Yingying," 12–27.

[6] This view was first put forward by the modern scholar Chen Yinke in 1948. For an extensive discussion of this theory as developed by him and others, see Lorraine Dong, "The Creation and Life of Cui Yingying," 27–48.

[7] *Ibid.*, 49–53.

[8] These four fragments are found as quotations in Dong Jieyuan's *Xixiang ji zhugongdiao*. They may be most conveniently consulted in *Dong Jieyuan Xixiang ji zhugongdiao*, collated and annotated by Ling Jingyan, 10, 36, 69, 91.

[9] This *guzi a* and its preface appear in Zhao Lingzhi's *Houqing lu*. In modern times it has been repeatedly reprinted; see, e.g., Liu Yongji, *Songdai gewu juqu luyao*, 56–66. For discussions of the genre *guzi a*, see André Lévy, "Un document unique sur un genre disparu de la littérature populaire", Hanan, *The Chinese Short Story*, 141–42; and Idema, "The *Wen-ching yüan-yang hui*," 92–95.

[10] The basic Chinese study on the all-keys-and-modes is still Zheng Zhenduo, "Song Jin Yuan zhugongdiao kao" of 1932, reprinted in his *Zhongguo wenxue yanjiu*. See also Li-li Ch'en, "Outer and Inner Forms of *Chu-kung-tiao*," and "Some Background Information on the Development of *Chu-kung-tiao*", West, *Vaudeville and Narrative*, 48–131; and our *Chinese Theater 1100–1450*, 197–201, 236–78.

[11] Wang Zhuo (fl. 1145), *Biji manzhi*, 115.

[12] Tanaka Kenji, "Gendai sankyoku no kenkyû," 11–21, 23–26; Idema, "Satire in All-Keys-and-Modes."

[13] These fragments have been reproduced photomechanically as *Liu Zhiyuan zhugongdiao*. A critical edition has been provided by Uchida Michio in "Kôchû Ryu Chi-en shokyûchô." The text has been translated into English by Doleželová-Velingerová and Crump as *Ballad of the Hidden Dragon*.

[14] The majority of these suites are found in various chapters of the mid-sixteenth-century *qu* anthology *Yongxi yuefu*. Numerous attempts have been made to reconstitute the original sequence of these songs, but many uncertainties remain. For a convenient reprint, see Zhu Pingchu, *Quan zhugongdiao*, 179–240.

[15] Idema, "Performance and Construction of the *Chu-kung-tiao*."

[16] *Dong Jieyuan Xixiang ji zhugongdiao*, collated and annotated by Ling Jingyan, 1–3. Another annotated edition has been produced by Zhu Pingchu as *Xixiang ji zhugongdiao zhuyi*. Dong's work has been translated into English by Li-li Ch'en as *Master Tung's Western Chamber Romance* and into Dutch by Idema as *Het verhaal van de westerkamers in alle toonaarden*.

[17] Zhong Sicheng, *Lugui bu*, 103.

[18] The single surviving copy of (probably) Zhang Yu's original edition has been photomechanically reproduced as *Ming Jiajing ben Dong Jieyuan Xixiang ji*. All later printings of Dong's work derive from Zhang Yu's edition.

[19] For a recent translation of this brief tale, see Karl S. Y Kao, *Classical Chinese Tales of the Supernatural and Fantastic*, 184–86, "The Disembodied Soul."

[20] For a translation of this tale, see, e.g., Elizabeth Te-chen Wang, *Ladies of the Tang*, 1–15, "Madam Willow."

[21] Cf. Tanaka Kenji, "Bungaku toshite no Tô Seishô," part 2, 98.

²² Idema, "Satire in All-Keys-and-Modes."

²³ *Ibid.*

²⁴ *Ibid.*

²⁵ Cf. Tanaka Kenji, "Bungaku toshite no *Tô Seishô*."

²⁶ For a more detailed discussion of the conventions of *zaju* and Wang Shifu's departures from these rules, see chap. 4.

²⁷ Cf. Tanaka Kenji, "Zatsugeki *Seishôki* ni okeru jimbutsu seikaku no kyôchô."

²⁸ Conflicting evaluations of Ming and Qing critics comparing Dong's and Wang's versions of our romance have been collected by Zhang Renhe in his "*Xixiang ji* lunzha," 18–20.

²⁹ For a spirited attempt to prove that Wang's version outdoes Dong's work in its ideological content, see Su Xing, "Wang Shifu zaju *Xixiang ji* fanfengjian zhuti de fazhan de shenhua: zaju *Xixiang ji* yu zhugongdiao de bijiao yanjiu." Almost all monographs on *The Story of the Western Wing* contain extended comparisons between the two works.

4

EXCEPTIONS TO THE RULES

In the preceding chapters we have noted a number of times that Wang Shifu's *Story of the Western Wing* belongs to a specific genre of traditional Chinese drama known as *zaju*, "comedy." While a discussion of some of its conventions was unavoidable in addressing questions of dating, authorship, and adaptation, a full appreciation of the play demands a more detailed discussion of the rules that govern *zaju* and the ways in which *The Story of the Western Wing* departs from them. If *zaju* is not the earliest form of theater in China, it is the first to have left a rich legacy of plays in written text: over two hundred scripts from the period 1250–1450 have come down to us, primarily in the form of heavily edited recensions printed in the early seventeenth century In contrast, we have only three scripts of the roughly contemporary genre *xiwen*, while the number of *chuanqi* that may safely be attributed to the first century of the Ming dynasty is also very limited. Among the most striking aspects of this large corpus of *zaju* scripts are a great thematic diversity and a remarkable degree of uniformity in terms of formal rules.

The uniformity may be indebted to some degree to later editorial practice, but in essence it appears to be an inherent characteristic of the genre right from its start in the middle decades of the thirteenth century.[1] As in all forms of traditional Chinese drama, the script does not assign dialogue and songs to characters in the play but to various role types (*jiaose*) who perform these characters. Actors and actresses specialized by training in a specific type of role much in the way that players in *commedia dell'arte* or in a nineteenth-century stock company did. One major difference in their training would be that the Chinese actor or actress also had to be a well-trained acrobat *and* a singer; their schooling would have been far more intensive.

In *zaju* there are three basic role types: *mo* (male roles), *dan* (female roles), and *jing* (clowns). Both men and women might specialize in any of these role types. A *mo* might play any male character of positive moral value, and further subdivisions of the *mo* were called up when a play featured more than one positive male character. One finds, for instance, designations like *ermo* (second male role) and *waimo* (extra male role). If the songs in any given *zaju* are assigned to the *mo*, this role type is designated *zhengmo* (male lead). The *dan* plays all positive female characters, and here too various further subdivisions are possible.

Whenever the songs are assigned to the *dan*, the role type is designated *zhengdan* (female lead). The *jing* performs villains, scoundrels, and comic bits. Specific social types that have only subsidiary parts are designated by their own terms—for example, a monk is played by a *jie* (bald one), a child by a *lai* (child).

The designations for role types vary slightly from genre to genre. In *chuanqi* the young male protagonist is usually played by the *sheng* (male lead).[2] The Hongzhi edition of *The Story of the Western Wing* may reflect the influence of this genre in its curious usage of designating Student Zhang's role type alternately as *mo* and *sheng*, though we prefer to understand the term *sheng* as "student" and translate it accordingly. *The Story of the Western Wing* is also exceptional for its preference for assigning text to characters rather than role types: whereas both Student Zhang and Oriole are identified by their role types (either *zhengmo* or *sheng* and *zhengdan*) and by their names, other characters are often identified simply by name. At the risk of confusing some of our readers, we have decided not to systematize our translation in this respect but to follow our source in all its inconsistencies in the possibility that there is some rationale for the alternate designations that is not apparent to us at this time.[3]

Each role type has its own basic costume, and actors and actresses were assumed able to perform any play in their repertoire at a moment's notice—which in general leaves little room for individualization of character through costume or makeup (the elaborate painted faces of Peking Opera appear to be a rather late and localized development). Therefore, in order to establish an identity within the play, each performer directly addresses the audience on his or her first entrance, delivering a brief and reliable exposition of name, background, and aims before engaging in conversation with any fellow performers, who are supposed *not* to have heard this exposition. In the case of the male and female leads, this direct address usually extends to the first few songs of the act. In late Ming editions of *zaju*, self-introductions usually open with two or four lines of verse, but this convention is not consistently observed in our edition of *The Story of the Western Wing* (nor, for that matter, in other early editions of *zaju*). The convention of a reliable self-introduction may strike many Western readers as unrealistic, but in fact it is no more unrealistic than the convention of the aside that we find both East and West. The traditional Chinese stage manages to avoid the highly contrived openings of traditional and modern plays in the West through the convention of the reliable self-introduction and has continued to use it up to the present day.

Zaju, like all other genres of traditional Chinese drama, is a form of ballad opera. Music and song are an indispensable part of any form of traditional Chinese theater, but unlike Western opera or musicals, the music is not composed afresh for each new play. The playwright writes his songs to existing melodies that he selects from a well-known and circumscribed body of tunes. Genres of drama in China are not primarily distinguished by content, as in the West, but by differences in music. As a rule each body of tunes has its own conventions for combining melodies into suites, for the dialect to be used in singing, and for the composition of the accompanying orchestra. If *xiwen* and *chuanqi* employ "southern tunes," *zaju* is distinguished by its use of *beiqu* or "northern music." As music, *beiqu* has not been preserved: all we have are some late notations of melodies and some isolated melodies that have survived because they were adopted into other musical traditions. As a result, any attempt to reconstruct the music will remain of doubtful validity.[4] Northern music provided the Yuan dynasty playwright with over two hundred tunes to which to write his lyrics;[5] however, the playwright could not choose his tunes at random. Each tune belonged to one of nine modes customarily employed in *beiqu*, and only tunes that belonged to the same mode could be combined into a suite. For each mode specific rules applied as to the sequence of tunes within a suite, and some tunes occurred only in set combinations.[6]

An ordinary *zaju* contains four suites of songs, each in a different mode. The first suite in practically all extant *zaju* belongs to the *Xianlü* mode, and the fourth to the *Shuangdiao*. The variation is greater for the second and third suites. In the second suite the *Nanlü* mode appears most often, but the *Zhonglü* mode and the *Zhenggong* mode also occur regularly. The third suite favors the *Zhonglü* mode, followed by the *Zhenggong* and *Yuediao* modes.[7] A Yuan dynasty treatise on singing associates each mode with a specific emotional mood, but in view of the wide variety of subject matter in *zaju* it seems highly unlikely that the emotional connotations of these widely used modes are very pronounced.[8] Within each suite the tempo probably starts out slowly, accelerates gradually until it reaches its highest pitch roughly two-thirds through the suite, and then abruptly slows down again, only to have the suite close with a brief accelerando.[9] The unity of the songs within each suite is compounded by the fact that the same rhyme is maintained from beginning to end.

All four suites of songs are assigned to a single performer, either the male lead or the female lead. Each suite may be prefixed by a demi-act, a "wedge" in Chinese (*xiezi*)—that is, a song to the tune "Shanghua shi" or "Duanzheng hao," usually with a reprise—sung by the lead or another performer. Even though plays containing two wedges occur, it is far more common to find only one wedge in a play.[10] The convention of assigning all four suites of songs, and therefore most of the text, to a single performer (related, perhaps, to the limited size of an ordinary *zaju* troupe) imparts a highly asymmetrical character to *zaju*: only one party in the dramatic conflict is allowed a full airing of feelings and only that party is allowed to develop into a well-rounded character, so that the opposing protagonist often remains a shadowy figure at best.[11] This imbalance may be remedied to some extent by assigning the other party lyrics, letters, or rhymed lines to recite.[12]

Early editions of *zaju* do not explicitly divide the text into acts; they only mark the conclusion of a scene by leaving the remainder of its final column of text blank. Even though a single suite of songs can be spread over a number of succeeding scenes, it is more common for a suite to be confined to a single major scene. Late Ming editors accordingly divided *zaju* texts into acts and demi-acts on the basis of the distribution of wedges and suites.[13] The Hongzhi edition of *The Story of the Western Wing* is the earliest preserved printing of a *zaju* in which the division into acts is explicitly marked (demi-acts, not marked, are still included with the full act they precede). But it appears that our anonymous editor had little experience in this practice: usually the legend Act *X* is placed at the beginning of the first scene of the act, but occasionally the legend appears just before the first song of the suite that is the core of the act concerned.

If *zaju* does not observe the rules of unity of time and place, it does exhibit unity of action. The action of the first three acts is tightly connected and usually builds to a logical climax in the third act. The fourth act may take place much later and occasionally resembles an epilogue rather than a conclusion. In both the plays of Zhu Youdun and late Ming printings of Yuan plays it is quite common to conclude the *zaju* with a passage in rhymed lines recited by a judge, an imperial emissary, or another person of authority, in which the action of the play is summarized one final time and the moral of the story is stated explicitly in case anyone has managed to miss it. In *The Story of the Western Wing* there is no such passage, even though Du Que would be suited to pronounce this rhymed homily Following the conclusion are a *timu* (title) and *zhengming* (name), each consisting of one or two parallel lines, one of which provides the abbreviated title by which the play is commonly known. In the Hongzhi edition of *The Story of the Western Wing*, however, the *timu* and *zhengming* of the first two plays are found following their respective first acts.

Although *The Story of the Western Wing* clearly belongs to the genre of *zaju*, it transgresses many of its rules. The first and foremost exception is of course the format of Wang Shifu's masterwork, the five-*zaju* cycle. As we have noted, in this respect *The Story of the Western Wing* is without contemporary parallel. The earliest datable imitation is Liu Dui's two-play cycle of *The Story of Jiaoniang and Feihong*, which was written in the early fifteenth century What we do find in thirteenth- and fourteenth-century *zaju* are groups of plays that derive their subject matter from popular story cycles like the saga of the Three Kingdoms, the court cases of Judge Bao, and the daring exploits of the noble bandits of the Liangshan moor. But though the modern scholar may arrange the plays in these groups in chronological order, no coherent cycle will result: every one of these plays has clearly been conceived as an independent work setting forth a single self-contained episode that is brought to a close in the fourth and final act of the play In contrast, *The Story of the Western Wing* devotes twenty-one acts to the exposition, development, climax, and conclusion of a single love affair. These twenty-one acts, however, are distributed over five *zaju*, which, while constituting a single play, individually maintain many of the features of an ordinary self-contained *zaju* in four acts.

This relative independence is underlined by formal features. Each play has its own "title" and "name," and in principle the sequence of modes within each *zaju* is the same as that within an ordinary *zaju*. The first acts of the first four plays of the cycle all open in the *Xianlü* mode. The fifth play is the only *zaju* from the period 1250–1450 to open in the *Shangdiao* mode. The *Shangdiao* mode was not popular and if used at all tends to appear in the second or third acts. Traditionally characterized as "sorrowful and longing," the *Shangdiao* mode is well suited to the contents of the act concerned; this may be a reason for its unique and startling occurrence in the first act. Three of the five plays—the first, the fourth, and the fifth—use the *Shuangdiao* mode in their final acts, which is the most common practice. In the second and third plays the *Yuediao* mode is used in the final acts, which is rather rare, and the *Shuangdiao* mode in the penultimate acts (act 4 in the second play and act 3 in the third). We may perhaps explain this use of the *Shuangdiao* mode with the fact that in these two plays, more than in the other three, it is the penultimate act that winds up the preceding action of the *zaju*, while the final act shares some of the characteristics of both an epilogue to action past and a prologue to action to come in the next *zaju* of the cycle.[14] In the second and third acts Wang Shifu employs modes that are frequently used for those acts, but we may note that the *Nanlü* mode, the mode most commonly used in second acts, is absent from *The Story of the Western Wing* As if to remedy this situation, a certain Student Wang of the fifteenth century composed a single act, intended to follow the third act of the first play, entitled *Oriole and Crimson Play Go.* This act depicts Crimson and Oriole in the garden late at night playing *go* until, surprised by Student Zhang, they retire. The song suite in this act, included among the prefatory materials in the Hongzhi edition, employs the *Nanlü* mode.[15]

A consideration of the distribution of modes in the five *zaju* cannot proceed, as we have just seen, in isolation from the contents of each play Even a perfunctory reading will show that in this respect too Wang Shifu conceives of each *zaju* as a relatively independent unit with its own unity of action and its own sequence of exposition, development, climax, and conclusion. The theme of each of the five *zaju* might be epitomized in sequence as infatuation, expectation, dissimulation, consummation, and suspicion. The first play begins with Student Zhang's arrival at the monastery and reaches its climax in the third act with the rudely disrupted exchange of poems between Zhang and Oriole. The second *zaju* starts out with the siege of the monastery and peaks in the fourth act when the widow goes back on her promise. The third play devotes its first two acts to the exchange of billets-doux and culminates in the third act in the famous scene of Oriole lecturing Student Zhang after she has lured him to her room. The fourth *zaju* of the cycle treats the consummation and discovery of their love affair, and climaxes in the third act with the parting of the lovers. The fifth and final play opens with Student Zhang's postponed return to the monastery; it peaks in the third act with Zheng Heng's firm determination to abduct his fiancée. Wang Shifu seems to have designed the climaxes as a progressive series: in each case Student Zhang has high hopes of approaching or obtaining Oriole, and in each subsequent case these high hopes seem to be ever more justified only to be completely shattered.[16] While Wang Shifu takes care to stress the relative independence of each play within the cycle, his primary concern is of course the continuous development of the story throughout the play The individual *zaju* are linked by the device of a two-line song to the tune of "Luosiniang shawei," which occurs after the final act of the first four *zaju* (in the first play these two lines are not explicitly named as such) and anticipates the continuation of the play in the next *zaju*. We may assume that the performer assigned to the song suite of the final act would also perform this short song, but this is specified only in the fourth play of the cycle.

But more important than this slight formal device of linkage is the fact that the final act of each of the first four *zaju*, while concluding the action of its respective part of the cycle, also acts as a bridge between plays that resolves the action of one play and serves as a prologue to the following play When, in the final act of the first *zaju*, Student Zhang and all the monks are overcome by Oriole's physical beauty, the siege of the monastery is the logical continuation of the disaster of the mass, since in popular Buddhist allegory our senses are bandits always ready to strike. The attempted seduction by zither playing in the final act of the second play prefigures the attempted seduction by love poems in the third *zaju*, which concludes its final act with Oriole's promise of the only effective medicine—herself—against Student Zhang's illness; and the affair is indeed consummated in the fourth play Student Zhang's dream of the soldiers' abduction of Oriole in the final act of this *zaju* may reflect his guilt on leaving her, but it also prefigures Zheng Heng's attempt to claim his fiancée in the last play of the cycle. This paradoxical tendency to stress both the relative independence of the individual *zaju* that make up *The Story of the Western Wing* and the interrelation between the individual plays may reflect the performance of the play that was originally intended to be spread over five consecutive days.[17]

Whereas all other plays in the cycle comprise four acts, the second play of the cycle is exceptional in having five. All other known five-act *zaju* are either relatively late works (there are three by Zhu Youdun) or heavily revised versions of early works (e.g., Ji Junxiang's *Orphan of Zhao*). During the last century of the Ming many editors of *The Story of the Western Wing* solved this anomaly by designating the second act of the fifth *zaju* as a wedge by simply assimilating its song suite into the first act.[18] This act contains both a full suite of songs in the Zhenggong mode and a wedge, however, so the designation as demi-act is clearly inappropriate. On the other hand, it is the only act to feature the monk Benevolent Perception, and we might assume it to be a later addition to *The Story of the Western Wing*, which originally might have dealt with the relief of the siege in a much simpler way Nevertheless, if this act is an addition to the original play, it must be a very early one, because *A Formulary of Correct Sounds for Great Peace* already refers to the fourth act of the fourth *zaju* as the seventeenth act of *The Story of the Western Wing*.

Wang Shifu's second major infringement of *zaju* conventions is his disregard of the rule that within an individual *zaju* all four song suites be assigned to a single performer, either the male lead or the female lead. Only two *zaju* from the cycle of five are regular in this respect: in the first play all four suites are assigned to the male lead, Student Zhang, and in the third *zaju* all four suites are assigned to Crimson. The three remaining plays are highly irregular. In the second *zaju* the first suite of songs is assigned to the female lead, Oriole, the second suite is assigned to Benevolent Perception, and the third is assigned to Crimson, while the fourth and fifth suites are again assigned to Oriole. In the fourth *zaju* the first suite of songs is assigned to Student Zhang, the second to Crimson, the third to Oriole, and the fourth and final suite again to Student Zhang. The fifth play distributes its four suites of songs over the same three characters: the first suite of songs goes to Oriole, the second to Student Zhang, the third to Crimson, and the final suite once more to Student Zhang. In consequence, performance of *The Story of the Western Wing* would have required an exceptional cast for its time. Most *zaju* companies, it appears, were small family troupes organized around a single star performer doubling as singer; but Wang Shifu's work requires at least two equally competent *dan* for the roles of Oriole and Crimson, one "weak *mo*" for the part of Student Zhang, and an altogether different actor to sing the role of Benevolent Perception.

The Story of the Western Wing not only disregards the rule that all suites within a *zaju* be assigned to a single performer but also breaks the rule that all songs within an individual suite be performed by the same character. Actually, *The Story of the Western Wing* so often departs from this rule that the editor of the Hongzhi edition has sensibly noted the singer's name or role type after the tune title of each song. (At times the editor even provides instructions on *how* the song is to be delivered.) It is of course impossible now to gauge the impact these seemingly modest departures might have had on audiences of *The Story of the Western Wing*, but in view of the general rigidity of these conventions it must have been considerable, especially since these infractions appear to be organized carefully to achieve maximum effect.

The care behind the infractions becomes even more self-evident when we take related features into account. The first *zaju* of the cycle starts out quite regularly. If all song suites are assigned to Student Zhang, Oriole recites a poem in an exchange with him in the third act, and both she and Crimson have a single short song near the end of the final act.[19] The second *zaju* assigns its first suite of songs to a female voice and returns to a male voice in the second act. In the three remaining acts the suites are assigned to a female voice in principle, but in each act Student Zhang is given a few songs to sing; moreover, in the fourth act Crimson too has a song, while in the final act Student Zhang is expected to play the zither and sing a zither song that does not belong to the suite. The third *zaju* constitutes a new beginning (perhaps to stress that once Student Zhang fails to achieve his desire by open means he will take recourse to illicit measures)[20] as once again all four suites are assigned to a single performer—this time to a female voice, Crimson. In both the first and second acts, however, Student Zhang is given poems to recite. In the third act he is almost silent, a dramatic move that accentuates how dumbstruck he is by Oriole's stern lecture. In the fourth act Student Zhang has one song to sing and a poem to recite. The fourth *zaju* thereupon assigns its first suite to a male voice, returning to a female voice, Crimson, for its second suite. The third suite too is assigned to a female voice, Oriole's, but two songs in it are given over to Student Zhang. The fourth suite of songs is again assigned to Student Zhang, but no less than five of the songs in it are sung by Oriole. Oriole then takes over for the first act of the fifth and final *zaju*; only one song in this suite is given over to Crimson. The second act calls for a male singing voice again, Student Zhang's, and the songs of the third act are assigned to Crimson. After each of the three principal singers has had one suite of songs to him- or herself, each in a context designed to give full rein to the character's specific capacities (the longing of the beautiful maiden and the talented scholar, the saucy girl servant's barrage of abuse), all three join in the final suite of the play, a suite assigned to Student Zhang but in which both Crimson and Oriole take part in turn, ending with Student Zhang and Oriole singing *unisono*.

Because the literary value of *zaju* texts in general and of *The Story of the Western Wing* in particular is so great and because the music to which it was once performed is irretrievably lost, modern scholars tend to study these plays primarily as literary documents, underestimating the requirements of the genre as musical theater. It appears that Wang Shifu (or whoever else is responsible for the shape of our play in the Hongzhi edition) was very much aware of the requirements of this side of his art. Precluding the possibility of internal rivalries and jealousies among star performers by an almost equitable distribution of suites, he carefully spaces his effects to achieve a maximal musical complexity in the grand finale of the play's last act. The departures from the rules of the genre in *The Story of the Western Wing* are usually interpreted as influence of southern drama (*xiwen* and *chuanqi*), in which all actors are expected to sing. Though the possibility of such an influence cannot be excluded, it does not seem necessary to assume that it was the direct cause of Wang Shifu's experiments. In at least one of his other plays Wang Shifu displays an interest in musical experimentation: his *Hall of Beautiful Spring* is one of the rare early *zaju* to employ the "Jurchen suite"[21] and may well have been designed expressly to accommodate it. In a way, Wang Shifu stays within the confines of the genre in *The Story of the Western Wing* by assigning songs only to those performers who sing complete suites—even a major character like Oriole's mother has no song of her own. In contrast to Zhu Youdun's experiments in the early fifteenth century, Wang Shifu's *Story of the Western Wing* neither adopts choral singing nor incorporates any southern tunes into its musical arrangement.

Late Ming editors of the play, after it had become closet drama, did their best to reduce the number of anomalies and reassigned as many songs as they could to the principal singer of the suite by any means possible. In this way they distorted a very important part of the craftsmanship of *The Story of the Western Wing* as musical theater. The distribution of songs in the Hongzhi edition makes perfect sense, both from the standpoint of the contents of the songs and from the standpoint of musical theater.

Notes

[1] Crump, "The Elements of Yüan Opera", Chung-wen Shih, *The Golden Age of Chinese Drama*, 20–46; Xu Fuming, *Yuandai zaju yishu*.

[2] Zeng Yongyi, "Zhongguo gudian xiju jiaose gaishuo", and our *Chinese Theater* 1 100–1450, 134–40.

[3] We have, however, provided the dramatis personae, appropriately cross-indexed, on p. xiv.

[4] Chung-wen Shih, *The Golden Age of Chinese Drama*, 180–97. For late notations of music for *The Story of the Western Wing*, see Yang Yinliu and Cao Anhe, *Xixiang ji sizhong yuepu xuanqu*; and Zhang Shibin, *Shen Yuan Bei Xixiang xiansuo pu jianpu*

[5] The earliest preserved formulary for writing *beiqu* is Zhu Quan's *Taihe zhengyin pu*, which carries a preface of 1398 but probably dates from a few decades later. The most authoritative modern Chinese formulary is Zheng Qian's *Beiqu xinpu*. Dale R. Johnson has provided an exhaustive descriptive catalog of tunes employed in Yuan *zaju* in his *Yuan Music Dramas*.

[6] For an exhaustive catalog of song sequences for each mode, see Zheng Qian, *Beiqu taoshi huilu xiangjie*. For a more systematic presentation of the main regularities governing the sequence of songs within each suite, see Johnson, *Yuan Music Dramas*, 7–24

[7] Chung-wen Shih, *The Golden Age of Chinese Drama*, 193.

[8] Yannan Zhi'an, *Changlun*, 160–61. Cf. Chung-wen Shih, *The Golden Age of Chinese Drama*, 193–94, and Johnson, *Yuan Music Dramas*, 86.

[9] Johnson, *Yuan Music Dramas*, 82–86.

[10] Ibid., 3–4.

[11] See Perng Ching-Hsi's fine discussion of characterization in *Double Jeopardy*, 85–120.

[12] Crump, "The Conventions and Craft of Yüan Drama."

[13] See Sun Kaidi, "Yuanqu xinkao", Zeng Yongyi, "Yuan zaju fen zhe de wenti", Idema, *The Dramatic Oeuvre of Chu Yu-tun*, 35–37.

[14] See Idema, *The Dramatic Oeuvre of Chu Yu-tun*, 252.

[15] This act is included in the prefatory materials of the Hongzhi edition and in some later editions. The authorship is disputed. The ascription to "Student Wang" is based on the final song of the introductory suite to Book the Second (translated below, p. 190). But since the author of that suite ascribes *The Story of the Western Wing* to Guan Hanqing, he may have Wang Shifu in mind when he speaks of "Student Wang." The anonymous *Lugui bu xubian*, 287, credits a certain Zhan Shiyu with *A Game of Go (A Supplement to the Western Wing)* (*Bu Xixiang yiqi*), which might refer to our text. See Fu Xihua, *Yuandai zaju quanmu*, 278.

[16] The relative independence of each *zaju* within the cycle is glossed over by many later editions that count all the acts consecutively

[17] The Hongzhi edition's presentation of the play in two books, each carrying its own introductory suite of songs, and the buildup of departures from the norm, which assigns all songs of a suite to a single performer, also strongly suggest that *The Story of the Western Wing* was originally meant to be performed on two consecutive days: the first two *zaju* on the first day and the three remaining plays on the second.

[18] Zhang Renhe, "*Xixiang ji* de banben yu tizhi."

[19] In the second act of the first *zaju*, one song is assigned to each Oriole and Crimson, who evidently at this point are not onstage. One possibility is that they are expected to sing these songs offstage; another possibility—since these songs represent Student Zhang's imagining both girls' reactions to his presence—would be that the male lead is expected to

sing both songs in the manner of Oriole and Crimson, respectively

[20] But see n. 17.

[21] Johnson, *Yuam Music Dramas*, 24, and West, "Jurchen Influence in the Northern Drama *Hu-t'ou-p'ai*."

5

AN INTRODUCTION TO THE WORLD OF
THE WESTERN WING

As a caveat to the reader, we should remark that what follows is not an extensive analysis of the text but is intended to be a general guide to important allusions and images in the play Our feeling is that a translation, like an original work of literature, should allow the reader to discover the text for himself. Furthermore, the intricacy of the language, the weight of the tradition of stage representations of characters, the multiple levels of puns, the complexity of allusions, while making for a profound and brilliant literary work, make any kind of cursory literary analysis in an introduction particularly selective and idiosyncratic. We have therefore adopted the rationale that by providing signposts for the educated and intelligent reader unfamiliar with Chinese or the tradition of Chinese literature, we might point the way beneath the superficial aspects of the text to deeper levels of signification.

In ancient Chinese cosmology, the world and its manifestations are created through the interaction of a binary pulse of natural forces known as *yin* and *yang* These forces are not contradictory or mutually exclusive but are in symbiotic movement throughout time. To each pole of this pair are assigned opposite attributes: to *yang* is assigned light, the sun, heat, maleness, the public world, generative force, and activity; to *yin*, darkness, the moon, cold, femaleness, the private world, receptivity, and passivity In the phenomenal world everything is constituted of a combination of these elements in their proper proportion, and being originally conceived as cosmological forces, their attributes were all of equal value. In the course of time, however, and through the trick of human language, those values associated with maleness and with *yang* became dominant as these cosmological pulses were reified through processes of symbolic correlation as the underpinnings of culture itself. The action of *The Story of the Western Wing* takes place in a world dominated by *yin* and the traditional symbols of that dark and female realm: water, the moon, and the monastery. Within this world unfolds a love comedy on two distinct planes: the astral and the terrestrial, mirror worlds of confinement and discovery for the young lovers. If the lessons of history and the accomplishments of males are told in a public forum that stresses the essentially *yang* world of the Confucian patriarchal system, it is certainly no coincidence that the comic reversal of a man's fall from his dutiful quest for legitimation and success should take place in a context in which *yin* and, by extension, women have dominion over his behavior.

The images that tie these two mirror worlds together are the Yellow River and its astral counterpart, the Heavenly or Silver River (our Milky Way). In the opening of the play Student Zhang introduces himself by describing at length the hardships he has had to face to maintain himself during his studies. In a seeming non sequitur, he suddenly switches to a direct lyric description of the Yellow River, which he must cross to reach East of Pu (Pudong) and his eventual but yet unknown destination, the Monastery of Universal Salvation. This switch has bothered critics for some time. Wang Jide, for instance, notes that it is "extremely odd but also based generally on the gist of Dong Jieyuan's text."[1] Geographically, of course, it is an accurate description of the point at which Student Zhang will cross the river, but it certainly sets the general mood of the story as well, and the "wind-tossed billows" of the river foreshadow the difficulties that the star-crossed lovers will face in the pursuit of love's fulfillment:

Where are the wind-tossed billows of the nine bends most conspicuous?

[(Student speaks:)] None of the waters of the world are as tricky as those of the Yellow River:

[(Student sings:)]
Only this place is paramount.
This river belts Qi and Liang,
Divides Qin and Jin,
Cuts off You and Yan.
Snowcapped waves beat the long sky,
At heaven's edge autumn clouds furl.[2]

The turmoil suggested in the final couplet above by the strong verb *pai* (to beat against, to slap) and the pun on *qiu* (autumn) and *chou* (sorrow) lends an emotional edge to two earlier puns in the middle couplet. Although Qin and Jin, a pair of ancient states in the Zhou dynasty, were physically divided by the Yellow River, in the metaphorical parlance of the stage a reference to the two states together also means a good marriage. In the scene where the monastery is surrounded by bandits who are seeking to steal Oriole away, for instance, the young girl suggests that she be given as a reward to whoever is able to drive them away:

Whosoever it may be—
If he establishes his meritorious service
And slays or drives away those traitorous troops
And sweeps away their malignant aura,
Then let us give as dowry our family reputation,
And with that brave I will gladly
Unite in wedlock,
As did the states of Qin and Jin.[3]

In the early history of China, the royal families of these two northern states intermarried as a matter of policy The phrase "Qin and Jin" has come to be used as a metaphor for matrimonial alliance arranged to provide security for the family and, by extension, a term for a happy marriage. Thus, the line may also be interpreted, "Our good marriage will be thwarted." In the second line of the couplet the place-names You and Yan may also be read as an adjective-noun phrase, *youyan*, which means "secret feast" or "secret meeting." Our young lovers seem to have no chance; authority, in the form of the old lady, will thwart their marriage chances and block their love trysts, and so hang the clouds of autumn, the gloom of sorrow, on a horizon of frustrated love.

Sexual punning is suggested as well in the next few lines of Student Zhang's long aria. The name of the Yellow River itself is a term for the flow of energy supposed to travel along the spine when semen is diverted during intercourse. The images of the recumbent dragon, the flying bolt, and the river breaking through its restraining dikes are all fit symbols for male lust and the rampant sexuality that will dominate the action of the play:

> Bamboo hawsers cable together the floating bridge,
> On the water a steel blue dragon reclines.
> East and west it breaches into the nine regions,
> North and south it threads together a hundred streams.
> A homing vessel: is it fast or not? How does one see it?
> Like a crossbow bolt's sudden leaving of the string.[4]

But it is the next song in the suite that establishes the mirror worlds of the play·

> Just as if the Silver River dropped through the nine heavens:
> From its deep fount beyond the clouds suspended
> To its entering into the Eastern Sea, it cannot but pass here.
> It irrigates the thousand kinds of flowers of Luoyang,
> Enriches the myriad-acre fields of Liangyuan;
> And once it floated a raft to the edge of sun and moon.[5]

The opening lines of this aria, adapted from the Tang poet Li Bo (701–62),[6] equate the Yellow River with its astral counterpart, the Milky Way The next two lines refer to the famous gardens of Luoyang and Liangyuan: the former renowned for its flowers, especially peonies,[7] and the latter, a garden constructed near modern Kaifeng by a prince of antiquity Both also denote pleasure precincts akin to the "Floating World" of Japan. As we shall see below, the peonies for which Luoyang was justly famous have a particular significance within the play

It is the final line, however, that serves to strengthen the associations drawn between the Milky Way and the Yellow River and ultimately sets the action of the play in two separate realms. It is an allusion to a story first found in *The Record of Wide Learning* (*Bowu zhi*), in which a man who dwells by the sea sees a raft float by every year in the eighth month. He prepares clothing and supplies and boards it one year. After a long period of travel, he finally arrives at a city with walls and residences, where he sees a woman weaving at a loom and meets a man leading an ox to drink in the river. When he asks where he is, he is told to wait until he has reached Shu (the area of modern Sichuan) on his return voyage and there to question a certain Yan Junping, the famous astrologer. He does as he is instructed, and Yan informs him that "on a certain day of a certain month a transient star encroached on the Islet of the Ox"—on a constellation in the Milky Way, that is. It is then that he knows he has actually floated beyond the confluence of the Yellow River and the Milky Way and out onto the Silver River itself and there encountered the Herdboy and the Weaving Girl (Chinese names for constellations roughly in the area of the stars Altair and Vega), two lovers separated by the Milky Way These celestial lovers are allowed to meet only once a year, on the seventh day of the seventh month, when magpies fly up from earth to form a bridge for them to cross. In later times and in the popular mind the traveler on the raft becomes associated with Zhang Qian, a famous explorer of the Han period who traveled extensively in Central Asia. Bearing the same surname as Zhang Gong, this explorer of wild and uncharted waters is an apt allusion to the young student and the adventure on which he is about to embark.[8]

More importantly, the allusion clearly lends a mythic dimension to our love story, establishing a strong link between the two domains of heaven and earth and between the pairs of lovers: Student Zhang and Oriole, and the Herdboy and Weaving Girl. This brings the earlier puns on Qin and Jin and on "cutoff secret meetings" more clearly into focus, and suggests that the river serves as paradoxical foreshadowing—it will transport the student to his loved one, but it also, like the Milky Way in heaven, signals separation and obstruction to the young lovers.

In the human dimension of this twofold world the monastery provides the perfect locale for the fall of a young Confucian gentleman. It is the home of men who have given up participating within the normal compass of human relations, as suggested by the term for becoming a monk, *chujia* (to leave home). In Confucian terms human identity is a function of one's role in a social and familial universe: a person is a person only when part of the normal family and social network, and a man can be a man only when he functions as son, husband, or father.[9] Therefore in Confucian eyes the monks and abbot of the temple, the *chujiazhe* (those who have left the family), have given up their gender identity and have been absorbed into a world of *yin*. Another indication that *yin* will dominate in the first part of the play is the setting, the Monastery of Universal Salvation, which was once supported and patronized by Empress Wu Zetian, the notorious female ruler who usurped the male lineage of the Tang.[10]

As a place where, theoretically, the urges of sexuality have been cleaned away, the monks' cloister as described in *The Story of the Western Wing* is a cauldron of barely concealed lust and homosexuality. It is the monks, for instance, who tell Zhang Gong that Oriole burns incense every night in the flower garden, a clue that they have been spying on her. And in the second act of the first play the student accuses the abbot, Dharma Source, of carrying on an affair with Crimson. In one of the many doublets in the text, Zhang's accusation is notable since it follows soon after another description of the abbot as virtue perfected:

(Male lead speaks:) What a fine monk!

> (Student sings:)
> What I see is a head like snow,
> Temple locks like frost,
> Face like a young boy's—a result of inner nurturing in younger years;
> His mien is proper and imposing,
> His voice is resounding and clear.
> All that's missing is a halo above his head
> To make him look just like the image of Sengjia in nirvana.[11]

Just a few minutes later he observes a halo of a different sort as the old man follows Crimson into the monastery to conclude arrangements for the memorial mass for Chancellor Cui:

> The dazzling face of this girl from the house of Cui
> Wouldn't be turning you on, would it, my old bald-pated one?
> How else could I so clearly see your head emitting such a slight
>   radiance?
> You are certainly playing a flashy role![12]

Zhang's accusations come after a rather testy exchange with the abbot about the integrity of the student's father and after the holy man's suggestion that Student Zhang might prefer to share his own couch. The portrait of the abbot represents the popular image of the sexual habits of monks. Within these walls Student Zhang comes to live as the only "real man" in a world otherwise populated either by ostensibly sexless beings or by women.

The situation is exploited to the full for its comic and erotic potential. The monastery is divorced from the everyday world; and it sequesters the members of the Cui family—a family made up, with a single exception, of women—who are bearing the casket of the dead patriarch back to their home for burial. Student Zhang, who lies to the abbot to secure a place for himself in the monastery after seeing Oriole, there sets aside his ambition to succeed in the examinations and forgets his lifelong goals. In one very fundamental sense, by stepping into the monastery he is also stepping out of the role that society has defined for him and is now free to pursue his own pleasures and fantasies, stripped of the responsibilities he would bear in the public world of the Confucian.

As the home of lustful monks and nuns, the monastery has long been associated with sexual deviancy in China. There is a tradition in later vernacular literature of monks and nuns engaging in illicit sexual acts both with each other and, in the guise of gods, with unsuspecting patrons of the temple. A cloistered and hidden place, the monastery has also long been an allegorical counterpart to the female sexual organ. In *The Story of the Western Wing*, for instance, the monastery is often equated in Zhang's fantasies and in his poetry with the grottoes of transcendent sylphs and other dark and secret places. Thus, coupled with the frequent comparison of the shaved heads of monks with the shiny *glans* of the penis, makes the monastery and its inhabitants powerful linguistic symbols with which to pun or create allegories of the act. Moreover, the monastery's isolated nature makes it the perfect location to carry on clandestine affairs. Its *yin* nature is all too clear: its inhabitants are participants in a neutered world of repressed sexuality, and its visitors are ruled by a matriarch. When Student Zhang steps inside its walls, he gives up his role in public, essentially male, culture, and his life is dominated by the tyranny of the matriarch, the vacillations of the young object of his lust, and the clever manipulations of a saucy and resourceful maidservant.

In the heavenly domain the play is dominated by the image of the moon. Like the common phrase "clouds and rain" (*yunyu*), the term "wind and moon" (*fengyue*) has a long tradition of use as a linguistic code for romantic trysts and sexual encounters. Much of the major action of the play takes place under moonlight, and the play itself is even known by the variant title *Waiting for the Moon*.[13] All of Student Zhang's visits to the flower garden are on moonlit nights; the mass for Oriole's father is held in the predawn morning of a night of full moon; and the moon is intertwined with the lovers' exchanges of poems, especially the ill-fated exchange in which Zhang misreads Oriole's intentions.

But the image of this wheel of ice in *The Story of the Western Wing* is also inextricably tied to the characterization of Oriole and the portrayal of her predicament. The moon plays a major part in her introduction and description in the words of the young student, the context of which is entirely one of otherworldly beauty and mystery. He first spies her when he is making the rounds of sites of interest in the monastery The steady cadence of his direct narration, in which each location in the temple is described in a single line, builds to a crescendo as he counts the arhats and makes his obeisances to the bodhisattvas. In the context of this religious visit and precisely at its climax, he suddenly encounters Oriole, who appears twirling a sprig of flowers, a daunting image of sexual congress and a brilliant spot of color in an otherwise colorless world:

> I've strolled through the grotto cells,
> Climbed the precious pagoda,
> And wound my way along twisting corridors.
> I've finished counting the arhats,
> Paid my respects to the bodhisattvas,
> Made my obeisances to the Holy One—

(Female lead enters, leading Crimson and twirling a flowering sprig. She speaks:) Crimson, let's go and play around in the Buddha hall.

(Male lead acts out seeing her:) Wow!

> [(Student sings:)]
> And now I run smack into my alluring karmic sentence from five
>   centuries ago![14]

Oriole and her maidservant are, of course clad in white. It is the radiant color of the sprig of flowers that accentuates her beauty and sexual allure and so takes Zhang aback. He first makes a rather flip comparison of her with the dangerous loves of Tushita Palace, home of lovely sylphs, but this first intimation that she belongs to another realm above is immediately overshadowed by his lengthy description of her all-too-worldly physical beauty In the end, however, he returns to his first comparison:

> Slowly, she meanders
> Until she reaches the doorway,
> And then a final step takes her far away.
> She has just shown her face for a moment
> But has driven to madness this laureate Zhang.
> Like a divine sylph returning to her grotto heaven,
> She leaves emptiness behind in the mists of willows,
> Where all that can be heard is the chattering of sparrows.[15]

The earlier concreteness of his physical descriptions gives way here to the vague haziness of newly greening willow branches and the singing of birds, the vestigial resonances of her lithe body and trilling voice. Having seen but a glimpse—in fact, he will catch only quick and shifting sights of her until the scene with the mass in the last act of the first play—he remembers her only as an apparition of a heavenly sylph now returned to her grotto. She has disappeared and left behind in the mortal world only the redolent odor of her presence and a faint tinkling:

> And the scent of orchid musk lingers still,
> The sound of hanging pendants moves slowly away
> The eastern wind sways, then drags up, strands of weeping willows,
> Floating threads catch and stir up petals of peach blossom;
> The pearly curtains now hide, now show, her lotus face.
> You say she is of the family of His Excellency, executive of Hezhong
>   Prefecture;
> I say she is an apparition of Guanyin, contemplating moonlight in
>   water.[16]

The shimmering vision of the white-robed Oriole reminds him of Guanyin, the

Buddhist bodhisattva known as the compassionate savior of humanity She too is
often associated with moon imagery.[17]

Later, when he steals into the flower garden to try to catch his first real glimpse
of Oriole, he shows every sign of the mortal suitor waiting in expectancy for the
manifestation of a heavenly lover:

> The jade vault is without dust,
> The Silver River drips light;
> Moon's color straddles the void,
> Flowers' shadows fill the courtyard.
> My silken sleeves grow cold,
> My fragrant heart is on alert.
> I cock my ear to listen,
> Walk with quiet step,
> Silent, so silent,
> In darkness so dark.
> Hiding, hiding,
> I wait and wait and wait.[18]

When she finally appears in the garden, he again compares her to divine beauties,
this time to the goddesses of the Xiang River and to Chang'e, the goddess of the
moon.

> It must be that this springtime beauty is fed up with confinement
> And has flown freely out of her Palace of Spreading Frigidity

Her whole face still covered with powder, draping gown baring one
shoulder, she lets her fragrant sleeves fall without word and trails her river-
goddess skirts without talking—she's just like the Consorts of the Xiang
Tomb, leaning against the red doors of Shun's temple, or like Chang'e in
the Moon Hall, barely visible in the Golden Hall of the Ecliptic Toad.
What a fine girl!

> I've just seen her lithe gracefulness
> And compare her to Chang'e in the Moon Hall, who is not so fine a
>   piece.
> Now blocked from view, now hidden, she threads the fragrant path;
> I can imagine how hard it is for her to walk on such tiny feet.
> A hundred seductions spring from the face of this delightful lass—
> Oh, it steals a man's soul away![19]

The original myths of the goddesses and divine beauties had become hope-
lessly intermingled and, as clearly shown here, were conflated by the late medieval
period. The Consorts of the Xiang Tomb were, in their original form, the
goddesses of the Xiang River, Xiangjun (Mistress of the Xiang) and Xiangfei
(Lady of the Xiang); they were also known by the style names Ehuang (Fairy

Radiance) and Nüying (Maiden Bloom).[20] The goddesses were assimilated into the legend of the great sage king Yao, as the filial daughters whom he gave in marriage to his successor, the sage king Shun. According to legend, Shun died while journeying in the south. His two consorts failed to reach him before his demise and so wept at his tomb, their tears staining the bamboos along the Xiang River—a legend of tragic love that explains the origin of the spotted bamboos of Hunan. In late medieval lore Ehuang was also another name for Chang'e, fairy goddess of the moon.[21] As Edward H. Schafer has pointed out, this is not unusual, given the traditional associations between water, the moon, and women.[22] Chang'e was renowned for her whiteness and fairness of skin, and it was believed that she lived in the moon accompanied only by a hare that ceaselessly pounded out the elixir of immortality beside a cassia tree.[23]

The myth of this nocturnal goddess was also conflated in popular imagination with a story about the Tang emperor Xuanzong (sometimes also called Minghuang), who once roamed in a celestial journey to the wheel of ice itself:

> Minghuang of the Tang roamed in the palaces of the moon where he saw a heavenly precinct, over the lintel of which a tablet read, "Precincts of Spreading Frigidity and Clear Nothingness." There were more than ten untouched beauties, dressed in snowy clothes and riding white simurghs that danced beneath the cassia walls.[24]

In these passages we can see an interwoven net of references emerging that traces a delicate tapestry of white light in the night and dark grottoes of mysterious beauty The constant references to these otherworldly women keep the image of Oriole as insubstantial as a mirage, whose shimmering beauty is caught in the next song:

> In night's depth mists of incense disperse through the empty
>   courtyard,
> The curtains of the door are stilled in the eastern breeze.
> Her bows finished, she leans on the curving balustrade
> And sighs deeply three or four times.
> The perfectly round moon is like a mirror suspended:
> This is neither the slightest cloud nor thinnest haze;
> But is all smoke of incense and human breath,
> Wafting inseparably upward together.[25]

But Chang'e is more than beauty, as the name of her abode suggests. Engraved on the educated reader's or onlooker's mind of course would be Li Shangyin's (812–58) poem about Chang'e, which stresses, among other things, her isolation and loneliness:

> Cloud-mother[26] screens the wind, lamp's shadows deepen,
>   The Long River gradually falls, dawn's stars sink;

Chang'e should now regret having stolen the magic herb,
In an azure sea of blue sky, in her heart, night after night.[27]

In this poem we see another phase of the myth. In one tradition, Chang'e was thought to be the wife of the archer Hou Yi. She stole from him an elixir of immortality, a gift from the Queen Mother of the West, and fled to the moon. Although her original intent had been to attain immortality, it cost her an eternity of loneliness, locked away in her cold palaces, deprived of love and companionship. This is clearly the image of Chang'e to which Oriole compares herself after the madam has gone back on her word to marry her daughter to Student Zhang:

([Female lead] speaks:) What good does it do to burn incense, now that the affair has fallen apart? O moon, how can I bear your fullness?

Clouds gather away in the clearing void,
The icy wheel suddenly wells up;
The breeze sweeps away tattered red,
Scattered into piles on the fragrant steps.
A thousand kinds of parting sorrow,
Myriad sorts of idle grief.

(Crimson speaks:) Sister, look at the bright moon. A full moon must have a breeze as well.

(Female lead speaks:)

Breeze and moonlight are there at heaven's edge,
But in this world of men there is nothing good.

Look in the human world:
A jade countenance is locked away within embroidered bed hangings
Out of fear that someone might sport with it.
Think of Chang'e:
Sinking in the west and rising in the east, who keeps her company?
How she resents her heavenly palace:
No Pei Hang has yet made his dream of cavorting with immortals.
These clouds are like the layers of my silken bed hangings that,
For fear Chang'e might be aroused,
Now close off the Palace of Spreading Frigidity.[28]

This song is an elaborate conceit that conflates the myth of Chang'e with an account found in a Tang classical tale about a scholar named Pei Hang. After failing in the examinations and roaming about, Pei visits his old friend Chancellor Cui (the same name as Oriole's father) and borrows money to return to the capital. On the way he encounters a beautiful woman on the boat to whom he sends a poem via her maidservant. She does not respond to his advances, but when he responds to her invitation to visit her chambers, which are bright and luminous, she explains to him that she is married. He treats her with utmost respect for the rest of the journey, and upon parting she gives him a poem:

Once you drink the chalcedony liquor, a hundred feelings are born;
When the dark frost is pounded to the end, then you will see Cloud's Blossom.
Indigo Bridge is indeed the cave of spiritual transcendents;
Why must you spur off, up to the jade capital?

Later, at the hostel at Indigo Bridge, Pei asks an old crone for a drink. She sends out a girl named Yunying (Cloud's Blossom) to serve him. He is so struck by the girl's beauty that he cannot proceed on his journey. When he wants to marry her, the old crone explains that she must first have a block of "magic cinnabar" ground to powder in a mortar and pestle made of jade. Pei sells all of his goods, his horse, and his servants in order to purchase the pestle and mortar. He grinds by day and sleeps by night, peeking once after dark to see a hare busy at the pestle. The old woman collects the powder daily, and after a hundred days, she has enough to consume as a proper dose. She then ascends to heaven, asking Pei to wait at the hostel. There he too is transported into the fairy precincts where he meets again the beautiful woman he first met on the boat, who turns out to be the elder sister of Cloud's Blossom. Finally he is transformed into an immortal.[29] The conflation and connection between the two stories are obvious in the symbols of the the hare and the elixir of immortality. Like Chang'e alone in her cold palace, Oriole hopes that a Pei Hang (Student Zhang) will rescue her from her isolation by equally industrious deeds with the pestle.

All of these allusions are interreferential, spinning about the mythic node of Chang'e, who is also known by the epithet Jade Lady. The student's description of Oriole as one of the several lunar women and the young girl's adoption of the moon fairy as a conscious persona point to the seamless identification of the moon with Oriole. This identification is an accepted tradition by the Ming, as a set of songs describing the vacillating thoughts of Oriole shows by its title, *A Boudoir Lament in the Palace of the Toad (Guiyuan changong).*[30] Only when we realize that in many cases the moon *is* Oriole can we understand the paradox of its continuous presence and its daily cycle of rising and setting: analogues of both her appearance in the play and the progress of their love. Virtually every appearance by Oriole in the play is in the luminosity of the moon. Even in the scene of the mass for her late father, the moon appears at the beginning of the act just as she does:

The wheel of the moon is high above the hall of the Brahma king;
Auspicious mists encage the azure tiles.
The incense smoke forms a canopy of clouds;
The chanted incantations swell into ocean billows.
The shadows of the pennants toss and flutter,
And all of the temple patrons are here.[31]

And it disappears again when she leaves at the end of the act:

> Better to not have a heart than to have one:
> "Those full of feeling are vexed by those without."
> I've been bustling around all night;
> The moon sinks, the bells sound out, the cock cries:
> True it is, "The jade person has gone back too hastily,"
> This good affair is concluded too soon.
> The ceremony finished, everyone disperses;
> All return to their homes in the dark.
> All befuddled, they've raised hell until dawn.[32]

Nowhere does the moon figure more importantly as a symbol of their love than in the famous scene in which Student Zhang misinterprets a poem sent to him by Oriole. By the time the verse reaches him, he has already exchanged other poems with her, including the one that follows here, in which it is clear that the moon has become a code for sexual congress:

> A night bathed in moonlight,
> A spring desolated by flowers' shadows;
> Why, under the hoary sickle,
> Do I not see the lady in the moon?[33]

He can hardly misinterpret Oriole's response to this poem, with its double entendre in the first line and in the last its indirect allusion to Chang'e's lonely sighing in the moon:

> Long has my orchid chamber been lonely,
> No way to pass the fragrant spring;
> I reckon that he who walks and chants
> Will take pity on the one who heaves a sigh.[34]

At this point, there have been no prohibitions to their meeting, except those normally in place for young people of opposite gender, and Oriole is clearly interested in the student. But after the madam goes back on her promise to have them married, Student Zhang continues his pursuit while the girl involves herself in a web of lies and self-deception. Here the image of the moon takes on yet another layer of meaning, symbolizing the waxing and waning of Oriole's responses to his overtures.

Finally, sick and despairing, he sends her a final poem, hoping that it will arouse her interest. The verse follows his attempt to seduce her with his zither playing, which despite its eventual success does not produce immediate results:

> The vexations of love's longing grow stronger;
> In vain I played the jasper zither.
> From happy affair to encountering spring,

> Your fragrant heart must also have been moved.
> Such passion cannot be denied;
> What need to cling to empty reputation?
> Do not betray the brightness of moon's blossom;
> But covet the heaviness of flowers' shadows.[35]

Despite Crimson's warnings that the love has ended ("The moon has darkened over the western wing"), Zhang holds out hope and appears to be rewarded with a titillating poem:

> Wait for the moon beneath the western wing;
> Welcoming the breeze, the door is half-opened.
> When separated by the wall, flowers' shadows move;
> I guess it is the jade one coming.[36]

Neither Zhang nor the reader at this point has any clue to the real meaning of the piece. His interpretation that the poem calls for a rendezvous is not only plausible but, considering the freight that the image of moon has carried to this point, the only likely reading:

> [(Male lead speaks:)] "Wait for the moon beneath the western wing" that's ordering me to come when the moon has come up. "Welcoming the breeze, the door is half-opened" that means she will open the door and wait for me. "When separated by the wall, flowers' shadows move; / I guess it is the jade one coming" that means she wants me to jump across the wall.[37]

But when Zhang Gong carries out these actions, he is berated by Oriole and Crimson for his presumption and even accused of forcible entry for the purpose of rape. Though on one level the poem Oriole sends surely expresses her real desires, she makes ironic use of the moon, an image that to this point has been used primarily for a romantic and sexual code; now she severely upbraids her lover and threatens him with exposure to the madam. Thus, the poem frustrates both the student and the reader, who have mistakenly placed their faith in the constancy of the moon, forgetting that like love and petulance it rises and sets, grows and diminishes.

Oriole is compared to women of antiquity as well as to the mythic and divine. The comparisons may be roughly categorized as negative and positive. Negative comparisons are to those beauties who can be described not only as alluring but also destructive. Such fear of female beauty (and the attendant fear of female sexuality) goes far back in Chinese written history, in whose pages a plethora of attractive women have led many a kingdom to its demise.[38] In *The Story of the Western Wing* it is clear that the author, while drawing primarily on the Dong Jieyuan text, is also continuing the description of Oriole found first in Yuan

Zhen's "Tale of Oriole," where she is described as a female demon (*youwu*). It is for this reason—sexual allure represented in unearthly beauty—that Oriole is finally rejected by the student of Yuan Zhen's tale.

The most significant actual comparisons in the play are made to the figures Xi Shi and Yang Guifei, who are inextricably linked with the phrase "toppler of state" (*qingguo*), a term used to identify women possessing the power, for instance, to distract a lord from his proper duties and thereby lead a kingdom to its downfall. In the case of Oriole the term is used in very limited circumstances: twice by Student Zhang, more notably when he first sees her and is caught off guard by her physical beauty, and again by Flying Tiger Sun, who, having heard rumors of Oriole's beauty, surrounds the monastery in order to carry her off as his "lady of the fortress"

(Clown, costumed as Flying Tiger Sun, enters and opens:) I am surnamed Sun, named Biao, and called the Flying Tiger. At this moment Emperor Dezong has ascended the throne and all under heaven is in turmoil. Because the commander-in-chief, Ding Wenya, has lost control, I, Biao, guard the river bridge and lead some five thousand men and horse in plundering the good citizens of their valuables and goods. Recently I learned that the daughter of the former chancellor Cui Jue, Oriole, who has the looks to topple cities and states and the face of a Xi Shi or Precious Consort Yang, is now staying at the Monastery of Universal Salvation. I've thought it over, and it seems that right now is just the time to exercise military might. When the commander-in-chief is not acting right, why should I alone be incorruptible? My troops listen to my orders: the men will all wear gags, the horses will all have bits. We will march this very night to Hezhong Prefecture. If I can snatch Oriole for my wife, then all my life's desires will be fulfilled.[39]

He calls her a beauty that can set empires awash, a reference to Li Yannian's sister, a performer so lovely that she was introduced to the Martial Emperor of the Han (Han Wudi, r. 140–87 B.C.) with the following poem:[40]

> In the north is a beautiful woman;
> Without compeer, she stands alone.
> A single glance topples a city,
> A second glance topples a state.
> Of course, one knows she can topple a city, topple a state,
> But such a beauty is not to be found again.

These allusions to Xi Shi and Yang Guifei provide two historical examples of women who actually brought the kingdoms of their lords to an end through their infatuating beauty Xi Shi was a beauty of the fifth century B.C. who was enlisted by a minister of the state of Yue, Fan Li, to subvert the state of Wu by distracting the king, Fu Chai, with her good looks and many charms. There are two accounts of her fate after the fall of Wu: one account says that she went away with Fan Li; another, that the people of Wu drowned her in the Yangtze. Whichever the case, in literature she has become the archetype of the destructive woman.

Yang Guifei was the young consort of the elderly Tang emperor Xuanzong. He first fell in love with her when he saw her plump, alabaster white body emerging from the hot springs at Huaqing Palace. Since she was married to one of his sons, she had to become a nun before she could become the emperor's concubine. As in the case of Oriole and Student Zhang, there are overtones of incest in his infatuation: Consort Yang had been Xuanzong's daughter-in-law, and in the play the old madam very cleverly establishes a brother-sister bond between our young lovers. There are other points in the text where Student Zhang makes much more subtle allusion to the similarities between Oriole and Yang Guifei: for instance, when he calls her "a flower that can speak," a reference to a famous anecdote about the aging Xuanzong's obsession with Precious Consort Yang.[41] According to legend, the emperor was so taken with her that he let the reins of government slip from his own hands into those of her evil cousin Yang Guozhong, whom the emperor had made a high-ranking minister. In the eyes of tradition, Xuanzong's passion for Consort Yang was also a direct cause of the rebellion of An Lushan, whose armies drove the emperor into temporary exile in Sichuan. While en route, the emperor was forced by his generals to command the death of his young mistress; she was strangled to death on the steps of a Buddhist monastery [42]

It is in light of these two legends that Oriole's own response to the siege of the monastery expresses an understanding that it is her very loveliness that will bring ruin to the temple. This final realization that she will be the death of all who surround her is both an echo and an acceptance of this basic fear of female sexuality While the ancient association between beauty and destruction is generally reflected in the background of this act, something else is hinted at as well. In his first encounter with the lovely Oriole, Student Zhang is overwhelmed by her physical beauty and, as we shall see below, becomes completely addled. When she later appears at the mass in the monastery, she drives the monks and acolytes wild, upsetting the gravest and most dignified of ceremonies and also thereby spreading the rumor of her beauty to Sun Biao, the bandit general. These passages clearly show that her physical beauty has the power to devastate the normal course of events and in a curiously symmetrical way to provoke punishment for her overt sexual attraction. Surrounded in the monastery, she sings:

> Those louts have heard a rumor on the wind,
> Saying, "The kohl of her eyebrows frowns darkly,
> And her lotus face engenders spring,
> Just like a city- and state-toppling Precious Consort Yang."
> Won't I be sending these three hundred monks to their deaths?
> Half a myriad of mutinous troops
> In half a second will cut them down like grass and root them out.
> For neither state nor dynasty have these louts trust or loyalty,

And they plunder the citizens at will.
Even this building constructed like a heavenly palace they will burn to
    the ground.[43]

Oriole lives a somewhat freer life in the monastery, and her normal place of residence—the isolated boudoir where she is surrounded only by female servants—is forsaken for a world that is still enclosed but in which she easily moves in the company of men. The siege by the bandit general, of which she here sings, may be seen both as a logical result of beauty openly shown and as an allegorical reprimand for the freedom that let her out. Her uncontrolled wanderings have stirred up the passions not only of the young scholar but of all the world that comes to know of her beauty She becomes in the play a "state-toppling beauty," bringing destruction on all who live close to her.[44] But the sexual allegory must hold as well. Given the clear association between the monastery and the female sexual organ, we should understand that it is aroused male lust that is banging at the gates of the temple.[45] This threat of violation implies a social message to readers and audiences—that beauty beyond the pale of its normal confines carries with it the danger of unwanted overtures, even rape.

The alluring Oriole is also compared (and even compares herself) to the "eastern neighbor," a figure first mentioned in Song Yu's "Rhapsody on Dengtu Zi's Love of Sex," ("Dengtu Zi haose fu"). In this rhapsody Song Yu (fl. 3rd century B.C.), accused by Dengtu Zi of being a lecher, responds by noting that of all the women in the world, the women of Chu are the most handsome. He goes on to describe a beautiful young girl, a neighbor to the east, who has made overtures toward him for three years—but to whose entreaties he has never assented. He points out that Dengtu Zi, however, has a clutch of children by a very ugly wife. Who, Song Yu asks, is the real lecher? Less negative than comparisons to either Yang Guifei or Xi Shi, there is still the implication of illicit intimacy here since the girl to the east actually climbed a wall to display herself to Song Yu. On the more positive side, invoking the name of a figure from one of Song Yu's poems brings to life the archetypal image of perfectly matched lovers, the king of Chu and the mysterious beauty of Shamanka Mountain, who figure in another rhapsody on sex and the divine, "Rhapsody on the High Terrace" ("Gaotang fu"). This rhapsody is also attributed to Song Yu, but actually dates from the second or first century B.C. It is this poem that first brings into the literary vocabulary the term *yunyu*, "clouds and rain," as a metaphor for sexual intercourse.

The most positive allusion drawn on for comparison to Oriole is that of Lady Wenjun, who eloped to become the wife of Sima Xiangru.[46] The story of these young lovers clearly provides the model for Student Zhang and Oriole, and sets the early parameters of the treatment of that story in later vernacular fiction.[47] The constituents of the tale as found in early sources may be summarized as follows: Sima Xiangru, the son of a rich family of Chengdu, fails in his first attempt to make a career at court despite his literary talents. He returns home to find the family estate in ruin and has to rely on the good graces of a friend, the magistrate of Linqiong, who finds a place for him to live in a public hostel but nevertheless treats him with utmost respect and courtesy A certain Zhuo Wangsun is impressed with Sima and invites him to a party at his house. While the poet is playing a zither for the guests' entertainment, Zhuo's recently widowed daughter, Wenjun, espies the talented young man and falls in love with him. Sima Xiangru bribes a servant to send her a love note, and they elope that night. Her father, extremely angry, cuts her off financially The lovers go back to the town of Linqiong and there open a wine shop. Their predicament naturally causes embarrassment for her father, who finally provides for the couple. Later Sima Xiangru's fame as a poet and man of letters spreads to court, and the emperor employs him as an envoy to the southwestern barbarians. When he is accorded highest honors by the officials in Shu, Zhuo Wangsun gives Wenjun her full dowry and inheritance. Sima returns to the capital, where he is appointed keeper of the funerary park of Emperor Wen and retires to Mouling.[48]

Of the many anecdotes about Sima Xiangru in the late Han miscellany *Xijing zaji*, one concerns Sima Xiangru's intention to take the daughter of a man from Mouling as his concubine.[49] Purportedly, when Zhuo Wenjun heard of it, she wrote a poem entitled "Lament on White Hair" ("Baitou yin"), in which she laments being rejected because of her age and expresses her longing for a true and lasting relationship. The significance of this spurious addition to the story (both transmitted texts of the lament are written in a poetic form that was not practiced in Wenjun's time) is that it changes the direction of the story from its original focus, providing a literary model for tales about women of good family who are courted and seduced by talented young scholars only to suffer the fear or actual ignominy of his selecting another young bride when away at a capital post.[50]

The adaptation of this model for the *The Story of the Western Wing* has allowed the playwright to retain Dong Jieyuan's version of the story in which Oriole, who originally plays the zither in Yuan Zhen's tale to express her unspoken feelings, is replaced by Student Zhang, who plays it to win her heart. This allows the use of the famous scene of this stringed seduction, of course; but through association with the tradition of the "Lament on White Hair," the adaptation also allows the playwright to exploit the dramatic potential of Oriole's possible rejection, which is part of the Tang dynasty tale and which provides background dramatic tension during the unfolding of the final acts after Oriole has given herself to the student and thereby risked ruining her reputation and standing in family and society She tells him after their first session of love-making:

> In a single second I have thrown away my body, precious as a thousand pieces of gold. My body and my life I entrust to you forever. May you never disdain me in the future and make me lament my white hairs.[51]

Oriole is certainly more than just a collection of allusions and suggestive descriptions. As we have seen, one early playwright notes that she is to be played by the *huadan*, or "flowery female lead," a role that usually specializes in courtesans and singsong girls. This appears to be a choice of role type that allows Oriole to emerge as a far rounder character than her male counterpart. In the play she is a bundle of contradictory feelings. She senses that her youth is passing, she falls madly in love with the young scholar, she is headstrong with her mother; and yet she is also extraordinarily passive and filial at times. Her sincere devotion to her father is clear in the text, and the suppression (or attempted suppression) of her feelings of love for the student seems to stem from a true desire to abide by her mother's wishes.

Her feelings for her mother are further complicated by something akin to a lack of self-esteem. We have only to note her conception of her mother's opinion of her—"worthless goods" to be sold at "two for the price of one"—to sense that Oriole's duty to her mother operates not in the realm of love and compassion but within the abused relationship of authority and filial response. The tension that develops between the filial devotion of the proper child and the demands and needs of sexual and emotional fulfillment exploits this boundary between feeling and duty to the fullest. It is aided by theatrical convention and the adoption of the flowery female lead to portray Oriole. It is most effective because the allure and sexuality normally presented in characters of romantic abandonment are displayed instead in the true and innocent longing of a young girl of good family Except for those moments when she realizes the effect of her beauty, Oriole's sexuality seems to be a mystery to her, something almost unconscious. Its charms are apparent to everyone else and are described exclusively by other characters in the play. But to Oriole, awakening sexuality remains a mysterious part of her contradictory and poorly defined, much less understood, feelings.

Oriole's inability to sort out these feelings leads her to charges of insincerity by the student and of lying by her maidservant. Yet if we were to accept a cynical point of view, she is the only one who stands to suffer loss in this love relationship. The student is a free agent, alone and directed toward a career. He can, if he chooses, be exploitative—seduce her and leave her behind as one more stop along the capital road or abandon her for a better match later. Dramatic conventions based on the *caizi-jiaren* stories (in which the male may either return to marry the woman or abandon her), allusions to dangerous and wanton women, and the use of the flowery female lead all suggest the possibility of rejection until the very end of the play Oriole's own fears, expressed so clearly after the seduction scene, echo the feelings of Zhuo Wenjun in her "Lament on White Hair." Here we might add that Oriole's acknowledgment of that similarity represents her awareness that they are acting out roles prescribed by the *caizi-jiaren* model, but it also signals a real change in her personality. While heretofore Oriole's indecisiveness has made her mistress of the situation, once her bargaining chip of chastity is played, she is completely at the mercy of the student. It is anxiety that stamps her feelings after the affair is discovered and Zhang Gong goes off to the capital—she waits as if in anticipation for the rest of that well-known story of use and rejection to unfold and for her lover to turn heartlessly against her. This anxiety also foreshadows Zheng Heng's return to claim her as well as Oriole's willingness to believe that the student has indeed taken another wife. In a turn of events typical in such stories, a beauty like Oriole, having been rejected, would settle for a dull second choice of a mate.

What seems like ambivalence toward the student—what he reads as heartlessness—is in fact the unresolved desire of a girl struggling to make a choice between love and responsibility. There are three points in the drama when Oriole is clearly ready to give herself to Student Zhang. The first comes when she sees him and first hears him chant his poem over the wall. The opening scene of the next act is given over to her expressions of love; but, the possibility of a relationship with him is endangered by the siege, for which she is ready to surrender either her body or her life. The second and most significant opportunity is when the old madam promises Oriole to Student Zhang if he can lift the siege. Oriole is plainly excited about this possibility, but it is ruined by the duplicity of her mother when she reneges on her promise. Finally, Oriole is seduced by Zhang's poetry and his zither, but at the crucial point she overhears him accuse her of lying.

Oriole's relationship with her mother makes these decisions even more difficult. There appears to be little mutual trust between the two women. It is apparent that Crimson's main task, from the old lady's point of view, is to follow Oriole around, making sure she stays out of trouble. Oriole's behavior has already occasioned one strong rebuke from her mother, but in Oriole's eyes (as she blurts out in a moment of exasperation) her mother simply considers her a piece of goods to be traded for status and family ties. Her bitter reaction to her mother's duplicity regarding the marriage promise is followed by an intriguing aria in which it is not the situation itself that comes under scrutiny but what she sees as a pathological and untrustworthy side to her mother—she is a liar:

> The old madam is a slippery bolt that can't be pinned down,
> A wordless riddle that can't be solved.
> In hidden corners she deceives people with honeyed words,
> But when she summons them, she makes them miserable.[52]

> [My mother] has felled him from the sky with honeyed words
> And has cheated me badly with false pretenses.[53]

She decries the fact that her mother's deceit is "as big as heaven." Earlier, when she learns that her mother is simply going to put on a small banquet to honor Zhang Gong, she laments to her maid that her mother has no real concern for her:

> She's afraid that I'm just goods to be sold at a loss;
> But when it's two for the price of one, then the deal is on.[54]

Even Crimson, after she discovers that the madam has gone back on her word, remarks that Oriole is merely "an article to be sold at a loss and even then rejected."[55] Lacking that basic level of trust between mother and child, they substitute for it a hierarchical relationship that not only abuses authority and power but precludes the trust that should develop within such a relationship by the exercise of humanity and compassion. It is small wonder that Oriole feels she is simply a commodity that can be offered for sale, withdrawn, and reoffered to someone of higher station if it will bolster family status.

As we have noted, although traditional morality may appear questionable to the modern reader, there is no doubt that in the world of the play (and in the society for which it was written) "marriage was the cornerstone of the social and cosmic order."[56] Under these circumstances—used by her mother as a tool to maintain family status, mistrusted by the man she loves, tailed everywhere by a maid in service to her mother—should Oriole choose passion that ends in rejection, then not only does she lose her self-respect and any chance of a good marriage, she also falls from her proper position in the family and in society—the governing context of her whole life.

The other partner in the twin analogues to the story of Sima Xiangru and Zhuo Wenjun is of course the student, and again the characterization draws heavily on the conventions of theater. There are basically two students in this play: the one who is full of self-confidence and acts responsibly in the public world; and the other who passively moans and groans over his love-longing in the monastery and the study. The sudden and dramatic changes in his character, shown through both his actions and his language, provide us with a figure whose very essence is inconsistency, at once the object of satire and scorn and a brilliant and talented young man.

The basic characterization of Zhang Gong is that of Dong Jieyuan's *Story of the Western Wing in All Keys and Modes*, which plays on the original Student Zhang of the Tang tale and on the traditional satires of students that were so firmly a part of Song and Jin farces. When Student Zhang makes his first entrance onstage, he sings a pedant's introduction, outlining how hard he has studied, how many difficulties his poverty has caused, and how determined he is to succeed. His facade, typical of the young scholar en route to the capital for the examinations, falls apart at the first sight of Oriole. There begins his descent into the world of *yin*, into sickness, and into what Crimson calls "addlepated silliness." In short, he loses all self-control. Part of the humor stems from his self-adopted pose as a celibate prude, a life-style that he calls up in an aria in the second act:

> When I saw any powdered faces before, I really was embarrassed,
> Or saw any painters of eyebrows, I really panicked.
> But when this man full of passion saw that passionate lass,
> It made my heart itch,
> Itch.
> It has stirred me up until my insides quiver,
> It has done me in until my eyes go crazy,
> And it has riled me up so, my heart is all aflutter.[57]

In the wonderful ambiguity of the opening lines the student refers to women's makeup and deftly alludes to the stories of He Yan and Zhang Chang, men whose names are synonymous with skirt-chasing and doting love for the fairer sex. He Yan powdered his face to make himself attractive to women, and Zhang Chang was so in love with his wife that he drew on her eyebrows himself. As Wang Jide pointed out in the early seventeenth century, this portrayal of Zhang Sheng as a celibate and a prude is certainly meant to echo that found in the Tang dynasty "Tale of Oriole."[58]

In the play the student's fall from grace is reflected in the register of his language. When he first sees Oriole, he is in the middle of a long aria describing the temple, composed in a style that, if not ponderous in its lyricism, is at least pedantic. Suddenly seeing her, he sings

> Stunning knockouts—I've seen a million;
> But a lovely face like this is rarely seen!
> It dazzles a man's eyes, stuns him speechless,
> And makes his soul fly away into the heavens.
> She there, without a thought of teasing, fragrant shoulders bare,
> Simply twirls the flower, smiling.[59]

He begins this song with a very colloquial interjection, *dianbula*, which has been variously understood as "frivolous or nonsensical," "unrestrained or romantic," "absolutely first-rate," although here it clearly means something like "fantastic" or "stunning."[60] The colloquial tone of the song gradually degenerates into the kind of lascivious yearning that critics have traditionally labeled "extremely vulgar" (*shuli*).[61] This mixture of registers of language and the descent from the pedantic patois of the scholar to the vulgarisms of the lecher are part and parcel of the picture of the fallen youth, whose descent is made all the more humorous by the strength and confidence of his original priggishness. The mixture of language levels throughout the rest of the first three and a half acts echoes the inconsistency in his actions: in the second act of the first play, for instance, when his elegant praise of the abbot turns into an accusation of lewd behavior. There are many points in the first part of the play in particular where Zhang's language stamps his lust. We can hardly reproduce in English the impact of the second "itch" in the aria above, which is meant to be sung as a single line, bearing all of the emphasis that isolation would give it.

But smitten he is, our young scholar, and he makes plans right away to move into the monastery The act in which he rents a room is important for understanding the character of Student Zhang. In it he not only first encounters Crimson, who is quite taken with his charm, but also demonstrates a vacillating, quicksilver temperament and a certain toughness that lies hidden beneath it. When Zhang visits the abbot about renting a room, he explains that he has nothing to present him but the gifts of a humble scholar. The abbot suggests that official corruption must have allowed the student's father to leave him rather well off. Zhang Gong makes a witty comeback using the metaphor of weights and measures that at once challenges the abbot and cleverly hints at the old man's craving for cash.[62] Bested, the monk proceeds to ask him where he would like his room. The student quickly responds with a litany of locations, including the western wing, "sung out," Jin Shengtan remarks, "like the sound of raindrops on banana leaves".[63]

> I do not want the refectory
> Or the hall of withered trees;[64]
> But far from the southern pavilions,
> Away from the eastern walls,
> Near to the western wing,
> Close to the main hall,
> Past the side rooms—
> Those are the places that are just right.[65]

Soon afterward, when Crimson makes her appearance to inquire about the mass for Oriole's late father, Zhang immediately assumes that she is taken with him and is flirting:

> This delightful lass's face is made up, oh, so lightly;
> She is wearing a set of plain white clothes.
> Her sparkling peepers are not of the ordinary kind:
> Stealing a glance
> Out of the corner of her eye, she strokes young Zhang.[66]

He suggests that if, through her intercession and to his good fortune, he should wind up with her mistress, he would take her for a concubine as well: "If I could share the same mandarin-duck bed-curtains with her passionate mistress, / Would I leave her just to pile up the quilts and make up the bed?"[67] As the young maid and the abbot leave to inspect the site of the mass, Zhang accuses the monk of lusting after the young girl. Again put in his place by the abbot, Zhang learns that the mass under discussion is to be said for Oriole's father, and he suddenly bursts out crying, beseeching the abbot to allow him to pay for part of the service to honor his own dead parents.[68] One minute flaunting his erudition before the abbot with the proper quote from the *Book of Poetry*, the next he excuses himself from the room "to change his clothes"[69] in order to waylay Crimson outside. He is proud and full of confidence when she appears, and he reels off a list of pertinent names and numbers:

> My surname is Zhang, my personal name is Gong, and I am known as Junrui. I hail originally from Western Luo and am just twenty-three. I was born on the seventeenth day of the first month, during the midnight hour. I have never been married.[70]

He finishes by asking her when her mistress comes out each night. Zhang's data are, in fact, the cyclical signs and other information needed for marriage divination. It is unseemly of a man to propose himself for a marriage match and especially unseemly to discuss the matter with a maidservant. Crimson readily rebuffs Zhang, scolding him with a list of classical citations about proper behavior that in effect parodies his erudite outburst in the abbot's cell. She then goes on to tell him that Oriole's mother is extremely severe. Learning of the old lady's strictures and seeing his bold, presumptuous gestures become the easy object of criticism and parody by a maid, Student Zhang goes into a tailspin of depression and longing:

> Having listened to this, my heart and bosom are bleak and blue;
> A whole heaven of sorrow have I pinched between my eyebrows.
> She said, "The madam's integrity is severe as ice and frost.
> If not summoned,
> Who dares enter the center halls?"
> Well, I wonder
> If your heart so fears the stern authority of your mother.
>
> You should never have turned around to look when you left![71]

These are the traits that will delineate his character until the affair is consummated later in the play.

We have identified elements in Zhang's characterization that can be ascribed to dramatic convention, to "The Tale of Oriole," to Dong Jieyuan's *Story of the Western Wing in All Keys and Modes*, or to new features added by Wang Shifu. Part of the traditional representations stem from farce skits in the *zaju* and *yuanben* variety shows of the Song and Jin. These include the convention of the *suan* (vinegar, vinegary), which was used to describe the role type of the witless student as portrayed onstage.[72] It is primarily Crimson who describes the student in this way She calls him *shajiao* (addlepated), a term that means something like a silly but lovable fool. It fits very well with the traditional caricature of the student. As Tanaka Kenji pointed out many years ago, the student is the perfect butt of satire. Learned but not wise in the ways of the world, free from family responsibilities but willing to throw his freedom away for the tyranny of a woman, he offers a good target for parody[73] Crimson makes excellent use of the stereotype to reinforce this image. When the bandits have been repulsed and Student Zhang is invited to a banquet in his honor, for instance, he asks Crimson to give him the once-over. She sings:

> Back and forth he watches his own shadow—
> What a pedantic scholar!
> What a foolish sourpuss!
> He has spent his time slicking up his pate,
> Brushing flies off all the time—
> Oily and glistening, it dazzles one's eyes;
> Sour and slick, it stings until one's teeth ache.

(Student speaks:) What has the madam put out for me?

([Crimson] sings:)
The meal has already been set:
She has rinsed off some pints of rice gone bad in the warehouse
And fried up seven or eight bowls of wilted vegetables.[74]

Crimson catches the essence of the crazed young pedant, all dandied up and strutting back and forth, admiring his costuming. Her fun continues in the last two lines of the verse when she recites the menu. The foods named will not be served, of course, but are a clever reference to the colloquial expression "salted pickle vat" (*suanji weng*), a common metaphor for students at that time: that is, he looks vinegary and crazed and will be fed accordingly with the rice and pickles from the public stores that the government doles out to students.

This satirical view of Student Zhang is repeated in other places as well. When, for instance, he misunderstands Oriole's note and goes to visit her in the garden, his obsession with his clothing is again ridiculed by Crimson when she sings, "I would have said that the wind swayed evening crows in the shade of the sophora tree, / But all the while it was the raven's-gauze hattails of the jade person."[75] Crimson is not all satire, however, in her opinion of the young student. She has a certain amount of affection for him, and she gives in twice to his entreaties to carry messages to Oriole: "I cannot withstand your honeyed words and hot entreaties!" When the student falls sick, she also rails at Oriole for the misery that she has caused him, claiming that she will be his death.

There are also moments when Crimson is disappointed with the student. The first comes when he offers her money for her help in setting him up with Oriole:

Bah! You starving, bankrupt sourpuss, you make no sense,
Flaunting as if you had family riches!
Did I come here scheming to get something from you,
Or to have you give your money and goods
To Crimson as a reward?
I don't give a damn about your gold.

You look on me as a spring-wind sprig of peach beyond the garden wall:
I'm not to be compared to those who lean against the gates to sell their charms.
I may be just a woman, but I have my pride.
I said to myself, "How pitiful this little one is,
All alone and by himself."

But now—

I'll have to change my thinking about that![76]

When he jumps over the wall to keep his supposed assignation with Oriole,

Crimson, convinced that his interpretation of the poem is correct, is surprised when Oriole attacks him. She comes partially to his defense and keeps him from any real harm, but her disappointment in him is nevertheless not difficult to see:

> Student Zhang, where's that big mouth of yours that you had when you were alone? You missed your chance to go ahead and embrace her! Wouldn't you be ashamed if we took you to court?
>
>> When no one was around, you knew how to idly rattle your teeth,
>> But on the inside it was all vain cunning and deceit.
>> Who would know that by the rockery
>> You did not remember "beneath the western wing"?
>> A perfumed and beautiful maiden has cloven the showy quince.[77]

Assuredly, as before, she is having him on; but the irony and comedy cannot conceal Crimson's real affection for the student, which surfaces most clearly when she defends the lovers to the madam and later disputes Zheng Heng's claim to Oriole.

Oriole, although sometimes a partner in the comic manipulation of Zhang, perceives him much as he perceives himself—as a dashing and brilliant young scholar. The influence of the Sima Xiangru legend has cast the student in a role readily accepted by both himself and Oriole. The legend is important in its own right and is well exploited for its seduction scene; but it is also simply a specific example of the more general theme of the *caizi-jiaren* stories that are rooted in the classical tales of the Tang and earlier. For it is really Zhang's cultural accomplishments that win Oriole over—his poetry chanted over the garden wall, his zither playing, and the poetic billets-doux he sends her in his passionate longing. Because Oriole is aware of spring's (and by extension youth's) passing, this model of the perfect scholar triggers a passion within her that has been long building and is—if we are to believe the play's subtle characterization of Oriole as a rather headstrong girl—barely suppressed. She has found the perfect match for her own talents.

Oriole's outward actions may demonstrate vacillation and even heartlessness, yet there is a remarkable consistency in her real feeling for the student. And if the Sima Xiangru–Zhuo Wenjun legend created the model for their roles, it has also provided the structure whereby setbacks in such model relationships do not abrogate the certainty of their outcome. This is why, for instance, the scenes of illness and passivity remain comic: the model generates a tension in the progress of their love but also provides a certain, indisputable climax to that love that never stands in doubt. If the audience can appreciate the strength of the feelings involved, they will also be able to laugh at the follies that passion creates.

If by the time of *The Dream of the Red Chamber* this *caizi-jiaren* model was seen as hackneyed,[78] *The Story of the Western Wing* represents one of the earlier written representations in vernacular literature. In the play this model is not just a literary or dramatic structure but also appears to provide the personæ consciously adopted by our young couple. After Zhang Gong has been aroused by Oriole's beauty, for instance, his next impression is of her poetic talent:

> Already struck by a vexing loveliness redundant upon her face,
> I'm now perplexed by the quick intelligence stored away in her mind:
> She has matched, oh, so well the meter of my new poem;
> Each word, one by one, tells true feelings—what a pleasure to hear.
>
> The lyrics are fresh,
> The prosody flows easily—
> No accident that she has been given Oriole as a name.
> If she were to fix her eyes on me,
> We would banter verses across the wall until dawn.
> Now rings true the saying, "Since ancient days the bright have loved
>   the bright."[79]

Later, when he receives her letter in the posthouse, he again vaunts her literary talents and skill.[80] This appreciation of talent is perfectly matched by Oriole's appreciation of his skill:

> Normally, whenever I saw a stranger,
> I would immediately scowl;
> Whenever I saw a traveler,
> I would instantly retreat.
> But since seeing that man,
> I have of a sudden wanted to get close.
> Thinking about his poem of last night,
> Using his earlier rhymes,
> I responded with freshness and originality
>
> He chanted the lines so evenly,
> Recited the words so true;
> His new poem that sang of the moon
> Far surpassed the palindrome woven into brocade.
> But who is willing to take the needle and draw the thread
> And transmit the utter devotion of this eastern neighbor?[81]

The characters so consciously adopt the stereotypes of the talented scholar and beautiful girl that no less an authority than Crimson accuses them of being poseurs who assume their roles out of perversity as much as passion. There are three separate points in the play where Crimson castigates them for playing too well, for failing to break out of their roles to act out real human feelings:

> It's not just this student alone
> But all young men of few years
> Who've only learned to suffer love sickness;
> [And young girls] of intelligent nature by virtue of birth,
> Dressed up in immaculate white—

Night after night they have to be all alone,
Our poet passionate,
Our beauty fickle.
Oh, aren't people's fates thwarted?[82]

And:

Beauties have always been unlucky,
Budding scholars are always weaklings:
One, a headless goose killed by gloom;
One, an article sold at a loss and even then rejected.[83]

And:

So haggard is our young Master Pan that his temples are streaked;
Our Du Weiniang is no more her former self.
Her—her belt is loosened, shrunk to nothing is her emaciated waist;
Him—he sleeps in a stupor, with no desire to look at canons or
    histories.
Her—she is unsettled, too listless to pick up her needlework;
Him—he played out on silk and paulownia a score of separation's
    grief.
Her—on flowered stationery she rubs out a poem of broken hearts;
Her—with her brush she writes out her hidden feelings;
Him—with his strings he transmits heart's affairs.
Both of them—both suffer alike from love's longing.

Now I believe that poets and beauties really exist,
But in Crimson's eyes they are a bit perverse—
It seems to me that passionate people who do not get their heart's
    desire are like this:
What I see is that they suffer so much, they become bewitched;
And what I find is that they never give a second thought
But immediately bury their heads to prepare for a wasting death.[84]

Crimson functions in the play as a spokeswoman for common sense and for human feeling stripped of all artifice and demands of social position. She disapproves of the student's and the young girl's role playing, and in the end she counsels Zhang to forget Oriole and get his studies under way Crimson, who of all the women has been the most doubtful of Zhang's resolve to stand by Oriole, is the one who urges him to leave her mistress's side.

Crimson's criticism of their role playing finds a parallel much later in *The Dream of the Red Chamber*, when Grandmother Jia lectures at length on the falseness of this convention of the talented beauty and young scholar:

"These stories are all the same," said Grandmother Jia, "—so tedious!

Always the same ideally eligible young bachelors and the same ideally beautiful and accomplished young ladies—at least, they are *supposed* to be ideal, but there's certainly nothing ideal about their behavior—in fact there's nothing very ladylike about them at all. Invariably, we are told how well-born they are. Their father has been a Prime Minister, or a First Secretary at the very least. They are always their father's only child and the apple of his eye. They are always amazingly well-educated, a model of decorum, a regular paragon of all the virtues—that is, until the first presentable young man comes along. As soon as *he* appears on the scene—it doesn't matter who or what he is—all their book-learning and the duty they owe their parents fly out the window and the next moment they are 'making their plans for the future' and generally carrying on in a way that would bring blushes to the cheeks of a cat-burglar—certainly not in the least like respectable, educated young ladies. You would hardly call a young woman who conducted herself like that a 'paragon,' however many books she might have read—any more than you would acquit a young fellow charged with highway robbery on the grounds that he was a good scholar. The people who make up these stories give themselves the lie every time they open their mouths."[85]

When, after Madam Cui discovers the affair and the student is more or less forced to leave the monastery to take the examinations as a condition of marriage, Zhang Gong moves back into the public world to assume his rightful position. It is interesting that neither the abbot nor the student's good friend General Du has lost any faith in the young student, but it is also understandable, since his weakness and passivity have been concealed from public view His successes in the world of culture outside are given but passing mention in the play, a sign that he plays out the *caizi-jiaren* model to the end. Time too is compressed in the last two acts so that he may reappear in the monastery to lay claim to Oriole. After the fourth play Oriole figures only once in her former role, and that is when she appears to Zhang in a dream, only to be dragged away by the soldiers of Flying Tiger Sun. This sequence is interesting as the mental actualization of what was only a possibility in real life. It can, as we have mentioned, represent Zhang's feelings of guilt about leaving; but if we read the original siege of the monastery as an allegory of unbridled lust, this dream can represent a fear on Student Zhang's part that Oriole will be taken by another. In any case, it is yet another intrusion of the world of *yin*—the dream state itself—and a nagging reminder that whatever his successes in the public world, this part of his life is unsettled.

In this public world too Zhang Gong can exercise parts of his personality and character that are largely obscured in the monastery. They appear briefly in his rebuttal to the abbot's accusations that his father was corrupt and again when he asks the madam point-blank why she has lied—both bold moves against age and authority. In fact, these incidents seem to strengthen the feeling that the Student Zhang who appears before the second act of the fourth play is partially acting out of a conscious adoption of the *caizi* persona and that his feelings, strong as they are, are merely momentary aberrations in an otherwise resolute personality fated for success.

The one character who owes most to the pen of Wang Shifu is Crimson, known in Chinese as Hongniang, the Red Maiden. A simple background figure in "The Tale of Oriole," she has been fleshed out in *The Story of the Western Wing* to become perhaps the most interesting of the three major personalities of the play Part of that interest and part of her own motivation in the play lie in her status as an indentured servant—a status so low that it allows her to speak with frankness and earthiness and grants her a far greater range of action than a girl of good station would have. The central importance of her role is suggested by the fact that many later adaptations of *The Story of the Western Wing* are simply called *Crimson*. The name itself is fraught with significance. Red is the color of life, of romance, and of marriage—"red dust" is the Buddhist term for the mortal world of desire and craving—and in this play, as in many other contexts, red is the color most often associated with sex and sexuality

As have we observed, Crimson clearly views the young lovers as poseurs who relate to each other only through the personae dictated by the *caizi-jiaren* model. But revealing such studied behavior on their part is only a measure of Crimson's systematic exposure of deceit and dissimulation throughout the play. At one time or another she accuses Oriole, the old lady, Student Zhang, and Zheng Heng of lying or of acting treacherously Deception and dissembling are part and parcel of all love comedies, and such revelations of hypocrisy are certainly to be expected in a love comedy set in a highly authoritarian society Ironically, it is Crimson's own cunning and her deception of Madam Cui that bring the play to a satisfactory conclusion.

The play hints at Oriole's headstrong nature several times and in places suggests that she has acted out of order. Crimson says so plainly at her initial meeting with Student Zhang when she explains that Oriole is kept under strict control:

> A few days ago Oriole sneaked out of the inner rooms and the madam discovered it. She ordered Oriole to stand in the courtyard below· "You are just a girl, but you left the inner chambers without requesting permission! If you had happened to encounter a visitor or a novice who had ogled you secretly, wouldn't you have been ashamed of yourself?"[86]

Crimson therefore has been assigned to keep her out of trouble. When Oriole first shows romantic interest in Student Zhang, she complains of Crimson's shadowing her every move:

> O Crimson,

I can only lie facedown on this fine silken pillow and drowse:
Were I just to leave the doors of my apartment,
Like a shadow, you'd never leave my side.

(Crimson speaks:) It has nothing to do with me! Madam ordered me to follow you around. (Female lead speaks:) My mother doesn't understand a thing. All this time she's been nothing but an obstacle to me.

(She sings:)
My little maid waits on me most diligently,
The madam ties me up most tightly:
"I'm so worried that my little girl will lose her honor!"[87]

Crimson happily accepts the responsibility of tracking Oriole's actions, and until the madam reneges on her promise of marriage, Crimson does in fact protect Oriole: hurrying her out of the flower garden when men appear, rebuffing Student Zhang's silly overtures, and herding Oriole back into her bedchamber. But she finally gives up the madam's injunctions in order to bring the two lovers together. While we might assume that love alone wins the servant's advocacy, there is a good deal of self-interest in Crimson's actions.

What she hopes to gain is not money—we have already noted above her fury at Zhang Gong's mention of monetary reward. She repeats her refusal later:

But the past has sunk away;
Let's talk only of today
When you meet tonight, I'll make it happen.
I don't scheme for your white jade or yellow gold;
I want only "flowers covering her head, brocade trailing the
    ground."[88]

These protestations that her only desire is to see Oriole married obscure her own interests in such a match. The advantages that she hopes to gain are clearly spoken earlier in the play when Oriole goes to burn incense in the flower garden:

(Female lead speaks:) Give me the incense. (Male lead speaks:) I'll pay attention to what she prays for. (Female lead speaks:) With this first stick of incense I pray for my deceased father's rebirth in heaven's realm. With this second stick of incense, I pray that my old mother will stay healthy. And with this third stick   (She acts out falling silent). (Crimson speaks:) Sister, don't utter a prayer with this stick of incense; I'll do it for you—I pray that my sister will soon find a husband who will take Crimson along too.[89]

Crimson, who senses Oriole's interest in the scholar and who, apparently because of her lower social status, is far more experienced than her mistress in matters of love, also sees a good match in Zhang Gong—not as a husband but as a man who will sign the writ of freedom (*congliang*) that is necessary to release her from indentured status. This is a precondition that slaves and courtesans must satisfy before they can become either the wife or the concubine of a person of good standing. Student Zhang has already suggested that such a course of action would be a reward for her services.[90] In the polygamous society of premodern China, of course, it would clearly be to Crimson's benefit to secure a suitable mate for her mistress since that would also mean a suitable master for herself; indeed, Crimson finds Student Zhang attractive:

> I have only to see him welcome me so politely with hands folded,
> And I say my "Myriad blessings, master."
> His raven's-gauze hat dazzles one's vision,
> His white gown is immaculate,
> His horn-decorated belt is a proud yellow leather strap.
>
> His gown and cap are spick-and-span, his face is handsome:
> He's sure to arouse our Oriole.
> On account of his exterior appearance
> And because of his inner talents,
> I, who have always had a hard heart,
> Am smitten as soon as I see him.[91]

There is little doubt that Crimson takes control of the lovers' relationship to realize her own end. When the match is endangered by the madam, for instance, her worry for Oriole is coupled with her own interests. "If you aren't married," she asks Oriole, "at the final exit what will you do about *me*?"[92] And when the madam acquiesces to the marriage, Crimson can finally see the outcome of her efforts:

> When you come back, the flutes and drums in the painted hall will
>   sound spring's daylight;
> A pair, simurgh mate and phoenix friend, will be arranged.
> Only then will I accept the red reward for being matchmaker,
> Only then will I drink the wine for thanking relatives.[93]

It would be wrong of course to view Crimson's actions entirely from the standpoint of self-interest. It is clear in her dealings with the two lovers that she has a great deal of affection for the both of them. It is equally clear, however, that as the go-between she also governs their lives and their feelings—to such an extent that when the repugnant Zheng Heng returns, she assumes the madam's rightful role and tells him, "I won't marry [Oriole] to you!"[94] We might ask how such power could fall into the hands of a single girl in a household in which, the play suggests, there are other servants. In *The Dream of the Red Chamber* such a question was indeed asked by Grandmother Jia:

"And for another thing: if these young women really belonged to cultivated, aristocratic households in which the girls and their mothers were all educated people, then even allowing for the somewhat reduced circumstances owing to their father's early retirement, you can be sure there would still be plenty of nannies and maids in attendance on them. So how is it that in all of these stories there is only ever a single confidante who knows what her young mistress is getting up to? What are all the other servants supposed to be doing all this time?"[95]

In the case of *The Story of the Western Wing*, the prototype of all of these later stories, it is precisely the madam's injunction to watch Oriole closely that leads first to Crimson's constant companionship and then gradually to her interest in the fate of the young couple. That interest is spurred by the old woman's breach of promise, an act that snuffs both Oriole's and Crimson's prospects. By carrying out these orders and by her efficient observation of Oriole's passion, her testing of its sincerity, her advocacy of Student Zhang, and her provision of opportunity for consummation of the affair, Crimson is able to overturn the deceit of the mother's broken promise. In fact, we might say that treachery and deceit are the primary issues of the third play, in which Crimson has the singing role. She acts as a kind of detective, exposing the real feelings of the characters and forcing them out of roles that either society or the conventions of love have determined for them. This is certainly the case with our two young lovers; it is also the case, as we shall see, with the old lady.

The first three acts of play III, in particular, center on the issues of treachery in human relations. In these acts the term *diandao* (upside down, topsy-turvy, or opposite of the truth) occurs no less than seven times. In her descriptions of Oriole, Crimson uses the terms *jiayi* (false feelings, false pretenses), *jiachu* (points of falseness), and *jian* (deceit, treachery, or feminine cunning). The madam is accused of treachery "as big as heaven" (*tianlai da*) and of "loss of faith" (*shixin*). Even Student Zhang is warned that he should "not let deceit run rampant under the guise of foolishness (*ni xiuyao daili sa jian*).

It is this deceit, this lying, this dissembling on the part of Oriole, the student, and the madam that Crimson must break through in order to bring the marriage to its rightful conclusion; she must have the trust and confidence of the two partners involved. Initially, Crimson sees no difficulties in bringing the two lovers together, and like Oriole she assumes that the madam will honor her original promise of marriage. When Crimson goes to invite Student Zhang to what she expects will be a wedding banquet, he asks if Oriole can be trusted. Crimson replies simply:

> Who has no trust?
> Who has no sincerity?
> You two will testify to that tonight.[96]

After her naive hopes for a quick match are shattered by the old woman, Crimson must both reassure Zhang Gong and win the confidence of Oriole.

Student Zhang is emotionally honest with her, but Oriole, partly because Crimson was originally the watchdog of her behavior, is reluctant to untangle her own mixed emotions—emotions that have been further complicated by her suspicion of Crimson.

After the banquet has dashed the hopes of all three, Crimson arranges for the student to play his zither in the flower garden. At that juncture still unsure of Oriole's real feelings, Crimson tells her that Zhang Gong is leaving, a point that is still ambiguous in the action of the play. When Oriole begs her to tell the student to stay, Crimson assumes that this plaint represents the girl's true feelings.[97] She also senses, however, that Oriole is not strong enough to act on her emotions but will instead play out her social role as a filial daughter:

(Male lead speaks:) Since missy does have some feelings of pity for me, can I trouble you to take this note here to let her know my innermost feelings?
(Crimson speaks:) I'm afraid that she will show a different face—

(Crimson sings:)
If she sees this poem,
Reads this lyric,
She will surely do a turnabout and put on a real act:

(Crimson speaks:) She will buckle on a different face [and say], "If I find out you bring me anyone's message

([Crimson] sings:)
How dare you act so rashly, you hussy!"
For sure she'll scoff and scoffing tear the paper to shreds.[98]

Crimson agrees to act as messenger, and her worst expectations come true. Oriole obviously enjoys the note—she is "never once annoyed" while reading it—but she berates Crimson immediately after she has done with it:

(Female lead shouts angrily:) Crimson! (Crimson winks to the audience and speaks:) Aw, shit!

([Crimson] sings:)
I suddenly wrinkle my jet brows.

(Female lead speaks:) Why don't you come here, you little hussy!

([Crimson] sings:)
All at once she droops her powdered neck,
Suddenly changes to a vermilion countenance.

(Female lead speaks:) You little hussy! Where did you get this? I am the daughter of a chancellor. Who makes sport of me with such a note? I'm not in the habit of reading such stuff! If I report this to the madam, she'll beat your bottom, you little hussy

Not to be outdone, Crimson counters by threatening to take the note directly to the old madam and accuses Oriole of projecting the responsibility for her own actions onto other people:

> It is clear that *you* transgressed the rules;
> There's no reason to savage *me*.
> You used someone else but, doing a flip-flop, are now the one offended—
> If you aren't in the habit, then *who* is?[99]

Crimson reassures Oriole of her intentions to see them married, yet she still accuses her of lying. This seemingly paradoxical attitude makes better sense if we understand that by now Crimson believes that she knows the true feelings of the young girl and will continue to act on her own knowledge of the situation rather than on the basis of Oriole's outward behavior:

> Because you fix your gaze on a tryst—a gaze as vain as waiting for
>   Mercury to appear—
> I've never been able to latch this side door tight.
> I really want you two to be man and wife, without any crisis or
>   hardship.
> At the head of the banquet mat I'll dress up
> And be a matchmaker whose mouth has been sewn shut.[100]

Crimson's chief criticism of Oriole centers not on her lying to Student Zhang but on her self-deception, her refusal to acknowledge her feelings and accept responsibility for their effects on others. Carrying messages back and forth on her behalf, Crimson feels particularly put upon being lied to. Twice she charges Oriole with double-dealing: that is, for telling Zhang Gong one thing in her notes but telling her, Crimson, something else face-to-face:

> You purposely stirred up rain and excited the clouds,
> And I, out of good intentions, delivered letters and transmitted notes.
> You refuse to examine your own crazy actions
> But want to search out faults in others.
> I'll take this hot moxa treatment just this once—
> But you're just too deceitful!

(Speaking as female lead, [Crimson] says:) "Student Zhang should act as a brother to me, his sister. How dare he do this?"

([Crimson] sings:)
In front of others, clever words and flowery speeches.

(Crimson speaks:) "If I see Student Zhang with no one present   "

([Crimson] sings:)

Then behind others' backs, sorrowful brows and teary eyes.[101]

Crimson is aware of course that it is sexual longing that is making the young girl such a guileful liar. She accuses her of being unable to "shackle that monkey of her mind and that horse of her desire" and of "preparing for a meeting of rain and clouds."[102] This fits with her belief that she has perceived the true nature of Oriole's feelings, her love and desire, and that lying and projecting her own faults onto others are simply Oriole's way of protecting her name and honor.

This belief is shattered in the third act of play III, set in the flower garden, when Student Zhang leaps the wall to what he believes will be a tryst. Hearing Oriole begin to curse the student, she comes to the realization that she has perhaps been wrong, that Oriole possibly has been telling the truth about her honor's prior claim over love. This would explain Crimson's sudden anger with Student Zhang. She sees that his brilliant interpretation of the poem betrays the flaw of pride in his scholarly abilities; certainly some of her anger must come from her realization that she was gullible enough to swallow his interpretation. But at the same time Crimson comes to understand that if Oriole's surface actions have been truthful and that if she has been on the square with Crimson, then she has conversely lied to the student and led him on:

(Crimson, discussing female lead, [sings]:)
All because you wrote a poem with multicolored brush
And wove palindromes into your brocade,
You have dispatched him to the point where he lies on his pillow, is
    glued to his bed,
Forgets to eat, neglects sleeping.

His grief is deep,
His illness is critical.
Last night, with hot anger, you reproved him face-to-face,
And today, with icy lines, you go at the man again.

(Crimson speaks:) How you reproved him last night!

(Crimson, discussing female lead, [sings]:)
Better you'd never waited for the moon, leaning on the wicker gate,
Or made poetic couplets in response to his rhyming words
Or listened to his zither with cocked ears.

([Crimson] speaks in imitation of female lead:) As soon as she saw him, she put on a show—and such a long speech: "Student Zhang, we are brother and sister—what are you after?"

([Crimson] sings:)
When angry, you trample him down;
When happy,

[(Crimson speaks:)] "Crimson, dear sister, go and see him."

([Crimson] sings:)
She coerces a serving maid.
That's insupportable!
She makes me as busy as a thread that never leaves the needle.
From now on, let her do it all herself![103]

Oriole lies to Crimson right up to the moment she is preparing to meet
Student Zhang for their first sexual encounter. As Crimson prepares to escort
Oriole to the tryst, Oriole tells her that she must get ready for bed:

(Female lead speaks:) Straighten up my bedroom, Crimson, I want to go to
sleep. (Crimson speaks:) If you are going to sleep, how will you dispose of
that student? (Female lead speaks:) What about that student? (Crimson
speaks:) There you go again. It's no joke to send a person to his death. If
you go back on your word again, I'm going to inform on you to the
madam and tell her you sent me with a note to set up a rendezvous with
him. (Female lead speaks:) You little hussy! You're really a pain in the
neck. I'm burning with shame—how can I go? (Crimson speaks:) What's
there to be ashamed of? Once there, just close your eyes. (Crimson,
pushing female lead, speaks:) Go on! Go on! The madam is asleep! (Female
lead acts out running [and leaves]. Crimson sighs and speaks:) My sister
may put on a strong show, but her steps have carried her there already [104]

We can almost hear the maid's sigh of relief when Oriole finally goes off to the
rendezvous. For the act of sex itself, which tends to strip away outward pretense,
not only moves Crimson's plan for their eventual marriage closer but also bonds
the two young women in a relationship of trust.

Crimson's contention with the old madam is somewhat more straightforward.
After Happy, the shadowy brother of Oriole, reveals that his sister has been
visiting the student at night, the madam, furious, summons Crimson.[105] Despite
her wiles, Crimson is fearful of the punishment awaiting her. She first tries to lie
to the old woman, who traps the maid into confessing that she did indeed leave
the girl alone with the student. Crimson then tries to blame the madam
circumlocutiously by putting the accusation into the student's mouth. When that
fails, she is forced to confront the old woman directly:

(Crimson sings:)
They don't recognize grief, don't recognize sorrow;
Their paired hearts are a perfect fit.
Madam, you'd better stop when it's right to stop.
Why must you suffer now to trace down every clue?
The proverb says, "A girl grown up should not be kept."

(Old lady speaks:) You hussy, you're responsible for it all! (Crimson speaks:) It is not Student Zhang's crime, or missy's, or mine—it's your mistake alone, madam.[106]

At this point Crimson openly challenges the madam by attacking her at her most vulnerable point: her supposed strictness in bringing up her child. First Crimson simply charges the madam with lying, bolstering her accusation with the standard quote from the Confucian *Analects* and imputing to her the violation of every standard of human behavior in not honoring her word. Then she accuses her of failing to send the student away, thereby keeping temptation within Oriole's reach. Finally she points out that if the madam fails to honor her original promise, she will be guilty of dishonoring the memory of her husband and of shaming Student Zhang, who will one day be powerful and in a position to take revenge; that if she were taken to court over the affair, she would be judged guilty on two counts: not controlling her family properly and ignoring a favor. Crimson's accusations are extremely effective because she aims them at a most sensitive spot: the madam's public face. That is, she calls attention to the fact that the madam has turned her back on human compassion in an attempt to satisfy society's sense of decorum, but fails even to do that. Only when threatened with public disclosure does she relent and consent to an engagement. In one very clever and logical string of arguments the maid has managed to show up the hypocrisy of a mistress who pretends in public to have her family in hand but who obviously has neither the personal compassion nor a close enough relationship with her daughter to guarantee that she will act out of love or a sense of reciprocal responsibility

We have discussed Crimson's affectionate but satirical relationship with the student: he is the single person who is honest with her, sharing with her his (literally) lunatic feelings and sorrows; she responds accordingly with mockery or warmth. But there is one special task she performs for him that is at once ironic and risqué: she acts as his instructress in love, his sexual informant. When Crimson first thinks that Zhang and Oriole will be married, she answers his questions about Oriole's sincerity with comforting words, then proceeds to give him some advice on lovemaking:

> As for your happy union tonight,
> How could our delicate Oriole
> Have had any experience?
> You must be tender and gentle
> When you twine your mandarin-duck necks below the lamp.
> After you've looked carefully at your wretch,
> You'll die of such happiness that it won't come off clean.[107]

She repeats this advice on what they both think will be the night of Zhang and Oriole's union:

The fine night goes on and on,
The quiet courtyard is deserted and still,
Flower stems bend low and rustle.
She's a young girl:
You should pamper her temper,
Massage her with words,
Blend with her moods.
Don't suppose her a broken willow or tattered blossom.

She's an, oh, so lovable, beautiful jade without flaw·
Her powdered face engenders spring,
Her cloudy locks are like piled-up raven feathers.
She's, oh, so timid, oh, so fearful,
And she does not scheme for free wine or idler's tea.
But once between the sheets, you should give it your all:
When your fingertips report back from duty worn out,
Then you can stack away your moans and sighs;
And when you are finished with your concerns and anxieties,
When you have cleared away frustrations and sorrows,
Then be prepared to be happily stuffed.[108]

There is little doubt that Crimson is sexually experienced and that a sense of bawdiness is part of her personality She knows that sex will cure Oriole's spring lassitude—"Her lingering illness would be cured / If only the smallest groove were opened down the rhinoceros horn"—and she accuses the student twice of impotence: once by calling him a "pewter spear that is easily bent" and once by remarking, "If you see that jade transcendent sylph, / You'll become all soft and paralyzed."[109] She also comments on his masturbating:

Our mandarin-duck pillows,
Our kingfisher-feather coverlets—
If you will be the one to have your heart's every desire,
Why should she have to rent them out to you?
What's to fear if you don't undress, but stay clothed?
Wouldn't that still be better than your hand grasping that little pinky
    down there?[110]

Saucy, impudent, bawdy, yet remarkably honest in her dealings with people, Crimson may be seen as a kind of central human essence around which revolve the roles the others deliberately adopt, which Crimson in turn sees through in her superior wisdom. This is evident in Crimson's use of theatrical terminology to describe the actions of the others. *Daban*, for instance—a theatrical term meaning to costume oneself as a particular role—she often uses in reference to Oriole (and once in reference to Dharma Wit as well). Other terms that Crimson uses of Oriole—*jiayi* (false feelings), for instance—are also generally employed for exaggerated expressions onstage. The term *zhuang* (to apply makeup), which is often used in reference to Oriole, can also means to put on one's theatrical face, either by pose or paint. While it is true that in China, as in many other cultures, theatrical terminology is commonly used in everyday language to indicate poses or gestures that are essentially false, in the case of *The Story of the Western Wing* exploitation of theatrical language is extremely self-conscious. We would suggest that it has to do with the fact that each of the major characters adopts a certain pose either based on social expectations or drawn from the literary and theatrical conventions for lovers. That most of these terms issue from the mouth of Crimson affirms that, as her name suggests, she represents guileless human nature in its basic truthfulness, a truthfulness that will eventually strip away the masks of pretense.

We have already seen how later editions of *The Story of the Western Wing* were bowdlerized by Jin Shengtan and how they came to be used as the bases of earlier Western translations. Like other early and middle Ming editions, the Hongzhi text, the basis of this translation and study, is not so squeamish about matters of romance and sex. The play is larded with erotic imagery and sexual innuendo, mainly in the form of puns. This is a point on which most Chinese and Western critics are silent. In China the ascendancy of neo-Confucianism after the fifteenth century, if it did not silence the earthy voice of Chinese vernacular literature, at least drove it into a kind of silent limbo.[111] In modern China an interest in sex is officially attributed to bourgeois decadence. While traditional critics are wont to shunt the issue aside by simply saying that a certain passage is "vulgar" (*li*), the silence of modern scholars, as philologically gifted as they are, is surely due to the fact that they too are heirs to the neo-Confucian tradition; in addition, they have had to work in an atmosphere that has been unforgiving in ferreting out bourgeois heresies. In the West indifference to the Ming editions and unfamiliarity with the code of erotic language in Chinese (of which, by the way, we claim no great knowledge) have been compounded by a general neglect of the text in the past two or three decades.

The setting of the courtship and seduction is the garden, specifically, the garden at night under the moon. If we trace the timing of the first three plays, we find that the entire process, from Zhang's first vision of Oriole to their night of shared love, takes place in the three nights of full moon in the second month (roughly equivalent to March or April of the Western calendar). The garden is a natural setting for love. In vernacular Chinese literature the garden, with its spring blossoms and spring breezes, often signals the advent of love.[112] In this play the garden is also associated with the *yin* phase of Student Zhang's life, when his actions are played out at night under a full moon—*yin* at its height—in contrast to his public life, which is carried out in the waning rays of autumn's sun and in the open world of nature.[113]

The principal feature of a garden is its flowers, and flowers have a special significance in the world of love. flowers are naturally associated with feminine beauty. As we have noted, Oriole is played by the flowery female lead; we imagine her costume was meant to play off her sensuality to its fullest. Such a role is usually assigned to actresses playing courtesans or singsong girls. The name itself stems from the common use of "flower" or "blossom" to designate women of pleasure. Though it is clear that Oriole is the daughter of a good family, her seductive nature is clearly suggested by the drooping garments that bare her fragrant shoulders for Student Zhang to see. We cannot help but wonder if this attitude, in addition to being a reference to the flowing robes of Guanyin, is also an oblique allusion to "The Song of the Women of Qin" ("Qinfu yin") by the Tang poet Wei Zhuang. In his poem, an account of the sack of Chang'an by rebels, Wei describes a young beauty so caught up in her own loveliness that she is unaware of the pillage and destruction going on outside the city gates—a very fit image for Oriole:

> In the western neighborhood is a girl, a true transcendent,
> One inch of crosswise wave cutting across the autumn waters;[114]
> Makeup finished, she simply faces springtime in the mirror,
> Young in years, she is unaware of events outside the city
> A brave leaps and bounds up the golden stairs.
> Her gown aslant bares half a shoulder; he wants to sully her.
> He pulls her by her clothes; she is unwilling and is sent out the vermilion
> gates:
> Red powder and fragrant rouges perish beneath the blade![115]

This certainly suits the portrayal of Oriole as an intensely sensual yet innocent young girl who is as beautiful as a divinity and yet unaware, except at very rare moments, of her effect on other people. But it is the flowering twig she twirls that triggers a flood of sexual imagery At crucial points in the play the image of red flowers floods the scene: a jumble of red petals is left behind on the path as she leaves and red blossoms scatter in the eastern wind, becoming the crimson print of the girl herself. The eastern wind, which blows from the quadrant of spring, at times is the object of the young girl's complaints—the red blossoms it tatters are a reference to her fading youth—and at times infuses the bedchambers of the monastery with the fragrance of flowers.

Flowers are also frequently associated in China with women of pleasure. The frequent occurrence of blossoms in our text reinforces a subtle structural element in the play that underlies the relationship between Oriole, the madam, and Crimson. This triangle is clearly congruent with the triangle of madam, singsong girl, and handmaiden that populates plays about courtesans in the Yuan and Ming period.[116] The comparison has been hinted at but never explicitly drawn; it certainly provides a hidden yet significant structure for the action of the play [117] In the courtesan plays, for instance, the madam is usually insistent that the courtesan marry the man of the madam's choice, usually an ugly merchant; the courtesan on the other hand has usually fallen in love with the poor scholar; and the maid acts as go-between for the scholar and the courtesan. We find close parallels in our play Madam Cui's insistence that Oriole marry the repugnant Zheng Heng is clearly based on the model of the madam and the merchant; Zhang Sheng is the poor and unknown scholar that Oriole refuses to repudiate; and Crimson acts as the liaison between the two in the face of the madam's wrath. This develops a certain logical tension in the play that the playwright exploits by having the lead role, Oriole, played by a flowery female lead, which usually specializes in prostitutes.

This underlying structure is further reinforced by Crimson, who in her counsels to young Zhang often reminds him that Oriole is no "roadside willow" or "tattered blossom" and should not be treated as such. Zhang is also referred to in the play as the *tanhua lang*, the "flower-plucking gentleman," a term used to designate the third-place candidate in the examinations. The play is unclear about his actual success, calling him both the flower-plucking gentleman and the head of the list, the top graduate. Part of the confusion arises because Wang carries over Dong Jieyuan's description of the student as a third-place candidate, a step necessary to keep the metaphor of sexual conquest ("plucking flowers") an active part of the play. Zhang is constantly called a "flower filcher" and a "plucker of blossoms" in the play, and Oriole is repeatedly referred to as a blossom. Zhang calls her a "flower that can speak," and several times Crimson refers to what she supposes is Oriole's acquiescence to Zhang's desire by describing her as "a flower with stem bent low," ready to "receive the eastern wind." The flower in fact is also an image of the female genitalia. Oriole's is a well-planned entrance, then, walking from the garden into the courtyard, twirling a sprig of red flowers in her hands and tantalizing Zhang Gong with the promise of things to come.

From the opening description of the Yellow River's irrigating the peony gardens of Luoyang, floral imagery leads us to the inevitable seduction scene. "flowers' shade" and "flowers' shadows" both refer to the female genitalia; "flower's heart" is a common term for the clitoris; and the red peony has especially come to symbolize the vagina in full flush of engorgement. All of these terms are used with some frequency in the play and figure in various contexts of the surface narrative. They anticipate the last blossoms of spring about to fall before warming winds from the east, but they also foreshadow the seduction scene itself:

> (Student sings:)
> Here to my breast I press her pliant jade and warm perfume—
> Ai,
> Ruan Zhao has reached Mount Tiantai.
> Spring has come to the realm of men, flowers sport their color!
> Gently she adjusts her willowy waist
> And lightly splits the flower's heart:
> Dew drips; the peony opens.[118]

By virtue of their fragrance, flowers are linked to physical descriptions of Oriole as well. Perfume, usually orchid musk, is an attribute of the sexually aroused body. The orchid itself, while used in descriptions of women's bedchambers also has another level of reference, as in Oriole's first response to the student's poems, "Long has my orchid chamber been lonely." Another major metaphor for her body is jade. Warm jade, soft jade, pliant jade, moist jade, jade that exudes a redolent odor of love—these are the descriptions of Oriole. This is not the green jade of jewelry shops but the wonderful white jade known in China as "mutton fat" because of its resemblance to the moist, glistening sheen of the congealed lard of lamb. The term "jade one" is also used reciprocally between Student Zhang and Oriole; and when it refers to him, it most certainly has a second level of reference to the penis, which in Chinese is called the "jade stalk" (*yuti*) or "jade stem" (*yujing*). When placed in concert, these images go far beyond the surface narrative to describe the anticipation of the sexual act itself. In Oriole's famous poem that lures Student Zhang to the flower garden, for instance, this second level of meaning is quite clear:

> Wait for the moon beneath the western wing;
> Welcoming the breeze, the door is half-opened.
> When separated by the wall, flowers' shadows move;
> I guess it is the jade one coming.[119]

The association of jade with physical love helps us understand the importance of the gifts that Oriole sends Student Zhang while he is away. Her love charm of a jade hairpin sent with the injunction "If you see another flower in a distant country, / Don't tarry there as you did here" implies a certain sense of urgency, as she senses she is playing out the role of the deserted woman so well defined by the negative side of the scholar-beauty model. As she sends him this philter she expresses her fear that he has thrown her "to the back of his mind."[120] On receiving the slender jade, Zhang correctly guesses it to be a token of her own body.[121]

> This jade hairpin—
> Long and slender like a bamboo shoot,
> Fine and white as an onion stalk.
> Its warm richness holds a fresh perfume;
> Shiny and pure, it is without blemish.[122]

The gifts sent by Oriole include another instrument of love, the zither. *Qinxuan* (zither strings) is a term used to refer to the frenum of the clitoris; and the zither is used as a symbol for a method of arousal. The scene of seduction by zither, as we have pointed out, may be read as a description of foreplay. There can be no mistake that when Crimson remarks on the scene, she has sexual arousal clearly in mind: "Because of a zither-playing hand at midnight, / A moon-loving heart has been aroused in spring chambers."[123] The zither, then, becomes a token of sexual love. Oriole dispatches the musical instrument to Zhang with the comment, "I only fear that his hands on the strings will lose their touch!"[124] Student Zhang again guesses its proper meaning: "This zither— / It tells me to close the doors and study restraining my fingers."[125]

Other explicit images that deal with sex are found in the references to grottoes and caves and to such phallic images as the red candles of the marriage chamber and the pagoda described as standing starkly in the burning sunlight of the courtyard after Zhang first spots Oriole on the temple grounds. Crimson, as we have seen, teases the student several times about impotence and masturbation. He himself, in anticipation of his tryst with Oriole, chants, "How I suffer from the great *yang* that now grows roots", and again, "I so despise the great *yang*'s coveting of battle, / I am unaware that the red sun sets in the west."[126]

"Suffering" from the great *yang* surely refers obliquely to the anticipation of his first sexual encounter, but it also must refer to the physically turgid male organ. The "great *yang*" of the second quotation has been changed by nearly every editor who has encountered it to the name of a legendary general, Lu Yang, who stayed the sun's decline so that he could finish battle with an enemy We feel, however, that the term should be maintained in its original form. It then refers indirectly to Student Zhang's prudery He has no physical control over his member; undone by lust, he has to endure this state until the tryst actually takes place. The allusion to Lu Yang may also generate echoes with the esoteric arts of sexual alchemy, in which the man attempts to maintain an erection until the woman has climaxed ("to stay the sun") and at the same time to control the emission of his own semen so that it can be diverted internally to flow up his spine (the "Yellow River") to be stored in his brain. At any rate, the passage remains an ironic and comic description of Zhang's mental and physical states of anticipation.

Most of the sexual punning and outright vulgarity in the text comes from the mouth of Crimson, ever ready with a quip. When Oriole first thinks that she might have a chance to marry Student Zhang, for instance, Crimson remarks:

Sister's face could be destroyed at the slightest touch. Student Zhang will be lucky!

> [(Female lead sings:)]
> You preposterous, lying little wench.
> You say that my face, so fittingly made up, can be destroyed by the
>   slightest touch![127]

Although Oriole's response is directed primarily toward the issue of putting on a false face, there can be little doubt that there is a pun on *mian* (face), which can mean "surface" and which may also refer to Oriole's hymen.

Crimson can be quite to the point at times; for instance, when Student Zhang is upbraided by Oriole in the flower garden, Crimson jumps in and curses him:

Who had you break and enter in the dead of night?
If it was not for fornication, then it was for theft!
You are a cassia-plucking man
Who's turned into a flower-filching lout!
You don't want to jump across the dragon's gate
But do want to learn how to mount a mare.[128]

According to Wang Jide, *pianma*, which we have translated "to mount a mare," means specifically to mount a horse from a running start. It is close to the modern term *qima* (to ride a horse), which is also a slang expression for sexual intercourse.

The maid is even more vulgar when Oriole's affair is discovered by the madam. Oriole begs her to cover up for her, and Crimson, in a fit of anger, replies,

On that night the moon had barely risen above the willow tops,
But you had already made a tryst with your lover after dusk.
I was so ashamed, I turned my head and bit the sleeve of my garment;
But when I fixed my eyes
And looked, I saw the tapering tips of your shoes.
One was so unrestrained in passion, she couldn't stop;
One fucked away with moaning sounds.
Ah, *then* why didn't you suffer the tiniest bit of shame?[129]

The word that Crimson employs here, *nou*, means to hoe; the Ming commentary tells us it is a homophonic replacement for another word, pronounced *niao* or *nao*, that is clearly the vulgar term for sexual intercourse (and still is in some southern dialects).[130] This is also one of three instances in which Crimson alludes to her voyeuristic tendencies.[131]

Crimson's rapier wit and bawdy sense of humor are also displayed in her satiric barbs at the repugnant Zheng Heng:

Let's not discuss high and low, far and near;
I'll spell it out clearly for you by breaking characters apart.

(Clown speaks:) What do you know, you little wench, about breaking characters apart? You tell me!

([Crimson] sings:)
Junrui is the character "similar to"
With an "upright man" at its side.
You are an "inch of wood," a "horse's door," a "corpse's kerchief."

[(Clown speaks:)] An "inch of wood," a "horse's door," a "corpse's kerchief"—you say that I am a boorish donkey's dick![132]

Crimson is engaging here in a popular form of wordplay known as *chaibaizi* (breaking apart characters), one of the chief jeux d'esprit of well-educated ladies, including prostitutes. The players describe characters part by part, assigning a meaning to each of the parts: for instance, the combination of *xiao* (similar to) and *ren* (man) describes the character *qiao* (handsome). Crimson's jibe at Zheng Heng may be explained thus: *cun* (inch) and *mu* (wood) combine to form *cun* (boorish, rustic); *ma* (horse) and *hu* (door) combine to form the word *lü* (donkey); *shi* (corpse) and *jin* (handkerchief) combine to form the slang word for penis, *diao*.

Despite these bawdy puns, however, the play remains a comedy that spells out a somewhat more delicate romance. One of the major tropes of the play is the story of King Huai of Chu and the spirit of Shamanka Mountain, recounted in Song Yu's "Rhapsody on the High Terrace." While visiting Shamanka Mountain the king took a noontime nap; a woman appeared to him, offering him a pillow, and the two made love. As she was leaving, she bade him goodbye with the following words: "I live on the sunny side of Shamanka Mountain, at the dangerous point of the highest hill. At sunrise I am the morning clouds and at sunset, the traveling rains. Morning after morning, sunset after sunset, I am below the Yang Terrace." From this story come many expressions—clouds and rain, Gaotang, Shamanka Mountain, spirit of Shamanka Mountain, Yang Terrace, even the name of the poet, Song Yu—that denote romance and the act of love and that have woven themselves into a dense pattern of allusions on which our text constantly draws.

Other allusions occur as well: He Yan, the face-powderer; Zhang Chang, the sketcher of eyebrows; Chang'e, the white, cold goddess of the moon. There appears to be good reason that *The Story of the Western Wing* was known as a lovers' bible. Not only did it provide models for action, but it also consolidated the vocabulary of romance, lust, and seduction, providing artists and actors onstage (and in real life) with a lexicon of love. Some of the more common phrases that occur in this text spell out the light, the color, and the fragrance of love and its union. We provide here a short list to help the reader understand some of the images and symbols at work in the allegory of love.

bimu yu	Pair-eyed fish	A perfect pair of lovers
canhong	Tattered red	A used woman
chuixiao	To play the flute	Fellatio
chunfeng	Spring breezes	1) Romantic ambience; 2) stirrings of love
daofeng dianluan	Upside-down phoenix, flip-flopped simurgh	Mutual oral sex
feng hua	Breeze and flowers	Romance
fengdie	Bees and butterflies	1) Go-betweens; 2) men flocking around a woman
fenxiang niyu	Powdery fragrance, moist jade	1) Makeup; 2) the female body
hualiu	Flowers and willows	A seductive woman

huaxin	Flower's heart	The clitoris, the vagina
jinlian	Golden lotus	Bound feet
lianli zhi	Intertwined branches	Lovers
mudan	Peony	The vagina
ousi	Lotus root fibers	Thoughts of love
qieyu touxiang	Pilfer jade, steal perfume	An illicit affair
shuangtou hua	Double-headed flower	A perfect pair of lovers
sinou	To hoe	To have sexual intercourse
tang	To press	To fondle
tongxin lou	Lover's knot	Lover's knot
xinyuan yima	Monkey of mind, horse of desire	Lust
yanlü yingchou	Swallow friends, oriole mates	A long-term sexual affair
yicui weihong	Lean on green, cuddle red	To cuddle
yuhuan	Jade circle	The female body
yunyu	Clouds and rain	A sexual tryst
yushui	Fish and water	Perfect concord

These few symbols of the strong passion of our lovers add fragrance and texture to the sensuous images of kingfisher feathers, mandarin-duck pillows, and the red and green hangings and trappings of the bedchamber. Literature is progressively discovered; we read a text through time. But our remembrance of it is synchronic and integral, creating a whole picture in our minds. And if the cool image of the moon and the plaintive sound of the zither are a major part of that memory, if they evoke the feeling our text describes as "a lonely cry on a moonlit night," then the smell and the texture and the vivid colors of other images in the play leave us as well with a remembrance of hot passion and the wonderment of love fulfilled.

Notes

[1] Wang Shifu, *Huitu xin jiaozhu guben Xixiang ji*, 1.7a. In his annotations, Wang Jide also cites Xu Wei's comment that in fact the long geographical description that follows echoes the course of Student Zhang's trip up the Yellow River.

[2] I.1.34a. All citations refer to the Hongzhi edition; they are noted as follows; e.g., I.1.34a:

        I: play I (of I to V).
        1: act 1 (of 1 to 5).
        34a: page number.

[3] II.1.61b.

[4] I.1.34a.

[5] *Ibid.*

[6] The poem is one of a pair on the famed Mount Lu:

> The sun sears Incense Burner, producing violet smoke;
> Far off, looking at the waterfall suspending what was a stream before,
> Flying currents plummet straight down three thousand feet;
> Could it be the Silver River falling through the nine heavens?

Incense Burner is a name of one of the peaks of Lushan.

[7] The peony is known, in fact, as "the flower of Luoyang" (*Luoyang hua*). Ouyang Xiu (1007–72), the Song statesman and scholar, wrote a long treatise on the peonies of Luoyang, identifying hundreds of varieties; for his "Luoyang mudan ji," see *Ouyang wenzhong gong quanji*, 72.1a–7a.

[8] The *Bowu zhi* is a collection of anecdotes traditionally attributed to Zhang Hua (232–300) but shown to be a compilation of diverse stories by a later editor or editors. The story of the raft is found on 3.3a; there are also references to Zhang Qian on 1.1b. By the late Six Dynasties these myths were conflated as indicated by the amalgamated story's appearance in the late seventh-century *Jing Chu suishi ji* (A record of the annual and seasonal customs of the areas of Jing and Chu).

[9] See, for instance, the famous Tang neo-Confucianist Han Yu's essay "On the Source of the Way" ("Yuandao"), in which he claims that the government should burn down Buddhist monasteries, destroy their texts, and "make real people of their people" (*ren qi ren*). See Han Yu, *Changli xiansheng wenji*, 11.4b.

[10] The classic work on Empress Wu is Fitzgerald, *The Empress Wu*.

[11] I.2.40b.

[12] I.2.43b.

[13] Because of the characteristics of Chinese grammar, the phrase *daiyue* can mean both to wait for the moon's appearance and to wait under moonlight. In the case of this play, in which all the trysts take place in the moonlight and in which Oriole is constantly compared to the moon, the ambiguity is quite functional.

[14] I.1.35b–36a.

[15] I.1.37b.

[16] I.1.38a.

[17] It is worth noting that this is also the first of several points in the play when the filial gestures of the young girl in mourning for her father are interpreted as sexual signals. See, e.g., play I, act 4, songs "Tianshui ling" and "Zhegui ling," where Zhang wrongly judges the tears Oriole sheds at her father's mass as a sign of romantic interest.

[18] I.3.49b.

[19] I.3.50b.

[20] The translations for these names are taken from Schafer, *The Divine Woman*; see esp. 48–53.

[21] *Ibid.*

[22] *Ibid.*

[23] In some traditions Chang'e is actually transformed into the hare.

[24] This story originated in the *Longcheng lu*, which has been incorrectly attributed to Liu Zongyuan. For a complete account of the affair, see the Song work by Wang Zhuo, *Biji manzhi*, 124–28.

[25] I.3.51a.

[26] That is, the mica that is used for panels in the folding screen.

[27] *Li Shangyin xuanji*, 299–300. See also James J. Y Liu, *The Poetry of Li Shang-yin*, 99.

[28] II.5.82a–83a.

[29] "Pei Hang," in *Taiping guangji*, 2.312–15.

[30] Wang Shifu, *Xinkan qimiao quanxiang zhushi Xixiang ji*, 2a–3b.

[31] I.4.53b.

[32] I.4.56a.

[33] I.3.51a.

[34] I.3.51b.

[35] III.1.93b–94a.

[36] III.2.100a.

[37] III.2.100b.

[38] In the *Book of Poetry*, for example, the ode "Zhengyue" (Mao no. 192) recounts the story of the woman Si of Bao, on whose account the last king of Western Zhou was besotted with love; it also spells out the dangers of "wise" women who can topple cities with their tongues as well as with their beauty. See also the song entitled "Zhanyang" (Mao no. 264). Legge, *The She King*, 314–20 and 559–64.

[39] II.1.57a–b.

[40] From the biography of the woman Li, consort to the emperor. Both she and her brother were performers. See Ban Gu, *Hanshu*, 8:3951. The words of Li Yannian's poem echo Mao no. 264; see n. 38.

[41] The anecdote refers to a feast that Xuanzong and his court ladies held to view the white lotuses that were in bloom. When everyone present sighed in admiration over their beauty, Xuanzong pointed out Yang Guifei to those around him and said, "But can they compare with my flower that speaks?" See Wang Renyu, *Kaiyuan Tianbao yishi*, 96.

[42] The stories and accounts of this beauty are too numerous to mention. For a general guide to the literature, including the Chinese texts, see Howard Levy, *Harem Favorites of an Illustrious Celestial*.

[43] II.1.60a.

[44] Wang Jisi interprets these lines as a concrete result of the expression "city- and state-toppling beauty"

> Wouldn't I then send not only these three hundred monks to their deaths,
> But even half a myriad of troops—
> In half a second they would be cut down like grass and rooted out.

See Wang Shifu, *Jiping jiaozhu Xixiang ji*, 57.

[45] See also above, p. 37.

[46] See the biography of Sima Xiangru in Sima Qian, *Shiji*, 5:2999–3074, translated by Watson in *Records of the Grand Historian of China*, 2:297–342, and by Hervouet as *Le chapitre 117 du Cheki*. Hervouet has also published an extensive study of the poet's life and works in *Un poète de cour sous les Han: Sseu-ma Siang-jou*. See also Idema, "The Story of Ssu-ma Hsiang-ju and Cho Wen-chün."

[47] Idema, "The Story of Ssu-ma Hsiang-ju and Cho Wen-chün," and his "Satire in All-Keys-and-Modes," esp. the section entitled "Social Satire and Sexual Allegory in the *Hsi-hsiang-chi chu-kung-tiao*."

[48] Abstracted from Idema, "The Story of Ssu-ma Hsiang-ju and Cho Wen-chün," 62–63.

[49] Liu Xin, *Xijing zaji*, 3.18b.

[50] Wang Jisi, "Cong *Fengqiuhuang* dao *Xixiang ji*," 17–24.

[51] IV.1.117a.

[52] II.4.79a.

[53] II.4.80a.

[54] II.4.76b.

[55] II.4.79a

[56] Idema, "Satire and Allegory in All-Keys-and-Modes."

[57] I.2.40b.

[58] Wang Shifu, *Huitu xin jiaozhu guben Xixiang ji*, 1.17b.

[59] I.1.36a.

[60] See Wang Jisi's note in Wang Shifu, *Jiping jiaozhu Xixiang ji*, 13, and Jiang Xingyu, "'Dianbula' wei meiyu meinü kao."

[61] Wang Jide, quoting Xu Shifan in Wang Shifu, *Huitu xin jiaozhu guben Xixiang ji*, 1.7b.

[62] I.2.41b–42a.

[63] "So cool it is, his singing it out like the sound of rain on banana leaves; so full of life it is, like the sound of a drum struck by scattered beans", see Wang Shifu, *Jiping jiaozhu Xixiang ji*, 18.

[64] The dharma hall.

[65] I.2.42b.

[66] I.2.43a.

[67] I.2.43b.

[68] This is another example of the lovers' lack of filial piety, especially Zhang's. It would be unthinkable for him to use such a solemn occasion of filial expression simply to ogle Oriole.

[69] Used to signal the need to use a toilet, like the phrase "to wash one's hands" in English.

[70] I.2.45b.

[71] I.2.46a.

[72] On the *yuanben* and other farce skits, see Hu Ji, *Song Jin zaju kao*; Crump, "Yüan-pen, Yüan Drama's Rowdy Ancestor", Idema, "Yüan-pen as a Minor Form of Dramatic Literature", West, *Vaudeville and Narrative*, 1–77.

[73] Tanaka Kenji, "Genbun kô."

[74] II.3.72a.

[75] III.3.104a.

[76] III.1.93a.

[77] III.3.105b.

[78] See chap. 54 of Cao Xueqin, *The Story of the Stone*, 3:30–31.

[79] I.3.51b.

[80] V.2.142a–b.

[81] II.1.59a–b.

[82] II.3.72b.

[83] II.4.79a.

[84] III.1.91b–92a.

[85] Cao Xueqin, *The Story of the Stone*, 3:30.

[86] I.2.45b–46a.

[87] II.1.58b–59a.

[88] That is, Oriole dressed up in wedding garments; see III.4.112a–b.

[89] I.3.50b.

[90] See above, p. 73.

[91] II.3.70b–71a.

[92] II.4.79a.

[93] IV.2.124a

[94] V 3.150b.

95 Cao Xueqin, *The Story of the Stone*, 3:30–31.

96 II.3.72b.

97 II.5.86b.

98 III.1.92b–93a.

99 III.2.96a–b.

100 III.2.98a.

101 III.2.98b–99a.

102 III.3.104a.

103 III.4.109a–b.

104 IV.1.113a–b.

105 One of the functions of Happy in the play is perhaps to act as a symbol of Oriole's own happiness. For instance, in the scene when she offers sacrifice at the temple after receiving the news that Zhang has passed the examinations, it is Happy who accompanies her. In this case, it is clear that Oriole has been betrayed by her own "happiness," an emotional state that, as Crimson points out, is all too apparent in her budding physical well-being.

106 IV.2.120b–21a.

107 II.3.72b–73a.

108 III.3.105a.

109 III.1.90b, III.4.110b.

110 III.4.111b.

111 It is interesting to note that the bulk of writing condemning the vulgarity and indecency of vernacular literature comes from the middle Ming period. See, e.g., Wang Liqi, *Yuan Ming Qing sandai jinhui xiaoshuo xiqu shiliao*, 11–21, 89–94.

112 Perhaps the most significant example is the play *The Peony Pavilion* (especially the scene "An Interrupted Dream"); see Tang Xianzu, *The Peony Pavilion*, 42–52.

113 There is an interesting contrast, for instance, between the monastery scenes in spring and the lovers' farewell scene at the ten-mile pavilion, set amid the sere grasses and red leaves of the fall.

114 That is, the expression in her eyes changing quickly.

115 See Wei Zhuang, *Wei Zhuang ji jiaozhu*, 471. Our reading of the poem differs with some commentators who read the line "His clothes off the shoulder, he wants to sully her", they see it referring to the coarse clothing of a country bumpkin. See, e.g., Chen Shunlie and Xu Dianxi, *Wudai shixuan*, 185.

116 See Zheng Zhenduo, "Lun Yuanren suoxie shangren, shizi, jinü jiande sanjiao lian'aiju."

117 As noted above, pp. 30–31, Chen Yinke has suggested that "The Tale of Oriole" might be about a courtesan. Historical evidence is lacking, but it seems more likely that what Chen perceives is the structure of the courtesan-scholar tale that provides an underlying pattern of significance. This certainly seems to be the case here.

118 IV.1.117a.

119 III.2.100a.

120 V.1.138b.

121 We might compare here as well his description of her long and delicate fingers that he calls "shoots of jade"—a clear use of metonymy for the body.

122 V.2.143a–b.

123 III.1.90b.

124 V.1.138b.

125 V.2.143a.

[126] III.2.102b.

[127] II.4.76a.

[128] III.3.106a.

[129] IV.2.122b.

[130] Wang Shifu, *Jiping jiaozhu Xixiang ji*, 129, and Wang Jide's comment in Wang Shifu, *Huitu xin jiaozhu guben Xixiang ji*, 3.31b; these two texts would prefer to read it in its bowdlerized form as "leaping the wall." Wang Jide, however, does refer to a "vulgar" commentary that says it means to seduce a woman.

[131] II.3.73a; IV.2.120a; IV.2.122b.

[132] V 3.149a–b.

TRANSLATION

The Story of the Western Wing

Newly Cut,

Deluxe,

Completely

Illustrated,

and

Annotated

新刊奇妙全相

註釋西廂記

Printed in the Year *Wuwu*
of the Hongzhi Reign
1498

Newly Cut, Large-Character, Folio-Size, Completely Illustrated, Expanded, Deluxe, Annotated Story of The Western Wing

Book the First

An Introduction to the Story of Oriole Cui and Student Zhang[1]

Banshe mode: "Shaobian"
On a day long ago Oriole Cui
Kept watch with unswerving devotion over her father's casket,
And a student in youth's flower roved in East of Pu—
Neither of them had yet sent a matchmaker forth.
Bandits arose, half a thousand men and horse,
And striking their drums, ringing their gongs,
They drew a tight circle around the monastery,
Almost scaring to death Dharma Wit, Dharma Source,
Benevolent Perception, Benevolent Brightness,
And the master of preachers in the ashram.
If General Du had not caused buckler and spear to retreat,
Would Master Zhang have consummated his marriage?
Predestined karma at Universal Salvation
And a passionate love waiting under the moon
Have been entrusted to the strongest pen of the present day!

"Shua hai'er"
This author caps all the personalities of the Central Plain with his rich talents
And brandishes the brush and ink, letting his compositions flow like water.
Before the cold window he reads his fill of five cartloads of books.
Past or present, none can reach his intelligence:
He has compiled the most charming affair of the last millennium
And spread this romance for all the world to know

---

[1] The text of this song suite is heavily damaged in the Hongzhi edition; for missing text, we have consulted the "*Xixiang bie diao*" in Wang Shifu, *Yuanben tiping Xixiang ji*, 2.62a–b.

Within is not half a speck of vulgar dust:
His bosom conceals only embroidered brocade,
His mouth spews forth colored rainbows.

"Fifth from Coda"
Fresh and original, the words are just right;
The melodies of the popular tunes are sweet.

1b   Breeze and flowers, snow and moon, he can stitch together into couplets.
He has composed sentences of chiming jade and ringing bronze
And brewed up a rendezvous of ample rains and abundant clouds.
The intent of it all
Is to make sure that this Shuang Jian gets the best of Feng Kui![2]

"Fourth from Coda"
His belly stuffed with myriads of books:
At heaven's edge, a student clad in cotton.
Our Zhang Junrui, whose ancestors lived in Western Luo,
Relied on a thousand poems chanted back and forth under the night moon
To get to inspect a circle of jade in the breezes of spring.
Such heroes rely on their ways with words
To suffer through sleepless nights and hungry days.

"Third from Coda"
This one flaunts his brutish rudeness
Inside the Buddhist monastery
And coerces amorous feelings
Within the traveler's lodge.
This lout is named Zheng
And is known as a yamen rat.
Can a frozen crow be the companion of a mandarin duck?
It is impossible for a common bird to roost with the phoenix.
He's just a child's game
Without the slightest hint of a warm and tender, gentle heart.
He's altogether an uncouth and addled dolt!

"Second from Coda"
The handsome one repairs the road to the Yang Terrace of Chu,[3]
The boorish one sets himself afire in the palace of the king of Han.[4]
Handsome and boorish don't belong together:
The boorish one is destined to do himself in below the fragrant steps;

---

[2] For the story of Shuang Jian and Su Xiaoqing, see pp. 20–21.

[3] Yang Terrace was the abode of the spirit of Shamanka Mountain, paramour of King Huai; see pp. 67, 96.

[4] Zheng Heng is compared here to a young man who burned himself to death in a Zoroastrian temple (the "palace of the king of Han") in despair over a lost love. See play II, act 4, n. 10.

The handsome one swears not to return if his name is not on the golden list.[5]
Boorish and handsome, they serve as exemplars for others:
The boorish should be taken as a warning;
But the handsome one is someone worth relying on.

"Coda"
A playboy from Five Hills has told me,
"Don't be stingy with money in your bag;
But spend your life in full enjoyment of this *Story of the Western Wing*,
So that when you die you'll become a romantic and rakish ghost!"

---

[5] I.e., he will not return if his name is not found on the list of those who passed the *jinshi* examinations.

[Eight Satiric Songs Against *The Western Wing*][1]

1a   "Manting fang"
The madam—no good at all!
An orphaned child, a widowed wife,
A young girl newly in mourning—
And you did not bury the casket
But left it fully exposed in the cells of monks.
You organized a grand mass,
And so sought out calamity and misfortune.
You broke the marriage contract
And so brought to ruin the bonds of decency
Isn't this for sure dissolving bad luck?
You stirred up the bees to buzz and the butterflies to flock:
Such an unwise parent!

"Manting fang"
Oriole—a bewitching devil!
Musk and orchid scent, a half share each,
Flower and moonlight, oh, so elegant—
You tied the knot without matchmaker or witness
And sent out feelings from the corners of your eyes.
Listening to the jasper zither,
You hustled in the evening and bustled in the night.
Burning midnight incense,
You were all aquiver and alarmed.
You're your family's misfortune.
Without reason you took your chic elegance
And worked it into a ridiculous reputation.

"Manting fang"
Crimson—ever ready to run!
You passed along letters and delivered notes,
Sent warmth and stole away the cold.[2]

---

[1] The original text has no title; but since the text begins after a lacuna of two pages, we assume that it was in the original edition. We have copied the title here from the text of Wang Shifu, *Yuanben tiping Xixiang ji*, 2.63b.

[2] I.e., passed messages between lovers but sweetened the messages so that each side would be somewhat more pleased with the communication.

Under a starry sky, by light of the moon,
You tricked Oriole
And made her, brokenhearted,
Wait into the depths of night.
You turned her into a moon incomplete, a blossom tattered.
You put on quite a skit, causing problems left and right,
But ended up as the matchmaker.

"Manting fang"

Student Zhang—no talent at all!
Your learning of brocade and embroidery
Was all lost to skirts and hairpins.
Waiting at the western wing, you sang about the breeze and chanted about the
   moon.
A look returned with a glance:
Writing a letter, your literary skill was like the sea;
But suffering from illness, your body was like a stick of firewood.
You almost ruined your reputation.
You did not at all think about "considering the wise wise, disesteeming sex"[3]
But ended up with the typical student's perversity

"Manting fang"
Playwright Wang—what a busybody!
Shopping for fame and eager for a reputation,
You extended what was short by adding on length.[4]
You pasted other folks' flesh on your own cheeks,
And hung out a sheepskin but sold dog meat.[5]
You don't have the inner qualities of a Zhu Xi,[6]
He doesn't have the deportment of the Masters Cheng.[7]
Too wild and crazy,
You've spent your whole energy
But will never make it to temple or hall.[8]

---

[3] *Analects*, 1.7: "Zixia said, 'A man who treats the wise as wise and disesteems sexual attraction can exhaust his strength in service to his parents, can exert himself in service to his lord, and is one whose words can be trusted in interaction with friends. Even though he is called unlearned, I would say he is learned.' "

[4] I.e., changed the facts of the situation to suit your taste.

[5] I.e., claimed another's property as your own and sold it under false pretenses; acted or did something under false pretenses.

[6] Zhu Xi (1130–1200) is the great and, since the Ming dynasty when his commentaries were prescribed for use, canonical neo-Confucian philosopher and scholar of the Southern Song.

[7] The two brothers Cheng Hao (1032–85) and Cheng Yi (1033–1107), famous philosophers of the Northern Song who were known for their strict behavior in daily life. We are not sure to whom the pronoun "he" refers at this point.

[8] I.e., his writings are unfit for either the state temple or the Bright Hall: they will never

"Manting fang"
Zheng Heng—what a muddlehead!
You shouldn't have run into the tree and killed yourself.
How can one recall your soul?
An unmarried man and a frustrated girl are not worth discussing—
Of course it is not moral!
If you had pulled yourself together
And sought another wife elsewhere
And, relying on your family's reputation,
Had picked another noble family—
Wouldn't that have been wonderful!
You killed yourself without reason
And showed off all the more your petty boorishness.

"Manting fang"
Guan Hanqing—how low!
He understands no nature or principle
But solely displays his poetic skills!
Without rhyme or reason he praises and blames the boorish and smart
And makes a show of his talent and learning.
His heaven-deceiving lies are no little thing.
The penalty of having his tongue ripped out
He'll not be spared after death!
He'll make people say,
He built a bridge in thin air.
Without any reason his pen became the sword that did him in.

"Manting fang"
That bald one—Dharma Wit!
He doesn't understand sutra texts
And cares not a whit for the sect of Zen.
He acted the matchmaker and became a witness, vainly welcoming and
    sending off![9]
He wanted only to plot for engagement wine and red gifts of cash.
All because he hid that Miss Cui away—but not out of sight—
The rebels nearly burned Universal Salvation to pure emptiness.
He simply stirred up those strong troops to action,
Showing off their heroic bravery.
Casually disregarding your own life, you fought in the vanguard.

"Manting fang"
General Du—You're inhumane!

---

be read in front of the emperor, the highest honor a man of letters could strive for.

[9] "To welcome the new and send off the old" (*yingxin songjiu*) is a common phrase used in vernacular texts for courtesans, pimps, or madams, who welcome new customers as they send the old ones away.

Without authorization you left the territory entrusted to you
And are incapable of safeguarding the people.
How can you be considered one who upholds the state and delivers those in
    danger?
You so casually brought your armies to bear!
If you had been defeated, you would have lost your own life;
And when you won, you made things good for someone else.
Did you consider "His words may be trusted"[10]
When you casually fought it out for no reason?
Wherein did you display any meritorious service?

---

[10] *Analects,* 2.22

Student Zhang Arrives at East of Pu[1]

VOLUME I OF THE DELUXE, COMPLETELY ILLUSTRATED, AND ANNOTATED STORY OF THE WESTERN WING

Burning Incense and Worshiping the Moon[2]

Act 1

---

[1] The illustrations and the accompanying sidebars are confused in the first two pages of the Hongzhi edition. The sidebar attached to the woodblock above actually belongs to the second illustration, a picture of Madam Cui, Oriole, and Crimson sauntering through the monastery. This caption reads, "The Old Lady, Deeply Affected, Wiles Away Her Time with Oriole and Crimson in the Buddha Hall." We have translated here the sidebar mistakenly attached to the second illustration, which refers to the illustration reproduced above.

[2] While the text begins with Act 1 (*diyi zhe*), the first scene is what later editorial convention calls a wedge; see pp. 44-45. While early texts clearly mark the end of scenes by such devices as leaving the remainder of a line blank, the conventions of dividing a play into acts and wedges is a later editorial practice. This text represents a mixture of earlier and later editorial custom. Those instances in which a line has been left blank or in which some other feature marks the clear end of a scene have been noted in our translation by the sign ❖❖❖ There are places in the text—notably the vulnerable first and last few pages— that are missing or are tattered. In those places we have followed the readings of Ling Mengchu's text as reproduced by Wang Jisi in his punctuated and annotated edition.

(Extra [female] dressed as old lady enters and opens. Two female leads [as Crimson and Oriole] and child [as Happy] follow her and enter. [Old lady speaks:]) Me, my maiden name is Zheng; my husband's surname was Cui. He was appointed to the rank of chancellor under the former emperor but unfortunately passed away on account of illness. We had only one daughter, a young girl whose milk name is Oriole and who is now nineteen years of age. Embroidery and other female skills, verse, lyrics, calligraphy, and ciphering—there is nothing in which she is not competent. When His Excellency was still alive, he promised her to my nephew Zheng Heng, the eldest son of Minister Zheng, as his wife. But since my child's period of mourning for her father has yet to be completed, they have been unable to consummate that union. There is also a little wench called Crimson, who has waited on my child since early youth. And a little fellow named Happy After my late husband left this world, my daughter and I set off to bear his casket to Boling for final burial but were unable to get through because the way was blocked. When we reached the prefecture of Hezhong, we lodged his casket here in this Monastery of Universal Salvation. It was restored by His Excellency, my late husband. This is an institution founded by Her Majesty Zetian.[3] In addition, the abbot, Dharma Source, is a monk who obtained his ordination with support from my late husband.[4] And so we have settled now into lodgings in the western wing. On the other hand, I have written a letter, now dispatched to the capital, summoning Zheng Heng here to help us bear the casket back to Boling. The waning of spring really gets to one. Crimson, if there's no one burning incense in the Buddha hall, go on with your mistress to wile away the time and have some fun. When my late husband was alive, as I recall, provisions before us filled a place ten feet square, our servants numbered in the hundreds. Today there are left only these few who are close family. Oh, how painful.

Xianlü mode: "Shanghua shi" (Old lady sings:)
In the capital did my lord and master's life come to a close;
Child and mother, orphan and widow, we've come to the end of our road,
And so we have lodged this casket in the palace of Brahma.
I'm filled with longing for the old graves at Boling,
And bloody tears sprinkle "azalea bird" red.[5]

31b

32a

---

[3] The notorious empress Wu, consort of the Tang emperor known posthumously as Gaozong, "Exalted Ancestor." She ruled from 684 to 701 and was known to posterity as Zetian Huanghou, "Resplendent Empress, Pattern of Heaven."

[4] *Tidu*, or "ordination of the shaven." A monk normally shaved off his hair after he had left his family and renounced lay life to enter the monastery. At that time a patron would provide him with living expenses and the means to purchase his certificate of ordination (*dudie*).

[5] This term, *dujuan*, refers to both the cuckoo and the azalea. According to popular lore, the cuckoo's mournful sounds were accompanied by tears of blood that stained the azalea red. Its sad call is said to imitate the phrase *buru gui*, "you'd better return home."

"Reprise" (Female lead sings:)
So it is: I meet with fading spring east of Pu Commandery;
The gates are closed with double bolts within this monastery
Blossoms fall, the water flows red,
My sorrows are a thousandfold;
But I have no words to lay plaint against the eastern wind.

(They leave together.)[6]

❖❖❖

(Male lead, dressed as a horseman, enters, leading a child actor, and opens:) I am Zhang Gong, known as Junrui. I hail from Western Luo. My late father, who was appointed minister of the Board of Rites, unfortunately died of an illness after he had reached an age of more than five times ten. One year later I lost my mother. With books and sword is this student tossed about the world. But as long as I have yet to achieve merit and fame, I will travel through the four quadrants. Now it is the first decade of the second month of the seventeenth year of Auspicious Prime,[7] and the emperor Dezong now reigns. I want to go to court to take the examinations. My road passes through the prefecture of Hezhong, and when I go through Pu Pass I'll find an old friend, Du Que, known as Junshi. He is both a compatriot and a fellow student of mine; from the very start we have been sworn brothers. Later he abandoned a civil career and opted for the army and was the highest graduate in the military examinations. He has been appointed Grand Generalissimo for the Subjugation of the West and now heads an army of a hundred thousand guarding Pu Pass. After I've seen my brother, I'll be off to the capital to seek advancement. I'm mulling over how, by windows lit by fireflies at the desk where snowlight reflects, I scraped away grime to polish forth radiance. From studies completed came a belly stuffed with literature, but still I'm tossed about on lake and sea. When will I achieve my grand ambition?

32b

A precious sword of priceless value hidden in autumn waters;
Spring sorrows lade my horse and press upon the embroidered saddle.

33a

[*Xianlü* mode:] "Dian jiangchun" (Student sings:)
I travel for study through the Central Plain,

---

[6] The abrupt switch to the female lead (Oriole) in the reprise is handled differently in other editions. In those texts Crimson appears onstage just after the song "Shanghua shi", the old lady's lament over spring and her orders to Crimson to take Oriole to the Buddha hall are also moved between the song and the reprise and are rounded out with the following lines:

(Crimson speaks:) As you say, madam. (Old lady leaves. Crimson speaks:) Missy, please   (Main female role dressed as Oriole enters. Crimson speaks:) Madam orders us to the Buddha hall to amuse ourselves a while.

[7] February 17–26, 801.

Heels without strings,
Like a tumbling weed.
My gazing eyes link with heaven:
"The sun is near, Chang'an is far."[8]

"Hunjiang long" (Student sings:)
Penetrating the *Poetry* and *Documents*, the classics and traditions,[9]
Like a bookworm I never emerged but labored over my boring and rubbing.
I stayed in the thorny enclosure until my seat grew warm[10]
And ground the iron inkstone until it was worn through.[11]
Before I can make the ninety-thousand-mile cloud-path journey of the *peng*,[12]
I'll first have to endure twenty years of snow-lit window and firefly light.
Lofty talent does not fit well into the schemes of the vulgar;
When time's athwart, there is no attaining the ambitions of a man.
In vain I whittle insects and carve seal-script characters[13]
And stitch together broken strips and tattered texts.[14]

33b

---

[8] A saying common among students seeking fame and fortune in the capital at Chang'an. It derives from a story about the youth of Emperor Mingdi (r. 323–25) of the Jin dynasty. When asked which was closer, the sun or Chang'an, he replied that the sun was: one could see it simply by raising one's head, but no one could see Chang'an. Students used his words to refer to their own dim prospects.

[9] The basic texts of the curriculum for the examinations. In addition to *The Book of Poetry* (*Shijing*), a collection of 305 early poems, and *The Book of Documents* (*Shujing*), a compilation of early historical records, students also studied *The Record of Rites* (*Liji*), a compendium of early ritual practices, *The Book of Changes* (*Yijing*), a manual of divination, and *The Spring and Autumn Annals* (*Chunqiu*), a bare historical chronology of the state of Lu for the period 722–484 B.C The "traditions" are three ancient commentaries to *The Spring and Autumn Annals*: *The Tradition of Master Zuo* (*Zuozhuan*), *The Gongyang Tradition* (*Gongyang zhuan*), and *The Guliang Tradition* (*Guliang zhuan*). In a more general sense, this is merely a term for the all of the works studied in the traditional curriculum.

[10] Originally a thorn and bramble fence constructed to keep examination candidates from crowding around the plaque announcing the roster of those who had passed. It also came to stand synecdochically for the examination ground itself.

[11] The story of the tenth-century student named Sang Weihan who stood for the examinations but was disqualified because his surname was a homophone for a word that meant "funeral" or "mourning" (*sang*). Having been advised to change to another career, he had an iron inkstone cast, vowing that he would not give up until he had worn it through grinding ink.

[12] *Peng* (usually translated "roc") is mentioned in the opening lines of the *Zhuangzi*: it was a bird so massive that it "rose on the whirlwind for nine thousand *li*" before it set off on its six-month journey to the south. The "cloud path of the *peng* journey" is a common Song and Yuan metaphor for the road to success in the examinations.

[13] "Carving seal-script characters and whittling insects" usually refers to the famous Han scholiast Yang Xiong (53 B.C–A.D 18), who remarked that writing rhapsodies and poems was the equivalent of carving intricate characters and images: time-consuming and interesting but not particularly worthy of effort.

[14] The following section does not appear in our text, but it does in others; it explains

34a   "You hulu" (Student sings:)
Where are the wind-tossed billows of the nine bends most conspicuous?

[(Student speaks:)] None of the waters of the world are as tricky as those of the Yellow River:

[(Student sings:)][15]
Only this place is paramount.
This river belts Qi and Liang,
Divides Qin and Jin,
Cuts off You and Yan.[16]
Snowcapped waves beat the long sky,
At heaven's edge autumn clouds furl;
Bamboo hawsers cable together the floating bridge,
On the water a steel blue dragon reclines.
East and west it breaches into the nine regions,
North and south it threads together a hundred streams.
A homing vessel: is it fast or not? How does one see it?
Like a crossbow bolt's sudden leaving of the string.

"Tianxia le" (Student sings:)
Just as if the Silver River dropped through the nine heavens:[17]
From its deep fount beyond the clouds suspended
To its entering into the Eastern Sea, it cannot but pass here.
It irrigates the thousand kinds of flowers of Luoyang,
Enriches the myriad-acre fields of Liangyuan;[18]
And once it floated a raft to the edge of sun and moon.[19]

---

the abrupt switch between the two songs:

> (Student speaks:) Well, traveling all the while, I've already reached Pu Ford.
> This Yellow River has nine bends, and this is precisely the the area of ancient
> Henei. Look at this grand sight!

[15] Although we have translated this as direct speech, these lines appear to be editorial comment rather than spoken text. Not only is the passage stylistically different from the language of the drama, but it is also printed differently: each line is composed of two columns of smaller characters, the standard layout for commentary. Spoken text is normally printed in smaller characters, but in single, not double, columns. The Dong Jieyuan ballad at this point reads: "And where is the Yellow River most mighty? Right here in Hezhong" (*Huang he nali zui xiong? Wuguo Hezhong fu*). In other cases in the Hongzhi edition where characters are printed two to a column, it is usually to rectify an error in the cutting of the block. Such cases seldom run to more than two characters in length.

[16] These are six of the *jiuzhou*, the nine ancient divisions in China's magical and cosmological geography.

[17] A line adapted from a famous poem by Li Bo, "Wang Lushan, qi'er." See p. 54.

[18] References to Luoyang and Kaifeng: the first renowned for its many flower, especially peony, gardens; and the second, for the famous gardens a feudal lord of antiquity

(Male lead speaks:) While I've been talking, I've reached the city Here's an inn. Lute boy, take my horse. Where's the innkeeper? ([Extra] male lead enters and speaks:) I'm the innkeeper of Head-of-the-List Lodge. If you, sir, want to stay, I have a nice clean room here.(Male lead speaks:) I'll take the finest room. You go feed the horse first, [lute boy]. Innkeeper, come, I want to ask you: is there a place here where I might wile away my time? Any famous mountains or spectacular spots or blessed places or precious wards will do.[20] (Extra speaks:) There's a monastery here called Universal Salvation; it is an institution founded by the august empress Zetian. Its architecture is not of the common kind:

> The ceramic-tiled halls draw near the blue empyrean,
> The relic-filled pagoda pierces the cloudy Han.[21]
> Whether coming south or going north,
> No matter of which of the three creeds or nine schools,
> All who pass gaze upon it in amazement.

It is only there, sir, that a man of your refinement can wander in pleasure. (Male lead speaks:) Lute boy, prepare my lunch for the upcoming noon period. I'll just go there and have a look and then come back.

([Male lead] leaves.)

(Child speaks:) I'll prepare some dishes, and after feeding the horse, I'll wait for big brother to come home.

([Lute boy and extra] leave.)

❖❖❖

(Clown, costumed as a bald one, enters and speaks:) I, Dharma Wit, am a disciple of the abbot, Dharma Source, of this Monastery of Universal Salvation. Today my teacher has gone out to a vegetarian meal and has made me stay here in the monastery. I am supposed to take note of anyone who comes looking for him and then report to my teacher as soon as he comes home, so I am standing in front of the temple gate to see if anyone will come by (Male lead enters and speaks:) Well, I'm here already. (He meets clown. Clown asks him:) Where are you from, traveler? (Male lead speaks:) Well, I've come from Western Luo. I have heard that your ashram is elegant and secluded, pure and refreshing, and so I have come partly to gaze upon the Buddha image and partly to pay my respects to your abbot. May I ask whether the abbot is here? (Clown speaks:) My teacher is not in the monastery. I am his poor disciple Dharma Wit. May I invite you, sir,

34b

35a

35b

---

constructed near modern Kaifeng.

[19] For this allusion and its significance to the play, see pp. 55–56.

[20] That is, famous Taoist or Buddhist temples.

[21] "Cloudy Han" is also a reference to the Milky Way; one tradition connects the Milky Way to the Han, instead of the Yellow, River.

to our ten-foot-square[22] for some tea? (Male lead speaks:) Since the abbot isn't here, there's no need to drink tea. Could I trouble you, my monk, to guide me around the monastery so I may gaze upon its wonders? (Clown speaks:) I'll go get the keys and open up the Buddha hall, the bell tower, the pagoda court, the arhat hall, the refectory; and when we have made our tour, my teacher should be back. (Male lead speaks:) The architecture is really fine.

> "Jiegao" [(Student sings:)]
> Having gladdened my heart by visiting the Buddha hall above,
> Here I am already at the monks' court below
> We pass close by the west end of the kitchen,
> The north of the dharma hall, the front of the bell tower.
> I've strolled through the grotto cells,
> Climbed the precious pagoda,
> And wound my way along twisting corridors.
> I've finished counting the arhats,
> Paid my respects to the bodhisattvas,
> Made my obeisances to the Holy One—

(Female lead enters, leading Crimson and twirling a flowering sprig. She speaks:) Crimson, let's go and play around in the Buddha hall. (Male lead acts out seeing her:) Wow!

> [(Student sings:)]
> And now I run smack into my alluring karmic sentence from five centuries ago!

> "Yuanhe ling" [(Student sings:)]
> Stunning knockouts—I've seen a million;
> But a lovely face like this is rarely seen!
> It dazzles a man's eyes, stuns him speechless,
> And makes his soul fly away into the heavens.
> She there, without a thought of teasing, fragrant shoulders bare,
> Simply twirls the flower, smiling.

> "Shangma jiao" [(Student sings:)]
> This is Tushita Palace,[23]
> Don't guess it to be the heaven of Separation's Regret.[24]
> Ah, who would ever have thought that I would meet a divine sylph?

[36a]

[36b]

---

[22] I.e., the abbot's room.

[23] The abode of the future Buddha, Maitreya, Tushita Palace (or Tushita Heaven) is a realm of utter bliss.

[24] In popular lore there were thirty-three heavens; Separation's Regret was the highest of them, the home of thwarted lovers obligated to endure eternal separation. In Yuan drama we find the common saying "Thirty-three heavens: Separation's Regret is the highest; / Four hundred and four ailments: the illness of love's longing is most bitter."

I see her spring-breeze face, fit for anger, fit for joy,
Just suited to those flowered pins pasted with kingfisher feathers.

"Sheng hulu" (Student sings:)
See her palace-style eyebrows, curved like crescent moons,
Invading the borders of her clouds of locks.

(Female lead speaks:) Crimson, look:

> Lonely, lonely monks' chambers where no one goes;
> Filling the steps, padded by moss, the red of fallen flowers.

(Student speaks:) I'm dying.

[(Student sings:)]
Bashful in front of others before she even speaks:
Cherry fruits split apart their redness,
Jade grains reveal their whiteness.
Time passes before she speaks.

"Reprise"
Just like the warbling sound of an oriole twittering beyond the flowers,
Each step she takes makes me tingle:
A waist just made for dancing, lovely and lithe,   37a
A thousand kinds of alluring charms,
Myriad kinds of graceful motions,
Just like a weeping willow before the evening breeze.

(Crimson speaks:) Someone's over there. Let's go home. (Female lead turns back
to look at student [and leaves with Crimson]. Student speaks:) Monk! Guanyin
just materialized! (Clown speaks:) You're babbling. This is the young daughter of
Chancellor Cui, executive officer of the prefecture of Hezhong. (Male lead
speaks:) Such a girl in this world! Isn't she a heavenly beauty, a real "state-
toppler"?[25] Needn't mention her figure—why, that pair of feet alone is worth a
hundred talents of gold. (Clown speaks:) She's so far away   you're here, she's
there   she's got a long skirt on—how do you know her feet are small?

"Houting hua" [(Student sings:)]
If it weren't for the softness of that fragrant path padded with tattered red,
How could it betray the light imprint of her foot as it treads the perfumed dust?
It's not necessary to say, "The corners of her eyes, there she lets passion
     linger,"
Because this single footprint relays all the feelings of her heart.   37b
Slowly, she meanders
Until she reaches the doorway,

[25] For this allusion to Li Yannian's sister, see pp. 65–66.

And then a final step takes her far away.
She has just shown her face for a moment
But has driven to madness this laureate Zhang.
Like a divine sylph returning to her grotto heaven,
She leaves emptiness behind in the mists of willows,
Where all that can be heard is the chattering of sparrows.

"Liuye'er" (Student sings:)
Ai, the gate shuts away the pear blossoms' courtyard deep,
The chalky walls are as high as blue heaven.
I hate heaven
That gives man no ease.
How hard it makes it on me to pass time—
Truly, how can I hold on?
Missy, you've brought out my monkey of mind, my horse of desire.

Made him horny

(Clown speaks:) Don't stir anything up. That's the daughter of the executive of Hezhong Prefecture, and she's already gone far away. (Male lead speaks:) She hasn't yet gone far,

38a

"Jisheng cao" [(Student sings:)]
And the scent of orchid musk lingers still,
The sound of hanging pendants moves slowly away.
The eastern wind sways, then drags up, strands of weeping willows,
Floating threads catch and stir up petals of peach blossom;
The pearly curtains now hide, now show, her lotus face.
You say she is of the family of His Excellency, executive of Hezhong
    Prefecture;
I say she is an apparition of Guanyin, contemplating moonlight in water.

(Student recites:)

    "For ten years I did not know the face of my lord and king"—
    Only now do I believe that a beautiful woman can lead a man astray

[(Student speaks:)] I'm not going to the capital! (Looking at clown, he speaks:) May I bother you, my monk, to let the abbot know that I would like to rent a monk's cell—no matter how small—where I might review the canon and the histories? That would be far better than the hubbub of a traveler's inn. I will pay rent according to accepted practice, and I'll move myself in tomorrow

38b

"Zhuan Coda" [(Student sings:)]
My hungry eyes have gazed until they are shot through,
My starving mouth has salivated until I swallow in vain.

In vain I am infected with a marrow-piercing love-longing;
How can I withstand her, who turned her autumn ripples on me as she left?[26]

[(Student speaks:)] Don't say it's just me—

[(Student sings:)]
Even a man of steel or stone would have had his feelings stirred, his emotions
    tickled.
Near the garden porch,
Flower and willow struggle in their seductiveness;
The sun at noon centers in the courtyard, the shadow of the pagoda is
    round—
Spring's radiance is before the eyes.
Alas, this person of jade has disappeared,
And the palace of Brahma
I take to be the Fount of Wuling.[27]

([They] leave.)   39a

Title: The old lady closes the springtime courtyard;
          Oriole Cui burns incense at night.

Name: Winsome Crimson is concerned for the memorial service;
          Zhang Junrui stirs up the mass.

---

[26] "Autumn ripples" is perhaps the most common metaphor in popular literature for
lovely eyes.

[27] The Fount of Wuling is a conflation of two popular stories: that of Tao Yuanming's
(365–427) idyllic paradise, the Peach Blossom Spring, that was discovered by a fisherman
from Wuling; and that of Liu Chen and Ruan Zhao of the Han, who went up to Mount
Tiantai to pick medicinal herbs and stayed to share a grotto with two transcendent
maidens. When they finally returned home, they met only their seventh-generation
descendents, so much time had passed.

Crimson Angrily Upbraids Student Zhang for His Questions

Act 2

(Clown has departed.[1] Old lady comes on and opens:) I've had no word from the abbot since he took my money a few days ago to perform a mass for His Excellency I've told Crimson to transmit these words of mine to the abbot: "When would it be best to hold a mass for His Excellency?" I want him to put everything in tip-top order and then report to me.

[(Old lady leaves.)]

❖❖❖

(Extra, dressed as abbot, enters and speaks:) I am Dharma Source and am the abbot of this Monastery of Universal Salvation. This monastery was built by Her August Majesty, Zetian. I was indeed ordained on the authority of His Excellency, Cui Jue, who also restored this monastery after it had fallen for many years into disrepair. Now the old widow and her immediate family are bearing the casket back to Boling; but finding the road blocked, they can go no further. The widow detests the boisterousness of the marketplace inn, and so she's using the western wing here. When the road is safe again, she will pack up and return to Boling for her husband's burial. In her management of all things the old madam is amiable and simple. She runs the household according to the book—what's right is right, what's wrong is wrong—and no one dares violate that. Yesterday I

---

[1] We assume that originally there was a comic interlude at the beginning of this act, so well known that it was not scripted. This occurs frequently: the farce skit *A Pair of Battling Quacks* (translated in Appendix I) is noted in this drama only by its title.

was invited to a vegetarian meal, so I don't know if anyone came to visit me or not. (He calls out clown and acts out questioning him. Clown [enters and] speaks:) Yesterday a budding scholar came from Western Luo just to see you, my master; but failing to meet you, he went back. (Bald one speaks:) Keep watch in front of the temple gate, and if he comes a second time, inform me. (Male lead [enters and] speaks:) After seeing that girl yesterday, I was awake all night long. If it had not been for that monk Dharma Wit   But that girl certainly was of a   40a
mind to look me over. Today I'm going to ask the abbot about renting a monk's cell where early and late I can practice the canon and histories. If that girl should happen out, then I can get a real eyeful of her.

[*Zhonglü* mode:] "Fendie'er" (Student sings:)
You were no help—
Oh, how I resent you, monk Dharma Wit!
Just rent me out the smallest guest room or monk's cell,
Then I'll be living just opposite that lovable wretch of mine.[2]
Although I may not be able to filch the jade or pilfer the perfume,[3]
I'll have these eyes that watch for traveling clouds all prepared.[4]

"Zui chunfeng" (Student sings:)   40b
When I saw any powdered faces before, I really was embarrassed,
Or saw any painters of eyebrows, I really panicked.[5]

---

[2] *Kezeng cai* (lovable wretch) literally means "hateful stuff" but is used as a strong term of endearment. Wang Jide explains, "Not to say 'lovable' but to say 'hateful' is to use an 'opposite term.' This is just like calling [a lover] a 'karmic injustice' (*yeyuan*) or a 'plaintiff' (*yuanjia*)—it is the height of love." See Wang Shifu, *Huitu xin jiaozhu guben Xixiang ji*, 1.17a.

[3] This is a common euphemism for illicit sexual encounters between young lovers. "Pilfering perfume" refers to an anecdote from the *Jin History* (*Jin shu*). The daughter of Jia Chong was enraptured with Han Shou, whom she saw at a banquet. Her desire was communicated by a maid to Han Shou, who began to visit the girl regularly in her chambers. The emperor had given Jia Chong a vial of perfume from Central Asia that once applied was said to stay on a person for a month. This his daughter stole and gave to Han Shou, who wore it among the courtiers. They told Jia Chong of Han Shou's wonderful scent, and thus the affair was sniffed out—and ended in marriage. "Filching jade" refers to a now unknown story about a certain student named Zheng. There are scattered references to the story in Yuan *sanqu* and dramatic texts, including a citation in Sun Jichang's "Gathering Titles of Comedies to Sing of Passion" ("Ji zaju ming yongqing"), where the title of a play is noted as *Guessing at the Jade-filching Mind and Perfume-stealing Character* (*Chuaizhe qieyu xin touxiang xing*). See Sui Shusen, *Quan Yuan sanqu*, 2:1238, and Wang Shifu, *Jiping jiaozhu Xixiang ji*, 23.

[4] "Traveling clouds," a reference to the object of Zhang's love, is adapted from Song Yu's "Gaotang fu," the source of the other famous phrase for sexual encounters, "morning clouds and evening rain," or simply "clouds and rain." See pp. 67, 96.

[5] The referent of these two lines is ambiguous. Powdered faces and painted eyebrows are metonymies for lovely women. They can also refer to skirt-chasers, however, like He Yan and Zhang Chang (see p. 72). This would appear to be more consistent with Student

But when this man full of passion saw that passionate lass,
It made my heart itch,
Itch.
It has stirred me up until my insides quiver,
It has done me in until my eyes go crazy,
And it has riled me up so, my heart is all aflutter.

(After male lead has greeted Dharma Wit, Dharma Wit speaks:) My teacher is expecting you at just this moment, sir. Please wait here a second and I'll report to him. (Bald one acts out coming out [of his room] and greeting him. Male lead speaks:) What a fine monk!

"Ying xianke" (Student sings:)
What I see is a head like snow,
Temple locks like frost,
Face like a young boy's—a result of inner nurturing in younger years;
His mien is proper and imposing,
His voice is resounding and clear.
All that's missing is a halo above his head
To make him look just like the image of Sengjia in nirvana.[6]

41a   (Bald one speaks:) May I invite you, sir, to my ten-foot-square? Yesterday I wasn't home, so I missed greeting you. Please forgive me. (Male lead speaks:) Long have I heard of your pure reputation, therefore I have wanted to come receive instruction beneath your dais. I couldn't know that I would be unable to meet you yesterday; that I can see you today is the greatest happiness of three lifetimes. (Bald one speaks:) From which commandery does your family stem? May I ask you your name? What has brought you here to this lowly place? (Male lead speaks:) My name is Zhang Gong, and I am known as Junrui.

41b   "Shiliu hua" (Student sings:)
Reverend, you ask for all the details of my life;
I will give you full account of all my secret feelings:
Western Luo was our home of old,
But official postings sent us through the four quadrants
Until we temporarily lodged in Xianyang.[7]
My late father, appointed minister of the Board of Rites, was a noted man;

Zhang's character in the "Yingying zhuan," where he declaims his puritanical morality; it would also appear more appropriate to this act in which both He Yan and Zhang Chang are later mentioned.

[6] Sengjia was a monk from the western regions who was thought to have been the avatar of Guanyin. He preached in the area of the Huai River and became extremely popular as a Buddhist figure in the Tang dynasty and afterward. There were large temples constructed in his honor in Luoyang and in Sizhou.

[7] An archaism for Chang'an, the capital of the Tang.

But after a life of five times ten years, an illness carried him away.

(Bald one speaks:) When His Excellency abandoned this world, he must have left you something.

([Student] sings:)
For his whole life he was upright and true, without any partiality;
He left me only the empty bag of this wide, wide world.

his desire to stay is suspicious if he has any other options

(Bald one speaks:) When His Excellency was in office, he must have mixed with the vulgar crowd and matched their brilliance.[8]

"Dou anchun" (Student sings:)
How could my late father have mixed with the vulgar crowd and matched their brilliance?
He was altogether as fresh as a breeze and as radiant as the moon.

42a

(Bald one speaks:) On this trip you must surely be on the way to court for the examinations.

([Student] sings:)
I have no mind to seek office;
But my mind is set on hearing your lectures.

(Male lead speaks:) I have come especially to visit you, my abbot. But, alas, since I am hurrying along the road, I have nothing proper to present you.

(Student sings:)
To size it up, the gift of a poor budding scholar can be only half a sheet of paper,[9]
I have no fourteen- or eighteen-carat gold.
But if you want to discuss the long and short of it,
I can still balance out in pounds and ounces.[10]

---

[8] From the *Laozi*: "Match their brilliance, share their grime." The last part of the sentence is omitted here, but it still implies corruption or greed on the part of Zhang's father.

[9] That is, poetry, calligraphy, or painting done by the young (and presumably soon-to-be-famous) scholar.

[10] Literally, "I have no seven-blue or eight-yellow." This is a difficult passage to render in English. According to Wang Jide, a treatise entitled *Gegu yaolun* (Essential discourses on investigating ancient things) under "Grades of Gold" listed a scale of one to ten, which reads: "Seven equals blue, eight equals yellow, nine equals purple, ten equals scarlet." But in other dramas it is clear that in the context of enumeration, the colors blue and yellow are also counters for sons and daughters. See Wang Shifu, *Jiping jiaozhu Xixiang ji*, 25. By extension, it may refer here to the fact that the student is unmarried. "To discuss longs and shorts" is to evaluate a person's merits or actions by any of several criteria. The student's response, couched in terms of weighing and evaluating, is a satirical rebuke of the monk

(Male lead speaks:) I'll just present one tael of white silver as a token gesture, to be used in common by the permanent residents. Please accept it with a smile. (Bald one speaks:) Since you are on the road, what need is there for this? (Male lead speaks:) Such a small trifle is not worth refusing, but it will do for a serving of tea during your lectures.

"Shang xiaolou" (Student sings:)
I, a student, come especially to visit;
Great master, how can you so modestly refuse?

(Bald one speaks:) Oh, I *dare* not accept it.

(Student sings:)
This cash is not enough to buy firewood by the bunch,
It won't amount to the grain for a vegetarian meal;
But it will provide for tea and water.

([Student] faces Dharma Wit and speaks:) This tael of silver is not a hefty present;

(Student sings:)
But if you'll be my advocate
And, face-to-face with that dazzling beauty,
Pass along my words,
I won't forget, in life or in death, any of you monks.

42b   (Bald one speaks:) You must want something. (Male lead speaks:) In my ignorance, I have an earnest plea: I detest the boisterousness of the inn and find it hard at any time to practice the canon and histories there. I want to ask you, my teacher, if I can rent a room and listen morning and night to your lessons. I'll leave it up to you to decide the monthly rent. (Bald one speaks:) Our monastery does seem to have some rooms. We'll let you take your choice.

"Reprise" [(Student sings:)]
I do not want the refectory
Or the hall of withered trees;[11]
But far from the southern pavilions,
Away from the eastern walls,
Near to the western wing,
Close to the main hall,

---

for being greedy: in paraphrase, "Although I don't have much money, if you have to evaluate my character, I'll come out all right in the end."

[11] "Hall of withered trees" comes from a story about monks who studied with the ninth-century Zen master Shishuang (Stone Frost) and were so enraptured by his lectures that they remained in their meditation postures for hours. They were called "the withered-tree assembly." The term simply refers to the dharma hall.

Past the side rooms—
Those are the places that are just right.

(Bald one speaks:) Those are no good; how about sharing my couch? (Male lead laughs and speaks:) What do I want with you?

(Student sings:)
Don't you bring up this ten-foot-square of the abbot.

(Crimson enters and speaks:) The old lady has sent me to ask the abbot when the   43a
mass will be said for His Excellency. I'm supposed to see to it properly and then
go and tell her. I'd better move along. (Acts out greeting bald one and speaks:)
Myriad blessings on you, abbot. My mistress has sent me to ask you when you
will say mass for His Excellency. She said, "See to it properly and then report
back." (Male lead speaks in an aside:) What a fine girl!

Crimson who he has liked all along?
—thinks is oriole?

"Tuo bushan" (Student sings:)
She has the meticulous behavior of one from a great family;
She doesn't have half a speck of flippancy.
She makes deep, deep obeisance before the reverend
And then opens her scarlet lips and speaks just so.

"Xiao Liangzhou" (Student sings:)
This delightful lass's face is made up, oh, so lightly;
She is wearing a set of plain white clothes.
Her sparkling peepers are not of the ordinary kind:
Stealing a glance
Out of the corner of her eye, she strokes young Zhang.

"Reprise"   43b
If I could share the same mandarin-duck bed-curtains with her passionate
    mistress,
Would I leave her just to pile up the quilts and make up the bed?
I'll entreat her mistress,
Entreat the madam;
And if they don't want to turn her loose,
I will myself sign a writ of freedom.[12]

(Bald one speaks:) On the fifteenth day of the second moon we can say mass for
His Excellency (Crimson speaks:) I will accompany you, my abbot, to the
Buddha hall to have a look and then withdraw to report to the madam. (Bald one
speaks:) Please sit here for a while, sir. I'll be back after I have accompanied this
girl to have a look. (Male lead speaks:) Why leave me behind? Let me go with
you, all right? (Bald one speaks:) Well, come along. (Male lead speaks:) Let the

---

[12] For this writ of freedom, see pp. 81–82.

girl go first, and I'll just trail closely behind. (Bald one speaks:) Here's a budding scholar who makes sense. (Male lead speaks:) May I say a word? (Bald one speaks:) Speak your mind.

"Kuaihuo san" (Student sings:)
The dazzling face of this girl from the house of Cui
Wouldn't be turning you on, would it, my old bald-pated one?
How else could I so clearly see your head emitting such a slight radiance?
You are certainly playing a flashy role!

44a   (Bald one speaks:) Sir, what kind of language is this? Fortunately that girl couldn't hear it. If she knew   What are you up to? (Crimson acts out entering the Buddha hall.)

"Chao tianzi" (Student sings:)
Getting through the main corridor,
She leads us into the grotto chamber:[13]
"Good things descend from heaven."

(Male lead speaks:) I'll watch the gate for you. Go on in! (Bald one speaks in anger:) Sir, this not in conformity with the words and deeds of the Former Kings! Aren't you sinning against the school of the Sage? Am I prepared at my age to perform such acts?

([Student] sings:)
Oh, such a fine performance of anger!

(Male lead speaks:) Well, if you're not going to do it, then forget it.

([Student] sings:)
One way or the other, I've ruffled this Tripitaka of the Tang![14]

(Male lead speaks:) You can't blame me for suspecting you.

([Student] sings:)
If it is such a great family,
How come they don't have a single boy
But send out a servant girl to settle affairs?

(Bald one speaks:) The old madam manages her household strictly and sternly

---

[13] "Grotto chamber" also refers to the honeymoon room, and as in most cases with such imagery, it can refer to the female sexual organs.

[14] Tripitaka (602–64), or Xuanzang, who made a pilgrimage to India from 629 to 645 to acquire Buddhist scriptures, was the most famous monk of his day. He later became the central character in the sixteenth-century novel *Journey to the West* (*Xiyou ji*), the story of his pilgrimage to the Western Paradise. This novel describes Xuanzang as a holy monk who had not spent a drop of semen in nine lifetimes.

Not a single male goes in and out. (Male lead speaks in aside:) Oh what a sly talker this bald prick is!

(Student sings:)
In front of me
You talk a good show
But stiffen up your forehead skin to fight back.[15]

(Bald one speaks to Crimson:) The vegetarian meal and the mass have both been   44b
prepared. On the fifteenth day please have the madam and the young mistress come and burn incense. (Male lead speaks:) Why? (Bald one speaks:) This is [to demonstrate] the perfect filiality of the daughter of Chancellor Cui, who wants to repay the benevolence of her parents; it is also [to mark] the sacrificial day at the end of the mourning period for His Excellency, the day on which she takes off her mourning gowns—so she is having this mass said. (Male lead acts out mourning and weeping.)

> Alas! alas! my parents,
> With what toil ye gave me birth!
> If I would return your deep kindness,
> It would be like great heaven, illimitable.[16]

The young mistress is only a girl, but even she has the heart to repay her parents. For many a year have I, this poor student, been tossed about on lake and sea. Since my parents left this world, I have never been able to pay them back even a bundle of spirit money. O my monk, I hope that you will act out of compassion and let me also contribute five thousand cash toward the cost of the vegetarian meal that I may posthumously offer up something to my parents. It won't make any difference if the madam knows, as I satisfy a son's heart. (Bald one speaks:) Dharma Wit, let this gentleman contribute to the cost. (Male lead asks Dharma Wit in an aside:) Will the young mistress come tomorrow? (Dharma Wit speaks:)   45a
Of course she'll come; it's about her parents. (Male lead speaks in an aside:) I've used this five thousand well!

"Sibian jing" (Student sings:)
On earth or in heaven,
Seeing Oriole sure beats singing a mass.
Such supple jade, such warm fragrance—

---

[15] The earlier references to shiny heads culminate in this pun; on the comparison of monks' heads to the shiny *glans* of the penis, see p. 56–57.

[16] From the poem "Liao'e," Mao no. 202 in *The Book of Poetry*. The poem is the lamentation of a son who has been prevented from performing the proper last rites for his parents. There is a slight change in the first line of the second couplet quoted, from *yu bao zhi de* (I want to repay this virtue) to *yu bao shen'en* (I want to repay deep favor); see Legge, *She King*, 350–52. Could this be an indirect plea to the monk to help Zhang in his advances toward Oriole?

Even if we don't embrace,
If I can just touch her once,
It will dissolve all worldly obstacles.

(Bald one says:) Let's all go back to my cell and have some tea. (They act out arriving there. Male lead speaks:) I'm going to change my clothes.[17] (Male lead acts out going out and speaks:) That wench is bound to come out. I'll wait here to ask her something. (Crimson takes her leave of bald one and speaks:) I won't have tea because the madam might wonder why I'm late. I'll go and report to her. (Crimson acts out going out. Male lead acts out going up to Crimson and greeting her. Male lead speaks:) Greetings, my girl. (Crimson speaks:) Myriad blessings, my sir. (Male lead speaks:) Aren't you the personal servant girl of the young mistress Oriole? (Crimson speaks:) Yes, I am. But, sir, why should you ask? (Male lead speaks:) My surname is Zhang, my personal name is Gong, and I am known as Junrui. I hail originally from Western Luo and am just twenty-three. I was born on the seventeenth day of the first month, during the midnight hour. I have never been married.[18] (Crimson speaks:) Who asked you about all of this? (Male lead speaks:) May I ask if your mistress ventures out regularly? (Crimson speaks angrily:) Huh! You are a gentleman of the books. Does the *Mencius* not say, "Is it not propriety that males and females shall not allow their hands to touch in giving or receiving anything?"[19] A gentleman "does not snap his sandals in a melon field nor adjust his cap beneath a plum tree."[20] Is it not said, "Look not at what is contrary to propriety; listen not to what is contrary to propriety; speak not what is contrary to propriety; make no movement that is contrary to propriety."[21] The old lady manages her household strictly and sternly; she has the integrity of ice and frost. In her house there's not a boy over five feet high to answer the door. As soon as a boy reaches twelve or thirteen, he does not dare enter the inner halls of his own accord without being summoned there first. A few days ago Oriole sneaked out of the inner rooms and the madam discovered it. She ordered Oriole to stand in the courtyard below· "You are just a girl, but you left the inner chambers without permission! If you had happened to encounter a visitor or a novice who had ogled you secretly, wouldn't you have been ashamed of yourself?" Oriole immediately acknowledged her faults and said, "From now on I'm going to turn over a new leaf. I won't dare run afoul

---

[17] A euphemism for going to the toilet.

[18] He is explaining the eight characters taken from the hour, day, month, and year of birth that are used for marriage divination. Of course, in traditional China, a land of arranged marriages, it was in extremely bad taste and was presumptuous to propose oneself for marriage; it was particularly unseemly to do so to a maidservant.

[19] From *Mencius*, 4.A.17: "Chunyu Kun said, 'Is it not propriety that males and females shall not touch when giving or receiving things?' Mencius replied, 'It is propriety.'"

[20] I.e., to avoid the mistaken interpretation of his actions as theft. This comes from the Han "Ballad of a Gentleman" ("Gu junzi xing").

[21] *Analects*, 12.1; see Legge, *Confucian Analects*, 250.

again." You see, when even her own daughter is treated like this, what do you expect to happen to a simple serving girl like me? You, sir, practice the way of the Former Kings and thus honor the propriety established by the Duke of Zhou.[22] Why meddle in something that doesn't concern you? If it were only me, well, I could forgive that. But if the madam were to find out about it, you wouldn't be let off so easily. So in the future ask only what may be asked and don't babble on about things you shouldn't ask about!

([Crimson] leaves.)

(Male lead speaks:) I will really have to suffer this love sickness!

"Shaobian" (Student sings:)
Having listened to this, my heart and bosom are bleak and blue;
A whole heaven of sorrow have I pinched between my eyebrows.
She said, "The madam's integrity is severe as ice and frost.
If not summoned,
Who dares enter the center halls?"
Well, I wonder
If your heart so fears the stern authority of your mother.

[(Student speaks:)] Oh, missy—

[(Student sings:)]
You should never have turned around to look when you left!   *her fault*
Even if I wanted to rid myself of love-longing now, how could I?
All for nothing has passion pasted up my liver,
Has desire stirred up my innards.
If it is impossible in this life to find a lover,
It is because in another I burnt a broken stick of incense.
But if I can get her, I'll carry her aloft in my cupped hands,
Keep her warm within the pit of my heart,   46b
And serve her always with my eyes.

"Shua hai'er" (Female lead sings:)[23]
At first that Shamanka Mountain was just as far away and cutoff as heaven,

---

[22] The Duke of Zhou was a son of King Wen and younger brother to King Wu, the founders of the Zhou dynasty. He acted as regent during the youth of King Cheng, the son of King Wu. He was greatly admired by Confucius and was widely credited with the standardization of, among other rituals, the wedding rites.

[23] This is the first instance in our play where someone other than the singing lead is assigned a song. Later editions assign these songs to Student Zhang, but in light of the fact that he admits in song "Fourth from Coda" to "fantasizing," we assume that this is a highly original attempt to show a character's imagined thoughts by having the one imagined sing from offstage. Another possible interpretation could be that the stage directions originally

But I am now there at Shamanka Mountain.[24]
Although this cursed body stands in this winding corridor,
My soul is already at his side.
All I wanted was to put aright the affairs of my heart and send them to this
    seeker of secret places,
But I was afraid that I might let the radiance of spring leak out to the high
    hall.[25]
The widow fears the dissipation of her daughter's spring heart,
Blames the yellow oriole for finding a match,
And resents the powdered butterfly for consummating a union.

"Fifth from Coda" (Crimson sings:)
My mistress is young in years
But stubborn in character.
If Master Zhang should get to hold her tight—
If an accidental encounter, she'll look till sated at Master He's powder;
Looking for a chance to meet, she'll steal away Han Shou's perfume.[26]
Just as you reach that still unattained romantic situation,
She'll turn you into a loving, a caring, a handsome husband.
So why fear a mother who now has the power to restrict her?

actually on his side?

47a   "Fourth from Coda" (Student sings:)
Her mother is too attentive;
I vainly fantasize.
My talent and her visage are just meant for each other!
Let her not wait until her eyebrows have faded before she longs for Zhang
    Chang,[27]
Or until the colors of spring have been blown to nothingness before she
    remembers Master Ruan.[28]
It's not that I am bragging:
She has virtue and looks,[29]

---

specified that the male lead should sing this song and the following one in the voices and characters of Oriole and Crimson. At any rate, it is clearly a case of the lead singer trying to imagine another character's psychological state.

[24] Since other texts assign these lines to Zhang, some commentaries, such as *Xixiang ji tongsu zhushi*, take this line to mean "I am on the other side of Shamanka Mountain now", that is, even further separated from her love. But our interpretation makes good sense, especially when read in tandem with the next couplet, in which Oriole clearly says that her soul has flown to his side.

[25] *Naitang* (high hall) is a standard term for "mother." Oriole is worried that any news of an illicit affair ("spring's radiance") would leak to her mother.

[26] See play I, act 2, n. 3 and n. 5 for these two allusions.

[27] See play I, act 2, n. 5.

[28] See play I, act 1, n. 27. In Chinese poetic language, spring's radiance or the colors of spring often denote sexual longing.

[29] A vague paraphrase from a section of *The Book of Rites* entitled "Marriage Rites,"

And I am "respectful, restrained, warmhearted, and good."[30]

"Third from Coda" (Student sings:)   47b
I can imagine how finely, finely sketched are her brows,
How lightly, lightly her face is made up.
The fragrance of powder and the jade luster of ointments are spread on her
    rouged neck;
Under the mandarin-duck embroidery of her halcyon skirt the golden
    lotuses are tiny;[31]
Protruding from the simurgh fretwork of her red sleeves, the jade sprouts
    are long.[32]
Don't imagine it; it makes things worse—
You've thrown down half a heaven of beauty,
And I've picked up a thousand kinds of worry.

(Male lead speaks:) I've completely forgotten to take my leave of the abbot! (He   48a
acts out greeting bald one [and speaks]:) May I ask you, sir, about the room? (Bald
one speaks:) A single cell in the western wing, the one in the corner of the pagoda
courtyard, is very quiet and secluded. It's really the place for you to stay. It has
just recently been cleaned, and you may come anytime. (Male lead speaks:) I'll go
back to the inn and move out. (Bald one speaks:) I'm going to my vegetarian
feast. (Male lead speaks:) You go on and have your meal; I'll go and get my
luggage. (Bald one speaks:) Well, if it's all worked out, I'm ready to go. Sir, we'll
expect you.

([Bald one] leaves.)

(Male lead speaks:) If I were in the bustle of the inn, I'd have no problem wiling
away my time. But if I move to such a secluded and elegant place in the
monastery, how will I be able to endure such dreary loneliness?

"Second from Coda" (Student sings:)
The courtyards are deep,
The pillow and mat are chilly,
A lonely shadow of a single lamp flickers on the study curtains.
Even though I should fulfill my present life's ambition,   48b
How will I make it through this lengthening night?

---

which enumerates the four things that women are taught before marriage: a wife's virtue,
a wife's words, a wife's labors, and a wife's looks.
    [30] According to *Analects*, 1.10, the four virtues of a gentleman. Roughly paraphrased,
the couplet means that they are a perfect match by the classical standards of orthodox
morality and personality traits.
    [31] Her small bound feet.
    [32] Her long fingers. The repetition of "jade" at this point suggests that Zhang is using
feet and fingers as synecdoche to talk about Oriole's lustrous body that is obscured by her
clothes.

Unable to sleep, like a hand turning over and over:
There will be no fewer than a myriad of long sighs and short moans,
Five thousand poundings of the mat and flippings of the pillow

"Coda" (Student sings:)
Charming and shy, a flower that speaks;
Warm and supple, a jade that has fragrance.
We met by accident, and I can't remember fully her feigned appearance;[33]
I can only tap my teeth, and slowly, slowly imagine.

(He leaves.)

---

[33] While other texts have emended *qiao* (crafty or dissembling) to *jiao* (charming), we have decided on the basis of the common use of *qiao* in such phrases as *qiaomo qiaoyang* (and its shortened version *qiao moyang*, both meaning to posture or to affect a certain behavior) to keep the original character as the preferred reading, especially in view of the fact that Oriole's actions are later the subject of suspicion and resentment because of their purposive ambiguity

Oriole, Burning Nighttime Incense, Sees Student Zhang and Returns to Her Chambers with Crimson

Act 3

(Main female lead comes on and opens:) The madam sent Crimson to question the abbot, but the little hussy never came back to report to me. (Crimson comes on and speaks:) I've finished reporting to the madam, so now I'll take the message on to missy (Female lead speaks:) You were sent to ask the abbot when the memorial mass would be held. (Crimson speaks:) I have just finished reporting to the madam and was on the verge of reporting to you, missy On the fifteenth day of the second month you and the madam are invited to burn incense. (Crimson laughs, saying:) Missy, you can't know what a funny thing I have to tell you about. That young scholar we saw in the temple yesterday was also in the abbot's cell today He went ahead of me and waited for me outside. He gave me a grave salutation and then said, "My surname is Zhang, my personal name is Gong, and I am known as Junrui. I hail originally from Western Luo and am just twenty-three. I was born on the seventeenth day of the first month, during the midnight hour. I have never been married." Now, missy, who ever asked him such a thing? He also asked, "Aren't you Oriole's private maid? Does missy come out a lot?" I came back only after he'd been bawled out properly by me! Sister, I don't know what he was thinking. This world is full of such addlepated jerks! (Female lead smiles, saying:) Crimson, don't mention this to the madam. It's getting late now Set up the incense table, and we'll go burn some incense in the flower garden.

(They leave.)

❖❖❖

49b   (Male lead enters and speaks:) I've just moved into the temple and am living quite close to the western wing. The monks told me that missy burns incense in the flower garden every night. The flower garden is right next to the temple. Before missy comes out I'll hide myself near the Taihu rocks[1] at the corner of the wall. When she appears, I'll get an eyeful of her. All of the monks in the twin corridors are sound asleep, the night is deep, people are still. The moon is bright, the breeze is fresh. Ah, what lovely weather! (He recites a poem:)

> In leisure I seek the abbot's cell for the noble monk's conversation;
> When depressed, I face the western wing to chant under the hoary moon.

[*Yuediao* mode:] "Dou anchun" [(Student sings:)]
The jade vault is without dust,
The Silver River drips light;
Moon's color straddles the void,
Flowers' shadows fill the courtyard.
My silken sleeves grow cold,
My fragrant heart is on alert.
I cock my ear to listen,
Walk with quiet step,
Silent, so silent,
In darkness so dark.
Hiding, hiding,
I wait and wait and wait.

"Zihua'er xu" (Student sings:)
I'm waiting for that chic, neat,
Lithe, and svelte
Little missy, Oriole.
After the first watch,
When the pipes of nature are silent,
I'll go straight to Oriole's courtyard.
If by chance I run across that wretch of mine in the winding corridors,
I'll clasp her tightly in my arms:
"I want to interrogate you about the lack of meetings, the surplus of separations,
50a   About showing your shadow but withholding your body."

(Female lead [enters] and speaks:) Crimson, go on up, and when you've opened the corner door, bring the incense table out.

"Jin jiaoye" (Student sings:)
Of a sudden I hear the corner door creak;

---

[1] These are strangely shaped rocks that were placed in gardens and ponds for effect. They were named after rocks found in Lake Taihu near Suzhou.

Where the breeze passes, flower's perfume is lightly borne.[2]
Standing on tiptoe, I fix my eyes carefully:
Her face is even more chic than when I first saw her.   50b

(Female lead speaks:) Set that incense table down closer to the Taihu rocks. (Male lead acts out watching her and speaks, [first reciting]:)

> It must be that this springtime beauty is fed up with confinement
> And has flown freely out of her Palace of Spreading Frigidity.[3]

Her whole face still covered with powder, draping gown baring one shoulder, she lets her fragrant sleeves fall without word and trails her river-goddess skirts without talking—she's just like the Consorts of the Xiang Tomb, leaning against the red doors of Shun's temple,[4] or like Chang'e in the Moon Hall, barely visible in the Golden Hall of the Ecliptic Toad.[5] What a fine girl!

"Tiaoxiao ling" (Student sings:)
I've just seen her lithe gracefulness
And compare her to Chang'e in the Moon Hall, who is not so fine a piece.
Now blocked from view, now hidden, she threads the fragrant path;
I can imagine how hard it is for her to walk on such tiny feet.
A hundred seductions spring from the face of this delightful lass—
Oh, it steals a man's soul away!

(Female lead speaks:) Give me the incense. (Male lead speaks:) I'll pay attention to what she prays for. (Female lead speaks:) With this first stick of incense I pray for my deceased father's rebirth in heaven's realm. With this second stick of incense I pray that my old mother will stay healthy. And with this third stick   (She acts out falling silent.) (Crimson speaks:) Sister, don't utter a prayer with this stick of incense; I'll do it for you—I pray that my sister will soon find a husband who will take Crimson along too. (Female lead sticks the incense [into a censer] on the table and makes obeisance and speaks [in verse]:)   51a

> The unending heartbreaks in my heart
> All lie in these two deep, deep bows.

(Female lead heaves a deep sigh. Male lead speaks:) The young miss leans against

---

[2] That is, the open doorway admits a breeze into the courtyard garden, which is surrounded by high walls, and carries with it the scent of Oriole's perfume.

[3] The legendary name of a palace in the moon where beauties dwelt; it is also associated with the moon goddess, Chang'e. See pp. 59–62.

[4] For the Consorts of the Xiang, see pp. 59–60. While there are other legends about the Xiang River goddesses, "leaning on the doors of Shun's temple" indicates that the singer has Ehuang and Nüying in mind. Red is the standard color of temple doors in China.

[5] Legend also has it that a toad that lived on the moon swallowed the lunar orb during eclipses.

the balustrade and heaves a deep sigh. It seems as if her feelings have been stirred.

"Xiaotao hong" [(Student sings:)]
In night's depth mists of incense disperse through the empty courtyard,
The curtains of the door are stilled in the eastern breeze.
Her bows finished, she leans on the curving balustrade
And sighs deeply three or four times.
The perfectly round moon is like a mirror suspended:
This is neither the slightest cloud nor thinnest haze;
But is all smoke of incense and human breath,
Wafting inseparably upward together.

(Male lead speaks:) Though I'm no match for Sima Xiangru, I can see that the little miss certainly has the mind of Wenjun.[6] I'll sing a quatrain to see what she has to say. (He recites a poem:)

> A night bathed in moonlight,
> A spring desolated by flowers' shadows;
> Why, under the hoary sickle,
> Do I not see the lady in the moon?

(Female lead speaks:) Someone's chanting a poem by the corner of the wall. (Crimson speaks:) Why, it's the voice of that twenty-three-year-old, as-yet-unmarried, addlepated jerk! (Female lead speaks:) What a fresh and original poem. I'll make up one on the same rhyme. (Crimson speaks:) The two of you make a nice couple—couplet. (Female lead recites a matching poem:)[7]

> Long has my orchid chamber been lonely,
> No way to pass the fragrant spring;
> I reckon that he who walks and chants
> Will take pity on the one who heaves a sigh.

(Male lead speaks:) That was a snappy response.

"Tusi'er" (Student sings:)
Already struck by a vexing loveliness redundant upon her face,
I'm now perplexed by the quick intelligence stored away in her mind:
She has matched, oh, so well the meter of my new poem;
Each word, one by one, tells true feelings—what a pleasure to hear.

---

[6] Sima Xiangru and Zhuo Wenjun were famous lovers of the Han dynasty who overcame parental opposition to marriage. As the prototype of the "talented scholar yet to achieve success and the perfectly beautiful young maiden" tale, the legend of these two lovers has exerted a tremendous influence on later love stories. For a detailed discussion, see pp. 35, 67–68, 76.

[7] I.e., she recites a poem extempore employing the same rhyme.

"Shengyao wang" (Student sings:)
The lyrics are fresh,
The prosody flows easily—
No accident that she has been given Oriole as a name.
If she were to fix her eyes on me,
We would banter verses across the wall until dawn.
Now rings true the saying, "Since ancient days the bright have loved the
    bright."

(Male lead speaks:) I'll rush out here and see what she'll say.   52a

"Ma lang'er" (Student sings:)
I pluck my gown up, about to walk—

(Female lead acts out seeing him.)

She welcomes me with a smile on her face;
But that unhelpful Crimson is just too unfeeling,
Even though she only follows orders.

(Crimson speaks:) Missy, someone's here. Let's go inside; otherwise, the madam
will take us to task. (Female lead looks back as she leaves.)

"Reprise" (Student sings:)
Suddenly I hear an alarming noise—
But it was just the flapping of a roosting bird rising on wing,
The quivering of a flowering branch shaking its shadow,
The jumble of falling red filling the path.

(Male lead speaks:) Now that missy is gone, what do I do with myself?

"Luosiniang" (Student sings:)
Left behind for no reason, the dewy chill, azure and transparent on the dark
    moss;
The light of the moon, clear and brilliant, winnowed by flowers.
In daylight cold and lonely, vainly suffering sickness,
Tonight I sicken with love-longing again.

"Dongyuan le" (Student sings:)
The curtain has been let down,
The door already bolted;
Just now I whisperingly questioned,
And there she answered in a voice so low
The moon bright, the breeze fresh, just at the second watch.
Oh, how frustrating!
She lacks the karma; I'm out of luck.

52b
"Mian daxu" (Student sings:)
Just as I was going back,
I stood still in the empty courtyard:
Branch tips of bamboo vibrated in the wind,
The handle of the Dipper was strung by clouds.

[(Student speaks:)] Oh,

[(Student sings:)]
The bleakness of this night is four-starred,[8]
What can I do if she cares not for me?
Even though the corners of her eyes relayed her feelings,
Our two mouths never spoke of what our hearts well knew

(Male lead speaks:) How will sleep ever come to my eyes tonight?

"Zhuolusu" (Student sings:)
Facing that single flickering blue lamp on its short stand,
Leaning against that chilling, cold screen with its old panels,
Neither does the lamp give light, nor do my dreams coalesce.
At the window, the freezing, chilling wind penetrates the widely spaced stiles;
Flapping and fluttering, the paper shreds chatter.
Alone on my pillow,
Desolate in my quilted burrow.
If you were a man with a heart of stone—
A man with a heart of stone would still be moved.

53a
"Reprise"
Resent, I cannot,
Hate, I will not;
I sit, but unsteadily,
I sleep, but unquietly
A day will come when—blocked by willows and shielded by flowers,
Obstructed by mists and screened by clouds,
When night is deep and people are quiet,
With ocean promises and mountain covenants—
Then, at that time,
In romantic and happy celebration,
With a future like a strip of brocade,
With our love wonderfully fulfilled,
Spring will blossom forth in our painted hall.

---

[8] There is a pun here. There are only four stars visible in the Dipper, which is partly obscured by clouds. But the word for star, *xing*, is also a measure word for a unit of 2.5 *fen*. Since ten *fen* (*shifen*) is also a Chinese idiom for 100 percent, "four-starred" can also be construed to mean 100 percent.

"Coda" [(Student sings:)]
The happiness of that day has now been fixed:
A single poem is clear evidence.
Never again will I seek in dreams the blue palace gates
But only wait beneath the peach flower tree.

(He leaves.)

The Old Lady and Oriole Perform the Mass

Act 4

(Bald one leads Dharma Wit onstage and speaks:) We begin our ceremony today on the fifteenth day of the second month. Monks, shake your dharma instruments![1] I've already invited the madam and the young miss to come burn incense, but I'll ask Student Zhang to burn his incense first before the madam appears. In case the madam should ask, I'll just say he is a relative of this poor monk. (Male lead enters and speaks:) Today is the fifteenth of the second month. The monks have invited me to go and burn incense, so I might as well go.

[*Shuangdiao* mode:] "Xinshui ling" (Student sings:)
The wheel of the moon is high above the hall of the Brahma king;
Auspicious mists encage the azure tiles.
The incense smoke forms a canopy of clouds;
The chanted incantations swell into ocean billows.
The shadows of the pennants toss and flutter,
And all of the temple patrons are here.

"Zhuma ting" (Student sings:)
Dharma drums and bronze clappers—
Spring thunder of the second month echoes in the corner of the hall;
The sound of bells and the invocation of Buddha—
A rainstorm from the blue sprinkles the branch tips of the pine.

---

[1] I.e., the various musical instruments and other paraphernalia used in Buddhist rituals.

144

At noble gates no old monk is permitted to knock,[2]
Because outside the gauze window Crimson would surely report.
My hungering eyes, suffering from love-longing,
Will look their fill when she appears.

(Male lead acts out greeting bald one. Bald one speaks:) Sir, burn your incense now, and if the madam should ask, just say you are my relative. (Male lead acts out burning his incense.) 54a

"Chenzui dongfeng" (Student sings:)
I only pray that all those now alive enjoy a ripe old age in this world
And that all those who have passed away will roam freely in heaven.
On behalf of the souls of my great- and grand- and father,
I venerate the three jewels: Buddha, dharma, and sangha.
While I burn this fine incense, I pray in secret:
All I want is for Crimson not to be so mean,
For the madam not to be so cross,
And for the dog not to be so vicious.[3]

[(Student speaks:)] O Buddha,

[(Student sings:)]
Bring our secret trysts and rendezvous to completion soon!

(Old lady, leading female lead, enters and speaks:) The abbot has invited us to burn incense. Missy, let's go. (Male lead acts out seeing her and, addressing Dharma Wit, speaks:) Because of your sincerity, a divine sylph has descended to this world. (Dharma Wit speaks:) He's at it a second time!

"Yan'er luo" (Student sings:)
I'd have said a jadelike heavenly sylph had left the azure empyrean,
But all along it was this seed of happiness who has come for the pure mass.
How can my body that is full of grief and full of sickness
Stand a face that can topple cities and topple states?

"Desheng ling" (Student sings:) 54b
It is just as if her sandalwood mouth were a dot of cherry,
As if her powdered nose were a tilt of rose quartz,

---

[2] We take this to be a double entendre. It means, of course, that no males may approach the Cui household; but it surely also refers to the image of penises that monks' bald heads evoke and to a story about the poet Jia Dao (779–843), who could not decide whether to use the line "The monk knocks at the moonlit gate" or "The monk pushes the moonlit gate" in one of his poems. This also explains the pun on "gauze window" and "Crimson [i.e., red] would surely report [i.e., leave telltale signs]" in the next line.

[3] A general allusion to the dogs that guarded family compounds and whose barking impeded illicit lovers' trysts.

Her face a pale white pear blossom,
Her waist a lithe and supple willow
Bewitching, bewitching,
Her face is winsomeness on winsomeness;
Graceful, graceful,
The whole bit is lovely.

(Bald one speaks:) Dare this poor monk say a single word to you, madam? I have a relative, a budding scholar full of learning. After his parents died, he had no way to pay them back, and so he has asked me if he might take part in this offering and make a belated sacrifice to his parents. This poor monk agreed to it, but I am afraid that you may take me to task over it. (Old lady speaks:) Your relatives are mine, abbot. Please introduce him to me. (Male lead makes obeisance. Old lady speaks. Seeing female lead, monks act out various comic routines.)[4]

55a   "Qiao pai'er" (Student sings:) The grand master is aged,
But on his dharma seat he stares at her fixedly.
The noted instructors are stupefied;
They drum Dharma Wit's head instead of their bronze chimes.

"Tianshui ling" (Students sings:)
The old ones and the young ones,
The boorish and the clever—
All are turned topsy-turvy
And make a greater ruckus than on Prime Eve.[5]
That sexy one—she is afraid others might catch on,
And so when she looks, it's just a glance stolen with teary eyes.

"Zhegui ling" (Student sings:)
It makes me wild and crazy;
My itching heart cannot be scratched.
Her weeping is like the warbling of an oriole in tall trees;
Her teardrops are like dew falling on flower tips.
That grand master is hard to copy,
Covering up with a face of compassion.
The monks who strike the cymbals are sorely vexed;
The acolytes who keep the incense going simmer inside.
The lamps' reflections shimmer in the wind;
The haze of incense wafts like clouds.

---

[4] These were probably standard farce interludes of monks besotted with lust and unable to perform their ritual duties correctly. There is a vivid rendition of the scene in Dong Jieyuan's all-keys-and-modes version; see Dong, *Master Tung's Western Chamber Romance*, 37–42.

[5] The carnivalesque celebrations of the first night of the full moon in the new year on the fifteenth of the first month, accompanied by drink, lanterns, music, and somewhat lascivious and riotous festivities.

Greedily watching Oriole—
The lamps die out, the incense disappears.

(Bald one speaks:) The wind has blown the lamp out. (Male lead speaks:) I'll light   55b
the lamps and burn incense! (Female lead says to Crimson:) That student has been
busy the whole night.

"Jinshang hua" (Female lead sings:)
A dashing appearance,
A youth of greening spring,
An inner nature perceptive and quick,
A talent and learning to cap the age.
Twisting and turning his body in a hundred posturings,
Right in front of us he runs back and forth to show off his wit and good looks.

(Crimson speaks:) I'll take a guess that that fellow—

"Reprise" [(Crimson sings:)]
Now at dusk,
Then in broad daylight,
And then when he blabbered outside the window,
And when night came, just getting to sleep in his study—
It was a million heavy sighs: he couldn't make it through to dawn.

(Student speaks:) Boy, that girl is really paying attention to me!   *crimson or*
                                                                      oriole?

"Biyu xiao" (Student sings:)
My emotions drawn to the tips of my brows—
You know my heart's threads.
What sorrow has seeded now sprouts in the heart—
I can guess her loving thoughts.
Oh, how vexing!
Clickety-clickety-clack clap the cloud clappers;
The practitioners cry out,
And the acolytes blow the pipes.
Don't wrest away my love![6]

(After bald one and monks do comic routines, various dharma instruments have   56a
been played, and abbot has shaken the bells and read out the sacrificial prayer,
they act out burning paper money Bald one speaks:) It has grown light. Would
you, madam, and the young lady please return to your residence? (Student
speaks:) Let's do it one more time! Oh, what am I to do with myself?

"Yuanyang sha" (Student sings:)
Better not to have a heart than to have one:

---

[6] I.e., they are bringing the ceremony to a close and are thereby making it impossible
for him to have any further chance of seeing Oriole.

"Those full of feeling are vexed by those without."[7]
I've been bustling around all night;
The moon sinks, the bells sound out, the cock cries:
True it is, "The jade person has gone back too hastily,"
This good affair is concluded too soon.
The ceremony finished, everyone disperses;
All return to their homes in the dark.
All befuddled, they've raised hell until dawn.

(They leave.)

The beauty and the poet are in the midst of greening spring;
  Meeting by moonlight, they desire to be married.
Unexpectedly, soldiers come to encircle Universal Salvation;
  Brokenhearted, who will rescue her from danger?

["Luosiniang shawei"][8]

A passionate beauty lacks karma, finds it hard to meet spring in the bridal chamber;
The interested young student lacks plans—can he withstand the Flying Tiger General?

VOLUME I OF THE DELUXE, COMPLETELY ILLUSTRATED, AND ANNOTATED STORY OF THE WESTERN WING

---

[7] This line is taken from a famous lyric by Su Shi (1037–1101). "Those without feelings" here refers not to Oriole but to the monks and acolytes who are concluding the ceremony and who, in great irony after their ribald display on seeing Oriole, are supposedly without human desire. Cf. the last line of the song "Biyu xiao" above.

[8] While this is not designated in the text as a "Luosiniang shawei," the first six characters of the two lines match the prescribed pattern for that song. We are puzzled by the second clauses of five characters each, but we assume on the basis of both the song's placement within the text and its obvious function that it is indeed the "Luosiniang" song.

56b

Student Zhang Promises the Old Lady He Will Repulse the Troops

VOLUME II OF THE DELUXE, COMPLETELY ILLUSTRATED, AND ANNOTATED STORY OF THE WESTERN WING

Icy Strings Spell Out Grief

Act 1

(Clown, costumed as Flying Tiger Sun, enters and opens:) I am surnamed Sun, named Biao, and called the Flying Tiger. At this moment Emperor Dezong has ascended the throne and all under heaven is in turmoil. Because the commander-in-chief, Ding Wenya, has lost control, I, Biao, guard the river bridge and lead some five thousand men and horse in plundering the good citizens of their valuables and goods. Recently I learned that the daughter of the former chancellor Cui Jue, Oriole, who has the looks to topple cities and states and the face of a Xi Shi[1] or Precious Consort Yang,[2] is now staying at the Temple of Universal Salvation. I've thought it over, and it seems that right now is just the time to exercise military might. When the commander-in-chief is not acting right, why should I alone be incorruptible? My troops listen to my orders: the men will all wear gags,[3] the horses will all have bits. We will march this very night to

---

[1] For Xi Shi, a beauty of the early fifth century B.C., see p. 65.

[2] For Yang Guifei, the young consort of the elderly emperor Xuanzong (r. 712–56), see pp. 65–66.

[3] These were wooden gags shaped like chopsticks with cords on either end that were tied behind the neck. It was a way to keep soldiers quiet while on march.

Hezhong Prefecture. If I can snatch Oriole for my wife, then all my life's desires will be fulfilled.

57b

(He leaves.)

❖❖❖

(Bald one enters in panic and speaks:) Who would have thought that Flying Tiger Sun would seal off the temple with his five thousand troops? They sound their gongs and beat their drums, shout out their battle cries and wave their battle flags, all to snatch away Missy Oriole for Sun Biao's wife. I dare not delay but must report to the madam now!

(He leaves.)

❖❖❖

(Old lady enters in panic and speaks:) What's to be done now? We'll go together to missy's sleeping chambers and discuss it there.[4]

([She] leaves.)

❖❖❖

(Together,[5] main female lead enters, leading Crimson, and speaks:) Since seeing Student Zhang, my spirit and soul have been set aflutter, my mind has been troubled, and I barely eat or drink. Already so brokenhearted by separation—how can I face this late spring weather? (She recites a poem:)

> Fine lines of verse, full of feeling, pitied the night moon;
> Fallen flowers, without a word, still resent the eastern wind.

58a

[*Xianlü* mode:] "Basheng Ganzhou" (Female lead sings:)
Listless, listless, growing ever thinner,
Already heartbroken, can I face the tatters of spring?
My gauze gown grows ever looser;
How many more dusky eves can I wile away?
The wind wafts up seal-script smoke,[6] the door curtain is left unfurled;
The rain beats the pear blossoms, the doors are securely locked.

---

[4] To repeat all of the information about Sun's encirclement here would lead to a considerably expanded scene onstage; other editions by later editors do actually repeat the information.

[5] The character *tong* in the stage directions seems superfluous here; other texts omit it. Since the preceding scene and this scene are supposed to take place at the same time, perhaps the word is meant to express simultaneous action.

[6] This may be a description of the design of the wafting smoke; but it may also refer to the incense burner itself, which was often grooved in the elaborate form of an ancient character. Incense, laid within the grooves and then burned, traced the form of the character in smoke and ash.

Without a word, I lean on the balustrade,
My gaze dying at roving clouds.

"Hunjiang long" (Female lead sings:)
Fallen flowers form battle arrays,
The wind tosses myriad specks—oh, how it saddens me.
Waking from a dream by the pond,
I bid spring adieu at the balustrade.
Powder of butterflies' wings delicately moistens snows of flying floss;
Mud for swallows' nests fragrantly teases dust of fallen flowers.
Tied to spring's heart, passions are short, willow withes are long;
Separated by flowers' shadows, he is far, but heaven's rim is near.[7]
Gone is the fragrance of the golden powder of the Six Dynasties,
Dwindled is the freshness of the spirit energy of the Three Chus.[8]

(Crimson speaks:) Sister, you're not feeling well. I will infuse your covers until   58b
they are, oh, so fragrant so that you may sleep a little.[9]

"You hulu" (Female lead sings:)
The halcyon-colored covers engender coldness and weigh down the embroi-
    dered mattress.
Don't infuse them with orchid musk,
For even if you infused them through and through with orchid musk,
I would still have to keep them warm alone.
Last night beautiful compositions from his brocade bag clearly seduced me;[10]
Today this person fit for the Jade Hall[11] is hard to approach.
All this time I sit, but unsteadily;
I sleep, but fitfully.

---

[7] As is the case with many songs in this drama, nearly all of these lines are either verbatim citations or close paraphrases of several poems and lyrics written on the theme of separation and love-longing. For a complete list of citations, see Wang Shifu, *Jiping jiaozhu Xixiang ji*, 48–49, 52–53.

[8] Despite the numbers, these do not appear to be specific references but are general allusions to the diminishment of beauty and energy that comes with age. There are vague associations between the Six Dynasties and ornate, decadent beauty and between the Three Chus and strong spiritual energy; but attempts to identify these allusions precisely have generally been failures, as Wang Jisi points out. See Wang Shifu, *Jiping jiaozhu Xixiang ji*, 53.

[9] I.e., the covers were infused with smoke from an incense burner; this was also a way to fumigate bedclothing.

[10] The poet Li He (791–819) would leave the house every day at dawn, riding a nag and followed by a servant boy with a brocade bag. When inspiration struck, Li He would write the verses down and throw them in the bag. At nightfall he would return home and work the verses into a finished poem.

[11] Jade Hall is a name that was given to the Hanlin Academy in the eleventh century. It became a standard metaphor in the dramatic tradition for men of talent and literary skill.

If I were to ascend a high place, I would still be suffering;[12]
Were I to walk around, I would still be depressed.
Each day I slumber in passion's hazy confusion.

"Tianxia le" (Female lead sings:)
O Crimson,
I can only lie facedown on this fine silken pillow and drowse:
Were I just to leave the doors of my apartment,
Like a shadow, you'd never leave my side.

59a   (Crimson speaks:) It has nothing to do with me! Madam ordered me to follow you around. (Female lead speaks:) My mother doesn't understand a thing. All this time she's been nothing but an obstacle to me.

(She sings:)
My little maid waits on me most diligently,
The madam ties me up most tightly·
"I'm so worried that my little girl will lose her honor!"

(Crimson speaks:) Sister, you have never been so listless and lackluster. Since you've seen that student, I sense an uneasiness in your heart—what do you do now?

"Nuozha ling" (Female lead sings:)
Normally, whenever I saw a stranger,
I would immediately scowl;
Whenever I saw a traveler,
I would instantly retreat.
But since seeing that man,
I have of a sudden wanted to get close.
Thinking about his poem of last night,
Using his earlier rhymes,
I responded with freshness and originality.

"Que ta zhi" (Female lead sings:)
He chanted the lines so evenly,
Recited the words so true;
His new poem that sang of the moon
Far surpassed the palindrome woven into brocade.[13]

---

[12] Traditionally, ascending to a high place is a prelude to writing poetry and a means to ease one's suffering by viewing nature. There are also overtones here of a famous Song poem that decries the fact that with each level of ascent there comes, paradoxically, a higher degree of sorrow.

[13] When, during the first half of the fourth century, Su Hui's husband Dou Tao was banished to Central Asia, she expressed her longing for him by weaving a palindrome of no less than 840 characters into a piece of brocade.

But who is willing to take the needle and draw the thread[14]
And transmit the utter devotion of this eastern neighbor?[15]

"Jisheng cao" (Female lead sings:)
Thinking of that lettered man of culture,
That enchanting man of elegance—
The fresh beauty of his face, the distinction of his bearing,
The warmth of his nature, the compliance of his feelings—
One cannot but recite his name, feel his stamp upon the heart.
He has studied so long that "his literary compositions blaze like a sky full of stars."
It was not in vain that "for ten years by the window no one asked of him."[16]

(Old lady and abbot enter together and act out knocking at her door. Crimson, after having looked, speaks:) Sister, the madam and the abbot are both outside the door. (After female lead has acted out greeting them, old lady speaks:) Do you know, my child, that at this moment Flying Tiger Sun has sealed off the temple gates with five thousand mutinous troops? He says that the kohl of your eyebrows frowns darkly, that your lotus face engenders spring, just like that city- and state-toppling Precious Consort Yang. He wants to snatch you away to become the lady of his lair! O child, what shall we do?

"Liuyao xu" (Female lead sings:)
Having heard what she says, my soul quits its husk
And leaves behind this body, doomed to destruction.
With the tips of my sleeves I wipe away the traces of my tears;
This has put me in such a place, I can neither go nor stay,
Have no gate by which to advance or retreat.
Where can I find someone close to help me escape this fix?
Orphan and widow, child and mother, we've nowhere to flee.
Truly, he who passed away first turned out to be the lucky one!
Within earshot, gongs and drums quake to the heavens,

---

[14] A conventional phrase for someone who acts as matchmaker.

[15] For the story of the eastern neighbor, see p. 67. Here, of course, the allusion to Song Yu's aloofness from the advances of his neighbor is meant to suggest the student's supposed aloofness from Oriole.

[16] Although taken from two different poems, these two lines are often cited in tandem as testimony to the brilliance of one unknown until he achieves success in the examinations:

> For ten years beneath the window, no one asked of him.
> Once he attained a name, he was known throughout the world.

and

> Peals of thunder for a thousand miles—so was the mandate driven.
> Starry constellations in the entire sky—so blazed his literary compositions.

The point is that Oriole sees his talent, so well hidden from everyone else.

Campaign dust clouds thicken as they spiral,
Showers of dust swirl in confusion.

"Reprise"
Those louts have heard a rumor on the wind,
Saying, "The kohl of her eyebrows frowns darkly,
And her lotus face engenders spring,
Just like a city- and state-toppling Precious Consort Yang."
Won't I be sending these three hundred monks to their deaths?
Half a myriad of mutinous troops
In half a second will cut them down like grass and root them out.[17]
For neither state nor dynasty have these louts trust or loyalty,
And they plunder the citizens at will.
Even this building, like a heavenly palace built, they will burn to the ground.
And though they have no Zhuge Liang,
60b   Still they will burn us out at Bowang.[18]

(Old lady speaks:) I am already sixty years old, and that's not young to die. But, child, what about you, who have yet to find a husband? (Female lead speaks:) I have a plan: give me up to that traitor as a wife. I hope that I can save my whole family (Old lady weeps and speaks:) Our family counts among it no man who ever committed a crime nor a single woman who ever remarried.[19] How can I bear to give you up to that traitor? Would that not defile our family record? (Bald one speaks:) Let's all go to the dharma hall. There, in both corridors, we will ask both monks and laymen if anyone has a good idea. We will discuss a solution together. (They all act out going to the dharma hall together. Old lady speaks:) What will we do, missy? (Female lead speaks:) It would be best to give me up to the enemy There are five advantages to that:

61a   "Houting hua" (Female lead sings:)
First, it avoids destroying my mother;
Second, it avoids turning these halls to ashen embers;
Third, the monks will be left alone and kept secure;
Fourth, my late father's coffin will be safe and sound;
And fifth, even though Happy is not grown up—

(Happy speaks:) Why am I so unimportant?

[(Female lead sings:)]
He is the posterity of the Cui family.
Should I, Oriole, out of consideration for my body alone,

---

[17] Wang Jisi interprets these lines differently, taking them as a concrete result of the expression "city- and state-toppling beauty", see p. 67 n. 44.

[18] A reference to a tale in the story cycle of the Three Kingdoms in which the sage Zhuge Liang defeats the superior forces of Xiahou Dun by setting fire to his encampment at Bowang.

Not gladly follow those mutinous troops,
Then all the monks will be splattered with blood,
The monastery will be destroyed by fire,
And my father's corpse will turn into fine dust!
Thus, any kinship with my beloved younger brother would be cut off,
And all my compassionate mother's grace would be hacked away.

"Liuye'er" (Female lead sings:)
From our whole family not an infant would be left—
And yet, to go with this army would also defile my family's reputation.
Better for me to seek my own end in a noose of white silk:
If you give up my corpse to those traitors,
It will surely keep harm at a distance and my body intact.

"Qing ge'er" (Female lead sings:)
O Mother, it will all turn out to be Oriole's sin;
It will be hard to explain it to an outsider in a single word.
O Mother, don't just cling to this body of Oriole's.

[(Female lead speaks:)] I have another plan, Mother.

(She sings:)
Whosoever it may be—
If he establishes his meritorious service
And slays or drives away those traitorous troops
And sweeps away their malignant aura,
Then let us give as dowry our family reputation,
And with that brave I will gladly
Unite in wedlock,
As did the states of Qin and Jin.[20]

(Old lady speaks:) That plan is a little better. Even though not a proper and exact match in status, it is still better than falling into the hands of traitors. Abbot, call out in the dharma hall, "Whosoever among the monks and laymen of either corridor has a plan to repulse the soldiers, the madam will send Oriole to him as wife—and throw in a dowry as well." (After monk has shouted and spoken, student enters, clapping his hands, and speaks:) I have a plan to turn the soldiers back. Why not ask me? (After [student] greets old lady, bald one speaks:) This is the same student who took part in that posthumous offering yesterday. (Old lady speaks:) Where lies your plan? (Student speaks:) "There is a brave man whenever there is great reward."[21] "If the rewards and punishments are clear, the plan is

61b

---

[19] There was a traditional objection against widows' remarrying in China, an objection especially pronounced after the rise of neo-Confucianism.
[20] On these two early northern states whose royal families frequently intermarried as a matter of state policy, see pp. 53–54.
[21] This is only the second line of a couplet; the first line reads, "There is a dead fish wherever there is scented bait."

62a   bound to succeed." (Female lead speaks in an aside:) I only hope that this student is the one who can drive them away (Old lady speaks:) I just promised the abbot a second ago that I would give Oriole as wife to anyone who could drive the traitorous soldiers away (Student speaks:) If it is really so, then let's not scare my wife anymore! Please go to your bedchamber. I myself have a plan to repulse the troops. (Old lady speaks:) Go on with Crimson, missy (Female lead speaks to Crimson:) How rare this student's good heart!

> "Zhuan sha" (Female lead sings:)
> All the monks flee for their own lives;
> Of all my relatives, who cares about us?
> This student, who knows me not at all, shows great concern for a perfect stranger.
> It is not just the pedantic discourse of a student;
> He'll keep "jade and rock from being burned together."[22]
> Even though he is no relative of mine,
> He takes pity that my life hangs in the balance.
> Whether the situation can be rescued or not
> Is temporarily in the hands of this budding talent.
> If you are truly capable of a "Rescript on Sending Out the Army"[23]
> And a "Letter to Scare the Barbarian"[24]—
> O Student Zhang—
> I only hope that you can wipe away five thousand men
> With the tip of your brush!

[(Oriole and Crimson leave.)]

62b   (Old lady speaks:) How is this going to be done? (Student speaks:) I have a plan. First I need to use the abbot. (Bald one speaks:) I can't fight! Please call out another, my budding talent. (The student speaks:) Don't be foolish! I don't want you to fight. But you go out and tell that rebel, "The madam really wants to deliver missy up to you, General. But she is still wearing mourning for her father and, alas, she has fainted out of alarm over the sounding gongs and beaten drums. If you want to become a bridegroom, you should lay down your armor, restrain your troops, and retreat the distance of one bowshot. Within a limit of three days her mourning will be completed; she will change her mourning garb for brightly colored clothing.[25] Then will missy be sent to you, General, with a dowry

---

[22] The rough equivalent of "throwing the baby out with the bath water"; that is, he will keep the bad and the good from suffering together.

[23] A memorial written by Zhuge Liang (181–234) after Liu Bei's death in 222 to persuade the new emperor of Shu-Han to carry on the battle his father had been engaged in.

[24] A letter that, in the tradition of drama and fiction, was dashed off by a drunken Li Bo but was so well written that it scared the unruly Koreans into submission.

[25] I.e., she will change into the bright red of a bridal gown.

thrown in. But if she is given up immediately, first, she will still be wearing mourning clothing, and second, she will be unlucky for you." Go tell him this. (Bald one speaks:) But after three days, then what? (Student speaks:) The plan follows.

63a

Title: Zhang Junrui smashes the rebel's plans;
        A wild monk gives vent to a murderous heart.

Name: Little Crimson invites a guest during the day;
        Oriole Cui listens to the zither at night.

Benevolent Perception and the Monks Fight Their Way Through to Pu Pass

Act 2

(Bald One faces a ghost door and shouts:) Would you, General, please come out and talk?[1] (Clown [as Flying Tiger Sun] enters, accompanied by soldiers, and speaks:) Send Oriole out quickly! (Bald one speaks:) Don't be angry, General. The madam has sent me here to talk to you. (He finishes reciting [a passage from] above.)[2] (Flying Tiger speaks:) Well, since it is like this, I'll give you three days' grace. If she's not delivered then, you'll die to the last man. Go and tell the madam that. Tell her to summon the nice, good-natured son-in-law that I am.

[(Flying Tiger leaves.)]

(Bald one speaks:) The troops have withdrawn. If she's not delivered up in three days, we're all dead. (Student speaks:) I have an old friend surnamed Du, named Que, who is called the White Horse General. He is now in charge of a hundred thousand men and is guarding Pu Pass. If a single letter goes forth to him, he will surely come rescue us: we are only forty-five *li*[3] from Pu Pass. But if I write the letter, who will I find to take it? (Bald one speaks:) If the White Horse General is willing to come, then what is there to fear from Flying Tiger Sun? We have an

---

[1] While this act is designated act 2 in the text, the assignment appears to be a later editorial decision: the acting is continuous, there is no scene break, and the characters have all remained onstage.

[2] I.e., the author doesn't want to repeat it in the text.

[3] A *li* is approximately one-third of an English mile.

acolyte here called Benevolent Perception, who wants only to drink and fight. If you try and make him go, he'll refuse; but if you can strike home with a few words, he will be willing to go. [(Student speaks:)] I have a letter to send to General Du. Who dares to go? Who dares to go? [(Benevolent Perception enters and speaks:)] I dare.

[*Zhenggong* mode:] "Duanzheng hao" (Benevolent sings:)
I do not recite the Lotus Sutra,
I do not practice the penitences of the emperor of Liang;[4]
I've thrown away the sangha hat,
Stripped off the monk's red robes.
A murderous heart has riled up my heroic gall;
A pair of hands has tightly grasped the black-dragon-tailed iron club.

"Gun xiuqiu" (Benevolent sings:)   64a
It is not that I am covetous,
Nor that I am daring;
But what do I know of sitting in meditation?
With bounding steps I'll slay straightaway out of the tiger's cave and dragon's
    pool.[5]
It is not that I am grabby,
Or that I keep things for myself;
But the vegetable-stuffed buns I've been eating these days
Are really tasteless.
No need to bake, deep fry, sauté, or roast those five thousand men—
The hot blood from their throats will slake my thirst for a time,
The raw hearts among their lungs and livers will temporarily stave off hunger.
What's so repugnant about that!

"Daodao ling" (Benevolent sings:)
That floating-granule soup with wide wheaten noodles[6]—
Let's add a little flavor to it.
Those sour yellow pickles and that rotten bean curd—
Don't mix them up to eat [but save them so that]
With ten thousand catties of black flour—no matter how moldy—
I can make a dumpling stuffing out of those five thousand men.
Don't delay me, for heaven's sake;

---

[4] The Lotus Sutra was and is extremely popular in the secular world. There are numerous translations of the text available in a variety of Western languages. The penitences he mentions were written by the Martial Emperor of the Liang dynasty (Wudi, r. 502–49), a devoted follower of Buddhism. These two texts represent what were, in the popular mind, two of the major devotional scriptures of Buddhism.

[5] I.e., out of dangerous situations.

[6] Wang Jisi suggests that this may be a soup into which a dough mixture is extruded through a sieve. See Wang Shifu, *Jiping jiaozhu Xixiang ji*, 63.

64b

Don't delay me, for heaven's sake.

The leftover meat I'll pickle with dark salt.[7]

(Bald one speaks:) Student Zhang orders you to take a letter to Pu Pass. Do you dare to go?

"Tang xiucai" (Benevolent sings:)

Why do you ask if I dare or not?

Here I inform the grand master: do you use me or not?

The fame of the Flying Tiger General has spread everywhere south of the Dipper.[8]

But that lout is capable only of lust and desire, competent only in avarice and greed.

He's not worth a thing.

(Student speaks:) You are one who has left your family—why don't you read the scriptures and practice the penitences? How come you fight?

"Gun xiuqiu" (Benevolence sings:)

I am not competent to discuss the texts of the sutras,

Too lazy to participate in meditation sessions;

But the point of my prohibition's knife[9] has recently been tempered into steel,

And not a half of speck of dust[10] sullies my iron club.

As for the others—the monks are no monks,

The laymen no laymen,

The women no women,

The men no men.

They are capable only of stuffing themselves on vegetarian fare

And lolling about in their cells.

What do they care that a monastery like the Tushita Heaven will be burned to nothing?

That one who is skilled at civil affairs and capable of military action is a thousand miles away,

65a

So here it all depends on this single letter that will save the oppressed and rescue the endangered—

I have the courage and will not be shamed!

---

[7] A rock salt that was distilled from brackish freshwater lakes, possibly one that was produced in the area now known as Mongolia.

[8] I.e., throughout the known world: the Dipper is at the northern pole of the stellar atlas.

[9] Actually, a "knife of cutting off" or a "knife of renunciation." It was carried by monks as a way of reminding them of the prohibitions of their chosen life. It was also used to cut out the material for their robes—a gesture, we suppose, that symbolizes cutting oneself off from the desires and human pleasures that mark life in the secular world.

[10] A reference to "red dust," a commonly used metaphor for the "dusty world of human desires."

(Student speaks:) What if they won't let you pass? (Bald one [i.e., Benevolent] speaks:) If they won't let me through, rest easy

"Bai hezi" (Benevolent sings:)
I'll have several small acolytes hold aloft pennants and Buddha parasols,
Some sturdy practitioners shoulder quarterstaves and pitchforks.
You line up the foot of the array and keep the monks orderly,
While I pierce through the enemy troops like a nail!

"Two"   65b
Those far off, with giant steps, I will sweep away with my iron cudgel;
Those nearby, with a flick of the wrist, I will cut down with my prohibition's
   knife.
The small ones—I'll pull them up and give them a toe kick!
The big ones—I'll squash them down and trample their skulls!

"Three"
With a single angry stare, roaring and crashing, I'll roil the breakers in the
   ocean;
With a single wave of the hand, thundering and smashing, I'll shake the
   cliffs in the mountains.
My feet will trample until the axis of the earth trembles, rattling apart;
My hand will pull until the gate of heaven collapses, splitting asunder!

"Four"
I've always been mean and bad;
I've never been flustered or shaken in my whole life.
I've forged myself into a tireless natural courage;
I have always been number one at halving nails and cutting iron[11]—
Not like those grass-teasing flower-fiddlers[12] who never think twice.
My mean nature gives everyone the chills.
Disregarding my own life, I raise my knife and wield my sword;
Fearing me even more, they rein in their horses and halt their chariots.

"Five"
I've always bullied the strong but feared the weak,
Eaten the bitter but never the sweet.
Don't gamble all just because of a marriage—
If General Du won't make buckler and spear retreat,
Then you, Laureate Zhang, will carry the wind and moon in vain!
I fooled you with insincere words just now![13]

---

[11] These are the names of two "strongman" skits in the variety show repertoire of the Song and Yuan.
[12] I.e., romantic souls who lust after sex.
[13] Wang Jide reads these lines a bit differently. He suggests that this is the monk warning Student Zhang that he had better be sincere in his request to bring General Du's armies to the rescue:

If by chance a mistake is made,
Then great indeed the embarrassment and shame!

(Bald one [i.e., Benevolent] speaks:) Give me the letter; you wait for an answer.

66a   "Coda"
You support my might by beating some drums,
Rely on Buddha's power, shout out a battle cry.
Under the embroidered flags far away you'll see brave me—
Me, making those five thousand rebels piss in their pants.

[(He leaves.)]

(Student speaks:) Madam, you and the abbot rest easy now When this letter arrives, we'll have good news. We

Strain our eyes to watch for the banner of victory,
Prick up our ears to listen for good news.

Just watch:

When one letter reaches there, they will come from afar,
Five thousand brave soldiers will draw ever closer.

[(They leave.)]

❖❖❖

(Extra male role, costumed as General Du, enters leading his soldiers. Reciting a poem, he opens:)

Drying our clothes in the forest, we detest the weakness of the sun;
Washing our feet in the pond, we hate the stench of fish.
The original beauty is in the root of the flower: a noble's son.
A tiger's body is originally striped: the scion of generals and chancellors.[14]

If you are toying with me just to carry off the affair of the marriage, then I'll toy with you on this trip and deliver your insincere words to General Du and deceive you. I'll make it so that he won't come to your aid; all of your plans will have been made in mistake, and the marriage surely will not happen. Won't that be a great shame?

See Wang Shifu, *Huitu xin jiaozhu guben Xixiang ji,* 2.19b.

[14] The first couplet of this poem is constituted of lines conventionally declaimed by monks. They are most certainly meant as a satirical comment on the fact that we have been presented here on the one hand with the case of an army that does nothing but stand by and watch the situation degenerate, much in the way monks are expected to behave, and on the other hand with a monk who takes on a role rightfully belonging to a military savant.

I am surnamed Du, named Que, called Junshi. I hail from Western Luo. In my youth I studied the Confucian arts together with Junrui, but later I gave up a civil career in favor of a military one. That year I succeeded in the military examination and was appointed Westward Campaigning General; and I hold a regular appointment as grand marshal of the army. Leading a hundred thousand troops, I guard Pu Pass. Someone from Hezhong learned that my brother, Junrui, was staying at the Temple of Universal Salvation. Junrui did not come see me, so I sent someone to invite him. Still he was not willing to come. I wonder why? I've just heard too that Ding Wenya has lost control of his troops and refuses to abide by the laws of our dynasty, plundering the common folk. But since I do not know what is rumor and what is truth, I dare not rashly raise my army yet. As Master Sun said, "Generally, as for the method of using troops: when a general receives an order from his lord, he unites his armies and assembles his hosts. Do not bivouac in low-lying territory. Join battle in well-roaded territory Do not tarry in isolated territory Lay plots in surrounded territory Battle only in territory where you will have no alternative. Some roads should not be followed. Some armies should not be struck. Some walled cities should not be attacked. Some territories should not be fought over. Some orders of the lord should not be taken. Those generals thoroughly acquainted with the advantages of the nine mutations, therefore, are those who know how to use their troops. To order troops without knowing the techniques of the nine mutations—even though one knows the five benefits, one will not be able to use personnel properly."[15] The reason I have not yet advanced my troops to subdue the rebels is, I do not know the lay of the land.[16] Yesterday I sent out spies, but they have yet to report back. Today I will go to my headquarters tent and see what intelligence there is to be communicated. (Foot soldiers come on, leading the monk Benevolent Perception, and open. Benevolent speaks:) It has taken me a day to get to Pu Pass from the Temple of Universal Salvation. I'm on my way to see General Du. (Foot soldiers report. General speaks:) Send him over here. (Bald one [i.e., Benevolent] finishes his formal greetings. Bald one speaks:) This poor monk is from the Temple of Universal Salvation. Flying Tiger Sun has just mutinied and sealed off our temple with five thousand rebellious troops. He wants to abduct the daughter of the late chancellor Cui to become his wife. The roving scholar Zhang Junrui has sent a letter which he has asked me deliver to Your Honor. He wants to ask you, General, to relieve this great distress. (General speaks:) Give me the letter. (Benevolent hands the letter over to him. General breaks open the letter and reads out loud:)

I, Gong, bow my head and make obeisance twice:

---

[15] A quote from the eighth chapter of the *Sunzi bingfa* (The strategy of soldiery by Master Sun), entitled "Jiubian," or "The Nine Mutations."

[16] An allusion to the line that follows the *Sunzi* passage he has just cited: "A general who is not familiar with the nine mutations, even though he knows the lay of the land, cannot obtain its full benefit."

Under the banner of my sworn brother, General and Grand Marshal.

Since blessed to part from you, him of rhinoceros emblem,[17] in the city of Luo, I have long been separated from knowledge of your actual condition, and so it has been for years and months. My partiality to your lofty virtue is as if engraved on my heart. I recall that in the past our beds were side by side as

we weathered storms together. Now I sigh over our present state, each at an edge of heaven. The feelings of a wanderer are born and reborn in my soul, and the sorrows of separation find no comfort in my thoughts while I am on horseback. I consider both my poverty, the ten years of eating naught but wild plants, and how I've wandered into difficulties in a strange district. And I envy how you, in mighty guidance of a million fierce troops, securely settle our borders. And so I know that you, mighty as a tiger, enjoy our emperor's emolument and gaze upon our emperor's face. Such great virtue surpasses the ordinary This makes me, this fractious one, desire to see your noble face, to gaze upon your noble missive, and thus to allow my heart to be soothed.

I dare to report that since leaving home I have wanted to visit your headquarters and lay out for you my affairs during our many years of separation. But, alas, when I reached the Temple of Universal Salvation in Hezhong Prefecture, I was suddenly beset with the "anxieties of picking firewood"[18] and was not yet able to come to you. Unexpectedly, a rebel general, Flying Tiger Sun, led a force of five thousand in a desire to abduct the daughter of the former chancellor Cui. Truly all is in urgent disorder, and my own fate also lies in perilous balance here. If by chance the court should learn of this, where would the guilt fall?

If you, General, sit and watch with no thought of rescue and consciously let these rebel troops go berserk, you will lose defense of the borders completely If you, General, would not cast aside the feelings of old friendship but

would bring a battalion of troops into the field, above you would repay the grace of the emperor, below you would rescue the distress of the black-haired citizens; and you would even cause the former chancellor, although he resides in the nine springs,[19] not to forget the General's virtue. I beseech you, General, to look with tigerlike stare at this letter I have dispatched so that I, your younger brother, can gaze with craned neck for the coming banners.

I am coarse and disrespectful and cannot overcome the shame I feel. I beseech your noble attention to this and only this. Zhang Gong makes obeisance twice.

Written on the sixteenth day of the second month.

---

[17] The head of a rhinoceros was a conventional emblem for military commanders. It is also a conventional synecdoche for all of a general's insignia.

[18] The phrase "too busy even to pick up firewood" is derived from the *Mencius*; it is simply a polite way of saying that troubles have kept him from writing.

[19] I.e., the world of the dead.

(General speaks:) Well, if it is really so, monk, go on ahead, and I will follow
(Benevolent Perception speaks:) You must come as quickly as possible,
General.

"Shanghua shi" (Benevolent sings:)[20]
That lout plunders the black-haired citizens, lacks virtuous actions;
You, General, guard the frontier regions and are rich in schemes and plans.
His heaven-reaching crimes are of a hundred thousand kinds:
If you don't control him, General,
But allow that marauder to give rein to his lawlessness,

"Reprise"
Then you will just be sitting idly by and waiting for the court's decision and
    deceiving the emperor.
But if you sweep away the malignant aura and make the hundred surnames
    happy,
Buckler and sword will cease,
Your great merit will be complete;
Songs and ditties will flow everywhere,
And your renown will be carried to the golden throne.

(General speaks:) Even though there is no imperial directive to issue soldiers   68b
forth, when a general is wielding field command, "there are some lord's orders
that are not accepted." My troops, listen to my orders! Quickly assemble five
thousand men and horses—the men will all wear gags, the horses will all have
bits—and under the stars we will march overnight to the Temple of Universal
Salvation in Hezhong Prefecture to rescue Student Zhang.

[(They all leave.)]

❖❖❖

([Flying Tiger Sun] enters, leading his foot soldiers, and opens.[21] General [Du
Que] leads his foot soldiers on. Riding a bamboo horse, he arrays his squadrons,
captures and binds [Flying Tiger Sun], and [all] leave.)

❖❖❖

(Old lady and abbot enter with Student Zhang. She speaks:) The letter was sent
out two days ago, and we still have no reply. (Student speaks:) Outside the

---

[20] Most other editions delete this short song suite, which is conventionally used for
scenes that, in later editorial convention, are marked as *xiezi*, "demi-acts" or "wedges."
See p. 44 and play I, act 1, n. 2.
[21] This scene was most certainly a pantomime performance of military arts. There must
also have been a declamation by Flying Tiger Sun in which he reintroduces himself and
reports the arrival of Du Que's army.

temple gates they shout battle cries and wave battle flags. Surely my brother has come with his troops. (After student has greeted general, he leads old lady to pay respects [to general]. General speaks:) I, Du Que, have failed in my protection, and so you, madam, have been alarmed. Please do not censure me for this. (After student has paid his respects to general, [he speaks:]) Since I have been parted from your noble visage, I have had no chance to listen to your advice. Now, seeing you today is like seeing the sun break through the clouds. (Old lady speaks:) It is as if our lives, mother's and daughter's, have been bestowed by you, General. How can we repay that? (General speaks:) It's nothing—just something in the line of duty Can I ask, brother, why you didn't come to my headquarters? (Student speaks:) I wanted to come; but I was suddenly struck with a minor illness and could not move, so I failed in my proper respects. Now, seeing that the madam was in distress—and she said that she would give her daughter in marriage to whoever could make the rebels withdraw—I made bold to write that letter and ask you, brother, to come. (General speaks:) How about this marriage? (The widow speaks:) How about a meal? (General speaks:) That's not needed. There are still some small groups of rebels at large, and I'll be off to apprehend them. Then will I return to visit you, my brother. Attendants, go and behead Flying Tiger Sun. (He recites a poem:)

> A brave general at this moment steps forward;[22]
> The mutinous rebels at this place meet their end.

(After they have taken the rebel, [general speaks]:) I originally wanted to behead you as a warning to the multitude, and only afterward send in a memorial. But since Ding Wenya has committed the crime of failing in his control, I am afraid that there may be those who might want to but have not yet rebelled. I will simply give the leaders a hundred strokes each; let all the others go back to their old encampments. (After Flying Tiger Sun has expressed his thanks, he leaves. After general goes back to the temple, general speaks:) The marriage to Student Zhang cannot be forgotten, since he was the one who devised the plan for repulsing the troops. Madam, you promised him face-to-face that the marriage would take place. If you do not go back on your word, then a chaste maiden will be married to a fine gentleman. (Old lady speaks:) I am afraid that my daughter is not good enough for Junrui. ([She] continues speaking:) I would like to ask you, General, to a feast. (General speaks:) I won't eat; I'm going back to the camp. I'll come another day for the wedding festivities. (Student speaks:) I don't dare delay you, brother, from your responsibilities. ([Student, old lady, and abbot] leave.) (General [speaks]:) Back to Pu Pass! (He recites:)

> As the horses leave Universal Salvation, the beat is tapped on golden stirrups;
> As the men march toward Pu Pass, they sing songs of victory.

> [(General and troops leave.)]

---

[22] We emend *jiangpan* (about to revolt) to *jiangjun* (general).

The Madam Sets Out a Banquet to Repay Student Zhang

Act 3

(Old lady enters and speaks.)[1] ([Abbot and student enter.] Old lady speaks:) Never will I dare forget the help and kindness that the two of you showed us. ([She] speaks again:) Student Zhang, don't stay in the monastery anymore. Just have your servant look after the horse there. You should stay in the study at our place. I have already cleaned it up, so move in immediately. Tomorrow I'll prepare a hasty dinner and have Crimson come tell you when it's ready. Be sure to come, because we'll have something to talk about.

(She leaves.)

(Student speaks:) This affair all depends on you, abbot. I don't know yet when the wedding will be. (Abbot speaks:) It has already been decided that Oriole will marry you, sir. ([He] recites:)

Because the war fires appeared,
A heart of rain and clouds was aroused.

(Student speaks:) I'll pack my bags and move into the flower garden.

[(They leave.)]

❖❖❖

---

[1] No text is provided. We surmise here a small monologue in which the old lady voices her doubts about the promise of marriage.

167

(Old lady enters and speaks:) I've prepared a small repast today and invited only Student Zhang so that I can repay him for his labors. I've told Crimson to hurry to the study and summon him and to make sure that he comes right away He can make no excuses.

[(She leaves.)]

(Student enters and speaks:) The madam told me last night that she would have Crimson summon me; where is she? I'm all dressed up and waiting for her. I've used up two bars of soap and been through two buckets of water; I've brushed my raven's-gauze hat until it glitters and glows. Where is Crimson? (Crimson enters and speaks:) The madam has sent me to summon Student Zhang. Come to think of it, if it hadn't been for Student Zhang's clever plan, none of us would have escaped with our lives.

higher opinion of him

7ob   [*Zhonglü* mode:] "Fendie'er" (Crimson sings:)
Five thousand rebel troops—
Like rolling up floating clouds, swept away in a moment's time.
Our whole household escaped from certain death.
Carefree, we arrange the delicacies of the mountains,
Set out the finest things from land and sea.
Zhang Junrui, it is right that we honor you.
What you wanted on an earlier day never came to pass;
Who would have thought that a single letter
Would turn into your engagement contract?

"Zui chunfeng" (Student sings:)
Today in the eastern apartment a tortoiseshell mat is spread:
That's much better than waiting by moonlight in the western wing.
Now there will be someone to warm my thin blanket and single pillow;
Nevermore will they be cold,
Cold.
I'll enjoy to the limit rich incense from the precious tripod,
The gentle breeze through embroidered curtains,
And the isolated quiet at the window of green.

(Male lead speaks:) Here she is!

"Tuo bushan" (Student sings:)
Can someone be walking in this out-of-the-way place?
Dotting the dark moss, the white dew is cold, cold.
Someone is coughing outside the window

(Student speaks:) Who is it? [(Crimson speaks:)] It's me, it's me. (Crimson acts out knocking at the door.)

([Student] sings:)
Parting her scarlet lips, she answers quickly.

(Student speaks:) Welcome, young lady

"Xiao Liangzhou" (Crimson sings:)
I have only to see him welcome me so politely with hands folded,
And I say my "Myriad blessings, master."
His raven's-gauze hat dazzles one's vision,
His white gown is immaculate,
His horn-decorated belt is a proud yellow leather strap.

"Reprise" (Crimson sings:)
His gown and cap are spick-and-span, his face is handsome:
He's sure to arouse our Oriole.
On account of his exterior appearance
And because of his inner talents,
I, who have always had a hard heart,
Am smitten as soon as I see him.

(Student speaks:) "Since they have come, give them repose."[2] Please come in the study and talk a bit. My young lady, why have you come here? (Crimson speaks:) I bear the strict mandate of the madam to invite you, sir, to have a few cups at a small repast. May you not refuse. (Student speaks:) Let's go! Let's go! Will sister Oriole be at the feast?

"Shang xiaolou" (Crimson sings:)
The word "invite" was barely uttered,
When the word "go" came hurriedly in response.
In front of me, he
Already calls Oriole "sister,"[3]
And his yes, yes, yesses come one after another.
The budding scholar hears the word "invite,"
And heeds it as the strictest order of a general
And, along with the Gods of his Five Innards, wants to follow whip and spur.[4]

[(Student speaks:) What's today's banquet really for?][5]

---

[2] *Analects*, 14.12, from a passage that is both ironic and appropriate to the current situation of the student: "So, it is like this: if distant people are not submissive, then perfect the virtue of your civilized accomplishments in order to make them come. Once they have come, then make them secure."

[3] This is a fine bit of foreshadowing. The terms "brother" and "sister" can be used by lovers as terms of intimacy; but they can also be used to establish familial relationships between individuals who are related by neither blood nor marriage. Such alliances placed the young men and women involved beyond the boundaries of acceptable marriage.

[4] The respective gods of the heart, liver, lungs, gall, and kidneys. In drama the term often has the meaning of a hungry or rumbling stomach.

[5] In a rare mistake, this line has been totally dropped from our text. We restore it as an essential part of the text on the basis of other editions.

"Reprise" [(Crimson sings:)]
First, to assuage those who were frightened;
Second, to express her thanks:
She's not inviting the neighborhood,

72a She's not gathering relatives and friends,
She's not accepting presents,
She's avoiding the monks,
But she invites you, brother,
And Oriole to become a couple.

(Student speaks:) Well, then, I am happy.

[(Crimson sings:)]
Just see: he's as happy as can be,
Strictly obeying orders.

(Student speaks:) I don't have a mirror with me on my travels; can you give me the once-over, missy? How do I look?

"Manting fang" (Crimson sings:)
Back and forth he watches his own shadow—
What a pedantic scholar!
What a foolish sourpuss!
He has spent his time slicking up his pate,
Brushing flies off all the time—
Oily and glistening, it dazzles one's eyes;
Sour and slick, it stings until one's teeth ache.

(Student speaks:) What has the madam put out for me?

([Crimson] sings:)
The meal has already been set:
She has rinsed off some pints of rice gone bad in the warehouse
And fried up seven or eight bowls of wilted vegetables.[6]

72b (Student speaks:) When I ponder it, I realize that after I saw that young lady in the temple, it never crossed my mind that I'd be able to bring off the marriage that I will today. It must have been determined in an earlier life. (Crimson speaks:) A marriage is not made by human effort; it is the will of heaven alone.

"Kuaihuo san" (Student sings:)
For humans, "if one thing is fine,
All things are fine;

---

[6] This is not the meal that has really been prepared, but it is a fine bit of sarcasm about the student's poor state. See pp. 74–75.

If one thing doesn't turn out,
Then nothing turns out."[7]
In the world, plants are actually without feeling.

(Male lead speaks:) And yet the earth produces trees with intertwining branches, and the waters give birth to double-headed lotuses.

([Student] sings:)
Yet still they come together!

"Chao tianzi" (Crimson sings:)
It's not just this student alone
But all young men of few years
Who've only learned to suffer love sickness;
[And young girls] of intelligent nature by virtue of birth,
Dressed up in immaculate white—
Night after night they have to be all alone,
Our poet passionate,
Our beauty fickle.
Oh, aren't people's fates thwarted?

(Student speaks:) Can your missy really be trusted?

(Crimson sings:)
Who has no trust?
Who has no sincerity?
You two will testify to that tonight.

(Crimson speaks:) I'll give you some good advice:

"Sibian jing" (Crimson sings:)
As for your happy union tonight,
How could our delicate Oriole
Have had any experience?
You must be tender and gentle
When you twine your mandarin-duck necks below the lamp.
After you've looked carefully at your wretch,
You'll die of such happiness that it won't come off clean.[8]

sounds like they will already be consummating

73a

(Student speaks:) Go on ahead, missy I'll come after cleaning up the study. What are the sights there?

---

[7] A common aphorism in Song and Yuan vernacular texts.

[8] This line, *haosha ren wu ganjing*, is difficult to translate. Normally, *haosha* means something that overcomes one by its beauty or accommodation: it is often used to make fun of a pair of lovers overcome by pleasure during their tryst. *Wu ganjing* means never to cease or never be let off the hook. But its denotative sense, "it won't be clean," certainly carries the implication that Zhang will be happy to find out that Oriole is a virgin.

"Shua hai'er" (Crimson sings:)
Could it be for us that "fallen red fills the ground, the rouge has turned cold"?
Don't miss this auspicious time and bewitching scenery
The madam did not send me to wile away the time—
Please, master, don't find an excuse to linger here.
At our place are waiting for you golden bed hangings filigreed with mandarin
     ducks and the night moon,
Pliant jade screens of peacocks in the spring breeze.
For music is played the melody "Union of Happiness"
There will be phoenix flutes and ivory clappers,
Brocade zithers and simurgh mouth organs.

73b   "Fourth from Coda" (Crimson sings:)
Betrothal presents surely aren't important;
This marriage has succeeded of its own.
The "banquet with your new bride"[9] is all set:
You clearly have become the guest who straddles the phoenix and rides the
     simurgh.
Tonight I will lie and watch the Herdboy and Weaving Girl.[10]
Don't fret:
It won't take half a length of your red thread[11]
To bring off a whole life's prospects.

(Students speaks:) Drifting about with books and sword, I have nothing to give as
engagement presents. What'll I do?

74a   "Third from Coda" (Crimson sings:)
We'll rely on your merit in extinguishing the bandits,
Your ability in recommending a general.
These two meritorious successes are like the red engagement gifts.
Why is our Oriole's heart full of compliance?
Simply because the million soldiers in Junrui's breast
Showed off the refulgence of his literary style!
You'll enjoy to the full a circle of pearls, a garland of halcyon feathers,
And wind up for good your yellowed scrolls and blue lamps.[12]

---

[9] A phrase from *The Book of Poetry*, ode 35, entitled "Gufeng" (Valley winds). It has an ironic double meaning here. While the line is often used alone and shorn of context, most readers would be able to finish the verse themselves: "Like an elder brother, like a younger brother, [you will be intimate]." Crimson, of course, is as oblivious to what the madam has in store for Zhang as the student is himself. See play II, act 3, n. 3.

[10] For the legend of the Herdboy and Weaving Girl and their special use in the play, see pp. 54–55.

[11] According to a classical tale of the ninth century, lovers destined to marry each other were tied together with a red thread by the Old Man under the Moon.

[12] I.e., the ancient texts that he reads at night under a lonely lamp as he prepares for the examinations.

"Second from Coda" (Crimson sings:)
Madam is all by herself;
You have no companions, brother.
Since she despises the bustle and hubbub, she seeks solitude and stillness.

(Student speaks:) What other guests are there?

([Crimson] sings:)
She has asked only you, a helpful and righteous traveler at leisure,
And avoids them, the meddlesome monks beneath the window
The order of the madam
Was not to let you beg off:
Please come immediately with me.

(Student speaks:) Go on ahead. I'll come right after you.

"Coda"
Don't be so shy, master,
The madam is waiting with all her heart.
The proverb says, "Respectfulness is not as good as obedience."
Don't make me come to summon you again.

(She leaves.)

(Student speaks:) Crimson is gone. I'll close the doors of my study. When I get to the madam's place, she'll say, "Student Zhang, you're here. Have a few cups and go on into the bedroom to consummate your union with Oriole." And when I get into the bedroom, I'll take off her belt, and slip off her gown, turn the simurgh upside down, turn the phoenix around, share with her the joy of fish in water, and fulfill our wish of being in flight together. I'll watch her cloudy locks droop low, her starry eyes glaze over. The blankets will heave in halcyon waves, her stockings will tattoo mandarin ducks.[13] And do you know if she will escape with her life or not? Just watch how it unravels in the next installment.[14] (He continues to speak:) Oh, praise that good monk Dharma Wit:

> All because of his mouth that preaches the dharma
> This heart that studies books was diverted.

[(He leaves.)]

---

[13] I.e., her crossed ankles will suggest the intertwining necks of mandarin ducks.

[14] This is a parody of the storyteller's point of suspense between storytelling sessions, in which the fate of a character is put in peril in the current session and remains unknown until the next. Here it is distinctly a parody, not a direct address to the audience, and is clearly meant to conjure up "petite" rather than real death.

At the Banquet the Madam Orders Oriole to Honor the Student as Her Brother

[Act 4]¹

(Old lady, arranging the table, enters and speaks:) Crimson went to summon Student Zhang. Why hasn't she come back yet? (Crimson [enters], greets old lady, and speaks:) Student Zhang had me come on ahead; he'll follow soon. (Student [enters] and greets old lady After he has finished his obeisances, old lady speaks:) If it had not been for you yesterday, how would we have seen today? You are the one, master, who has given life to our whole family I have only been able to lay out a small repast. In no way is it a fitting repayment; please don't feel we're slighting you. (Student speaks:) "If one person has blessings, everyone shares in them."² The defeat of this rebel is all to the madam's good fortune. If by sheer chance General Du had not arrived, none of us would have had the skill to avoid death. But these are all past matters and need not now hang upon our lips. (Old lady speaks:) Bring on the wine. Master, drink this cup to its full! (Student speaks:) "When an elder bestows something, a junior dares not beg off."³ (Student acts out drinking the wine. After he hands the cup to old lady, old lady speaks:) Please sit down, sir. (Student speaks:) I, your junior, will stand in waiting at your seat. I have already overstepped the bounds of propriety; how dare I presume to sit opposite you, madam?(Old lady speaks:) Is it not said, "Respect-

---

¹ The designation for act 4 is placed just before the song suites that are introduced by this scene. Since the scene should not be split, we have moved the designation here but have also marked it where it occurs in the original text.

² A citation from "The Punishments of Lü" ("Lü xing") in *The Book of Documents*.

³ A phrase of common parlance, drawn originally from *The Book of Rites*.

fulness is not as good as obedience"? (After thanking her, student sits down. Old lady speaks:) Crimson, go and call missy to pay her respects to the young master. (Crimson faces a ghost door and calls out:) The madam is entertaining a guest in the rear chambers and summons the young miss to come out. (Female lead responds and speaks:) I am a little queasy; I can't go. (Crimson speaks:) Can you guess who's been invited? (Female lead speaks:) Who's been invited? (Crimson speaks:) Student Zhang's been invited. (Female lead speaks:) If Student Zhang's been invited, I'll just have to go, sick as I am. (After Crimson acts out a comic routine, female lead [comes on] and recites a poem:)

> The expulsion of catastrophe for the entire family Cui
> Lay entirely in the half-sheet letter of Student Zhang.

Act 4[4]

[*Shuangdiao* mode:] "Wu gongyang" (Female lead sings:)
Aside from that noble laureate Zhang, who knows so many people,
How could anyone else have caused buckler and spear to retreat?
We set out wines and fruit,
Arrange mouth organs and songs.
Seal-script smoke so faint
And the fragrance of flowers so slight
Are dispersed on the eastern wind to fill curtains and hangings.
He saved my whole family from catastrophe:
Sincerest diligence—that's the proper ritual;
Respectful admiration—that's what's appropriate.

"Xinshui ling" (Female lead sings:)
At the azure-gauze window I have just drawn a pair of moths,[5]
From my silken gown I have brushed away a film of powder's fragrance,
I have delicately dabbed on beauty spots with my fingertip.
If I had not been awakened,
I would still be asleep, pressed beneath the embroidered coverlets.

(Crimson speaks:) Sister's face could be destroyed at the slightest touch. Student Zhang will be lucky!

"Reprise" [(Female lead sings:)]
You preposterous, lying little wench.
You say that my face, so fittingly made up, can be destroyed by the slightest touch!

(Crimson speaks:) Sister, you have the natural style of a noble lady of the house.

76a

---

[4] See n. 1 above.

[5] I.e., sketching her eyebrows shaped like the arching wings of a moth.

([Female lead] sings:)
Don't babble on,
Don't be one who runs off at the mouth.
How do I know what his luck will be?
But a noble lady of the house is something I can surely manage.

(Crimson speaks:) Both of you suffered before; now you're finally happy

"Qiaomu cha" (Female lead sings:)
My love-longing was because of him;
His love-longing, because of me.
But from now on, love's longing will be cured for us both.
When it's time to fete him, then we should, by rites, celebrate.[6]

76b   Oh, my mother is *too* kind.

(Crimson speaks:) If indeed she is going to match you and Student Zhang, then why didn't she have a big feast and invite the relatives and friends? What is she doing with such a small repast? (Female lead speaks:) You don't understand the madam.

"Jiao zhengpa" (Female lead sings:)
She's afraid that I'm just goods to be sold at a loss;
But when it's two for the price of one,[7] then the deal is on.
On the basis of his recommending that the general root out the rebels,
He should be entitled to live on our family fortune.
But what is she willing to spend
To have us tie the knot?
Let it be!
My old mother, so perceptive about human affairs, is too cautious:
She's afraid of being taken in by him.

(Student speaks:) I have to change my clothes. (He acts out bumping into female lead.)

"Qing Xuanhe" (Student sings:)
Outside the door, in front of the curtain, she moves away on tiny feet;
I see only her eyes turn their autumn billows on me.
Who would have thought that her quick and knowing mind would see through my tricks so speedily?[8]
It startles me so much that I back off,
Back off.

---

[6] I.e., when it is time to reciprocate his good will, it should be done with the proper celebration dictated by etiquette and ritual.

[7] I.e., when she can both thank Zhang Gong and marry off Oriole at the same time.

[8] She sees that he has excused himself from the room to get a chance to see her alone.

(Student sits down and acts out greeting female lead. Old lady speaks:) Come   77a
here, daughter, and pay your respects to your *elder brother* (Student speaks in an
aside:) Huh! That's a bad sign. (Female lead speaks:) Huh! My mother has
changed her stripes. (Crimson speaks:) They'll have to go through that love-
longing again!

"Yan'er luo" (Student sings:)
It startles me so that all flustered and flurried, I cannot move;
All dead and deflated, I have no retort;
All stupefied and startled, I cannot reply;
All weakened and wilted, I almost fall over in my seat.

"Desheng ling" (Student sings:)
Who could have thought this seasoned old madam
Would make Oriole greet me as younger sister to older brother?
White and boundless rise the waters at the Indigo Bridge,[9]
Crackling and popping burn the fires at the temple of Zoroaster.[10]
Clear, clear azure the freshening waves,
Smashing and roaring, pull the pair-eyed fish apart.[11]
Why so sudden   ?

(Male lead speaks:) When I hear the old lady finish speaking, oh—

([Student] sings:)
Wrinkling, crinkling, I lock both my brows in frowns.

(Old lady speaks:) Crimson, bring in some warmed wine and hand missy and her   77b
brother a cup.

"Tianshui ling" (Female lead sings:)
Here I droop my powdered neck low,
My mothlike brows furrow tightly,
My fragrant heart has no recourse.

---

[9] There are two incidents in dramatic texts that refer to an Indigo Bridge. Here the
story alludes to a certain Wei Sheng who made a tryst with a woman to meet under the
Indigo Bridge. He waited there, even though flooding waters began to rise, until finally he
drowned, still clinging to a piling. The other incident is explained above, p. 62.

[10] The story of a king of Shu who hired a wet nurse to care for his new daughter. The
wet nurse brought her young son to the palace with her, but after several years, as he
approached manhood, he was forced to leave. He dwelt in a Zoroastrian temple, where he
grew sick over thinking of the young princess. She went to see him but found him asleep.
She then placed in his arms some ear ornaments that they had played with as children. On
awakening the boy was so distraught that he killed himself by burning the temple down
around him.

[11] A legend that probably grew from the peculiar shape of bottom fish. Pair-eyed fish
are flat fish that have only a single eye each. They must swim in matched pairs to have two
eyes.

Does the saying "Seeing each other, they have much to say" mean anything to
me?
Starry eyes are all hazy and glazed,
My sandalwood mouth sighs,
78a   I choke with resentment and cannot breath—
This banquet was surely called under false pretenses![12]

(Female lead acts out offering a cup of wine. Male lead speaks:) I don't have
enough room for this. (After old lady entreats him, female lead speaks:) Crimson,
please take this tray of cups.

"Zhegui ling" (Female lead sings:)
He really can't swallow the jade liquor in golden billows.
Who would have thought that "under the moon, below the stars"[13]
Would change to "the southern branch in a dream"?[14]
Teary eyes I stealthily wipe
Until, unnoticed, they have soaked through my fragrant silks.
There he is, too tired to open his eyes,
Turning to a deflated and paralyzed lump.
Here I cannot raise my hands,
Cannot straighten my shoulders.
I am infected with a critical disease—
Surely I won't live.
Oh, you are the end of me.
What kind of cunning is this?

78b   (Old lady speaks:) Give him another cup. (After Crimson has given him another
cup, Crimson speaks to female lead in an aside:) Sister, what will we do about this
misery?

---

[12] All other texts have emended the phrase *minghe* (to call together) to *wuhe* (a gathering
of crows), a far more common saying used to indicate a raucous and disorganized
congregation or a meeting that comes together and then separates quickly; here, in other
words, a hurried meal and then separation. We would like to suggest, however, that this
may be a phrase meaning to call birds into a gathering, just as crows, ducks, and other birds
are still lured by hunters who imitate their calls or use live decoys. This would certainly fit
the current context, a meeting in which one is confronted with a situation different from
what one had expected when lured there.
[13] A term for the perfect conditions for a romantic liaison.
[14] From the story "Nanke taishou zhuan" by Li Gongzuo (fl. 800). The hero of the tale
falls asleep under a tree and in a dream is transported to the country of Acaciapeace
(Huai'an). There he is married to the daughter of the king and given the title of Grand
Protector of Southern Branch (*Nanke taishou*). Upon awakening, he finds an anthill at the
base of the acacia under which he has been sleeping. He knows then that his glorious love
and his exalted career have all taken place in the anthill under the southern branches. So
have the student's hopes of a romantic liaision been dashed.

"Yueshang haitang" (Female lead sings:)
Now this misery is still bearable,
But later, when one mulls it over, then what will happen?
I have a desire to speak my inner thoughts,
But, alas, my mother is sitting here beside me.
And now, thrown apart,
An inch between us might as well be a mile!

"Reprise"
One cup of gloomy wine is passed before my parent.
Bowing his head, silent and frustrated,
Is he unable to stand his face flushed with red of drunkenness
And so thinks the glazed cups too large?
No, it is because of me!
A heart overcome with wine would be better.

(Old lady speaks:) Crimson, take missy back to her bedroom. (Female lead acts
out taking her leave of male lead and departing. Female lead speaks:) My mother
really is a case of the mouth not according with the heart.   79a

"Qiao pai'er" (Female lead sings:)
The old madam is a slippery bolt that can't be pinned down,
A wordless riddle that can't be solved.
In hidden corners she deceives people with honeyed words,
But when she summons them, she makes them miserable.

promised oriole to whoever saved them?

(Crimson speaks:) Missy, don't blame anyone else:

"Jiang'er shui" (Crimson sings:)
Beauties have always been unlucky,
Budding scholars are always weaklings:
One, a headless goose killed by gloom;[15]
One, an article sold at a loss and even then rejected.

[(Crimson speaks:)] If you aren't married,

[(Crimson sings:)]
At the final exit what will you do about *me*?

"Dianqian huan" (Female lead sings:)
The boisterous loud laughs of a minute ago

---

[15] Wang Jide explains "headless goose" as a person without direction who wanders
about lost; it stems from the common phrase "head goose" to denote the lead bird of a
migratory flock. Wang thinks this refers to the absence of Oriole's father, who would
never have allowed such ingratitude. The reading we have adopted, however, fits much
better with the penultimate line of the final song in the suite ("She has felled him from the
sky with honeyed words"). See Wang Shifu, *Huitu xin jiaozhu guben Xixiang ji*, 2.38a.

Have all turned into the many tears of the Constable of Jiangzhou.[16]
If it hadn't been for this single letter that smashed five thousand rebel troops,
How could our whole family have survived?
If he wasn't thinking of marriage then, what was he thinking of?
That's hard to feel out now
The old lady's deceit is as big as heaven.

79b

The fulfillment of that day was due to you, my mother;
The destruction of today is due to you, this Xiao He![17]

"Li ting yan dai xiepai sha" (Female lead sings:)
From now on my jade countenance will be a desolate spray of pear blossoms;[18]
My lip rouge, a pale cluster of cherries.
When will I ever recover from this love-longing?
Dark and dank, it will come as deep as a black ocean;
White and boundless, it will come as thick as the earth;
Infinite and azure, it will be as broad as the blue heavens.
My longing gaze will be as high as the Taihang Mountains,

80a

My thirsting thoughts as deep as the Eastern Sea.
Oh, how mean and cruel.

[(Female lead speaks:)] O Mother—

[(Female lead sings:)]
You pinched the calyx of the trembling and quivering flower of doubled
    heads,
Cut the knot of the fragrant and redolent lover's-heart belt,

---

[16] From the last line of the "Ballad of the Pipa" ("Pipa xing") by Bo Juyi. As the constable of Jiangzhou, Bo tells the story of a pipa player who had once been the rage of the capital but was married off to a merchant only to float endlessly along the canals and rivers of China. He first hears her playing a melody and then asks her to tell him her life's story. After telling her sad story, she plays with such intensity that Bo weeps into the folds of his blue magistrate's gown.

[17] This is an adaptation of the aphorism "Success came from Xiao He and disaster too came from Xiao He." It refers to the career of the great general of the Han, Han Xin, who was first promoted and later beheaded by Xiao He. Han Xin (d. 193 B.C.) was one of the ablest advisers of Liu Bang (256–195 B.C.), founder of the Han dynasty. During the wars between Liu Bang and Xiang Yu (232–202 B.C.), hegemon-king of Western Chu, when Liu Bang's fortunes were at their lowest ebb, Xiao He urged Liu Bang to raise Han Xin from common soldier to commander-in-chief. After Xiang Yu's defeat, Liu Bang, suspicious of Han Xin's military prowess, had him executed by Liu's wife and Xiao He. Since Xiao He was also noted for his severity as compiler of the Han law codes, this adaptation of the quote has clearly caught the image of the madam torn between being a mother concerned about her daughter's happiness and being the severe arbiter and protector of the family's reputation.

[18] A conflation of a couplet from Bo Juyi's "Song of Unending Sorrow" "A jade countenance, lonely and desolate, streaked with tears:/A sprig of pear blossom carries the rain of spring."

Snapped the branch of the long and supple intertwined rose-quartz bush.
My white-haired mother bears no burden,
But this girl of greening spring has been frustrated.
My mother has kicked apart a future that spread before us like a piece of
    brocade.
She has felled him from the sky with honeyed words
And has cheated me badly with false pretenses.

[(She leaves.)]

(Male lead speaks:) I'm tipsy and will take my leave. But I'd like to say something to you directly, madam. Would that be permissible? Before, when the rebel bandits were putting real pressure on us, what you said was that whoever could repulse the rebels would get Oriole as his wife. I, with this "commiserating heart"[19] of mine, stepped forward and agreed. I wrote a letter to General Du, hoping that we could alleviate your distress, madam. You ordered me to a banquet today—I thought that it was the day of our happy celebration. Who would have thought that you, madam, would have us treat each other as younger sister and elder brother? I did not come here to stuff my mouth. If this affair truly won't come to a harmonious end, then I will leave this very day (Old lady speaks:) Master, even though you have been helpful enough to save our lives, when missy's father, the late chancellor, was alive, he promised her to my nephew, Zheng Heng. I have already, this very day, sent a letter to the capital summoning him, but he has not yet arrived. What will we do when this young man arrives? It would be best to reward you handsomely with gold and silk so that you may select the daughter of a powerful family or noble house and find another match. What is your noble opinion, sir? (Student speaks:) Since you will not give her up, why should I crave the color of your gold and silk? Isn't it said, "In books there is a girl, her face like jade"?[20] I have to take my leave today (Old lady speaks:) Stay a while; there is still some wine left here today Crimson, help elder brother back to the study to rest. We'll have more to say tomorrow

[(Old lady leaves.)]

(Crimson acts out helping student. Student recites:)

It is my lot to suffer through nights in the Buddhist temple;
Lacking karma, it is hard for me to meet spring in the bridal chamber

[19] According to the *Mencius*, the commiserating heart is the seed of compassion and benevolence. It is exemplified in the story about a person who saves a young child he sees crawling toward a well: he does it without expecting a reward, motivated simply by a heart of goodness.

[20] From a passage in a poem entitled "On Urging Study" ("Quanxue pian") by Emperor Zhenzong (r. 998–1002) of the Song. It reads, "In taking a wife, don't begrudge having no good go-between; / In books there is a woman with a face like jade."

(Crimson speaks:) You should really have drunk less. (Male lead speaks:) Did I really drink anything? (Male lead kneels before Crimson and speaks:) Because of your missy, day and night I forget to eat and I give up sleep. My soul is wearied, my dreams are broken, and I'm constantly distracted as if I'd lost something. Ever since I saw her in the temple and we traded verses across the wall, I have suffered interminable miseries in hopes of breeze and moonlight. Barely had we achieved some success when the old lady changed her stripes. Now I am at wits' end. When will all of this end? <u>Young lady, please have pity on me and tell my thoughts to your missy so she may know my heart.</u> And now, right in front of you, I will take off my belt and hang myself. (Student recites:)

Alas for my ambitions, pricking thighs and hanging from rafters;[21]
I'm in danger of becoming a ghost away from home, far from my village.

(Crimson speaks:) Is firewood so cheap on the streets that we can cremate your addled pate? Don't be so foolish. We should think of a way out. (Male lead speaks:) Where are you going to get a plan? I will raise an altar and appoint you *my* general!

---

[21] Conventional phrases describing the hardships of students. Su Qin, the famous rhetorician of the Warring States period, supposedly pricked his thigh with an awl to keep himself awake while studying. Likewise, a certain Sun Jing tied his hair to a rafter to keep himself from nodding off to sleep.

Hearing the Student Strum the Zither, Oriole Tiptoes to the Window to Listen

(Crimson speaks:)[1] I see you have a bagged zither. You must be skilled at that. My missy is devoted to the zither. Tonight when I go with missy to the flower garden to burn incense, you should start playing when you hear me signal you with a cough. I'll see what she has to say when she hears it. I'll also tell her what you said. If anything comes of it, I'll come back tomorrow to tell you in person. I'm afraid that the madam may be looking for me right now, so I'll go back.

[(Crimson leaves.)]

(Student speaks:) There's a lot to what Crimson says. It's getting late. Can't you come out more quickly, moon? I've already burned my incense　　Ah! Now, they've sounded the watch　　Ah! Now they've sounded the bell　　(He acts out tuning the zither and [speaks]:) Ah, zither, you and I have been constant companions on our wanderings. The success of tonight all depends on your demonic quality, your golden chord marks, your jade bridges, your snake-patterned bellows in crinkled lacquer, your scorched tail of Yiyang wood,[2] and

---

[1] As in other cases, the editor has arbitrarily placed the act division marker here. There is no discontinuity in the text; the characters are still onstage from the last scene, although it appears that they have moved (probably by doing a figure eight onstage) into the student's study.

[2] Cai Yong (132–92) once rescued a piece of tung wood from someone's fireplace and had it made into a zither. It turned out to have a superb sound, but the tail of the zither was scorched. The southern slopes of Yiyang produced the finest wood known for zithers.

183

your icy strings. O heaven, can't you loan me a favorable breeze to blow the sounds of my zither into those handsome little jade-sculpted, powder-molded, music-loving ears of my little miss? (Female lead enters, leading Crimson. Crimson speaks:) Missy, let's go and burn incense. What a clear moon! ([Female lead] speaks:) What good does it do to burn incense now that the affair has fallen apart? O moon, how can I bear your fullness?[3]

> [*Yuediao* mode:] "Dou anchun" (Female lead sings:)
> Clouds gather away in the clearing void,
> The icy wheel suddenly wells up;
> The breeze sweeps away tattered red,
> Scattered into piles on the fragrant steps.
> A thousand kinds of parting sorrow,
> Myriad sorts of idle grief.

82b

[(Female lead speaks:)] O madam

> (Female lead sings:)
> "Every single thing has a beginning,
> Few have their proper ending."[4]
> He has turned into a lover in a mirror's reflection,
> And I into a beloved one in a painting.
>
> "Zihua'er xu" (Female lead sings:)
> All that's left to do is remember him in my heart,
> Idly call out his name in my mouth—
> We can meet only in dreams.
> Yesterday my mother threw open the eastern apartments;[5]
> I wondered why she made such a feast of roasted phoenix and boiled dragon
> And in all confusion
> Had me wear halcyon sleeves to serve with diligence goblets of jade.
> Couldn't that be called great hospitality?
> But because we were given family rank as brother and sister,
> We could not join as fish in water.

83a

(Crimson speaks:) Sister, look at the bright moon. A full moon must have a breeze as well. (Female lead speaks:)

> > Breeze and moonlight are there at heaven's edge,
> > But in this world of men there is nothing good.

---

[3] The term for full moon, *tuanyuan*, also means a happy reunion.

[4] From ode 255 of *The Book of Poetry*, this has generally been understood in later times as an aphorism: everyone starts out good, but not everyone winds up that way.

[5] From the story about the Han minister Gongsun Hong (200–121 B.C.), who, after he had risen to a high post from obscurity, opened up the eastern quarters of his residence to travelers and worthy men: Oriole's mother, that is, has invited Student Zhang to move into the study and has provided him with a feast.

"Xiaotao hong" (Female lead sings:)
Look in the human world:
A jade countenance is locked away within embroidered bed hangings
Out of fear that someone might sport with it.
Think of Chang'e:
Sinking in the west and rising in the east, who keeps her company?
How she resents her heavenly palace:
No Pei Hang has yet made his dream of cavorting with immortals.[6]
These clouds are like the layers of my silken bed hangings that,
For fear Chang'e might be aroused,
Now close off the Palace of Spreading Frigidity

(Crimson acts out coughing. Male lead speaks:) They've come. (He acts out   83b
tuning his zither.) (Female lead speaks:) What's that sound? (Crimson acts out a
comic routine.)

"Tian jing sha" (Female lead sings:)
Could it be that our precious hair ornaments are set ajangling by our steps as
    we walk?
Could it be that our girdle pendants clink and tinkle as we trail our skirts?
Could it be that the iron horses[7] are stirred by the wind before the eaves?
Could it be that the golden curtain hooks hung in pairs
Are jingling and chinking as they beat against the door posts?

"Tiaoxiao ling" (Female lead sings:)
Could it be the night-struck bell in the Brahma palace?
Could it be the scattered bamboos rustling behind the curved balustrade?
Could it be the sound of ivory rulers and scissors keeping time?
Could it be the long dripping of the clepsydra echoing in catchpot's bronze?
Hiding myself, I listen again, east of the wall
All the time it was someone tuning a zither near the western wing.

"Tusi'er" (Female lead sings:)
When the sounds are virile, they are like the cacophony of the blades and
    spears of ironclad cavalry.
When the sounds are serene, they are like the rippling of fallen flowers on   84a
    flowing waters.
When the sounds are raised, they are like a crane's cry in a void of clear breeze
    and bright moon.
When the sounds are lowered, they are like the cooing of lovers' whispers
    heard through a small window

"Shengyao wang" (Female lead sings:)
There, his longing is limitless;

---

[6] For this conflated myth of Chang'e and Pei Hang, see pp. 61–62.
[7] I.e., wind chimes.

Here, I have already understood his intentions:
The lovely simurgh and fledgling phoenix have lost their mates.
Before his song is even finished,
My feelings have grown intense.
But alas, the shrike goes west and the flying swallow east[8]—
It's all told in what's unspoken.

(Female lead speaks:) I'll listen closer at the study window   (Crimson speaks:) Missy, listen right here. I'll have a quick look at what the madam is doing and then be right back. (Male lead speaks:) There's someone outside the window   It must be missy. I'll retune my strings, do another tune, and sing a song entitled "The Phoenix Seeks Its Mate." Long ago Xiangru carried off his affair because of this song. I may not be a match for Sima Xiangru, but I hope that missy has the intentions of Wenjun. (He sings the song:)

> There is a beautiful woman, oh,
>   Seeing her, I cannot forget.
> If I don't see her for a single day,
>   I long for her as though crazed.
> The phoenix flies, soaring, soaring, oh,
>   Seeking its mate within the four seas.
> Alas, that wonderful person, oh,
>   Is not at the eastern wall.
> I string my zither to take words' place, oh,
>   So I may spell out my subtlest feelings.
> When will I be accepted, oh,
>   And my vacillations eased?
> Oh, to be a match to her virtue, oh,
>   And lead each other by the hand.
> If we cannot fly together, oh,
>   It will destroy me utterly.[9]

84b

(Female lead speaks:) How well he plays! The words are sorrowful, the intention is keen, chilling and cold as a crane's cry in the sky   It makes me weep all unawares.

"Ma lang'er" (Student sings:)
This is to make her ears keenly perceptive
As I give plaint to my innermost feelings.
One who loves music—a fragrant heart will naturally understand;

---

[8] This is the opening line of "A Song of the Life of Oriole" ("Yingying benzhuan ge"), a ballad attributed to the Tang writer Li Shen and preserved in fragments in the all-keys-and-modes ballad by Dong Jieyuan (*Xixiang ji zhugongdiao*). See pp. 30–31.

[9] This is, of course, the text of the song that Sima Xiangru is supposed to have played to win the heart of Zhuo Wenjun. See p. 68.

One moved by feeling—a heart will be broken by pain.

"Reprise"
Now this piece and its original mode
Are not the same, beginning and end:
It is neither "Hearing a Bell in the Clear Night"
Nor the "Yellow Crane and the Drunken Gaffer",
Nor is it "Weeping for the Unicorn and Grieving for the Phoenix."[10]

"Luosiniang" (Female lead sings:)
With each and every word, the watch lengthens, the clepsydra drips for an   85b
  eternity;
With each and every sound, my gown grows roomier, my belt looser.
All the grief of parting and the sorrow of separation
Have turned into this single tune.
O Student Zhang,
It makes one love you even more.

(Male lead speaks:) Oh, the old lady has turned her back on favor, and, missy, you too have lied to me. (Female lead speaks:) You resent me wrongly:

"Dongyuan le" (Female lead sings:)
This was all my mother's clever scheme;
It was not my deception at all.
If I had my way, I would pray to imitate the simurgh and phoenix;
But my mother day and night compels me to a woman's labors.
If I'd ever had any breathing room,
O Student Zhang, you wouldn't curse me when no one's there.

"Mian daxu" (Female lead speaks:)
Through loose shades the wind is light;
In the secluded room the lamp is clear.
It's just a single thickness of red paper
And a few wide-apart stiles—
But isn't it the same as being separated by myriad screens of cloudy mountains?
How to find someone to transmit messages
So that even if separated by the twelve peaks of Shamanka Mountain,   86a
He would already have gone to Gaotang to meet me in his dreams?

(Crimson speaks:) The madam is looking for you, missy We have to go home.

"Zhuolusu" (Female lead sings:)
I see her running toward me, all panting, out of breath.
Oh, how it makes me overflow with rage;
It startles me so that I am filled with fear.

---

[10] These are all titles of songs within the traditional corpus of zither music.

Before I have turned around,
That girl is already shouting at the top of her voice.
I grab her tightly
And have to shut her up,
Afraid that she will bury me in front of the madam.

lies}
86b   (Crimson speaks:) Why are you so infatuated with that zither? Student Zhang
told me to tell you that he is going away (Female lead speaks:) O dear sister,
when you see him, make him stay another stretch. (Crimson speaks:) What are
you saying now? (Female lead speaks:) Go—

"Coda" (Female lead sings:)
Just say, "Others have lately been babbling to the madam;
No matter what, we won't have you miss the mark.
Forget about my unreliable, cruel mother—
How could you be willing to leave me, this sincere person?"

[(They leave.)]

"Luosimang shawei"
Because of a seductive tune that teases grief and entices feelings
They can't avoid the symptoms of neglecting sleep and forgetting meals!

Volume II of the Deluxe, Completely Illustrated, and Annotated Story of the Western Wing

Newly Cut, Large-Character, Folio-Size, Completely Illustrated, Expanded, Deluxe, Annotated Story of The Western Wing

Book the Second

[Untitled]

[*Xianlü* mode:] "Basheng Ganzhou"
A marriage made in heaven:
A student from Western Luo,
A beauty in Universal Salvation,
Meeting each other in Pu Commandery,
Intelligent and in the spring of their youth.
Waiting for the moon, chanting poems, their gorgeous rhymes are true:
He's no less than Sima Xiangru of the Han;
She's an equal to Zhuo Wenjun.

"Hunjiang long"
Barely had they a concord of feeling,
When Flying Tiger stirred up a malignant atmosphere at the Yellow River Bridge.
The monks had nowhere to flee.
The madam said with full sincerity,
"To whoever it may be who establishes his meritorious service
By sweeping away this mist and dust,
I am willing to give my dear daughter in marriage."
Student Zhang accepted:
"I have an old friend from my carefree days
Who's called the White Horse General."

"Jin zhan'er"
Quick as fire, he wrote his letter
And immediately extinguished smoke and dust.

Who could have thought that [the madam] would accept a favor but not repay it?
He had to wait until the illness of love's longing was at a dire point
And he was about to die
Before she finally let him savor the joys of marriage.

"Zui fugui"
That bald monk Dharma Wit[1]
Saved the monastery·
He took the letter to ask the marshal for his tiger's strength.
His whole body was hacked and broken,
Like a bucket of blood;
He had a head but no ears
And barely escaped with his life!
Vain were the sufferings of that damned monk,
Hot was the desire of that rejected student!

"Coda"
The old composition of Master Dong
And the new tunes of Guan Hanqing
Are collated in this full edition of The Western Wing
The latecomer author, Student Wang, had a lot to say
And added A Game of Go.[2]
Fresh and original, this tale is known throughout the world,
And in this romantic performance
The souls of Oriole Cui and Student Zhang come back to life forever!

---

[1] While Dharma Wit does perform these heroic deeds in the Dong Jieyuan Xixiang ji zhugongdiao, in this play it is of course Benevolent Perception who races with Zhang's letter to Du Que.

[2] This is an incidental act that was supposed to follow play I, act 3. We have not translated it because it is clearly of inferior quality and is disruptive to the play as preserved in the Hongzhi edition.

Crimson Takes Student Zhang's Letter to Oriole

VOLUME III OF THE DELUXE, COMPLETELY ILLUSTRATED, AND ANNOTATED STORY OF THE WESTERN WING

Feelings Transmitted by Lines of Poetry

Act 1

(Female lead enters and speaks:) I haven't seen Student Zhang since I listened to him play the zither last night. I'll send Crimson now to his study to see what he has to say (She acts out calling Crimson. Crimson enters and speaks:) Missy is calling me. I don't know why, but I'd better go and see. (Female lead speaks:) I'm feeling so poorly, why haven't you come to check on me? (Crimson speaks:) You're thinking of stu—— (Female lead speaks:) What stu—— (Crimson speaks:) How stu——studiously I'll watch over you, missy (Female lead speaks:) I'm begging you to do something for me. (Crimson speaks:) What's that? (Female lead speaks:) Go and find out what Student Zhang has to say and then come tell me. (Crimson speaks:) I won't go! If the madam finds out, it will be no laughing matter. (Female lead speaks:) Dearest sister, I'll bow to you twice if only you'll go. (Crimson speaks:) Rise up my governess; I'll go, I'll go. I'll say, "Student Zhang, your illness is surely grave, but sister suffers no less." (Crimson recites:)

Because of a zither-playing hand at midnight,
A moon-loving heart has been aroused in spring chambers.

"Shanghua shi" (Crimson sings:)
Needlework my sister has no mind to take in hand;
Fragrance of powder and rouge dissipated, too listless is she to apply them again;
Spring grief weighs down the tips of her brows.
Her lingering illness would be cured
If only the smallest groove were opened down the divine rhinoceros horn.[1]

[(Crimson leaves.)]

(Female lead speaks:) Crimson is gone. I'll see what she has to say when she comes back, and then I'll make up my mind.

[(Female lead leaves.)]

❖❖❖

91a (Male lead enters and speaks:) This suffering will be my death. I haven't been able to see my missy since that night she listened to my zither. I told the abbot to go and tell them, "Student Zhang is gravely ill." Why hasn't anyone come to check on me? Well, the best idea is to try and get some sleep. (Crimson enters and speaks:) I've been ordered by my missy to go and check on Student Zhang, and I'd better go. Well, how could we have kept anyone in our family alive if it hadn't been for Student Zhang?

[*Xianlü* mode:] "Dian jiangchun" (Crimson sings:)
The temporary shrine of the chancellor
Is lodged in this Buddhist monastery.
Because of his funeral rites,
A young daughter and orphaned child
Were about to go along with the army to their deaths![2]

"Hunjiang long" (Crimson sings:)
Thanks to Student Zhang for extending his will:
As soon as his letter arrived, it raised an army,
Showing clearly that fine writings have their use
And proving that heaven and earth are impartial.
If he had not trimmed the shoots and extirpated the roots of those five
    thousand rebels,
Quite likely they would have extinguished the gates and destroyed the doors
    of this, our whole household.
Oriole and Junrui

---

[1] The rhinoceros was considered a divine animal by the Chinese, and its horn was thought to be an aphrodisiac. Running from tip to tail of the horn is a white groove, symbol of sexual love between men and women, best known by its appearance in the poetry of Li Shangyin (812–58.)

[2] Because the news of Oriole's beauty, which caused such a ruckus at the mass, spread far and wide, leading to Flying Tiger Sun's siege of the monastery.

Were promised to be man and wife.   91b
The madam has broken her promise
And come up with all kinds of pretexts
To destroy the bond of wedlock
And turn them into brother and sister.
Now any chance of marriage is completely removed:
He has deranged the brocade and embroidery in his breast;[3]
She has drenched with tears the rouge on her face.

"You hulu" (Crimson sings:)
So haggard is our young Master Pan that his temples are streaked;[4]
Our Du Weiniang is no more her former self.[5]
Her—her belt is loosened, shrunk to nothing is her emaciated waist;
Him—he sleeps in a stupor, with no desire to look at canons or histories.
Her—she is unsettled, too listless to pick up her needlework;
Him—he played out on silk and paulownia a score of separation's grief.
Her—on flowered stationery she rubs out a poem of broken hearts;
Her—with her brush she writes out her hidden feelings;
Him—with his strings he transmits heart's affairs.
Both of them—both suffer alike from love's longing.

"Tianxia le" (Crimson sings:)   92a
Now I believe that poets and beauties really exist,
But in Crimson's eyes they are a bit perverse—
It seems to me that passionate people who do not get their heart's desire are
    like this:
What I see is that they suffer so much, they become bewitched;
And what I find is that they never give a second thought
But immediately bury their heads to prepare for a wasting death.

(Crimson speaks:) I'm already here at the flower garden. I'll wet a spot with
spittle to dissolve the window paper and see what he's doing.

"Cunli yagu" (Crimson sings:)   92b
I'll wet the paper window and make a hole
And with silenced voice peep inside—
Probably he has slept in his clothes,
Since the front fold of his silken robe is rumpled.

---

[3] I.e., his talent and learning.
[4] Pan Yue (247–300), who is better known in drama as Pan An, was a prodigy whose
hair turned gray at the age of thirty-two. As a youth he was so handsome that women
would wait by the roadside to throw fruit in his chariot as he passed through the streets of
the capital at Luoyang.
[5] Du Weiniang was a beautiful courtesan of the Tang for whom a song title ("Du
Weiniang qu") was named. After the late Tang period, her name simply became a term for
a beautiful girl.

There's the taste of sleeping alone:
Cold and lonely threads of thoughts
And no one to wait on him.
Observe his washed-out appearance,
Listen to his feeble and weak breathing,
Look at his yellow and emaciated face.

[(Crimson speaks:)] O Student Zhang,

[(Crimson sings:)]
If you don't die from depression, you'll die from love's suffering.

"Yuanhe ling" (Crimson sings:)
My golden hairpin knocks on the leaf of the door—

(Male lead asks:) Who is it?

[(Crimson sings:)]
I am the Agent of the Five Plagues, spreading love's longing!
Thinking of when night was deep, when breezes were fresh and moon was
    bright—
My young miss has sent Crimson to check on you.

(Male lead speaks:) Well, since you are here, you must have a message.

([Crimson] sings:)
To this day my mistress has yet to spread on her rouge or powder;
But she has recited aloud a thousand times "Doctor of Letters Zhang."

(Male lead speaks:) Since missy does have some feelings of pity for me, can I trouble you to take this note here to let her know my innermost feelings? (Crimson speaks:) I'm afraid that she will show a different face—

"Shangma jiao" (Crimson sings:)
If she sees this poem,
Reads this lyric,
She will surely do a turnabout and put on a real act:

93a

(Crimson speaks:) She will buckle on a different face [and say], "If I find out you bring me anyone's message

([Crimson] sings:)
How dare you act so rashly, you hussy!"
For sure she'll scoff and scoffing tear the paper to shreds.

(Male lead speaks:) I'll reward you later, my girl, handsomely with gold and silk.

"Sheng hulu" (Crimson sings:)
Bah! You starving, bankrupt sourpuss, you make no sense,

Flaunting as if you had family riches!
Did I come here scheming to get something from you,
Or to have you give your money and goods
To Crimson as a reward?
I don't give a damn about your gold.

"Reprise"
You look on me as a spring-wind sprig of peach beyond the garden wall:
I'm not to be compared to those who lean against the gates to sell their
    charms.[6]
I may be just a woman, but I have my pride.
I said to myself, "How pitiful this little one is,
All alone and by himself."

[(Crimson speaks:)] But now—

[(Crimson sings:)]
I'll have to change my thinking about that!   93b

(Male lead speaks:) Please, sister, have pity on me, all alone, by myself. (Crimson
speaks:) Aren't you nice now! You write, and I'll take it for you. (Male lead acts
out writing. Crimson speaks:) Oh, you've written that well. Read it aloud and let
me hear it. (Male lead reads out loud:)

I, Gong, with a hundred obeisances, present this letter

To the dressing table of the fragrant one.

Since I have been separated from your mien, the geese have been rare, the
scales have disappeared,[7] and my sadness and grief I cannot overcome.
Who would have thought that the madam would turn a favor into a
grievance and thus change our former bond? How can this not be a breach
of trust? As a result, my eyes are fixed on the eastern wall,[8] and I resent that
I cannot grow wings to fly to your dressing table. My frustrations are
complete, my thoughts exhausted, and my life hangs every moment in the
balance. I avail myself of Crimson's visit to send a few words, to give
expression to my simple heart. If, by some miracle, you feel a little pity,
please write to me so that I can still nurse myself back to health.

I write this in haste, and I humbly beg you to forgive my carelessness.

I have also written a poem in regulated style in lines of five characters that
I have copied for your perusal.

---

[6] Both lines refer to prostitutes.
[7] Geese and carp are letter carriers. According to one old tale, a migrating goose that
was shot down was found to have a letter tied to its foot. According to another story, a
letter was discovered in the stomach of a carp when it was served at table.
[8] See p. 67.

([Male lead] recites a poem:)

The vexations of love's longing grow stronger;
In vain I played the jasper zither.
From happy affair to encountering spring,
Your fragrant heart must also have been moved.
Such passion cannot be denied;
What need to cling to empty reputation?
Do not betray the brightness of moon's blossom;
But covet the heaviness of flowers' shadows.

94a

"Houting hua" (Crimson sings:)
I thought he straightened out the flowered paper to sketch out a draft,
But actually he soaked the frosty hairs[9] in ink, and without study
He first penned several lines of a conventional opening
And then inscribed a five-character eight-line poem.

impressed?

[(Crimson speaks:)] And in no time at all,

[(Crimson sings:)]
The flowered note and brocaded characters
Were folded into the double diamond of joined hearts:
Oh, too romantic, too devoted,
Too smart, too much the rake!
Even though it's just a show,
Smaller abilities cannot achieve this.

"Qing ge'er" (Crimson sings:)
Upside down he writes the two words "mandarin duck, mandarin duck",
Only now do I believe that "in the heart, in the heart, there is intent."[10]

[(Crimson speaks:)] I'll see if she's happy or angry

[(Crimson sings:)]
And from it get some notion.
Set your worries aside, scholar!
I am willing to undertake this.
I will not shirk my responsibilities
But will in my own statement
Say, "The one who played the zither last night has told me to show it to you."

94b   (Crimson speaks:) I'll take this for you. You, sir, should be concerned about your career. Don't fritter away your energies.

---

[9] A brush from the finest hairs of a rabbit's autumn down, which grows only after the frost has fallen.

[10] A famous line from the "Great Preface" to *The Book of Poetry* that reads, "In the heart it is intent; put in words, it is poetry."

"Jisheng cao" (Crimson sings:)
Your hand that pilfers perfume
Should prepare to snap the cassia branch.[11]
Don't let any lascivious lyrics defile your dragon-and-snake script,[12]
Or lotus root fibers bind the wings of the giant *peng* bird,[13]
Or a yellow oriole snatch away the ambition of a great swan.
Don't let this one beauty between halcyon hangings and brocade curtains
Ruin you, [one of the] three scholars of Jade Hall and Golden Horse [Gate].[14]

(Male lead speaks:) Be careful, sister! (Crimson speaks:) Don't worry! Don't worry!   95a

"Coda" [(Crimson sings:)]
Like Shen Yue, beset by many illnesses,
Like Song Yu, sorrowed without peer:[15]
A figure worn thin by love-longing.
I, before your brows and eyes had finished transmitting your passions,
Had already marked it well in my heart, day and night.
How dare I be rash, since "there is a beautiful jade at hand"?[16]
⌈ I will see that it reaches its proper destination, this sheet of paper,
And by use of the arguments from the tip of my tongue,
Along with your heart's affairs within this note,
⌊ I'll make her come and pay you a visit.

(Male lead speaks:) Missy, take the note away! I won't brag, but it is a marriage charm. When you report back tomorrow, there must be some progress. [(Crimson recites:)]

---

[11] A common term for passing the examinations, especially as the number one candidate.

[12] The extraordinary grace and beauty of fine calligraphy.

[13] *Ousi* (lotus root fibers) is exactly homophonous with a term for the loving thoughts of a happy couple; it hence refers to the entanglement of love's thoughts. The great *peng* bird, as explained in play I, act 1, n. 12, is a metaphor for a student's ambitions for a successful career.

[14] Men of eminence and renown. The Golden Horse Gate was one of the portals of the Han court. It was flanked by two bronze horses and was where officials assembled when summoned to court. The Jade Hall, as noted above, is another name for the Hanlin Academy. The line is quoted from a congratulatory verse (*kouhao*) by the Song scholar Ouyang Xiu (1007–72), written to preface the performance of a comedy at a banquet he was attending with two friends (hence, "three scholars").

[15] Shen Yue (441–513) was a renowned literary figure of the Six Dynasties period. He once wrote a letter to a friend complaining of the illnesses that accompany old age ("Yu Xu Mian shu"). In drama this complaint is picked up and conversely applied only to young men who age before their time. The second line of the couplet is a reference to the songs *The Nine Disputations* (*Jiubian*) of Song Yu, traditionally noted for their sad and doleful nature.

[16] A clever use of *Analects*, 9.12: "'If there is a beautiful piece of jade at hand, would you store it safely in a box or seek a good price and sell it?' The master replied, 'Sell it, sell it. Just wait for the right price.'"

So, don't worry or fear now·
Good news is bound to come.

([Crimson] leaves.)

(Student recites:)

Send a romantic traveler like Song Yu
To a sequestered maiden East of Pu.

[(Male lead leaves.)]

Student Zhang Watches the Sun Sing and Goes Happily to His Tryst

Act 2

(Female lead [enters] and speaks:) She's been waiting on the old lady and has had no time or opportunity, but she'll be here about now I got up a little too early, and I'm worn out. I'll sleep some more. (Crimson enters and speaks:) On the orders of my young mistress, I went to check on Student Zhang but then had to attend the madam. Now I'll report to my young mistress. I don't hear a sound: she must have gone back to sleep. I'll go inside and see.

[*Zhonglü* mode:] "Fendie'er" (Crimson sings:)
Breeze stilled, hanging screen undisturbed,
Through gauzy windows scatters perfume of musk and orchid.
I open the vermilion leaves and shake the doubled rings aclatter;
The scarlet candlestand is high, the golden lily is small,[1]
The silver lamp still glitters.
Before I tap lightly upon the warmed bed-curtains,
I'll first lift this plumrose, silken-soft hanging screen and steal a peek.

"Zui chunfeng" (Crimson sings:)
All I see are her hairpins drooping, their jades slipping askew,
Her coif awry, the clouds disheveled.
The sun is high, but still she is not bright-eyed.
Oh, she is really lazy, lazy—

---

[1] The golden lily is the brass plate on top of the candlestand upon which the candle is actually placed.

A long while to raise her body,
Many times to scratch her ears,
A single sound of lengthy sigh.

(Crimson speaks:) I'd like just to give her the note, but I'm afraid that my young mistress will put on some show or another, so I'll place this note on her makeup box and see what she says when she finds it. (Female lead acts out facing the mirror. She acts out finding the note and reading it.)

"Putian le" (Crimson sings:)
Still traces of last night's toilet, raven clouds drooping,
Cheeks of powder so lightly spread,
A coif of clouds now disheveled—
She picks up the note
And closes the makeup box.
She slits open the envelope and reads with care,
Over and over, back and forth, never once annoyed.

(Female lead shouts angrily:) Crimson! (Crimson winks to the audience and speaks:) Aw, shit!

([Crimson] sings:)
I suddenly wrinkle my jet brows.

96b   (Female lead speaks:) Why don't you come here, you little hussy!

([Crimson] sings:)
All at once she droops her powdered neck,
Suddenly changes to a vermilion countenance.

(Female lead speaks:) You little hussy! Where did you get this? I am the daughter of a chancellor. Who makes sport of me with such a note? I'm not in the habit of reading such stuff! If I report this to the madam, she'll beat your bottom, you little hussy (Crimson speaks:) My mistress, you ordered me to go, and he had me bring it to you. I don't know how to read a single character—how do I know what he wrote?

"Kuaihuo san" (Crimson sings:)
It is clear that *you* transgressed the rules;
There's no reason to savage *me*.
You used someone else but, doing a flip-flop, are now the one offended—
If you aren't in the habit, then *who* is?

(Crimson speaks:) Sister, let's not argue. Before you have time to explain it to the madam, I will take this note to her and confess everything. (Female lead acts out pulling Crimson back [and speaks]:) I was only joking with you. (Crimson speaks:) Let go! I'll see my bottom beaten! (Female lead speaks:) How is Student Zhang these days? (Crimson turns her back and speaks:) I'm not going to tell. (Female lead speaks:) Dear sister, please tell me.

> "Chao tianzi" (Crimson sings:)
> Student Zhang these days—
> His face is so emaciated that it's really ugly to look at.
> He never thinks of drink or food;
> He's afraid of being moved about.
> Day and night his eyes are fixed on a tryst:
> He neglects sleeping, forgets to eat;
> From yellow dusk to freshest dawn
> He stares at the eastern wall with tear-filled eyes.

97a

(Female lead speaks:) Call a good physician to examine his condition. (Crimson speaks:) His condition cannot be cured by taking medicine.

> ([Crimson] sings:)
> To stabilize his illness,
> He'll have to sweat beads of romance.

> "Sibian jing" (Crimson sings:)
> You are afraid of people's sneers:
> If the madam ever saw through all this,
> Would you and I be safe?
> What do you care that *he* is at a crisis point?
> We've sucked him into climbing the pole,
> And now, having pulled away the ladder, you just look on.

(Female lead speaks:) Crimson, if it weren't for consideration for you, I'd go to the madam. Then we'd see if he had the face to see the madam. Even though my family is indebted to him, there are only the affections of brother and sister between us. How could there be anything else going on? Crimson, please keep your mouth shut. If anyone else knew, then what would happen? Give me my embroidery-pattern brush, and I'll write back to him and tell him not to act like this anymore. (Female lead acts out writing. She acts out getting up [and speaks]:) Take this, Crimson, and say that the young lady expects the young gentleman to abide by the proper rites of brother and sister. It has to be like this, without any other overtones. If this happens once more, then I'll have to let the madam know—and then she'll have something to say to you too, you little hussy!

97b

> "Tuo bushan" (Female lead and Crimson argue. [Female lead leaves. Crimson sings:])
> You little child, your mouth knows no restraint;
> Without exception, your words destroy
> Instead of throwing a tantrum, quit thinking about that budding scholar

And be more or less a model girl!

"Xiao Liangzhou" (Crimson sings:)
Because of you he is coupled in dreams but alone after he wakes.
He neglects his sleep, forgets to eat,
His silken gown cannot bear the fifth-watch cold.
His sorrow is infinite;
Tears of desolation streak across his face.

98a

"Reprise"
Because you fix your gaze on a tryst—a gaze as vain as waiting for Mercury to
    appear²—
I've never been able to latch this side door tight.
I really want you two to be man and wife, without any crisis or hardship.
At the head of the banquet mat I'll dress up
And be a matchmaker whose mouth has been sewn shut.³

[(Female lead leaves.)]

(Crimson speaks:) If I don't go, she'll say I disobey her. That student is waiting for
me too. I'd better go.

([Crimson] leaves.)

❖❖❖

(Male lead enters and speaks:) I asked Crimson to take the poem, but she hasn't
brought an answer back yet. This dispatch of my letter will surely bring off the
affair. She should be coming about now (Crimson enters and speaks:) I'd better

98b

go report back to Student Zhang. Oh, missy, you're far too spoiled. How can
you get today's heart from yesterday's?

"Shiliu hua" (Crimson sings:)
Today in the upper room where you make your evening toilet, apricot
    blossoms fade,
And yet you still fear the single layer of your gown.
But amid the clear dew and bright moonlight, that whole zither-listening heart
Last night did not fear spring's chill.
You came close to being a "gentleman's choice morsel."⁴

---

² Mercury appears infrequently and is extremely difficult to observe when it does
appear.
³ One interpretation of this song is that Crimson has been running back and forth
through the night, trying to set the lovers up with each other, but has only been cursed for
her efforts on Oriole's behalf. The last three lines are an attempt on her part to assure her
mistress that she wants them to marry and that she will not spill any secrets of the affair.
⁴ What we have translated here as "gentleman" is the term *xiansheng*, which in the
original passage from *Analects*, 2.8, actually means elders: "Zixia asked about filiality, and
the Master said, 'It is the face one puts on that is difficult. That younger people should take

At that time why weren't you ashamed?
Because of such a sour, such a vinegary, such a crazy lout
Across the wall, you came close to turning into a husband-longing mountain.[5]

"Dou anchun" (Crimson sings:)
You purposely stirred up rain and excited the clouds,
And I, out of good intentions, delivered letters and transmitted notes.
You refuse to examine your own crazy actions
But want to search out the weak points in others.
I'll take this hot moxa treatment just this once—
But you're just too deceitful!

(Speaking as female lead, [Crimson] says:) "Student Zhang should act as a brother to me, his sister. How dare he do this?"

([Crimson] sings:)
In front of others, clever words and flowery speeches.

(Crimson speaks:) "If I see Student Zhang with no one present   "   99a

([Crimson] sings:)
Then behind others' backs, sorrowful brows and teary eyes.

(Crimson acts out greeting male lead. Male lead rises and speaks:) You're here, missy My heaven-supporting pillar,[6] how did the great affair go? (Crimson speaks:) It didn't help a bit—but don't get all addled. (Male lead speaks:) My note was a marriage charm, so it must be that you did not give it your whole heart. You did it purposely! (Crimson speaks:) I didn't use my whole heart? Well, heavens   that note of yours   listen well:

"Shang xiaolou" (Crimson sings:)
It is because you have a niggardly fate,
Not because I disobeyed!
That note became naught but your confession,
Her arrest complaint, and my case file.
If she had not shown understanding,
Displayed some consideration,
Forgiven insolence,

(Crimson speaks:) You would have suffered punishment as demanded by rights. What guilt does this lowly maid bear?

---

on the burdens of affairs or give their elders wine and food to eat—is this really filiality?'"
One favorite technique in drama is to quote phrases from the *Analects* out of context and give them a satirical twist.

[5] Sometimes also called husband-longing rock: a woman who stood so long watching for her husband that she metamorphosed into stone.

[6] It was commonly believed that heaven was supported by eight pillars.

([Crimson] sings:)
You almost pulled "your mother"[7] into the crime.

"Reprise"
Rendezvous will be rare from now on,
And meetings will be impossible.
The moon has darkened over the western wing;
The phoenixes are gone from the loft of Qin;[8]
The clouds have gathered away at Shamanka Mountain.
You run away,
I run away
99b   Master, don't be so insensitive,
But leave now that the party has fallen apart!

(Crimson speaks:) It's just this: don't declaim your innermost feelings again. I'm afraid that the madam may be looking for me, so I'm going back. (Male lead speaks:) Once you've gone, missy, whom can I find to vindicate me? You have to find some solution to make it possible to save my life. (Student acts out kneeling down and holding Crimson back.) (Crimson speaks:) You are a reader of books, Student Zhang. Why don't you understand the significance of this? The affair is as clear as possible.

"Manting fang" (Crimson sings:)
Don't let deceit run rampant under the guise of foolishness!
You want the beautiful fulfillment of love and passion,
But that will cause the ruin and destruction of my bones and flesh.
The madam watches while stroking her cudgel:
A coarse hempen rope cannot pass through the eye of a needle.
You want me to be your *postillon d'amour* while walking on crutches
And the peddler of your sweet talk while my lips are stitched together.

(Crimson speaks:) If I go, my mistress will explode like salt thrown into the fire, and then

([Crimson] sings:)
100a   I'm treading on the triggers of traps.

---

[7] I.e., "your mother from an earlier life." There are overtones here of a stronger curse: "your fucking mother."

[8] From an ancient myth about two lovers, Xiao Shi and Nongyu. Xiao Shi was a "master of the pipes," able to summon peacocks and cranes to the courtyard with his music. One of the daughters of Duke Mu of Qin, Nongyu, fell in love with him, and he took her as a wife. He taught her birdcalls, and after several years she could imitate the cries of the phoenix. She drew these auspicious birds there in flocks, and Xiao built a dais for the birds where the couple also lived. After a period of time, Xiao Shi and Nongyu flew off with the phoenixes. Here, of course, the line means that such a perfect marriage as that of these two mythic figures does not appear in the cards for our young lovers.

[(Crimson speaks:)] If I don't go   (Male lead kneels down, weeps, and speaks:)
My life lies in your hands, missy

([Crimson] sings:)
I've no defense against your honeyed words and hot entreaties;
It makes it hard, either way, for me to do what a person should.

(Crimson speaks:) I have no way to explain. But missy has answered your letter.
You read it for yourself. (Male lead acts out accepting it. He acts out opening it
and reading it [and speaks]:) Oh, what a happy affair. I pinch some earth to use as
incense to burn, and finish the three obeisances. If I had known missy's letter was
coming, I would have gone out to receive it. Please don't fault me for not
receiving it with proper courtesy Little girl, joy to you too. (Crimson speaks:)
What? (Male lead speaks:) Your young mistress's curses for me were all feigned.
The meaning of the letter is that she summons me to the flower garden tonight
and with her to tra-la-la-la, tra-la-la-la   (Crimson speaks:) Read it out loud to
me. (Male lead speaks:) It is a four-line poem:

> Wait for the moon beneath the western wing;
> Welcoming the breeze, the door is half-opened.
> When separated by the wall, flowers' shadows move;
> I guess it is the jade one coming.

(Crimson speaks:) Why do you think she orders you to come? Read it out aloud   100b
for me. [(Male lead speaks:)] "Wait for the moon beneath the western wing"
that's ordering me to come when the moon has come up. "Welcoming the
breeze, the door is half-opened" that means she will open the door and wait for
me. "When separated by the wall, flowers' shadows move; / I guess it is the jade
one coming" that means she wants me to jump across the wall. (Crimson
speaks:) She orders *you* to jump across the wall? Can you really pull that off? Does
it really say this? (Male lead speaks:) I am a member of the Society for Solving
Riddles, a romantic Sui He,[9] a rakish Lu Jia.[10] How could I have failed to
understand it? (Crimson speaks:) Look, my sister pulls her tricks even in front of
me!

"Shua hai'er" (Crimson sings:)
Has anyone ever seen a sender of letters lead fish and geese astray?
She may be young, but her, oh, so subtle heart is full of twists.

(Crimson speaks:) She wrote

---

[9] Sui He was a rhetorician and persuader in the service of Liu Bang. At one crucial
moment during the war between Liu and Xiang Yu, Sui He talked Yingbu, one of the
Chu generals, into switching allegiance to Liu Bang.
[10] Lu Jia was another rhetorician in the service of Liu Bang. Following the establishment of the Han dynasty he persuaded Zhao Tuo, the king of Southern Yue (modern
Canton and surroundings), into becoming a vassal of the Han.

[(Crimson sings:)]
"Wait for the moon beneath the western wing" she'll wait until late at night;
She ordered you to jump across the wall—what feminine cunning.[11]
All the time those poetic lines enfolded a third-watch date;[12]
In that note lay the ambush of Nine Mile Mountain.[13]
In her straits she deludes others:
You will meet rain and clouds, and in confusion find quietude;
I deliver notes and letters, and from trouble filch rest.

101a "Fourth from Coda" (Crimson sings:)
The sheen of the paper is as bright as a jade platter;
The fragrance of the characters spews musk and orchid.
Isn't it spring sweat that has soaked through beside the lines?
A whole envelope of passion's tears, the red seal is still moist;
A full paper of spring's heart, the black ink is yet to dry
From now on, suspect no hardships;
Put your worries aside, my scholar.
In all probability you'll catch the golden bird and raven coils.[14]

101b "Third from Coda" (Crimson sings:)
In front of others she is particularly affectionate;
But in front of me, completely offhanded—
It is simply the case that Meng Guang has already received the plate of Liang
    Hong.[15]
Toward others—honeyed words and comely language, warmth in the deepest
    winter;
Toward me—filthy language that hurts, a chill in midsummer.
I will be the first to see,

---

[11] The line actually reads, "By the side of woman [*nü*] is work [*gan*]"· that is, it describes the character *jian*, which means cunning deceit.

[12] Crimson is playing on the phrase *sangeng zao*, rendered here "third-watch date." The original pun is based on an exchange between the fifth and sixth Zen patriarchs. The master gave his disciple three kernels of nonglutinous rice (*sangeng*) and a jujube (or red Chinese date, *zao*). The sixth patriarch quickly guessed the homophone—his master wanted him to come early (*zao*) to a meeting at the third watch (*sangeng*).

[13] According to the lore of drama and fiction, Liu Bang's ablest general, Han Xin, ambushed Xiang Yu at Nine Mile Mountain during the final phase of the wars between Xiang Yu and Liu Bang and inflicted a crushing defeat on him.

[14] We take *ya* (childish) primarily as a pun on *ya* (raven), with the understanding that it refers to both Oriole's hairdo and that of a child; that is, Crimson, who will become Zhang's concubine.

[15] Meng Guang was a woman so deeply in love with Liang Hong (fl. first century) that out of respect she always served him with "the platter lifted level with her eyebrows." Here it is a jibe at Oriole, who has already made an assignation with Student Zhang while trying to keep Crimson in the dark.

To see how you, this Qiannü of departed soul,[16]
Will deal with Pan An, showered with fruit.[17]

(Male lead speaks:) I am just a reader of books—will I be able to jump across into the flower garden?

"Second from Coda" (Crimson sings:)
The flowers across the wall are now bending over;
The door awaiting the breeze is only half-closed.
The trick for pilfering perfume you must use now—
How can you jump across the dragon's gate if you fear the height of this wall?[18]
If so you hate the dense flowers, you'll find it hard to snap a branch off the transcendent's cassia tree.[19]
Set aside your worries; don't tarry out of fear.
If you don't go,
She'll gaze until her overflowing autumn waters[20] are just sockets,
And frown until her lightly sketched spring hills[21] have all faded away

10za

(Male lead speaks:) I've gone to the flower garden twice already, and nothing came of it. What will happen this time? (Crimson speaks:) This time will be different!

"Coda" [(Crimson sings:)]
Of course, you've gone there twice,
But I'll bet this will be the time.
Bantering poems across the wall was all foolishness;
But what will come to fruition is in this single note!

[(Crimson leaves.)]

(Male lead speaks:) Alas. Everything has its allotted fate. Who would have thought that missy would be so good to me? I am a member of the Society for Solving Riddles, a romantic Sui He, a rakish Lu Jia. Once there we'll fall kerplunk to the ground. This shitty day, try as it might, won't get any later. Heaven, you hold all things for men: why wrangle about this single sun? Go down! Go down! (Student recites:)

---

[16] For Qiannü, heroine of "The Disembodied Soul," see p. 36.
[17] See play III, act 1, n. 4.
[18] To "leap the dragon's gate" means to pass the examinations. Fish that swam the Yellow River upstream and passed its rapids were believed to turn into dragons.
[19] A reference to both success at the examinations and the cassia tree in the moon, where the moon goddess, Chang'e, lives.
[20] Her eyes.
[21] Her eyebrows.

> When reading books throughout the day, I feared the yellow dusk;
> Unaware of its sinking in the west, I reluctantly closed the door.

102b

> But desiring to go to a tryst beneath the crab-apple flower,
> How I suffer from the great *yang* that now grows roots.[22]

(Male lead speaks:) Ai, it's just now noon. I'll have to wait a while. Now look again: the sun just won't go down, no matter what. [(Student recites:)]

> Azure heaven for a thousand miles without clouds,
> Vainly wearying body and mind of the tired traveler.
> I so despise the great *yang*'s coveting of battle,
> I am unaware that the red sun sets in the west.[23]

[(Male lead speaks:)] Aiya, fortunately it has tilted to the west. I'll have to wait longer.

> For no reason at all, the three-footed crow[24]
> As a perfect circle shines shimmering, shimmering;
> How can I get Hou Yi's bow
> To shoot this single wheel down?[25]

(Male lead speaks:) Thanks to heaven and earth! The sun's gone down, and now they strike the watch. Ai, now they strike the bell. I pull the door to my study closed behind me. When I get there, I'll pull myself up by the weeping willow and in one fell swoop leap across the wall.

[(Male lead leaves.)]

❖❖❖

---

[22] The sun (the great *yang*) is moving so slowly that it appears to have grown roots and become immobile.

[23] For this difficult passage, see the discussion on p. 94.

[24] It was anciently believed that the sun was inhabited by a three-legged crow.

[25] According to an early myth, there were originally ten suns in the sky, which came out in turn. When all ten appeared together, the great archer Hou Yi shot down nine of them and so saved the earth from being burned.

Oriole Gets Angry at the Student for Jumping over the Wall; Crimson Orders the
Student to Kneel and Take His Punishment

102b

(Crimson enters and speaks:) My missy ordered me to deliver a letter today to
Student Zhang. She put on all kinds of airs in front of me but all the time in that   103a
that poem of hers had secretly made a tryst with him. She didn't say anything to
me, so I'll pretend ignorance and ask her to come out to burn incense. Tonight
she made her evening toilet differently from on other days. I'll see how she
deceives me when the moment actually arrives! (Calling, Crimson acts out
something and [speaks]:) Sister, let's go and burn incense!

Act 3

(Female lead [enters] and recites:)

> Flowers' perfume thickly layered, gentle breezes soft;
> No one in the courtyard, the pale moon is full.

(Crimson speaks:) Sister, tonight the moon is bright, the breeze is fresh. What a
wonderful starry sky!

[*Shuangdiao* mode:] "Xinshui ling" (Crimson sings:)
The evening breeze, cold and piercing, penetrates the window's gauze;
Latched with golden hooks, the embroidered screens are furled.
On the door shutters freeze the evening mists;
On the tower corner collects lingering sunset rosiness.

209

She's just faced the caltrop flower[1]
And finished her evening toilet in the upper room.

"Zhuma ting" (Crimson sings:)
Far from clamor and noise,
The tender green pond hides away sleeping ducks.
A natural, elegant seclusion,
Pale yellow willows bear up roosting crows.

103b   Her golden lotuses trample sprouts of peonies;
Her jade hairpins catch on the brier-rose trellis.
The night is cool, the mossy path slippery;
Pearls of dew soak through wave-crossing stockings.[2]

(Crimson speaks:) As I see it, neither that student nor my young missy will be able to keep it together until evening.

"Qiao pai'er" (Crimson sings:)
Ever since that sun appeared, they have longed for moon's brilliance;
Struggling through a quarter hour, it seemed a summer's length.
Over the tips of willows, the slanting sun slowly, slowly goes down—
"Oh, let the god whip it on."[3]

"Jiao zhengpa" (Crimson sings:)
104a   She's costumed herself all falsely[4]
To prepare for a meeting of rain and clouds at Shamanka Gorge.
All because of that swallow mate and oriole partner,[5]
She is unable to shackle that monkey of her mind and the horse of her desire.

(Crimson speaks:) Not only is my young mistress suffering, but that student hasn't even tasted water or rice for the last few days

([Crimson] sings:)
Because my sister pales the moon and shames the flowers.
Whether true or false,
Now her true nature cannot be guessed,

---

[1] A bronze mirror, so named for the decoration on its back.

[2] An allusion drawn from Cao Zhi's (192–232) "Rhapsody on the Spirit of the Luo River" ("Luoshen fu"), in which the poet describes a goddess treading over the water of the Luo in her silk stockings. She was, of course, unattainable; the allusion here is meant to suggest Oriole's aloofness from the student.

[3] The god is Xihe, charioteer of the sun.

[4] On one level this line means that Oriole has made herself up to be especially beguiling; but on a second level it is clearly a comment on her attempt to dissemble her real feelings from Crimson.

[5] Depending on context, swallow mates and oriole partners may refer to either lovers or potential husbands.

And all he can do is thrash around wildly [6]

(Crimson speaks:) Sister, you stand here by the rockery. I'll open the side door of the temple and see if anyone could be listening to us. (After winking [at the audience, Crimson speaks]:) That addlepated lout hasn't shown up yet. Psst, psst. (Male lead enters and speaks:) This is just the right time to go! Psst, psst. (Crimson speaks:) That prick's here. Psst, psst.   104b

"Chenzui dongfeng" (Crimson sings:)
I would have said that the wind swayed evening crows in the shade of the
    sophora tree,
But all the while it was the raven's-gauze hattails of the jade person.
One hides himself beside the curving balustrade;
One stands by the rockery with her back turned.
There's no polite conversation,
And neither ever addresses the other.

(Crimson speaks:) That prick's here. (Male lead speaks:) Missy, you've come! (Male lead acts out embracing Crimson. Crimson speaks:) You animal, it's me! You ought to keep a careful lookout. What if I had been the madam? (Male lead speaks:) I've suffered so much, my eyes are dizzied, and I embraced you all too rashly. I hope you will forgive me.

([Crimson] sings:)
Even if you embraced me all too wildly,
You'd better keep your eyes open.

[(Crimson speaks:)] It must have been because

[(Crimson sings:)]
You, poor devil, were so starved that your eyes were dizzied.

(Male lead speaks:) Where is your missy? (Crimson speaks:) By the rockery. But I ask, did she really summon you here? (Male lead speaks:) I am a member of the Society for Solving Riddles, a romantic Sui He, a rakish Lu Jia. No doubt, in one fell swoop we'll fall to the ground! (Crimson speaks:) Don't come in through the door. She'd only say that I let you in. Go jump across the wall. This one acrobatic trick will help the two of you get married tonight. I'll tell you what to do, and you act accordingly·

"Qiao pai'er" (Crimson sings:)
See how pale clouds encage the brilliance of the moon,
Like red paper protecting a silver candle;[7]

---

[6] Another interpretation of these two lines is: "Because he could not guess her true nature, / He did all those crazy things [such as kneeling before me, not eating, etc.]."

[7] I.e., the lights arranged in the honeymoon chamber.

Willow skeins and flower clusters unfurl their screens,
Green sedge unrolls a pad of embroidered couch.

105a   "Tianshui ling" (Crimson explains female lead to student, [singing]:)
The fine night goes on and on,
The quiet courtyard is deserted and still,
Flower stems bend low and rustle.
She's a young girl:
You should pamper her temper,
Massage her with words,
Blend with her moods.
Don't suppose her a broken willow or tattered blossom.

"Zhegui ling" [(Crimson sings:)]
She's an, oh, so lovable, beautiful jade without flaw·
Her powdered face engenders spring,
Her cloudy locks are like piled-up raven feathers.
She's, oh, so timid, oh, so fearful,
And she does not scheme for free wine or idler's tea.
But once between the sheets, you should give it your all:
When your fingertips report back from duty worn out,
Then you can stack away your moans and sighs;
And when you are finished with your concerns and anxieties,
When you have cleared away frustrations and sorrows,
Then be prepared to be happily stuffed.[8]

(Student acts out jumping across the wall. Female lead speaks:) Who is that?
(Male lead speaks:) Me, your student. (Female lead speaks angrily:) Student
Zhang—what kind of person are you? Here I am burning incense, and you come
without any reason. If the madam should hear of this, what kind of explanation
could you give? (Male lead speaks:) Ai—she has changed her stripes!

"Jinshang hua" (Crimson sings:)
Why does the matchmaker's heart know no alarm?
Truly husband and wife are of one mind.
Here I'll just sneak up on tiptoe
And listen stealthily—
One stands ashamed,
105b   One is enraged!
Student Zhang is without a single word;
Ai—Oriole has changed her stripes!
He is silent and still, in the dark and confused;
She rattles and prattles, goes on without end.

---

[8] The term used here, *chengda*, means both to prop up from the inside and to be in fine
fettle, to be satisfied.

She has suddenly brought to a halt Sui He
And squashed Lu Jia.
With folded hands and bowing body,
He feigns deafness, plays dumb.

(Crimson speaks:) Student Zhang, where's that big mouth of yours that you had when you were alone? You missed your chance to go ahead and embrace her! Wouldn't you be ashamed if we took you to court?

"Qingjiang yin" (Crimson sings:)
When no one was around, you knew how to idly rattle your teeth,
But on the inside it was all vain cunning and deceit.
Who would know that by the rockery
You would not remember "beneath the western wing"?
A perfumed and beautiful maiden has cloven the showy quince.[9]

(Female lead speaks:) Crimson! A thief! (Crimson speaks:) Who? (Male lead speaks:) It's me. (Crimson speaks:) Student Zhang, what errand has brought you here? (Female lead speaks:) Let's drag him in front of the madam! (Crimson speaks:) If we do that, it will damage his reputation. Let's you and me interrogate him this time. Student Zhang, come forward. (Student acts out kneeling down. Crimson speaks:) Kneel down! You have studied the books of the sage Confucius; you should be familiar with the principles of the duke of Zhou. What concern brought you here in the dead of night?   106a

"Yan'er luo" (Crimson sings:)
It's not that we are faking a tribunal—
We speak some earnest words.
I would have said that your culture and learning were as deep as the sea;
Who would have guessed that your sexual daring was as wide as the heavens?

(Crimson speaks:) Do you understand your crime, Student Zhang? (Male lead speaks:) I do not understand my crime.

"Desheng ling" (Crimson sings:)
Who had you break and enter in the dead of night?
If it was not for fornication, then it was for theft!
You are a cassia-plucking man
Who's turned into a flower-filching lout!
You don't want to jump across the dragon's gate
But do want to learn how to mount a mare.

(Crimson speaks:) Missy, please pardon this student out of consideration for Crimson. (Female lead speaks:) If it weren't out of consideration for Crimson, I'd

---

[9] This is the *mugua*, a quince grown in southern China that has a beautiful skin but is completely inedible; good to look at but, like the student, useless.

have you off to the madam to see if you had "the face to meet the elders of East of the River."[10] Rise!

106b
([Crimson] sings:)
Thank you for you wisdom, missy,
And for forgiving him on my behalf.
But if the court had conducted the inquiry carefully

(Crimson speaks:) You are just a budding talent and should be exerting yourself to the utmost beneath the cold window. Who made you break and enter someone's flower garden in the dead of night? If what was on your mind was not fornication, then it was petty theft.

([Crimson] sings:)
Sir, prepare your delicate skin for a sound thrashing![11]

(Female lead speaks:) Student Zhang, you have favored me by saving my life, and this favor should be repaid. But how can you act this way when we are brother and sister? How could you be at ease if the madam were to find out about this? Don't ever do this again. If you do it once more, you will not escape so cleanly.

[(Female lead leaves.)]

(Male lead speaks, facing a ghost door:) *You* made me come. How come you gave me such a lecture? (Crimson pulls male lead around and speaks:) Shame on you.
107a   Tsk, tsk. Is this our romantic Sui He, our rakish Lu Jia? (Student speaks:) I've wronged my society! Today my hopes are dashed to the ground.

he mis-interpreted!

"Li ting yan dai xiepai sha" (Crimson sings:)
Don't quote again "A quarter hour of spring night is worth a thousand in gold,"[12]

---

[10] Following his crushing defeat at Nine Mile Mountain, Xiang Yu, in retreat from Liu Bang, was driven to the banks of the Raven River. According to "The Basic Annals of Xiang Yu" in *The Records of the Historian* (*Shiji*), when asked by a boatman to cross over and rule the land east of the Yangtze, from which he hailed, Xiang Yu replied, "I crossed the Yangtze and came west with eight thousand young men from East of the River. If I returned to East of the River today, even if their fathers and brothers should take pity on me and make me king, what face would I have to see them? Even if they should not speak of it, am I alone without a sense of shame in my heart?"

[11] The second referent here is masturbation.

[12] This is a paraphrase (with characters inverted to match the rhymes of the play) of the first line of a poem by Su Shi that will reappear in this and later acts. The poem is called "Spring Night" ("Chunye"):

A quarter hour of spring night is worth a thousand in gold;
The flowers have a fresh fragrance, the moon is dark.
Songs and pipes on the dais of the loft—a sound reedy and thin;
A hanging swing in the courtyard—the night is deep and dark.

But start preparing "Beneath the wintry window, another ten years of
   solitude."[13]
A Fellow of the Society for Solving Riddles
Has missed the beat on "Welcoming the breeze, the door is half-opened,"
Has been screened out by a mountain—"When separated by a wall, flowers'
   shadows move"—
And has been in deepest darkness while "waiting for the moon beneath the
   western wing."
You may pat on the powder of Master He,
But she'll have sketched Zhang Chang's eyebrows herself.
A vinegary pedant who would force passion—
This will dry out your heart entangled in clouds and enmeshed in rain,
Fill with remorse your gall to filch jade and pilfer perfume,
Cross out your talk of stroking the green and cuddling the red.

(Male lead speaks:) Let me write another note and trouble you to take it so that I
can express my innermost feelings.

([Crimson] sings:)
Forget now lascivious lyrics!
Quit forever those love notes!
You still don't have a knack for the rules of romantic lyrics.
From now on, be filled with remorse, my Zhuo Wenjun;
You'd better leave to study, my Sima Xiangru.

[(Crimson leaves.)]

107b

(Male lead speaks:) Missy, you're the death of me. I'll never dare think this
thought again. Alas, my illness grows deeper every day. What will I do? When I
got her note in the night, I was overjoyed; but when I forced myself to come
here today despite my illness, I encountered another spell of temper. I'd better go
back to my study and there drown in depression. It's clear that I'm finished.
(Student recites:)

The fruits of the cassia, in idleness I wander by;
The flowers of the sophora, in illness I watch.

[(Male lead leaves.)]

---

[13] See play II, act 1, n. 16.

Crimson Takes a Prescription to Student Zhang on Oriole's Behalf

Act 4

(Old lady enters and speaks:) This morning the abbot sent someone to tell me that Student Zhang is seriously ill. I ordered the abbot to send for a physician to examine him. At the same time I sent Crimson to see elder brother and to ask whether he needed any medicine; and to ask what medicine the physician prescribed; and what the symptoms and his diagnosis were. She was then to report back to me.

([Old lady] leaves.)

❖❖❖

(Crimson [enters and] speaks:) The madam said that Student Zhang is very ill. It's even worse since he had to suffer our tantrum last night. Oriole, you're going to be the death of him! (Female lead [enters and] speaks:) I've written a note, but I'll say that it is a prescription, and I'll have Crimson take it to him. Then his symptoms will immediately be relieved. (Female lead acts out calling Crimson. [Crimson] speaks:) Sister, why are you calling me? (Female lead speaks:) Student Zhang is very ill, but I have a good prescription. Please take it to him. (Crimson speaks:) Here we go again! Girl, don't be the death of him! (Female lead speaks:) Dear sister, please go and save his life. (Crimson speaks:) In the whole world, only you can save him from his illness. The old lady has already sent me, so I'll take your note along too.

([Crimson] leaves.)

(Female lead speaks:) Crimson has gone; I'll wait for her in my embroidered chambers.

([Female lead] leaves.)

❖❖❖

(Male lead [enters and] speaks:) Since suffering through that scene in the flower garden last night—what with my old symptoms—I'm evidently done for. The madam tells me that the abbot has called a physician to examine me. But these shit conditions can't be cured by just any physician. If only I could swallow down one drop of my missy's sweetly, sweetly delicious, aromatically, aromatically perfumed, piercingly, piercingly cool, dripping, dropping, lovable spittle, then this fucking illness would be over. (Extra male role does his routine.[1] Bald one, leading in clowns costumed as physicians, enters. After [clowns] have finished the skit *A Pair of Battling Quacks*, they leave.[2] Bald one speaks:) Now that you've taken your medicine, I'll report to the old lady and then be back in a moment to check on you.

([Bald one] leaves.)

(Crimson enters and speaks:) This is how my mistress sends them to their deaths. She's making me go again to ask about him and give him this prescription. It will only make him sicker. I'd better go. (Crimson recites:)

> In strange lands it is easy to catch the illness of separation's sorrow;
> But even a miraculous prescription cannot cure a man of a broken heart.

[*Yuediao* mode:] "Dou anchun" (Crimson, discussing female lead, [sings]:)
Because you wrote a poem with multicolored brush[3]
And wove palindromes into your brocade,[4]
You have dispatched him to the point where he lies on his pillow, is glued to
    his bed,
Forgets to eat, neglects sleeping.
You have so broken him down that his temples are like a sorrowing Pan
    An's,[5]

---

[1] In other texts the extra comes onstage to discuss the illness, then goes out to invite the two physicians to come treat the patient.

[2] See Appendix I for a translation of the single extant example of this skit.

[3] From a story about the Six Dynasties poet Jiang Yan (444–505), who dreamed that Guo Pu (276–324) appeared to him in a dream and said to him, "I have a pen that you have kept for several years, and now I'd like it back." Still dreaming, Jiang Yan then searched around in his clothing and found a multicolored brush that he gave to Guo Pu. From that time on, Jiang Yan lacked all creative skill and was unable to compose poetry The multicolored brush became a standard metaphor for creative literary power.

[4] See play II, act 1, n. 13.

[5] See play III, act 1, n. 4.

His waist is like a sick Shen Yue's.[6]
His grief is deep,
His illness is critical.
Last night, with hot anger, you reproved him face-to-face,
And today, with icy lines, you go at the man again.

(Crimson speaks:) How you reproved him last night!

"Zihua'er xu" (Crimson, discussing female lead, [sings]:)
Better you'd never waited for the moon, leaning on the wicker gate,
Or made poetic couplets in response to his rhyming words
Or listened to his zither with cocked ears.

([Crimson] speaks in imitation of female lead:) As soon as she saw him, she put on a show—and such a long speech: "Student Zhang, we are brother and sister—what are you after?"

([Crimson] sings:)
When angry, you trample him down;
When happy,

[(Crimson speaks:)] "Crimson, dear sister, go and see him."

([Crimson] sings:)
She coerces a serving maid.
That's insupportable!
She makes me as busy as a thread that never leaves the needle.
From now on, let her do it all herself!

[(Crimson speaks:)] This is all the fault of the madam:

([Crimson] sings:)
She's turned his ocean of righteousness and mountain of favor
Into a faraway river and a distant peak.

(Crimson greets student [and speaks]:) Brother, how is your illness? (Male lead speaks:) It's going to kill me. If I die, missy, you'll be summoned before King Yama's palace,[7] and you won't be spared being called a conspirator. (Crimson sighs and speaks:) No one in the whole wide world who has ever suffered love-longing has been as addlepated as you!

"Tian jing sha" (Crimson, discussing student, [sings]:)
His heart does not keep to the ocean of learning or the forest of letters;
His dreams never leave the shadows of willows or the shade of flowers.
He has set his mind only on filching jade and pilfering perfume,

---

[6] See play III, act 1, n. 15.
[7] King of the underworld.

And there too he has failed to achieve anything.
Ever since the crab apple blossomed, he has been longing himself into his
present state!

(Crimson speaks:) What is the reason you are so sick? (Male lead speaks:)All 110a
because—in front of you I'm afraid to lie—because of your governess. When I
returned to my study last night, every breath was a single death. I've saved her,
but I'm being killed by her. From antiquity the saying's been "A foolish girl, a
faithless man," but today that's reversed.

"Tiaoxiao ling" (Student, explaining to Crimson, [sings]:)
I've figured it out here myself:
This illness comes from lechery
The bones of my corpse poke out, invaded by a ghostly illness.
Even though budding talents have always been this way,
This lousy love-longing is just too silly.
Merit and fame—these I've already failed to achieve;
The bond of marriage—now I moan and groan over and over again.

(Crimson speaks:) The madam ordered me to come and ask what medicine you
might need, brother. The young missy extends her regards twice, thrice. I also
have a prescription that she sends to you, sir. (Male lead acts out panic and
speaks:) Where? Where?(Crimson speaks:) It employs a number of ingredients,
each with its own use. Let me explain them to you:

"Xiaotao hong" (Crimson sings:)
Cassia flowers sway their shade in the dead of night;
Vinegar soaks the one who "ought to return."

(Male lead speaks:) Cassia flowers are warm by nature, ought-to-return vivifies 110b
the blood—what is the method of their use?

([Crimson] sings:)
Facing the rockery, she turned her back and hid in the shade,
So the ingredients of this prescription are the hardest to find.
One or two doses will make people so.

(Male lead speaks:) What should I shun?

(Crimson sings:)
To be shunned is the "knowing mother," not yet asleep;
To be feared is that "Crimson" might blurt it out.
Once taken,
It will surely "make the gentleman" "completely well."[8]

---

[8] This is a complicated aria employing a kind of entertainment, a jeu d'esprit that
occurs as early as the *bianwen* texts of the late Tang and was also a common feature of the
urban stage in China. In this aria the names of six medicines are used in a way that plays on

(Crimson speaks:) My mistress wrote this prescription out in her own hand. (Male lead acts out looking at it. Bursting out laughing, he arises. Male lead speaks:) If I had known earlier that sister was coming, I would have gone out of my way to greet you, my girl. (Crimson speaks:) What's this—again? This is twice now! (Male lead speaks:) You don't know what the poem means. Your missy will tra-la-la with me. (Crimson speaks:) Aren't you missing something?

"Gui santai" (Crimson sings:)
Sir, you are really stupid;
Don't dissemble the fool.
What a laugh, you lunatic laureate—
With nowhere else to hear good news,
You want to extract it from this note.
Having gotten this scrap of paper, you'd better be careful of the needle in floss.
If you see that jade transcendent sylph,
You'll become all soft and paralyzed.
My young mistress forgets favors;
Truly she is an ingrate who leads people on for nothing!

111a

(Crimson speaks:) What does she say in the letter? Please read it out to me. (Male lead speaks, reciting:)

Don't let idle matters torture your bosom
And without reason ruin your heavenly endowed talents.

---

their common names and to a certain extent on their properties. In the first line there is a pun on the word *yaoying* (waving shadows) and *yao yinzi*, something that is added to medicine to make it more palatable. Cassia flowers (*cinnamomum cassia*) are used as both a medicine and a flavoring for medicine. "Ought-to-return" of the second line is usually identified as *angelica polymorpha*, a stimulant taken by women to help with menstrual problems and to stimulate the generative organs. "Vinegar" is a common pejorative applied to young and callow students. *Yin* (to hide) also means a storage vessel buried in the ground. "Knowing mother" is *anemarrhena asphodeloides*, a drug used primarily as an expectorant but also as a powerful diuretic. "Crimson" (literally, the red maiden) is the common ladybug, used for some medicinal purposes. It may also refer to the bloodstains left on the bedclothes after a maiden's first intercourse. "Make-the-gentleman" is *quisqualis indica*, a strong vermifuge that is used to get rid of intestinal parasites such as worms. "Completely well," *can*, is ginseng (*shen*), a powerful stimulant. The aria may be roughly paraphrased as follows:

Cassia flowers added to the medicine for draughts deep in the night,
Angelica root soaked in vinegar,
Taken face-to-face from the storage pit in the rear of the false rocks—
This is the prescription that's hardest to find.
Don't take this powerful diuretic before you go to bed;
I guarantee this vermifuge [will get rid of what's eating you] and a little bit of ginseng
    [will stimulate you].

We hope that this imperfect match will give some idea of the humor of this otherwise enigmatic passage that speaks so eloquently to the curative powers of Oriole.

My intention then was to keep my reputation intact;
Could I have kept it from being your disaster today?
Respectful of your ample virtue, I cannot follow the rites;
I humbly offer you a new poem that can stand as a go-between.
And I send word to Gaotang: do not write any rhapsodies,[9]
For tonight, truly, rain and clouds will come.

(Male lead speaks:) This rhyme is not to be compared to the one day before yesterday. Your missy is coming for sure. (Crimson speaks:) But if she comes,

"Tusi'er" (Crimson sings:)
Your body lies covered by a strip of cotton sheet,
Your head is pillowed on your three-foot jasper zither.
When she comes, how will she be able to sleep with you?
She'll be so cold, she'll tremble and shiver, quiver and quake:
You won't be able to talk about a "perfect companion."

"Shengyao wang" (Crimson sings:)   111b
If indeed your heart is set on it,
Her heart is set on it.
Yesterday, "in the courtyard with its swings, deep in the dark night,"[10]
The flowers cast their shadows,
The moon cast its shadow—
"A quarter hour of spring night equals a thousand in gold,"[11]
What need to "recite a poem to one who understands"?[12]

(Male lead speaks:) I have ten ounces of patterned silver. Please rent me a set of bedding.

"Dongyuan le" (Crimson sings:)
Our mandarin-duck pillows,
Our kingfisher-feather coverlets—
If you will be the one to have your heart's every desire,
Why should she have to rent them out to you?
What's to fear if you don't undress, but stay clothed?
Wouldn't that still be better than your hand grasping that little pinky down there?
If by chance you are married, then you'll be greatly blessed!

(Student speaks:) I look like this because of missy Hasn't she lost a bit of her elegance because of me?

---

[9] A reference to Song Yu's "Rhapsody on the High Terrace", see pp. 67 and 95–96.
[10] A reference to Su Shi's poem "Chunye", see play III, act 3, n. 12.
[11] See n. 10 above.
[12] Probably a reference to the common saying "Drink wine when you meet one who knows you; recite poetry to one who understands."

112a   "Mian daxu" (Crimson, discussing female lead, [sings]:)
The jet of her brows: spread-out halcyon on distant mountains;
The expanse of her eyes: unsullied autumn waters.
Her body like congealed cream,
Her waist like a supple willow.
Handsome her face, quick her heart,
Her postures warm and tender, her character subdued.
She may not know about hot dharma moxa or the divine needle,[13]
But she still surpasses Guanyin, who saves the world from bitter troubles.

(Male lead speaks:) I will never forget you if this affair is brought off.

"Reprise" (Crimson sings:)
In vain your mouth moaned and groaned,
Bitterly in dreams you hunted and sought.
But the past has sunk away;
112b   Let's talk only of today.
When you meet tonight, I'll make it happen.
I don't scheme for your white jade and yellow gold;
I want only "flowers covering her head, brocade trailing on the ground."[14]

(Male lead speaks:) I'm afraid that the madam may confine her so she can't come out. (Crimson speaks:) Fear only that missy is not willing. If she has set her mind on it, then you rest easy!

"Coda" [(Crimson sings:)]
Even if the madam locks up the gate day and night,
Whatever happens, Oriole will make you content.

(Student speaks:) Don't let her be unwilling like last night. (Crimson speaks:) Pull yourself together.

([Crimson] sings:)
Once she's here, can "willing" or "unwilling" be up to her?
When you see her, whether or not to be intimate will depend on you!

[(They leave.)]

❖❖❖

"Luosiniang shawei"
Because of tonight's exchange of words and sending of letters,
We'll watch tomorrow's transporting of clouds and clutching of rain!

---

[13] These terms refer to two traditional medical cures—moxabustion and acupuncture—although there are also clear sexual overtones here.

[14] I.e., Oriole dressed in the traditional wedding garb of long, colorful skirts.

Title: The madam orders up a doctor;
          Oriole Cui sends a poem of love.

Name: Little Crimson inquires about medicine;
          Zhang Junrui suffers longings of love.

VOLUME III OF THE DELUXE, COMPLETELY ILLUSTRATED, AND ANNOTATED STORY OF THE WESTERN WING

Crimson Coerces Oriole to Go to Her Tryst with the Student

VOLUME IV OF THE DELUXE, COMPLETELY ILLUSTRATED, AND ANNOTATED STORY OF THE WESTERN WING

A Clandestine Meeting of Rain and Clouds

Act 1

(Female lead enters and speaks:) Last night Crimson took my note to Student Zhang, setting a tryst to see him tonight.[1] I'll wait until Crimson comes, and talk it over with her. (Crimson enters and speaks:) Sister ordered me to deliver a note to Student Zhang in which she promised a rendezvous tonight. But I'm afraid that young mistress of mine is lying again, and that will finish him off. It's no joke anymore. I'll see what she says when I get there. (Female lead speaks:) Straighten up my bedroom, Crimson, I want to go to sleep. (Crimson speaks:) If you are going to sleep, how will you dispose of that student? (Female lead speaks:) What about that student? (Crimson speaks:) There you go again. It's no joke to send a person to his death. If you go back on your word again, I'm going to inform on you to the madam and tell her you sent me with a note to set up a rendezvous with him. (Female lead speaks:) You little hussy! You're really a pain in the neck. I'm burning with shame—how can I go? (Crimson speaks:) What's there to be

---

[1] "Last night" and "tonight" may refer to the nights of performance rather than time within the play, since the action seems to run on without interruption.

ashamed of? Once there, just close your eyes. (Crimson, pushing female lead, speaks:) Go on! Go on! The madam is asleep! (Female lead acts out running [and leaves]. Crimson sighs and speaks:) My sister may put on a strong show, but her steps have carried there already.

"Duanzheng hao" (Crimson sings:)
Because of sister's jadelike spirit and flowerlike appearance,
He's been longing for her day and night without a break.
Let her one sincere heart erase all her heaven-cheating deception!
She leaves her painted chambers and goes to his study room;
She departs the cave of Chu and goes to Gaotang.
Learning to filch jade and attempting to pilfer perfume:
The handsome lass of Shamanka Mountain and King Xiang of Chu.
King Xiang of Chu must already be on the Terrace of Yang!

[(Crimson leaves.)]

❖❖❖

(Male lead [enters] and speaks:) The note that Crimson gave me last night   114a
promised that I would succeed tonight. The first watch has just ended, but I still
don't see her. Don't lie anymore, missy. (Student recites:)

This fine night in the world of men, is it still or not?
The comely lass from heaven above, will she come or not?

[*Xianlü* mode:] "Dian jiangchun" (Student sings:)
Standing still on quiet steps,
The night is deep, and fragrant incense mists
Are spread over this realm of gold.[2]
Desolate and lonely is the study;
Drowned in depression is a roving reader of books.

"Hunjiang long" (Student sings:)
Where are the colored clouds?   114b
The moonlight is like water, soaking tower and terrace;
The monks are in their meditation cells;
Ravens caw in courtyard sophoras.
Wind plays the sounds of bamboo:
I take it for the echo of her golden pendants.
Moonlight moves the shadows of flowers:
Can it be the jade person coming?
My damned eyes suspended in expectation,
My passionate breast burning in anxiousness,

---

[2] A common term for a Buddhist temple.

My heart and body a single piece—
I do not know how to deal with them.
I had best sheepishly lean on this gate and wait.
In utter silence, the blue-green simurgh brings no letter,
The yellow dog carries no news.[3]

(Student speaks:) She's on my mind every minute twenty-four hours of the day.
But how could you know?

115a   "You hulu" (Student sings:)
Love thoughts, drowsy and confused, my eyes too tired to open,
From my solitary pillow
My dream soul flies to the Terrace of Yang in Chu;
Could I have known my suffering for her would go on day and night?
Better never to have met this city-toppling vamp.
When people commit transgressions, they must chastise themselves,
Without being afraid to reform.
I intended to keep my heart alert, "treating the wise as wise and slighting sex,"[4]
But I had no defense against the way that she would suddenly come to mind.

115b   "Tianxia le" (Student sings:)
I can only lean firmly against the gate, hands propping my chin;
I have no way of guessing
Whether she will come or not.
The madam's side, I guess, is hard to leave.
I gaze for her until my eyes are worn through,
I long for her until my heart grows constricted.
Probably my "karmic enemy" is not at liberty.

(Male lead speaks:) If she's not here by now, then isn't she just lying again?

---

[3] Blue-green simurghs were the messengers of the Queen Mother of the West. The
birds once visited the Martial Emperor of Han's palace on the seventh day of the seventh
month and presaged a visit by the Queen Mother herself. The simurgh is a messenger,
then, but one that is a harbinger of a visit by the sender. The reader should note that the
seventh day of the seventh month is also the one day of the year that the Herdboy and
Weaving Girl meet. The dog of the second couplet is the fabled Yellow Ear (Huang'er) of
the Six Dynasties poet Lu Ji (261–303). He carried messages home for his master, who was
stationed in the capital.

[4] These three lines are adapted from the *Analects*. The first is a paraphrase of *Analects*,
1.8: "The Master said, 'If a gentleman is not taken as weighty, then he provokes no awe
and his learning will not be solid. One should make conscientiousness and sincerity one's
mainstay. Have no friends but one's equals. If wrong, reform without fear.'" The second
is from *Analects*, 1.7: "Zixia said, 'A man who treats the wise as wise and disesteems sexual
attraction can exhaust his strength in service to his parents, can exert himself in service to
his lord, and is one whose words can be trusted in interaction with friends. Even though
he is called unlearned, I would say he is learned.'"

"Nuozha ling" (Student sings:)
If she's really willing to come,
Then morning's radiance has left her noble quarters.
If she'll really be here,
Then spring will burst forth in my simple study.
But if she does not come,
Like a rock I'll sink into the great ocean.
I count the steps she has to go
And wait, clinging to the window sill.
Please tell her, her of many talents:

"Que ta zhi" (Student sings:)
"Of that cruel lecture you gave me,
I have no memory in my heart.
Now that I've won your change of mind and turn of heart,
Night has gone and the daylight is here.
Vainly I have cast amorous glances
By now for half a year—
I barely made it through those times!"

(Student speaks:) Young lady, if you don't come this time,

"Jisheng cao" (Student sings:)
I'm set to suffer,
Prepared to be borne away.
Well, I've forced myself to live on water and tea in a strange land,   116a
All because that detestable creature taught my heart to bear torture[5]
And manipulated this sincere heart until just a carcass was left alive.
If one were to order the Bureau of Astronomical Observations to compute my
    sorrows of this half year,
Truly it would be more than ten loads in a heavy wain.

(Crimson enters and speaks:) Missy, I'll go over; you stay here. ([Crimson] acts
out knocking on the door. Male lead asks:) Who is it? (Crimson speaks:) Your
mother from your former life. (Student speaks:) Missy, come on, I'm waiting.
(Female lead greets male lead. Male lead acts out opening the door. Male lead
kneels and speaks:)[6] What abilities do I, Zhang Gong, have that a divine sylph
should trouble herself to descend from heaven? Am I sleeping or dreaming?

"Cunli yagu" (Student sings:)
All of a sudden I see her detestable countenance—

(Male lead speaks:) Was I ever sick?

---

[5] For "detestable creature," see play I, act 2, n. 2.

[6] The logical order of the stage directions is reversed here; this is probably a mistake for
"Male lead acts out opening the door. Female lead acts out greeting male lead."

[(Student sings:)]
She has cured 90 percent of my queasiness.
Since I was chastised earlier,
Who could have expected tonight's joyous loving?
Oh, missy, you are so considerate,
I, this untalented Zhang Gong, must kneel and make obeisance.
This small student lacks Song Yu's face,
Pan An's looks,
Cao Zhi's talents.[7]
Sister,
Please take pity on me, who has to live as a traveler!

116b   "Yuanhe ling" (Student sings:)
Her embroidered shoes, barely half a span,
Her willowy waist just fills a single armful;
Bashful and embarrassed, she refuses to lift her head
But keeps grasping the mandarin-duck pillow
Her cloudy coif seems to let slip its golden hairpins:
How it suits her, the bun at her nape awry.

117a   "Shangma jiao" (Student sings:)
I loosen the knotted buttons,
Untie her silken waistwrap;
Orchid musk spreads through my secluded study
O cruel one, you can really make me suffer.
Ai,
Why aren't you willing to turn your face to me?

"Sheng hulu" (Student sings:)
Here to my breast I press her pliant jade and warm perfume—
Ai,
Ruan Zhao has reached Mount Tiantai.[8]
Spring has come to the realm of men, flowers sport their color!
Gently she adjusts her willowy waist
And lightly splits the flower's heart:
Dew drips; the peony opens.

"Reprise" (Student sings:)
I just wet the tip, and she becomes numb all over:
Fish and water find harmonious concord;
From the lovely fragrance of the tender pistil the butterfly collects at will.

---

[7] The son of Cao Cao (155–220) and a famous poet from the late Han and Three Kingdoms period.

[8] See play I, act 1, n. 27; note that, like Peach Blossom Fount, Mount Tiantai may allude to sexual union.

Partly resistant, partly eager to give,
Now alarmed, now full of love—
A sandalwood mouth kisses fragrant cheeks.

(Male lead kneels and speaks:) Thank you, missy, for not rejecting Zhang Gong. Tonight I was allowed to share your pillow and mat, and on another day I shall repay this favor like a devoted servant.[9] (Female lead speaks:) In a single second I have thrown away my body, precious as a thousand pieces of gold. My body and my life I entrust to you forever. May you never disdain me in the future and make me lament my white hair.[10] (Male lead speaks:) How would I ever dare   117b
such a thing! (Male lead acts out inspecting her handkerchief.)

"Houting hua" (Student sings:)
Its spring silk was at first sparkling white,
But now I see a red fragrance has sprinkled its tender color.

(Female lead speaks:) Oh, how embarrassing! Why are you inspecting it?

([Student] sings:)
Below the lamp I steal a glance;
I place it next to my breast.
Oh, how marvelous!
My whole body feels great;
I do not know whence spring came.
But this incapable budding talent Zhang,
This lonely traveler from Western Luo—
Ever since I encountered your beauty,
I longed for you so much that I couldn't get you off my mind.
I was anxious and saddened by obstacles;
My love-longing had no relief.
O my loved one,
How grateful I am for not being chastised.

"Liuye'er" (Student sings:)
I will treasure you as my own precious heart,
Since I've sullied your pure whiteness.
I forgot to eat, neglected to sleep, vented heart's suffering;
But if I had not endured it with a true heart and struggled through with sincerity,
Would it have been possible that from the bitterness of our love-longing such
sweetness would come?

---

[9] The Chinese text actually reads, "On a later day I will repay you as a dog or a horse", that is, in a subsequent incarnation he will be reborn as a dog or a horse and will serve her with the unquestioning devotion of these animals—a conventional phrase used to express gratitude.

[10] On the "Lament on White Hair," see p. 68.

"Qing ge'er" (Student sings:)
We've consummated tonight's, tonight's joyous loving;
My soul has soared beyond welkin's, welkin's clouds.
From the moment I saw you, my passionate darling,
118a   My emaciated carcass has been thinning to a hemp stalk;
Tonight's harmonious concord—I still can't believe it.
Dew drips on fragrant dust;
The wind is quiet on still steps.
Moonlight shoots into my study;
Clouds lock away the Yang Terrace.
I ask for a clear answer;
I still believe you've come in last night's dream[11]—
Oh, stubborn sorrow!

(Female lead speaks:) I'm going back lest the madam look for me when she awakens. (Student speaks:) I'll see you out, missy.

"Jisheng cao" (Student sings:)
How elegant!
Too beautiful!
As soon as I see her, I suffer.
Don't see her for a second: she has you wondering;
See her for just a while: she's got you in love.
Tonight we met within bed-curtains of azure gauze;
When will I again untie your waistwrap of fragrant silk?

(Crimson speaks:) Come bow to your mother. Student Zhang, my congratulations. Missy, we'd better go.

[(Female lead and Crimson leave.)]

118b   (Student recites:)

The gathering is finished, each goes his way;
How shameful to hear the ashram bell ring after the meal:
For ten years darkened by dust and grime,
But now at last encaged by azure gauze.[12]

"Coda" (Student sings:)
Spring desires shone through her creamy breasts,
Spring colors spread across the jet of her brows.

---

[11] In a rare oversight, Wang Shifu here makes reference to a dream sequence that occurs in the all-keys-and-modes but not in the drama. In that sequence, Zhang Sheng, ill, dreams that he has consummated his union with Oriole, only to be disappointed when he awakens.

[12] For the story of Lü Mengzheng, see pp. 19–20.

Now devalued are the jade and silk of the human realm:
Apricot-flower skin and peach-blossom cheeks
In the color of the moonlight,
Oh, so lovely, display the more their red and white.
She descends from fragrant steps and lazily paces the dark green moss.
What moves me are the arched shoes, phoenix-beak narrow!
Alas, small fry like me are without talent;
Thank you, my lovely, for deigning to love me.

(Male lead speaks:) If you don't reject me, missy, please be of like heart of passion.

([Student] sings:)
You must do your best to be here earlier tomorrow night!

([Student leaves.])

The Old Lady Sends Happy to Summon Crimson in Order to Ask about Oriole

Act 2

(Old lady, leading young child, enters and speaks:) These past few days I've been keeping an eye on Oriole, and I've noticed that she is flustered when talking but that her energies are doubled. Her slender waist is unlike earlier days. Could she have had the daring to do it? (Happy speaks:) Last night, when you were asleep, I saw sister and Crimson go to burn incense. They stayed out a long time; I finally went to sleep. (Old lady speaks:) Crimson shoulders the responsibility for this affair. Call Crimson! (Young child calls Crimson. Crimson [enters] and speaks:) Brother, why are you calling me? (Young child speaks:) Mother knows you and sister went into the flower garden. Now she's going to thrash you. (Crimson speaks:) Missy, you've dragged me into it now. Brother, go on ahead; I'll be there shortly (Crimson acts out calling female lead. [Female lead enters.] Crimson speaks:) Sister, the affair is out in the open. The madam is calling for me. What shall I do? (Female lead speaks:) Dear sister, please keep the lid on it. (Crimson speaks:) Oh, fuck! Well, *you've* been quite circumspect! I'm going to say that you've done it. (Female lead recites:)

As soon as the moon is round, dark clouds will obscure it;
When flowers blossom, violent rains are called forth to ruin them.

[*Yuediao* mode:] "Dou anchun" (Crimson sings:)
I told you to go by night and return by light

232

So it might "last as long as heaven and earth."[1]
Because you clutched the rain and transported the clouds,
My heart was always in my mouth.
You should have gone between moonrise and starset—
Who told you to sleep there all through the night?
The old madam's wiles are manifold,
Her temper is violent.
There will be no use now for my clever words and flowery speech
That turn nothing into something!

"Zihua'er xu" (Crimson sings:)
The madam has guessed that this bankrupt sourpuss has become her new son-in-law,
That missy has become the lovely bride,
And that this little hussy has been their secret go-between.
Now your spring mountains let their halcyon green fall slack,
Your pupils lie frozen in their autumn waters.
Other changes aren't worth mentioning:
Just try to fasten the belt of your skirt
Or button the frogs across the front.
Compared to your earlier and slimmer self,
You've gained a lot of energy
And a special kind of romantic charm.

(Female lead speaks:) Answer carefully when you get there, Crimson. (Crimson speaks:) When I get in front of the madam, she'll surely ask, "You little hussy,

"Jin jiaoye" (Crimson sings:)
"I ordered you to guard and observe her wherever she went or stayed!
Who told you to lead her on to mischief and to let her wander astray?"
If she questions me on this point, how can I plead innocence?
"You should sentence her on the count of conspiracy!"

(Crimson speaks:) It is fitting that you be chastised. What did I scheme for?

"Tiaoxiao ling" (Crimson sings:)
Within the embroidered bed-curtains you were "bound together round and
round,"[2]

---

[1] From the last couplet of Bo Juyi's "Song of Unending Sorrow" ("Changhen ge"), a ballad of Tang Xuanzong's love and loss of the Precious Consort Yang. After the two lovers have met again on a magic isle, she tells him of her desire for eternal love; but the poem ends: "Heaven goes on, earth endures, but there is a time they will end; / This vexation threads on and on, and will never be broken."

[2] Both lines of this couplet refer to sexual activity. The first line is from Mao no. 118 of *The Book of Poetry*, the first stanza of which reads:

And you had it all: the upside-down phoenix and flip-flopped simurgh.
But outside the window I lightly coughed a number of times,
Standing on the dark green moss until my embroidered slippers were frozen
  through.
Today my tender skin will be raised in welts by a thick cudgel.
O sister,
All my good offices—
What did I do them for?

(Crimson speaks:) Sister, please wait here. I'll go over there. If I can talk her
around, then don't be happy; if I can't, then don't be upset. (Crimson acts out
greeting old lady. Old lady speaks:) Why don't you kneel down, you hussy? Do
you know with what crime you are charged? (Crimson speaks:) I do not know of
any crime. (Crimson kneels down and speaks:) I do not know of any crime! (Old
lady speaks:) You still stubbornly deny it. If you tell the truth, I'll let you off; if
you don't tell the truth, I'll beat you to death, you hussy! Who ordered you to go
with sister to the flower garden? (Crimson speaks:) We never went! Who saw us?
(Old lady speaks:) Happy saw you go. You still deny it? ([Old lady] acts out
beating Crimson. Crimson speaks:) Don't sprain your hand, madam. Please stay
your rage and stop your anger to listen to my story

120b   "Gui santai" (Crimson sings:)
  Sitting at night, just finished with our embroidery,
  I was idly chatting with sister,
  And our talk turned to brother Zhang's long illness.
  The two of us, without telling you,
  Went to visit him in his study.

(Old lady speaks:) What did he say when you asked about him? (Crimson speaks:)
He said

([Crimson] sings:)
Said, "The madam—the affair is finished!—
She's turned favor into a feud
And midway changed my joy into grief."
He said, "Crimson, you go on ahead for the while,
And let your young mistress stay behind for a time."

(Old lady speaks:) But she's just a young girl! Why did you let her stay behind?

Round and round, the firewood bound,
The three stars are in the sky
What night is tonight?
The night I see this good man.

The song has traditionally been read as expressing the joy of a happily married couple. In
popular literature, the first two words of the opening line, "round and round" (*choumou*),
have come to stand for sexual congress.

"Tusi'er" (Crimson sings:)
I thought it was only for the divine needle and hot dharma moxa;
Who expected swallow friendship and oriole mating?
The two of them have been sleeping together for over a month now;
What need is there to inquire into the facts one by one?

[handwritten margin note: throwing oriole under the bus? (lie?)]

"Shengyao wang" (Crimson sings:)
They don't recognize grief, don't recognize sorrow;
Their paired hearts are a perfect fit.
Madam, you'd better stop when it's right to stop.
Why must you suffer now to trace down every clue?
The proverb says, "A girl grown up should not be kept."[3]

(Old lady speaks:) You hussy, you're responsible for it all! (Crimson speaks:) It is   12ra
not Student Zhang's crime, or missy's, or mine—it's your mistake alone, madam.
(Madam speaks:) Now this hussy fingers me! How could it be my mistake?
(Crimson speaks:) Trust is the root of man: "To be a man and be without trust—
I do not know if such is possible. A large cart without crossbar, a small cart
without yoke—how can one drive them?"[4] When earlier the troops sealed off
Universal Salvation, you promised that you would give your daughter to whoever could make the troops withdraw. If Student Zhang had not admired the
beauty of the young mistress, would he have been willing to go to the trouble of
devising a plan to make the troops withdraw? But when the troops withdrew and
we all were safe, you, madam, went back on your earlier word. Can that be
anything but a breach of trust? Once you were unwilling to conclude the affair as
promised, then you should have rewarded Student Zhang with gold and silk and
sent him on his way. You should not have kept him here and asked him to stay in
the study and so cause a frustrated girl and single man to steal glances at each
other. That's why you have this affair, madam. If you don't put this affair to rest
right now, madam, first of all, you'll dishonor the chancellor and secondly, when
Student Zhang is a famous name in the world, will he accept having been
dishonored after bestowing such a favor? If you take the matter to court, then
you, madam, will be sentenced for failing to keep strict control in the family. If
the court inquires further into the case, they will find out that you, madam,
turned your back on what was right and ignored a favor. How can you maintain
your reputation as a woman of wisdom? I, Crimson, would not dare presume to
decide what's right, but I hope that you, madam, will give the matter your
consideration. The best would be to pardon this small transgression and complete
the grand affair. "Moisten to remove a blemish" isn't that the best way out?

"Ma lang'er" (Crimson sings:)
That budding talent is a champion of cultured writings;

---

[3] From a common saying: "There are three things that should not be kept: old
silkworms should not be kept, old people should not be kept, and a girl grown up should
not be kept."

[4] From *Analects*, 2.22.

Elder sister is a leader among noble maidens:
One is thoroughly versed in the three creeds and nine schools;
One is perfectly adept at patterning and embroidery.

"Reprise"
It is a fact,
So don't neglect
To promptly act.
Why turn a benefactor into an enemy?
He called out his old friend, the White Horse General,
To behead that rebel and robber, the Flying Tiger.

"Luosiniang" (Crimson sings:)
Because you are completely at odds with Laureate Zhang,
You bring shame and disgrace on Chancellor Cui.
In the end it will involve your own flesh and blood:
Madam, you should consider it with utmost care.

(Old lady speaks:) What this little hussy has said is right. I ought not to have raised such a good-for-nothing daughter! If I were to take it to court, I would defile our family reputation. Enough! Our family counts among it no man who has transgressed the law, no woman who has married twice. I'll have to give her to this scoundrel. Crimson, call that hussy here! (Crimson greets female lead and speaks:) Congratulations, sister. She had the cudgel out as quick as a flash, but she swallowed my line. I didn't have much to fear. Mother is calling you now and wants to complete your union. (Female lead speaks:) How embarrassing! How will I be able to face the madam? (Crimson speaks:) What is there to ashamed of in front of your mother?

"Xiaotao hong" (Crimson, scolding female lead, [sings]:)
On that night the moon had barely risen above the willow tops,
But you had already made a tryst with your lover after dusk.
I was so ashamed, I turned my head and bit the sleeve of my garment;
But when I fixed my eyes
And looked, I saw the tapering tips of your shoes.
One was so unrestrained in passion, she couldn't stop;
One fucked away with moaning sounds.
Ah, *then* why didn't you suffer the tiniest bit of shame?

(Female lead acts out seeing old lady. Old lady speaks:) Oriole, how have I raised you that you would commit such an act now? It must be my bad karma. Who is to blame? If I were to take it to court, I would disgrace your father. This is not the act of a member of the chancellor's family. Enough! Enough! Who has been so unlucky to bring up a daughter like mine? Crimson, go the study and summon that beast! (Crimson acts out calling student. [Male lead enters and speaks:]) Missy, why are you calling me? (Crimson speaks:) Your affair is out in the open. Now the madam calls you to betroth the young lady to you. My young mistress

has already confessed, so you'd better go on. (Male lead speaks:) I'm so scared! 123a
How can I see the madam? Who squealed to her? (Crimson speaks:) Don't feign
such scruples. Just go on.

"Xiaotao hong" (Crimson, scolding female^{Male} lead, [sings]:)[5]
Since the affair has leaked out, how can it be stopped?
It was I who confessed all.
Our family will provide the tea and the wine to bring it to an end.[6]
Don't be sorrowed:
There is no need for an engagement contract or use of a go-between.
I'm giving up my instructorship and won't take any more students[7]—
You turned out to be a sprout that wouldn't bud.
Bah, you're just a pewter spear that looks like silver.[8]

(Male lead acts out greeting old lady Old lady speaks:) Oh, what a fine and 123b
budding talent! Haven't you ever heard, "If it is not the virtuous behavior of the
Former Kings, I do not dare practice it"?[9] I'd like to take you to court, but I'm
afraid of disgracing our family record. Now I give Oriole to you as wife. But for
three generations our family has not welcomed a son-in-law clad in white.[10]
Tomorrow you will leave for the capital to take the examinations. I will watch
over your wife. If you obtain an official position, then come see me. If you fail,
don't bother. (Crimson speaks:) Student Zhang, my congratulations!

"Dongyuan le" (Crimson sings:)   by fulfilling?
A single stroke of the pen wipes out love's longing;
Now you can unfurrow the earlier wrinkles on your brow
Your beautiful love and secret joy have just stirred,
And since you can do it

[(Crimson speaks:)] Student Zhang, just look:

[(Crimson sings:)]
Does such a lovely face as this
Need someone else to enjoy it?

(Old lady speaks:) Have your baggage ready tomorrow We'll prepare fruits and

---

[5] "Female lead" is obviously an error for "male lead."

[6] Normally, the young man's family prepared tea and wine when asking for the girl's
hand in marriage.

[7] Roughly equivalent to "I've had it with you."

[8] Something that looks like the real thing but is not. We read this as a reference to the
"spear that is too easily bent," a barb directed at Zhang's manhood.

[9] From the "Section on Grandees" ("Qingdaifu zhang") in *The Classic of Filial Piety*
(*Xiaojing*), the most elementary of exemplary texts in the Confucian canon.

[10] I.e., one who has yet to pass the examinations and don the robes of office—a student
or a commoner.

wine and invite the abbot to come along with us to see Student Zhang off at the ten-mile pavilion.[11] (Female lead recites:)

> "Go tell the willows on the banks of the western river,
> 'Prepare your green eyes to see the traveler off.'"[12]

1242   "Coda" (Crimson sings:)

When you come back, the flutes and drums in the painted hall will sound spring's daylight;

A pair, a simurgh mate and phoenix friend, will be arranged.

Only then will I accept the red reward for being matchmaker,[13]

Only then will I drink the wine for thanking relatives.

[(All leave.)]

---

[11] Mileage was marked every five *li* along major roads. This refers to a pavilion erected at the first ten-*li* marker outside of town.

[12] This last line is lifted from a poem by a Jin poet of the twelfth century who recited it on the way to his execution.

[13] The "red reward" was red patterned cash given to the matchmaker on the third day after the marriage, when the man's family gave a banquet for the parents, the matchmaker, and the parents of the wife. This banquet was called "wine for thanking relatives."

Oriole Sees the Student Off and Weeps as They Part

Act 3

(Old lady and abbot enter. [She] opens:) Today we are sending Student Zhang off to the capital. I've arranged for a banquet at the ten-mile pavilion. The abbot and I have gone ahead. What's keeping Student Zhang and missy? (Female lead, [leading Crimson], and male lead, [leading lute boy], enter together. [Female lead] speaks:) Today I'm seeing Student Zhang off to the capital to take the examinations. Already upset by emotions of separation, I encounter now this atmosphere of late autumn. How vexing! (Female lead recites:)

> Grief and happiness, gathering and separation: a single cup of wine.
> South, north, east, and west: a myriad-mile journey.

[*Zhenggong* mode:] "Duanzheng hao" (Female lead sings:)
A sky azure and clouded,
An earth flowered yellow;
The western wind is stiff, northern geese fly southward.
At dawn what dyes the frosted woods the flush of drunkenness?
It will ever be the tears of separated lovers.

"Gun xiuqiu" (Female lead sings:)
I am vexed that our meeting was so slow
And resent that your departure is so quick.
The willow threads are long, and the jade colt is hard to fetter;[1]

---

[1] *Liusi* (willow threads) is an exact homophone for a phrase meaning "intent to keep

I am vexed that I cannot hire the sparse woods to hold back the slanting
   sunbeams.
The horse proceeds slowly, slowly;
My carriage follows swiftly, swiftly
We had scarcely reported our evasion of love's longing;
Just broaching the theme, we are separated again.[2]
As soon I heard the word "leaving" spoken,
My golden armbands grew loose.
From far away I had only to see the ten-mile pavilion,
And my jade white flesh wasted away
Can anyone understand this vexation?

(Crimson speaks:) Sister, you're not made-up today (Female lead speaks:) O
Crimson, how can you understand my heart?

"Daodao ling" (Female lead sings:)
Seeing them preparing the carriage, the horse,
I couldn't help my simmering, boiling anger.
What desire did I have
Daintily and prettily to make myself up with moles and beauty spots?
All prepared are the quilts and the pillows,
But I'll have to sleep in drowsy confusion.
From now on, my gown and my sleeves
Will be soaked from the constant wiping of countless tears.
Oh, it kills one with depression!
Oh, it kills one with depression!
Later on, letters and messages
You must hurriedly, hastily send to me.

125a   (They act out arriving.)

(After they greet old lady, she speaks:) Student Zhang, you sit with the abbot.
Missy, you sit over here. Crimson, you bring the wine. Come forward, Student
Zhang. You are a member of the family now Don't keep such a distance! Today
I give Oriole to you. Don't disgrace my child in the capital. Put all your energies
into becoming the head of the list. (Male lead speaks:) Relying on your ample
support and on the talents in my heart, I will find obtaining official position no
more than picking up a mustard seed. (Bald one speaks:) Madam, you've made
the right decision. Student Zhang is not one to fall behind others. (After offering

---

one behind." "Jade colt," while referring to Zhang's horse, is also a common trope for the
sun.
   [2] "Broaching the theme" (*poti*) is the point in a poem where the main theme is
introduced; it is also the second stage of the so-called eight-legged essay required of
examination candidates. A rough paraphrase would read, "We had just gotten started
when we had to part."

a cup of wine, he sits down. Female lead heaves a sigh.)

"Tuo bushan" (Female lead sings:)
Felled by western winds, yellow leaves fly in confusion;
Tinged by cold mists, sere grass spreads afar.
At the feast mat he sits stuck at the side,
Wrinkling sorrowed brows, as if nearly dead and buried.

"Xiao Liangzhou" (Female lead sings:)
I see him stop his welling tears, daring not let them fall
Lest others know
Suddenly seeing each other, we bow our heads,
Heave heavy sighs,
Rearrange our garments of plain silk.

"Reprise"　　　　　　　　　　　　　　　　　　　　　　　　　　125b
Even though later we'll become a fine couple,
How can we keep now from grievous weeping?
My mind's like a fool's,
My heart as if drunk—
Last night and today
Pare away the small round of my waist.

(Old lady speaks:) Missy, offer a cup of wine. (After Crimson has passed her the wine, female lead acts out offering a cup. She heaves a heavy sigh [and speaks]:) Please drink this wine.

"Shang xiaolou" (Female lead sings:)
Before the joy of our union ended,
The sorrow of separation had taken over.
I call to mind our secret passion of earlier evenings,
Our marriage of last night,
And our separation of today.
I have known full well, these last few days,
The flavor of love's longing;
But it turns out nothing when compared to the grief of separation—
That is tenfold more!

"Reprise"
Those young in years
Lightly part for distant places.
Those shallow in feeling
Easily discard their partners,
Never thinking of thigh pressing thigh,
Face hugging face,
Hand holding hand.
For you to be the son-in-law of Chancellor Cui

Means glory for the wife, honor for the husband.
For me, finding a double-headed lotus[3]
Far outstrips passing the examinations as head of the list!

126a (Crimson speaks:) Sister, you haven't eaten breakfast. Drink some gruel. (Female lead speaks:) Crimson, how can I choke down any gruel?

"Manting fang" (Female lead sings:)
You offer me food too insistently!
We were face-to-face for only a moment,
Then parted in an instant's time.
Were it not that mother and child must exercise restraint at this banquet,
I'd have a mind to "lift the tray as high as my brows."[4]

126b "Reprise"
Even though we've been together only an hour or so,
By rights we should eat as husband and wife at the same table.
Such romantic signals from the eyes
Trip thoughts of the feelings behind them
And nearly turn me into a husband-watching rock.

(Old lady speaks:) Crimson, offer a cup of wine. (Crimson finishes the action of offering wine.)

"Kuaihuo san" (Female lead sings:)
The wine and food that will be brought
Will taste like earth and mud.
Even if they were earth and mud,
At least they'd have the taste of earth and the smell of mud.

"Chao tianzi" (Female lead sings:)
What fills jade cups, warm and overflowing,
127a As crystal clear as water,
Are mainly tears of love's longing.
The tea and food before my eyes,
Of course I want to eat,
But vexation fills my sorrowed stomach.
Empty fame on the horns of a snail[5]
And profit as tiny as a fly's head
Tear the mandarin ducks apart.

---

[3] A single stalk of lotus with two flowers—a metaphor for a marriage of perfect happiness.

[4] See play III, act 2, n. 15.

[5] Both phrases meaning useless ventures. "Horns of a snail" alludes to a story from the *Zhuangzi* in which two kingdoms were established on the separate horns of a snail. The kingdoms gradually destroyed each other fighting over the territory between the horns.

One here,
One there—
One passing of the cup is one drawn-out sigh.

(Old lady speaks:) Get my carriage ready; I'm going back first. Young lady, you may follow later with Crimson.

[(Old lady leaves.)]

(Male lead acts out taking leave of bald one. [Abbot speaks:]) I have nothing to say about your trip, but I'm set to buy a list of those who've passed the examinations. Don't let this monk be missed at the wedding banquet. Be careful, sir! Take care when riding. (Monk recites:)

From now on, I've no mind to venerate the sutras and penitences;
I'll only listen for the first sound of springtime thunder.[6]

[(Bald one leaves.)]

"Sibian jing" (Student sings:)   127b
In a wink the cups and platters are scattered about;
Your cart heads east,
My horse faces west.[7]
Both sides tarry and linger; in the setting sun, mountains stretch their halcyon
    green athwart.
Where will I stay tonight?
Even in a dream, hard it would be to track me down.

(Female lead speaks:) Student Zhang, whether you get an office or not, come back as fast as you can! (Male lead speaks:) Missy, your heart is troubled—but once gone I will snatch the head of the list clean away! Truly it is, "If there is a road that leads to the blue empyrean, I will arrive in the end; if my name is not on the golden plaque, I vow not to return!"[8] (Female lead speaks:) I have nothing else to give you for your trip but a quatrain I have improvised to send you off. (Female lead recites:)

I'm rejected and discarded; where are you now?
In those times you drew close to me of your own accord.
Now you will again bring out the passion of former times
    And love whoever is before your eyes.

---

[6] The announcement of the list of successful candidates in the spring.

[7] These lines are taken from the famous ballad "Southeast the Peacock Flies" ("Kongque dongnan fei"), the story of a happy couple forced to separate by the young man's mother; they eventually commit suicide when the young woman's mother tries to marry her off to a wealthier family.

[8] A common vow of the candidates who went to the capital for the examinations; only a small minority actually passed.

(Male lead speaks:) You are mistaken, missy. Would I, Zhang Gong, dare love anyone else? Allow me to add a quatrain to bare my heart. (Male lead recites:)

128a

> A human life is naught but constant distant partings.
> Who among all is the closest to my heart?
> Had I not met her, she who understands my music,
> Who, who would have loved me, this ever-sighing one?

"Shua hai'er" (Student sings:)
I weep red tears, soaking my lapels and sleeves
Wetter than the Constable's blue gown.[9]
The shrike goes eastward, westward flies the swallow·
Before I have set out, you ask when I will return.
Although we will be parted a thousand miles from this very moment on,
Let us drink to the end this one cup of life's wine.
Flushed with wine before I even drink—
From my eyes blood flows,
And within my heart all turns to ash.

129a

"Fifth from Coda" (Female lead, counseling student, [sings]:)
When you reach the capital, adapt yourself to the local clime;
While on the road, be moderate in your food and drink.
Always take good care of yourself, pace your body's strength;
Go to sleep early in the rain and dew of desolate villages,
Rise late in the wind and frost of country inns.
Astride your horse in the autumn winds—
That is the hardest time to take proper care,
When you most need help and support.

"Fourth from Coda" (Female lead sings:)
To whom can I lay plaint of my anxiousness and sorrow?
My love-longing is known only to me.
Old heaven does not care if one grows haggard:
My tears will fill the nine curves of the Yellow River to overflowing;
My hatred will press the three peaks of the Flowery Marchmount down.[10]
And when evening comes, I will lean depressed on the western loft
And watch to the end this evening light, this old road,
This sere grass, this long dike.

"Third from Coda" (Female lead sings:)
Happily smiling, together we came;
Bitterly weeping, alone I return.

129b

Returning home, if I go within the silken bed-curtains,

---

[9] See play II, act 4, n. 16.
[10] Huashan, the Flowery Marchmount, one of the five sacred peaks of China, is located south of Puzhou, just across the Yellow River. It figures as a prominent landmark of the area.

Yesterday's embroidered quilt, warm with fragrance, keeps spring behind.
That tonight's halcyon blanket grows cold, you will know in a dream.
It is not my intention to cling to you;
But when I see you clutch the saddle to mount the horse,
I cannot stop tearful eyes and sorrowed brows.

(Male lead speaks:) Do you have any words to give me in counsel?

"Second from Coda" (Female lead sings:)
Don't worry that your texts are equal to the task but your luck is not;
I only fear that you'll divorce your wife and take another.
Don't you let fish and geese go through a whole spring without messages;
Here I will have the blue simurgh send letters to you without fail.
"If my name is not on the golden plaque, I vow not to return"
Is good and well, but remember this:
If you see another flower in a distant country,
Don't tarry there as you did here.

"First from Coda" (Female lead sings:)   130a
Blue mountains screen the one I'm sending off,
The sparse woods refuse to do me favors,
As a thin mist and evening haze hide him from my view
Evening light, old road, no human speech;
Ripening millet, autumn winds, listen to his horse whinny
Why am I so loath to mount my carriage?
So swiftly I came;
How slowly I leave.

(Crimson speaks:) The madam has been gone a good long time. Sister, let's go home.

"Coda" [(Female lead sings:)]
Amid four bounds of mountain colors,
In the single lash of the lingering rays,
A vexation that encompasses all the human realm fills my bosom.
How can a carriage so small
Cart it all away?

(Crimson and female lead leave.)

(Male lead speaks:) My boy, let's do the first leg quickly and find a place to stay for the night. (Male lead recites:)

My tears surge like flowing waters;
My sorrows fly with countryside clouds.

[(Male lead and lute boy leave.)]

The Student Dreams in the Inn that Bandits Pursue Oriole and that She Goes Out to
Repulse Them

Act 4

(Male lead, leading servant, enters on horseback and opens:) We are already thirty
miles from East of Pu. Strawbridge Inn lies ahead. We'll stay there tonight and go
on early tomorrow. This horse refuses to run, no matter what I do! ([Male lead]
recites a poem:)

> A single lash of journey's color urges the departing horse;
> Ten thousand pecks of traveler's sorrow draw out a new poem.

[*Shuangdiao* mode:] "Xinshui ling" (Student sings:)
Gazing at East of Pu: the monastery is obscured by evening clouds.
Pained by feelings of separation: half of the forest is yellowed leaves.
The horse is slow, its rider is listless;
The wind is strong, the ranks of geese are awry.
Separation's vexation doubles and doubles
At the broaching of the theme: the very first night.

(Male lead speaks:) Calling last night's enjoyment to mind, who could imagine
today's lonely desolation?

"Bubu jiao" (Student sings:)
Last night the perfume of the halcyon quilt was thick, infusing us with orchid musk.

246

Leaning on the coral pillow, we arched our bodies,
Pressing cheek against cheek.
The more inspected in detail,
The more astounding my detestable one.
Letting down her cloudy locks with jade combs aslant,
She was just like the new moon half-spewed forth.

(Male lead speaks:) Here we are already. Where's the innkeeper? (Innkeeper
enters and speaks:) Sire, please take our finest room.   131a

[(Innkeeper leaves.)]

(Male lead speaks:) Lute boy, take the horse. Light the lamps. I don't want to eat
anything at all; I just want to sleep. (Servant speaks:) I'm worn out too. I just want
to rest. ([Servant] acts out spreading his blankets at the foot of the bed and sleeping.
Male lead speaks:) Can sleep come to my eyes tonight?

"Luomei feng" (Student sings:)
In the traveler's lodge, I lay on a lonely pillow;
Autumn crickets sound from surrounding fields.
What urges sorrow on is a paper window torn by the wind.
The quilt of the lonely sleeper is thin, and I shiver:
Piercing, chilly cold—will I ever get warm?

(Male lead acts out sleeping. Female lead [enters] and speaks:) After I had taken
leave of Student Zhang at the long pavilion, I couldn't get him off my mind. While
the madam and my serving girl were both asleep, I secretly fled from the city to
catch up with him so we might travel together.

"Qiaomu cha" (Female lead sings:)
Fleeing through deserted faubourgs and open fields,
I can't control the beating of my heart.
Puffing and panting, I can't put two breaths together.
Hurry, hurry and catch up!
"Beat the grass, you'll scare the snakes."[1]

"Jiao zhengpa" (Female lead sings:)   131b
He is now dragging my heart toward him,

---

[1] From an old anecdote about a person who accuses a yamen clerk of corruption. The
magistrate who reviews the case knows that he himself is as corrupt as his underling, so he
writes on the accusation, "Although you have beaten the grass, I am the one who is the
startled snake!" Xu Wei, the Ming dramatist, has pointed out, however, that this saying was
already divorced from its original connection with corruption by the fifteenth century.
Oriole is using it in two senses here: to scare the snakes out of her path; and to caution herself
to make sure that no one else knows she is chasing after Student Zhang: "If I beat the grass,
I'll stir up the snakes!"

And so I cannot avoid this distant road.
I have deceived the madam, who is so adept at restrictions,
And evaded the serving girl, who is constantly at my side.
I'm thinking about his wounded sighs as he came to mount his horse
And how I wept until I seemed a fool.
Of course my heart is not depraved;
But from our parting to sun's first setting,
I've been so sorrowed, I've come to a dangerous peak,
And so emaciated, I've reached the point of snapping.
We've only been separated half a day,
And already my halcyon skirt has grown three or four pleats too large.
Has anyone ever been ground down like me?

"Jinshang hua" (Female lead sings:)
Our destined marriage
Had just been safely settled,
When, alas, fortune and fame
Forced us apart.
From insufferable sorrows
I had barely wakened,
When a longing from which there's no escape
Started all over again.
A pure frost cleanses azure waves;
White dew falls on yellowed leaves.
Up and down, down and up, the road sinks and turns;
Winds rise from every direction in the fields,
Scurrying wildly left and right.
Here I flee and race—
Where does he rest in his weariness?

132a

"Qingjiang yin" (Female lead sings:)
Sheepishly he sits silently in the room of an inn,
Facing in depression a year-long night.
Evening rains urge on the cold katydids;
Morning winds blow away the remnant moon.
Where will he sober up from wine tonight?

(Female lead speaks:) He's in this inn. I'll have to knock on the gate. (Male lead speaks:) Who's knocking? It's a girl's voice. I'll open the door and look. Who could it be at this time?

"Qing Xuanhe" (Student sings:)
If you are human, hurriedly declare yourself;
If you are a ghost, disappear immediately!

(Female lead speaks:) It's me! The madam was sleeping, and I was thinking, Now he's gone, when will I see him again? So I came to go on with you.

([Student] sings:)
Hearing this, I pull her by her fragrant silken sleeves[2]—
So, it was you all the time!

(Male lead speaks:) Missy, such ardor is hard to find.

"Qiao pai'er" (Student, pitying female lead, [sings]:)
Your character is such, you really give it your all.
You haven't given a thought to your clothes:
Your embroidered shoes have been stained by dew, water, and mud,
And the soles of your feet ruined by walking.

(Female lead speaks:) It was all for you. I didn't care how far it was! (Female lead sobs.)

"Tianshui ling" (Student, explaining female lead, [sings]:)   132b
I imagine how you neglected sleep and forgot to eat,
Your perfume dissipating, your jade diminishing.
"Flowers open, flowers fall,"
But I still feel that's off the mark[3]—
Rather: the pillow cold, the covers chilly;
The phoenix alone, the simurgh lonely;
The moon so round by clouds obstructed.
I conjure up what pain you must have felt.

"Zhegui ling" (Student sings:)
A human life, I think, suffers most bitterly from separation.
How touching! A thousand miles of passes and mountains
You've traversed all alone.
Could such soul-baring dedication
Be rewarded with treacherous infidelity?
Even though for a while the flower is tattered, the moon is incomplete,
Don't ever think you'll be "a sunken jug, a broken hairpin."[4]

---

[2] To test whether she's real and not a ghost.

[3] Flowers will grow in the next spring, but the person will be gone.

[4] From a ballad by Bo Juyi, "Pulling a Silver Flask from the Bottom of the Well" ("Jingdi yin yinping"), that recounts the story of a girl who elopes with a young man but is forced, after living with him for five years, to leave him because they have not been formally married. The pertinent lines read:

> From the bottom of the well a silver flask pulled;
> The silver flask starts up, the woven cord breaks.
> On a stone the jade hairpin honed;
> The jade hairpin, about to take shape, snaps in the middle.
> And what of the flask's sinking and the hairpin's snapping?
> They are just like my parting today from you, my lord.

I don't fancy the high and mighty,
Don't envy the proud and opulent.
Alive, we'll share the same blanket;
Dead, we'll share the same grave.

(Extra clown and party, costumed as soldiers, enter and shout. [Extra clown] speaks:) We saw a girl crossing the Yellow River a moment ago, but we don't know where she went. Bring a torch! It's clear that she's fled into this inn. Bring her out! Bring her out! (Male lead speaks:) What do we do now? (Female lead speaks:) You stand back. I'll open the gate myself and confront them.

"Shuixianzi" (Female lead sings:)
Stubbornly you surround the Monastery of Universal Salvation, set to work
    with spades and picks;
Cruelly, you grab our throats, pull out swords and axes.
Rebellious hearts and gluttonous eyes are by nature deformed.

(Student speaks:) Let me confront them. (Female lead speaks.)

([She] sings:)
Don't speak;
Stand back.

(Extra speaks:) Whose daughter are you to cross the Yellow River in the dead of the night? (Female lead speaks:) Don't talk nonsense.

([Female lead] sings:)
General Du—you know him as a hero—
He'll glance just once and turn you into salted pickles;
He'll point just once and transform you into blubber and blood.
He'll come riding a white horse!

(Extra grabs female lead and leaves [with clown and party]. Student speaks:) Ai, so it was a dream all the time. Let me open the gate and look—all I see is a whole heaven of dewy vapor, a whole earth of frosty flowers. The morning star has just appeared, and the remnant moon is still bright. (Student recites:)

Without reason swallow and magpie clamor on the highest branch;[5]
    On a single pillow a dream of mandarin ducks fails to coalesce.

"Yan'er luo" (Student sings:)
Green, so green, the wall is high, the willows are half-hidden;
Still, so still, the gate is closed, the night is clear autumn.
Sparse, so sparse, on tips of forest trees, winds that fell the leaves;
Dark, so dark, at the edge of clouds, a moon that penetrates the window

---

[5] A magpie's screech signals the arrival of a lover.

"Desheng ling" (Student sings:)
What startled me awake were quivering bamboo shadows: dragons and snakes
   set loose;
A flutteringly empty Zhuang Zhou: a dream of butterflies.[6]
Thrumming, humming, the urger of weaving never rests;[7]
Sounding, resounding, the sound of fulling blocks never breaks off.[8]
Painful, sensitive, the wound of parting;
Vexing, guiling, such a fine dream was hard to give up.
Chilling, chilling, cold moans:
That lovely and dainty jade person—where is she now?

(Servant speaks:) It's dawn. Let's do the first leg of our journey now and cook later.
(Male lead speaks:) Innkeeper! Here's the money for the room. Please saddle my   134a
horse. ([Student] recites:)

> She grasps his hands at time of parting, sends her husband off;
>   He grasps the saddle, and before she speaks, her soul is lost.
>   "Raise your head, and the sun is near, Chang'an far away!"
>   "Dusk after dusk, dawn after dawn, do not lean at the gate."

"Yuanyang sha" (Student sings:)
Willow strands are long,
Near to catching up my emotions;
Water sounds are muffled,
Like a person's sobbing.
Slanting moon, last of the lamp,
Half-bright, not extinguished.
Truly it is said, "Old hatreds go on and on,
New sorrows knot in profusion."
My hatred stuffed with parting's sorrow,
What fills my chest cannot be washed away
Unless brush and paper replace throat and tongue.
My thousand kinds of longing—to tell to whom?

"Luosiniang" (Student sings:)
All because of a single office, half a position,
We're kept apart by a thousand mountains and myriad waters.

---

[6] The well-known story of Zhuangzi's butterfly dream: when he awakes, he does not
know if is Zhuangzi, who has dreamed of a butterfly, or a butterfly, who is dreaming that
it is Zhuangzi.
  [7] Crickets, whose thrumming call sounds like a shuttle thrown quickly through a loom,
were called "urgers of weaving."
  [8] A set element of autumnal verse: the blocks upon which winter clothing was cleaned
for wear.

[(Both leave.)]

Title: Little Crimson brings the happy affair to completion;
          The madam inquires into the facts of the case.

Name: At the Long Pavilion she pours the wine of parting;
          At Strawbridge Inn he dreams of Oriole.

VOLUME IV OF THE DELUXE, COMPLETELY ILLUSTRATED, AND ANNOTATED STORY OF THE WESTERN WING

Oriole Orders the Lute Boy to Take Clothes, Stockings, and Other Things to the Student

VOLUME V OF THE DELUXE, COMPLETELY ILLUSTRATED, AND ANNOTATED STORY OF THE WESTERN WING

A Reunion Ordained by Heaven

Act 1

(Student, leading servant, enters and opens:) Since taking leave of missy in late autumn, half a year has flashed by. Thanks to the protection of my ancestors, I passed the examinations on my first try and attained the highest rank, head of the list! I am now waiting in the hostel for a formal appointment by imperial decree. I am afraid that missy may be worrying about me, so I've composed a letter and will have the lute boy take it to her. I'll inform the madam that this small student did succeed, so she can put her mind at ease. Lute boy! Come here! (Servant enters. [Male lead] speaks:) Bring me the perfect treasures of the literary studio.[1] I will write a letter home; I want you to take it with all dispatch to Hezhong Prefecture. When you see missy, tell her, "My master was afraid that you might be anxious and so especially dispatched me ahead of him to deliver this letter. Please let me have a letter of reply as soon as possible." Oh, how swiftly have the days and months gone by.

"Shanghua shi" (Student sings:)　　　　　　　　　　　　　　　　　　135a
When first we met, a rain of red, full and dancing, covered the green moss;

---

[1] Paper, ink, brush, and inkstone—the four treasures of the studio.

After I took my leave, yellowed leaves soughed and sighed, and clotted the evening haze.
Today I see a plumblossom open: separated for half a year!

(Male lead speaks:) Lute boy, remember well the words with which I enjoined you.

([Male lead] sings:)
Just say, "And so he especially sends this letter."

(Servant speaks:) I've got this letter in hand and in haste I am off to Hezhong Prefecture.

([They] leave.)

❖❖❖

(Female lead, leading Crimson, enters and opens:) It's been a quick half year since Student Zhang left for the capital, and we've had no news at all. I've been feeling blue lately I'm too lazy to lift my dressing mirror, and my waist has so wasted away that my madder skirt is too big. Oh, it frustrates one!

[*Shangdiao* mode:] "Ji xianbin" (Female lead sings:)
Although he is gone from my eyes,
Still he is in my heart.
Barely has he left my heart,
When there—again on my brows!
I forget, and then he's back;
These awful longings have no end, have no rest.
In all, how can a single inch of brow's peak
Withstand those, those many furrows there because of him?
New sorrow has just tied on to old sorrow,
And it's so damned mixed up, there's no dividing new from old:
Old sorrow weighty and heavy, like the mountains of the Great Range;[2]
New sorrow endless and infinite, like the stream of the Heavenly Moat.[3]

(Crimson speaks:) Sister, normally the point of your needle is never turned down; in truth, you were never idle at your embroidery frame. Now you are completely listless and weary Earlier, if you felt blue, a little rest would normally fix you up, but not this time. You've really wasted away to nothing!

"Xiaoyao le" (Female lead sings:)
Whenever I lost weight before,
It was just a trifling matter;
But this time it is more shocking.

---

[2] The Taihang Mountains.
[3] The Yangtze River.

135b

(Crimson speaks:) Sister, you are so depressed. Let's go somewhere to have some fun and enjoy ourselves.

> ([Female lead] sings:)
> Where can I forget my anxiety?
> When I want to look out, I climb the dressing loft alone,
> My hands roll up the beaded blinds and put up the jade hook:
> Vacantly, my gaze stops at mountains' brilliance and water's beauty,
> Where I see blue mists hiding the trees,
> Sere grass stretching to heaven,
> A boat athwart in the countryside ford.

(Female lead speaks:) Crimson, these clothes don't look like anything I'd wear anymore. (Crimson speaks:) Sister, your waist is so slim, it won't support your clothes.   136a

> "Gua jinsuo" (Crimson sings:)
> Skirt tinted by pomegranate flowers—
> Sleeping has worn rouge creases in it.
> Buttons knotted into cloves
> Overlap the lotus button loops.
> Pearl after pearl slipping from a string—
> Your tears have soaked perfumed silken sleeves.
> You frown over your willow-thin waist;
> You're thinner than a chrysanthemum.

(Servant enters and speaks:) As ordered by my master, I've come to bring this letter to the young mistress. A moment ago I saw the madam in the front rooms. She was very happy and ordered me to go inside and see the young mistress. I'm in the rear apartments already (He acts out coughing.) (Crimson asks:) Who is outside? ([Servant] acts out greeting her. Crimson greets servant. Crimson smiles and speaks:) When did you get here? Of course! Last night it was announced by the sputtering lamp; today the happy magpie screeches.[4] And just while sister is so frustrated. Did you come by yourself or with brother? (Servant speaks:) Brother obtained an office and ordered me to bring a letter. (Crimson speaks:) Just wait   136b
here. Come inside after I've told sister. (Crimson acts out greeting female lead. Female lead speaks:) What's with the little wench? (Crimson speaks:) Sister, my heartfelt congratulations! Congratulations! Your husband has obtained an official post. (Female lead speaks:) This little wench is fooling me because she sees that I'm depressed. (Crimson speaks:) His lute boy is waiting outside the gate. He has already seen the madam, who sent him on to see you. He brings a letter from your husband. (Female lead speaks:) Good grief! How many days have I been waiting? Call him in! (Servant acts out entering and greeting female lead. Female lead speaks:) When did you leave the capital, lute boy? [(Servant speaks:)] Over a

---

[4] Conventional auspicious portents of a lover's return. See below, play V, act 2, n. 3.

month ago. When I left, brother had been paraded through the streets and bastinadoed. (Female lead speaks:) You beast! You don't understand. The head of the list basks in glory and is paraded in the streets for three days.[5] (Servant speaks:) You're right, madam. Here's your letter. (Female lead acts out accepting the letter.)

"Jinju xiang" (Female lead sings:)
At first I lost my charms because he went away,
And now you bring a letter here—
That again intensifies my condition.
The promise he made was never kept.[6]
Silently I bow my head;
The letter rests in my hands, tears clot in my pupils.

(Female lead acts out opening the letter.)

137a   "Cu hulu" (Female lead sings:)
Here, as I open the letter, I open it in tears;
There, as he wrote the letter, he wrote it in tears.
Before the point of his pen had touched paper, his tears had already flowed;
Teardrops still stain this letter that you bring.
With newer stains I soak the older:
Truly, a single layer of sorrow is now doubled.

(Female lead acts out reciting the letter.)

I, Gong, with a hundred obeisances, present this letter

To the dressing table of the fragrant one.

Since our separation in late autumn, half a year has gone in a flash. Thanks to the protection of my ancestors and the virtue of you, my worthy wife, I have passed the examinations in the highest category At present I am housed in the Hostel for Gathering Worthies to wait upon my formal appointment by imperial decree. Precisely because I have feared that the madam and you, my worthy wife, would be anxious about me, I specifically ordered my lute boy to deliver this letter with all due haste. I hope that this will free you from worry Even though my body may be far away, my heart

---

[5] We have attempted here to reproduce a pun that revolves around the young boy's failure to understand the classical phrase *kuaguan youjie*, which means to parade through the streets to show off one's office. He has misunderstood *kuaguan* as a slangish way of saying *gun*, "club" it was common practice in vernacular to split a single word into two syllables, the first using the initial of the word and the second the final, as in the case of rendering *kong* (hole) as *kulong* While this is not a perfect phonetic match, we assume that this is the basis of his error.

[6] I.e., the promise she asked for before he left: "No matter whether you obtain an office or not, please hurry back!"

is always near. Alas, that we cannot fly like two birds on a single wing or nest together like orioles. As one who esteems fortune and fame over favor and love, I am truly guilty of shortsighted greed. When in the future we meet face-to-face, I must offer my apologies for my inadequacies. Here below I have completed a quatrain for your inspection.

([Female lead] recites the poem:)   137b

>   He who plucked a flower in the fairy precincts of the jade capital
>   Sends word to the modest and retiring lady of East of Pu:
>   In a day I will bow to imperial grace and be clothed in daytime brocade;[7]
>   Do not, for any reason, affect to lean by the gate.

(Female lead [speaks]:) I'm overcome with joy "He who plucks the flower" means he is the third name on the list![8]

"Reprise" (Female lead sings:)
On that day he hid in moonlight by the western wing,
But on this day he shines at the banquet in the Jasper Forest.[9]
Who could have hoped that the feet that leapt the eastern wall would dominate the tortoise's head?[10]
Who would have said that the heart that loved flowers could nurture a hand that plucks the cassia branch?
In a thicket of rouge and powder was hidden brocade and embroidery.
From now on, the evening dressing loft will become the Loft of Impartiality [11]

(Female lead speaks:) Have you eaten? (Servant speaks:) I will tell you, madam,

---

[7] To return home in glory. Xiang Yu is credited with the remark, "Not returning home when rich and powerful is like walking at night in clothes of brocade."

[8] In the earlier version of the story by Master Dong, Zhang is specifically designated as the number three candidate, colloquially known as the "flower-plucking gentleman." Wang Shifu has changed his place to that of head of the list, or the number one candidate. This contradiction is allowed to remain in the drama in order to keep the phrase "flower-plucking gentleman" in this poem. Since plucking flowers has been consistently used as a metaphor for illicit sexual congress, it is necessary that it be mentioned in the poem as a rationale for the suspicions that develop in Oriole's mind—suspicions that he has snatched another blossom, that is, taken another woman and forgotten about his lonely Oriole. Successful candidates were extremely desirable as sons-in-law to powerful families, and fiction and drama are rife with tales of young men who sacrifice earlier lovers for power in the capital.

[9] The Park of the Jasper Forest was on the western edge of Kaifeng; it was where the emperors of Northern Song held banquets for the successful candidates.

[10] To "stand alone on the tortoise's head" means to pass the examination as the head of the list: he was asked to stand forward of the other candidates on the steps of the imperial dais, in which were carved an ascending dragon and a giant tortoise. The candidate's position was literally on the tortoise's head.

[11] The examination halls.

138a   I've been standing idly in front of the hall since morning. How could I have I eaten? (Female lead speaks:) Crimson, get him something to eat quickly. (Servant speaks:) Many thanks, madam, for your generosity. I'll eat right here while you write a letter. That Student Zhang, he ordered me to bother you about a letter of reply. It's very urgent. (Female lead speaks:) Crimson, bring brush and inkstone! (Crimson does an action. Female lead speaks:) The letter is done. I've nothing else to express my thoughts with except a single undershirt, one waist wrap, one pair of stockings, one jasper zither, one jade hairpin, and one mottled bamboo brush. Lute boy, pack them carefully. Crimson, get ten ounces of silver and give them to him for his travel expenses. (Crimson speaks:) How can your husband lack these things if he has obtained an office? Why are you sending them? (Female lead speaks:) You don't understand:

138b   "Wuye'er" (Female lead sings:)
This undershirt—
If he keeps it on while sleeping,
It will be as if he is in bed with me.
As long as it sticks to his skin,
I can't believe he won't long for my warm pliancy.

(Crimson speaks:) What does he need this waist wrap for?

[(Female lead sings:)]
If it never leaves his front or back,
Then it guards his left and right,
Tied securely around his heart.

(Crimson speaks:) What about these socks?

[(Female lead sings:)]
They'll keep him from straying from the straight and narrow!

(Crimson speaks:) He has his own zither there; why take him another?

"Houting hua" (Female lead sings:)
First, his five-word poem pursued me hotly;
Later, his seven-string zither completed our union.
How could he have grown cold to the purport of his poem?
I only fear that the hands on the strings will lose their touch!

(Crimson speaks:) What's the significance of the jade hairpin?

[(Female lead sings:)]
Of course, I have my reason:
Now that his fortune and fame are achieved,
I only fear that he will throw me to the back of his mind.

(Crimson speaks:) What's the need for this mottled bamboo brush?

[(Female lead sings:)]
In autumn on the banks of the Xiang River,
In those days Ehuang sorrowed for Shun of Yu.[12]
Today Oriole is anxious for Junrui.
This bamboo from the foot of Mount Nine Suspicions[13]
And the sleeves of the perfumed silken robe   139a

"Qing ge'er" (Female lead sings:)   139b
Both alike have been soaked by tears, soaked by tears.
The tear marks, tear marks, are still visible as of old:
Eternal passions all sorrow alike.
My tears crisscross as they flow;
My spite and envy cannot be controlled.
Tell the scholar these reasons over and over;
Don't let him forget the old

(Female lead speaks:) Please pack these things carefully. (Servant speaks:) I
understand.

"Cu hulu" (Female lead, counseling lute boy, [sings]:)
When you sleep each night in country inns,
Don't use this bundle as a pillow
Lest some oily fat soil the goods inside beyond repair.
If by chance water soaks them or rain wets them, don't wring them out;
I'm afraid you won't be able to iron out the creases.
Guard every item, every article, with care.

"Jinju xiang" (Female lead sings:)
My letter sealed to the foot of a goose—it is now finished.
My passion bound to another's heart—when will it end?
Chang'an, at the edge of heaven when I gaze—
Around the whole circle of the western loft I have leaned to stare;
But my man is unseen, the waters flow by in vain.

(Servant speaks:) Madam, I take my leave and depart right away. (Female lead
speaks:) Lute boy, when you see your master, tell him   (Servant speaks:) Tell   140a
him what?

"Langlilai sha" (Female lead sings:)
He sorrows there on account of me;
I lose weight here because of him.
As he drew near parting, that clever tongue that deceives others

---

[12] For Ehuang, one of the Consorts of the Xiang, see pp. 59–60.
[13] The name of the mountain at whose foot Ehuang wept until her tears spotted the
bamboo; in keeping with the general tenor of the act, it also suggests Oriole's concern that
Zhang remain faithful to her.

Fixed as the date of return the ninth day of the ninth month.
But unawares, we have already passed the period of the small spring.[14]
Now I regret that I sent my husband away to seek fame and glory.

(Servant speaks:) I've got the letter of reply, and now I'll report in great haste to brother.

(They all leave.)

---

[14] The ninth day of the ninth month is known as Doubled Yang, a time when people traditionally got together. A "small spring" is what we call an Indian summer.

Student Zhang Orders the Lute Boy to Pack the Things Oriole Sent in a Wicker Basket

Act 2

(Student enters and speaks:)

> Don't laugh when the tiger is painted but yet unfinished:
> It will scare others as soon as fangs and claws are in place.

When I passed the examinations, I was appointed by imperial decree Compiler of the State History in the Court of the Forest of Pens.[1] It has been more than two months now. How can they understand my heart? What writings have I been able to complete? I dispatched my lute boy to deliver the good news, but he still hasn't returned. I haven't been able to sleep these past few days, and I can't abide food. I have been granted leave and am recuperating in this posthouse pavilion. This morning the Court of the Grand Physicians sent someone to check on me, and he prescribed a medicine before leaving. Even Bian Que of Lu himself couldn't cure my illness.[2] Since I left missy, my heart hasn't had a single day's ease!

[*Zhonglü* mode:] "Fendie'er" (Student sings:)
Since I arrived at the capital,
My longing heart has been like this from dawn to dusk.

---

[1] There is a certain irony in Zhang's appointment to a position in which he works on historical texts that formulate moral opinions about men of the preceding court of the same dynasty.

[2] A legendary physician of the Spring and Autumn period.

Stretched out across my heart lies my Oriole.
The best physician was invited:
When he took my pulse,
He had it right at all points.
My first thought was to refute him;

141a   But the truth he had diagnosed,
And there was no need for an examination.

"Zui chunfeng" (Student sings:)
He said, "To treat various diseases, I have prescriptions and skills;
But to cure love-longing, I have neither herbs nor pills."
O Oriole,
If you knew I was suffering love's longing,
I'd gladly die,
Die,
Homeless in the wide world.
All alone, cast as a traveler—
For nearly half a year.

(Servant enters and speaks:) I thought brother had been appointed to office, but he has been sick all the while in this posthouse pavilion. I'd better take him the letter of reply ([Servant] acts out greeting him. Male lead speaks:) You're back!

"Ying xianke" (Student sings:)
I was marveling at the prescient magpie screeching on the flowered bough
And the happy spider hanging from the blinds.[3]
They respond exactly to the report of the lamp last night on its short stand.
If it's not a lyric from a broken heart,
Then it's a poem from a broken heart.

(Servant speaks:) I have a letter here from the young madam. (Male lead acts out accepting it.)

[(Male lead sings:)]
When she wrote it, her passionate tears must have been like threads.
If not, then why are the tearstains on the envelope still wet?

141b   (Male lead acts out reading the letter aloud.)

I, your unfortunate serving maid, woman of the Cui clan, make obeisance to offer up

---

[3] This derives from the following lines by the early Han rhetorician Lu Jia: "The magpie chatters away: a traveler will arrive. The spiders gather: every affair will turn out happily." The word for daddy longlegs (*xizi*) is a true homophone for a word that means "the happy one", thus, spiders have come to be omens of auspicious events.

To the writing table of the talented gentleman Junrui.

From the time your voice and face left, time has passed unnoticed. But my heart's intention of reverent respect has never slackened in the slightest. Even if it is said, "The sun is near, Chang'an is far away," why did no geese or carp appear? Could it have been that your heart was set on flowers and willows and rejected the intentions of love and devotion of me, your serving maid? Precisely when I was pondering this, your lute boy arrived, and I saw the traces of your brush. Only then did I know that you had succeeded in the examinations, and I was so overjoyed that I nearly went mad. Your talents and reputation, sir, certainly bring no disgrace to the family record of the chancellor. Now your lute boy returns, and I have nothing to send as a gift except one jasper zither, one jade hairpin, one mottled bamboo brush, one waist wrap, one undershirt, and one pair of stockings to give momentary expression to my true sincerity. These hastily drafted characters lack all deference, and I humbly beg your indulgent forgiveness for my inadequacies. Utilizing the rhymes of your poem, I have ventured to add a quatrain.

142a

([Male lead] recites a poem:)

I've leaned the full circle of the balustrade watching for the man of talents;
    Don't love the "flower maidens" of the capital!
  In sickness I received your letter and knew you were of the first rank,
So before the window, gazing in the mirror, I try out my new adornments.

(Male lead speaks:) You, my elegant and charming, oh, so elegant and charming young miss! For such a girl, I, Zhang Gong, would die a fitting death.

"Shang xiaolou" (Student, vaunting Oriole's writings, [sings]:)
This could serve as a history of characters
Or should be a monumental inscription.
It has Liu's bones, Yan's force.
Zhang Xu, Zhang Dian,
Xianzhi, Xizhi[4]—
They had their time;
She now has hers.
A beautiful person, talented mind,
My Oriole is without peer on earth!

"Reprise"   142b
I will hold it like a mandala,
Use it like an amulet charm:

---

[4] These were all paragons of calligraphic skill: Yan Zhenqing, Liu Gongquan, Zhang Xu, Zhang Dian, and Wang Xizhi and his son Wang Xianzhi.

More lofty than a golden seal,
Weightier than gold and silk,
More noble than golden riches!
If this had been stamped with a chop,
It would have dispatched the head clerk,
Sent out a bailiff.
This is an official, in haste unstamped, notice for a rendezvous!

(Acting out taking the undershirt, male lead speaks:) Don't talk about her writings, just look at her needlework—truly exceptional in the human realm!

"Manting fang" (Student sings:)
Of course this makes me, Student Zhang, love you even more:
Capable of competing with professional needleworkers
Or being a teacher of the female crafts.
In a thousand ways meticulous, every stitch is right.
Just imagine: for length you had no model;
143a   For girth you guessed the size of my waist;
For fit you had no one to try it on.
When you were making it, I think,
Your heart used every care.

(Student speaks:) These few things my young lady sent me all have a special meaning. I have guessed every one of them.

"Bai hezi" (Student sings:)
This zither—
It tells me to close the doors and study restraining my fingers,
Devote my mind to poems set to music,
Compose and nurture a heart of sages and worthies,
Clean and purify the ears of Chao and You.[5]

"Second Coda"
This jade hairpin—
Long and slender like a bamboo shoot,
Fine and white as an onion stalk.

---

[5] This song is a set of double entendres, all enjoining Zhang to remain faithful. "Restraining fingers" needs little explanation: "zither strings," as mentioned in chap. 5, is a euphemism for the frenum of the clitoris. "To devote oneself to song" refers obliquely to *Analects*, 2.2: "The songs are three hundred in number but can be summed up in a single phrase: 'Keep to the straight and narrow'", that is, don't think about other women. Chao and You are Chao Fu and Xu You, two hermits of antiquity Xu You was approached to assume rulership of the state, but he refused and went to a stream to wash the words from his ears. Chao Fu, who had brought his ox to drink from the stream, led the animal upstream of Xu You for fear of its being contaminated as it drank. The allusion is an injunction, then, to maintain purity and not to succumb to the blandishments and proposals of other women.

Its warm richness holds a fresh perfume;
Shiny and pure, it is without blemish.

"Third Coda"
This mottled bamboo brush—
When on frosted branch a phoenix couple roosted,
For some reason their tears spotted and soaked the rouge.
Then Ehuang by Emperor Shun's death was hurt,
Now it makes a chaste maiden long for her lord.

"Fourth Coda"
This waist wrap—
In her hand a boll of cotton,
Below the lamp how many threads?
Expressing the sorrows in her belly,
It is a true match for affairs in her heart.

"Fifth Coda"
These padded stockings—
The stitches are finer than nits,
The stuffing more pliant than down.
"Since you know the rites, don't stray from the straight;
I wish that you would act like this."

(Male lead speaks:) Lute boy, what did the young madam say to you at your departure? (Servant speaks:) She wanted you not to seek another good match. (Student speaks:) Missy, don't you know my heart yet?

"Kuaihuo san" (Student sings:)
Chilling, chilling cold: a traveler's inn.
Plashing, splashing wind: threads of rain.
The rain drizzled;
The breeze was light.
When I returned from the dream,
There were so many affairs that wounded the heart.

"Chao tianzi" (Student sings:)
My four limbs I could not move;
Try as I might, I couldn't gaze as far as the monastery in East of Pu.
The young madam must, when you saw her,
Have had another message you haven't delivered.
Am I a rakish official,
A romantic scholar?
Could I be willing to wear tattered flowers or snap an old branch?
From that time until to now,
What idle rumors could there have been?

"He shengchao" (Student sings:)
There was no lack of prime ministers' families
Or beauties in search of husbands.
From time to time, should one among them be like you,
Could I find the same warm pliancy?
Or such talent and thoughtfulness?
The very thought of you, Oriole,
Makes me think of you in my dreams, long for you in my sleep.

(Male lead speaks:) Lute boy, put all these clothes and things you brought
neatly away

"Shua hai'er" (Student sings:)
Shake out a cane box in my study;
Spread some paper out inside the box.
Be careful when you place them there:
When you take the bundled clothing, don't let rattan splinters snag the cotton
    thread.
If placed high on a clothes rack, I fear their color will fade;
If placed carelessly in a bundle, I'm afraid they will fold into creases.
It has to be like this: they must be lovingly protected.
You can't simply be so-so.

"Second Coda" (Student sings:)
Just newly wed, barely married,
I came here for fortune and fame.
In Chang'an I remembered anxiously the monastery in East of Pu.
Last night we loved "at night as the peach blossoms opened in the spring winds",
Today I sorrow "when the *wutong* leaves fall in the autumn rains."[6]
Such is my sorrow·
My body may be distant, but my heart is near;
Whether sitting or walking, I think only of you.

"Third Coda" (Student sings:)
This passion, high as the heavens and thick as the earth,

[6] Another reference to a passage from Bo Juyi's "Song of Unending Sorrow," in which the broken emperor Xuanzong wanders through the old gardens of his newly recaptured palaces, visiting spots he once frequented with his young consort:

> Lotus blossoms in Taiyi pond, willows at Weiyang Palace:
> Lotus blossoms like her face, willows like her eyebrows.
> Facing them, can I not weep?
> In spring winds, on nights when the peach blossoms opened;
> In autumn rains, at the time when *wutong* leaves fell.
> In the Western Palace, the Southern Garden, grow many autumnal grasses,
> Fallen leaves fill the steps, the red is unswept

144b

Will last until the sea dries up and rocks rot away.
When will come an end to the anxieties of this moment?
They will last until "the candle turns to ashes—only then will my eyes be free
  of tears"—
Until "the silkworm is worn out—then the threads of longing will stop in my
  heart."[7]
I'm not to be compared to an unfeeling philanderer
Who slights the mutual harmony between man and wife
Or breaks apart a mating pair of phoenix and simurgh.

"Fourth Coda" (Student sings:)   145a
Without hearing the message of the yellow dog[8]
It was hard to send a poem on a red leaf.[9]
The post route is long; I met no plum-flower messenger.[10]
All alone and three thousand miles away from home—
Every hour of the day my heart returned to you.
Leaning on the balustrade, I watch,
Listen to the river's sounds roaring and surging,
See the mountains' color, uneven and mottled.

"Coda"
Anxious, yes, anxious when I was ill;
Happy, yes, happy now you've arrived.
By the time the soul-catching letter of this Zhuo Wenjun arrived,
This Sima Xiangru, suffering a ghostly illness, was almost dead with anticipation.   145b

(They leave.)

❖❖❖

---

[7] From a poem by Li Shangyin, "Untitled" ("Wuti"): "When spring silkworms die, only
then are their threads finished; / When the waxen candle turns to ash, only then do its tears
dry."
[8] See play IV, act 1, n. 3.
[9] From the story about a certain Yu You of the late ninth century, who found a red leaf
on which a poem had been written floating in a canal flowing out of the imperial palace.
He wrote a poem on another red leaf and set it adrift upstream of the imperial palace. As
it floated inside, it was picked up by Lady Han. She was later released from the imperial
seraglio and became Yu You's legal wife. At their wedding, they each took out a red leaf
to show to the other and remarked, "Let us thank our go-betweens."
[10] I.e., someone bringing a message. A certain Lu Kai (early fifth century), who was
stationed in southern China, once sent the following poem to Fan Ye (398–445) in
Chang'an:

> When I met a messenger going north,
> I plucked a branch of plum blossoms:
> Down south we have got nothing else,
> So I send you this single sprig of spring.

does happy
exist just
for seeing
them speak
out once

(Female lead and Happy enter. [Female lead] speaks:) Recently I've heard that Student Zhang has succeeded in the examinations and has won the rank of flower-plucking gentleman but has not yet been appointed to any position of authority Today is the fifteenth day of the sixth month, on which the god is invited to return to the temple hall. Happy, go and prepare incense and money, a sedan chair and horse,[11] so that I can accompany others to the shrine over there and there consult the fortune blocks. That he may be protected by the gods is my heart's desire.

[(They leave.)]

---

[11] All made of paper and to be burnt in sacrifice.

Zheng Heng Argues with Crimson about Oriole's Marriage

Act 3

zheng heng is a foolish character?

(Clown, costumed as Zheng Heng, enters and speaks:) I am Zheng Heng, known
as Bochang. My late father was minister of the Board of Rites, but unfortunately
he died early Several years later I also lost my mother. When my father was still
alive, he arranged for me to marry my aunt's daughter, Oriole. Since my aunt's
husband unexpectedly passed away and since Oriole's period of mourning had not
yet been completed, we never married. My aunt and Oriole were bearing the
casket back to Boling for burial, but the road was blocked, so they couldn't
continue on their journey. A few months ago my aunt wrote a letter summoning
me to help her bear the casket back. Since there is no one else in my family, my
departure from the capital was delayed. After I arrived in Hezhong Prefecture, I
discovered that Flying Tiger Sun had wanted to carry off Oriole as his wife and that
she had been promised by my aunt to a certain Zhang Junrui because he made the
rebellious troops withdraw If I hadn't heard this news when I got here, I would
have gone over to see her. But since I've heard it, it would be foolish of me to rush
right over there. This whole affair devolves on Crimson. I've ordered someone to
summon her here just to tell her that her brother is here from the capital and that
I don't dare go see my aunt. When Crimson comes to my lodging, I'll tell her what
to say to my aunt. The fellow I sent has been gone a long while: it appears that she
and my aunt are talking it over. (Crimson enters and speaks:) Brother Zheng Heng
is in his lodging and dares not come see the madam. Instead, he has summoned me
to talk it over. The madam ordered me to go and see what he says. (She acts out
greeting clown and [speaks]:) Brother, myriad blessings. The madam said, "Now

147a

that brother is here, why doesn't he come to our house?" (Clown speaks:) What face do I have to see my aunt? What was the reason I summoned you here? When my aunt's husband was still alive, he gave his promise to this marriage. Now I've arrived and the period of mourning for my aunt's husband is already completed. I'm relying on you, particularly, to go and inform the madam to select a lucky day to consummate this affair so that I may be buried together with your mistress. If she doesn't bring it to its rightful conclusion, we'll find it hard to say hello even if we stumble across each other on the road. If you say you are willing to do this, I'll reward you most handsomely (Crimson speaks:) Don't bring this topic up again. Oriole has been given to someone else. (Clown speaks:) Isn't it said, "A single horse does not carry two saddles"? Can it be possible that Oriole was promised to me when her father was alive but that the madam would go back on her word after Oriole's father died? That goes against all rule and reason! (Crimson speaks:) It is not like that. Where were you, brother, when Flying Tiger Sun appeared with his five-thousand-man cavalry? If it hadn't been for that student, who would be left of this household? Now when peace reigns undisturbed, you come along to claim the bride. Could you have claimed her if she had been carried off by those rebels? (Clown speaks:) It would make some sense if she were given to a really wealthy family But to give her to such a bankrupt sourpuss and starving pedant—and I of all people have to give way to him? As a humane person, I'm capable of humanity; my status derives from the roots of my status. Moreover, I'm a relative—he doesn't even have her father's mandate!

(Crimson speaks:) But should he give way to you? Shut up!

[*Yuediao* mode:] "Dou anchun" (Crimson sings:)
You show off your "humane personality capable of humanity",
You rely on your "status derived from the roots of status."
Even if you had office piled on office,
No one would tell you to add the bond of wedlock to the bond of blood.[1]

147b

You never brought lambs and geese or invited a matchmaker,
Offered riches and silks or asked for confirmation.
You have barely washed off the dust of the road,
But want immediately to cross the gate.[2]
You'd rudely defile her golden room and silver screen,
Rudely besmirch her brocade blanket and embroidered pad,

"Zihua'er xu" (Crimson sings:)
Rudely befoul her combed clouds and brushed moon,
Rudely shame her coveted jade and loved perfume,
Rudely vulgarize her ample rains and abundant clouds.

---

[1] Before the fourteenth century, third-generation relatives were not supposed to marry. The proscription was lifted in the mid-1300s.

[2] To get married.

When in the beginning the three materials were first divided,[3]
The two forms first separated[4]
Into *qian* and *kun*,[5]
The pure became *qian*,
The murky became *kun*:
Man in the middle is a muddle of both.
Junrui is a gentleman, one of the pure poor;
Zheng Heng is a small man, one of the murky crowd.[6]

(Clown speaks:) And when the rebels appeared? Could he repel them alone?
What nonsense! (Crimson speaks:) I will tell you about it: 148a

"Tian jing sha" (Crimson sings:)
The Flying Tiger General, holding the bridge,
Rebelled in East of Pu and plundered the populace.
Five thousand rebels laid siege to the gates of the monastery;
And with his double-edged sword across his saddle,
Sun loudly shouted, "I want Oriole
As the lady of my fortress!"

(Clown speaks:) Five thousand rebels—what could he do alone? (Crimson speaks:)
At the height of the rebels' siege, the madam panicked, conferred with the abbot,
clapped her hands, and loudly called out, "If anyone in the two galleries, whether
monk or layman, can repel the rebellious troops, I will give him Oriole as wife!"
Suddenly a traveler responded with the words, "I have a plan to repel the troops;
why not ask me?" The madam was overjoyed and asked what his plan consisted
of. ([Speaking as] student, [Crimson] says:) "I have an old friend, the White Horse
General. He is now in charge of a hundred thousand men and is guarding Pu Pass.
If I write a single letter and have someone deliver it, he will surely come to rescue
us." And indeed the letter went forth, the troops came, and our distress was
immediately relieved.

"Xiaotao hong" (Crimson sings:)   148b
If it had not been not for that talented poet from Luoyang adept at composition,
Who quick as fire wrote a letter
When the White Horse General arrived
And annihilated mists and dust,
The madam and the missy both submitted in their hearts.

---

[3] Heaven, earth, and human beings.
[4] Heaven and earth.
[5] *Qian* and *kun* are the names of the first two hexagrams in *The Book of Changes*. They
represent a binary pair of generative cosmic forces roughly equal to those of *yin* and *yang*,
i.e., the male and female elements of heaven and earth as cosmic energy.
[6] The Confucian tradition divides men into two classes: the gentleman (*junzi*), who acts
out of a sense of what is right, and the small man (*xiaoren*), who acts only out of self-benefit.

Because he is authority without cruelty,[7]
His words were full of trust.[8]
No one dares slight such a person!

(Clown speaks:) I've never heard of him! Don't know whether I've met him. And you, you little wench, make such a fuss over him. (Crimson speaks:) There you go, cursing me too!

"Jin jiaoye" (Crimson sings:)
He relies, for his disquisitions, on nature and reason, on the *Analects* in the
    traditions of Qi and Lu;[9]
For his composition of lyrics and rhapsodies, on the writings of Han and Liu.[10]
He knows the Way and its principle;
He acts a man, respects others.

149a   Our family keeps its trust and knows to repay favor with favor.

"Tiaoxiao ling" (Crimson sings:)
If you are 10 percent,
He's a hundred times a hundred.
How can a firefly compare to the wheel of the moon?
Let's not discuss high and low, far and near;
I'll spell it out clearly for you by breaking characters apart.

(Clown speaks:) What do you know, you little wench, about breaking characters apart? You tell me!

([Crimson] sings:)
Junrui is the character "similar to"
With an "upright man" at its side.[11]
You are an "inch of wood," a "horse's door," a "corpse's kerchief."

149b   [(Clown speaks:)] An "inch of wood," a "horse's door," a "corpse's kerchief"— you say that I am a boorish donkey's dick![12] My ancestors are a family of chancellors, and I still have to give away to that starving fellow, that bankrupt gent

---

[7] From *Analects*, 7.8.

[8] From *Analects*, 1.6. These are both classic descriptions of the Confucian gentleman.

[9] Two different schools of interpretation of the *Analects* in the Han period.

[10] Han Yu (768–824) and Liu Zongyuan (773–819), great masters of prose and poetry of the Tang dynasty and leading figures in the revival of neo-Confucianism.

[11] This popular form of entertainment and word play was one of the chief jeux d'esprit of well-educated ladies, including prostitutes. The players describe characters part by part, assigning a meaning to each of the parts. For instance, the combination of *xiao* (alike, similar to) and *ren* (man) describes the character *qiao* (handsome).

[12] *Cun* (inch) and *mu* (wood) combine to form *cun* (boorish, rustic). *Ma* (horse) and *hu* (door) combine to form *lü* (donkey). *Shi* (corpse) and *jin* (kerchief) combine to form the slang word *diao* (penis).

all clad in white? Those who hold office, hold office!

"Tusi'er" (Crimson sings:)
Relying on teachers and friends, he, as a gentleman, cultivates his essentials;
Leaning on your father and brothers, you abuse power and bully people.
During the days and months of pickled vegetables, he did not begrudge his
poverty;[13]
Governing the hundred surnames, renewing the citizens, he will find his name
spread afar.

"Shengyao wang" (Crimson sings:)
This lout reasons falsely,
Based on prejudice and bias.
You say only officials are suited to being officials;
You let your mouth run off
Without considering your lot.
You say that the poor will always be poor,
But isn't it said, "Generals and ministers come from humble homes"?

(Clown speaks:) This affair is all the work of that abbot, that bald ass, that son-of-
a-bitch! I'll go over it very, very slowly with him tomorrow!

"Ma lang'er" (Crimson sings:)
As one who has left his family, ruth and compassion are his root,
Good deeds are his gate.
Your death-dealing eyes don't recognize a good man;
Your calamity-calling mouth doesn't know proper measure.

(Clown speaks:) It's the last will of my aunt's husband. I'll pick a lucky day, bring   150a
along a goat and some wine, and then I'll see how my aunt deals with me.

"Reprise" [(Crimson sings:)]
You blow your top, act the boor, throw a tantrum—
What of your compliant friendliness and warm helpfulness now?
You'll force your way in, coerce her to become your wedded wife,
And without a ceremony coerce a harmony of Qin and Jin.[14]

(Clown speaks:) If Auntie doesn't give in, I'll have twenty or thirty cronies lift
Oriole into the palanquin; and when she gets to my lodgings, then off with her
clothes. And when you finally catch up, I'll give you back a used woman.

"Luosiniang" (Crimson sings:)
You're definitely the legal son of Chancellor Zheng,

---

[13] The meager fare of the poor: a common metaphor for poverty, with satiric overtones
when used in reference to students; see p. 75.
[14] See pp. 53–54.

Definitely not some uncouth slave-born soldier of Flying Tiger Sun.
Such an ugly face, such a filthy body, such a deathly lot—
You'll end up without a family to take you in!

150b   (Clown speaks:) You little wench, you've evidently accepted my invitation to surrender! I'm not going to talk to you anymore. Tomorrow I will take her to wife, take her to wife! (Crimson speaks:) I won't marry her to you, won't marry her to you!

"Coda" [(Crimson sings:)]
If the beauty is willing and the gentleman handsome, how could I bear not to cheer?

(Clown speaks:) Just cheer once, and let me hear it. (Crimson speaks:) Your fucking face—

([Crimson] sings:)
You're fit only to steal the ashes of Han Shou's perfume,
The powder from Master He's left cheek.

[(Crimson leaves.)]

(Clown speaks, acting out taking off his clothes:) That wench must have performed with that sourpuss! Tomorrow I will go to the gate myself and see Auntie. I'll act as if I don't know a thing, and I'll say that Student Zhang has become the live-in son-in-law of Minister Wei. My aunt believes any kind of rumor. And she has really loved me since I was young, so we'll be able to work it out. More than anything else, this set of clothes will surely move her. Ever since we lived together as children in the capital, we have been accustomed to hunting for lines and picking words.[15] Auntie's husband promised Oriole to me in marriage; who dares keep me away with words? Once I start creating a ruckus, we'll see where Oriole goes! (Clown recites:)

151a   I'll take my mind that suppresses the good and bullies the noble,
And for a while make it a heart for abundant clouds and ample rains.

[(Clown leaves.)]

❖❖❖

(Old lady [enters] and speaks:) Zheng Heng arrived last night. He did not come see me but sent for Crimson to inquire about the marriage. If I follow my heart, it is

---

[15] That is, picking out a few important sentences or words from texts that one should have read completely, then stitching them together into deficient literary works. Here it seems to refer to a game that they played as children—totally appropriate to their age—but there is also the suggestion that Zheng Heng's own literary talents have never gone beyond that point. This is quite a contrast to the fine literary pieces that have passed between Zhang and Oriole during the progress of their love.

right for me to give my child to him. Even more so since the chancellor had promised, when still alive, to give her to him. I have acted against the words of my late husband, and that is a lapse in my governance of the household. They may have committed the act, but I've made up my mind to give her to Zheng Heng. If he complained, I wouldn't blame him. I'll have some some food prepared to go with the wine: he'll probably come to see me today (Clown [enters] and speaks:) Here I am! No need to announce me; I'll go on in and see madam. (He acts out kneeling. He acts out weeping. Old lady speaks:) My child, why didn't you come and see me when you arrived? (Clown speaks:) What face did your child have to see you, Auntie? (Old lady speaks:) Oriole   because of what happened with Flying Tiger Sun, I couldn't wait for you. There was no other way of relieving the danger but to promise her to Student Zhang. (Clown speaks:) Which Student Zhang? That must be the head of the list! I saw the plaque announcing it in the capital. He's twenty-four or -five years old? This Zhang Gong from Luoyang, basking in glory, was paraded through the streets for three days. On the second day the cortege passed before the house of Minister Wei. The minister's daughter is eighteen. She had built a bunted loft on the imperial street, and she threw a ball that hit him squarely. I was riding along on a horse, watching, and she almost hit me! More than ten sturdy maids of that household dragged that Student Zhang on his heels into the house. He shouted, "I have a wife. I am the son-in-law of Chancellor Cui." That minister is very powerful, and they just didn't listen but kept on dragging him inside. This must have been his unavoidable fate. The minister said, "My daughter has built this bunted loft in accordance with an imperial decree, so you order your young lady Cui to be your concubine. You married her after seducing her—you shouldn't have taken her at all." It caused quite a stir in the capital. That's how I came to know about him. (Old lady speaks angrily:) I thought that budding talent wasn't fit to be supported, and now he has indeed betrayed our family. This household, that of a chancellor, has refused for generations to give a daughter away as a concubine. Since Student Zhang has taken a wife by order of imperial decree, you pick out an auspicious day, my child, and a good hour, and on the authority of your aunt, and in accordance with what was, then enter our family as a live-in son-in-law (Clown speaks:) What if Student Zhang complains? (Old lady speaks:) Leave that to me. Tomorrow—pick out an auspicious day and a good hour—and cross the gate quickly

[(She leaves.)]

(Clown speaks:) She fell for my trick. Prepare the banquet, the wedding gifts, and the gratuities! Within a day, I'll cross the gate.

(He leaves.)[16]

❖❖❖

---

[16] These next three scenes would probably make better sense as the leading scenes of the following act. We would prefer to transpose them there, but we lack the clear-cut evidence for such an emendation.

(Bald one enters and speaks:) Yesterday I bought a list of those who had passed the examinations, and I saw that Student Zhang—the very first name, the head of the list—has been appointed prefect of Hezhong. Who would have thought that the madam would so lack determination that she would promise marriage again to Zheng Heng? The madam refused to go out and welcome Student Zhang, but I am on my way to the ten-mile pavilion with some delicacies to welcome the official.

(He leaves.)

❖❖❖

152b   (General Du enters and speaks:) As appointed by imperial decree, I am in charge of the troops at Pu Pass and oversee the affairs of Hezhong Prefecture. Mounted, I govern my army; dismounted, I govern the citizens. Who would have thought that my brother Junrui would succeed in his first attempt at the examinations and be appointed prefect of Hezhong? I have yet to be able to welcome him. Evidently he'll be at the madam's house, determined to avail himself of this opportunity to consummate this marriage. I'll go straightaway to the madam's house with a goat and wine to both congratulate the head of the list and act as best man, and so complete this great affair for my brother. Servants, where are you? Bring my horse; I'm on my way to Hezhong Prefecture!

(He leaves.)

❖❖❖

(Old lady enters and speaks:) Who would have thought that Student Zhang would betray our family and become a son-in-law to Minister Wei's family? I'll not betray the last will of my late husband now but summon Zheng Heng again to be my son-in-law Today is an auspicious date: let him cross the gate! Prepare the banquet— Zheng Heng must be on the way!

[(She leaves.)]

The Old Lady Summons Crimson to Verify Zheng Heng's Tale for the Student

(Student enters on horseback and speaks:) I, this humble official, by imperial decree have been appointed prefect of Hezhong. Today I return home clad in brocade. My young lady's golden cap and sunset rose stole—bring them here![1] Who would   153a
have thought this day would ever happen? When I see her, I'll present them to her with both hands. (Student recites:)

> My literary compositions crowned of old all within *qian* and *kun*;
> My name is newly vaunted beside the sun and moon.

[*Shuangdiao* mode:] "Xinshui ling" (Student sings:)
With jade whip, on proud steed, I departed the august metropolis,
A damned fine and dashing personality from the Jade Hall:
Today a third rank official,[2]
Yesterday one cold scholar.
By personal appointment of the imperial brush
My name has been noted in the Forest of Pens.

"Zhuma ting" (Student sings:)
I, Zhang Gong, as if simpleminded,[3]

---

[1] These are the colored hat and robes that according to the sumptuary laws Oriole was entitled to wear as the wife of a high official.

[2] I.e., step three (from the top) in the Chinese nine-step ranking of civil officials.

[3] See *Analects*, 2.9, where Confucius discusses his favorite disciple, Yan Hui: "I can talk

Have at last realized my ambition with a three-foot Dragon Spring[4] and ten
    thousand scrolls of books.
You, Oriole, blessed with luck,
Have received upon my request the five-colored patent of nobility and the
    seven-perfumed carriage.[5]
Though glorious, I cannot forget I once rented a monk's cell;
When sorrowed, I still remember where I inscribed my poem.
From the time I left for the examinations,
My dream soul never left that road that ran to East of Pu.

153b   (Male lead speaks:) Take my horse! (He acts out greeting old lady [and speaks]:)
Madam, the new head of the list and prefect of Hezhong, your son-in-law, Zhang
Gong, pays his respects. (Old lady speaks:) You are a son-in-law by imperial decree!
How can I accept your greetings?

"Qiao pai'er" (Student sings:)
I bow my body reverentially and ask after your well-being.
Madam, on whose account is this expression of compassion turned to rage?
I see all the maids and servants staring at me—
Could there be something wrong with me?

(Student speaks:) When I left, you saw me off yourself. To my unconquerable joy,
154a   I have now succeeded in the examinations and attained office. How is it possible,
madam, that you run counter and are not pleased? (Old lady speaks:) How can you
still think of our family? Is it not said, "None do not have a beginning, but rare are
those who have a proper end"? My only daughter may be slovenly and ugly, but
her father was chancellor at the prior court. If it had not been for those rebels, you'd
never have had the power to break into our family But now you've suddenly
dismissed us from your concerns and have become the live-in son-in-law of
Minister Wei! How can this be proper? (Male lead speaks:) Who have you listened
to, madam? If this is true, heaven will not cover me, earth will not bear me up, and
I'll suffer from carbuncles and boils big and small.

"Yan'er luo" (Student sings:)
If you're speaking of scenes of silken whips and high-class ladies,

---

all day with Hui, and he never disagrees; it is as if he were simpleminded. When we withdraw
and I observe his private actions, they are sufficient to bring to light what we have discussed.
Hui is not simpleminded."

  [4] That is, his sword. A sword and books were standard equipment for the struggling
young scholar hoping to prove himself a man equal to his ambitions. Dragon Spring was the
name of a famous sword of antiquity.

  [5] The patent of nobility, written on a piece of silk of many colors, was sent to officers
of rank five and above. The "seven-perfumed chariot" was originally a palanquin of Tang
princesses decorated with seven precious jewels. Later the term came simply to mean the
conveyance of any lady of noble station.

Then indeed they did fill the pleasure quarters.[6]
But I have always cherished the old favors from here—
How would I be willing to seek a marriage partner elsewhere?

"Desheng ling" (Student sings:)   154b
Haven't you heard, "A gentleman decides at the outset"—
How could I forget the place where I found favor?
What terrible scoundrel acted out his jealousy
And came running to you to get in my way, madam?
He could not get the lovely lass
And so day and night plied his schemes.
The villain who said this
Will sooner or later mount the wooden donkey [7]

(Madam speaks:) Zheng Heng told me that the embroidered ball had hit your horse and that you had become a bridegroom. If you don't believe me, then summon Crimson and question her! (Crimson enters and speaks:) I have to see him! So he really did obtain an office and come back. Heavens! This will be a confrontation of right and wrong! (Male lead, turning his back, questions her:) How is missy, Crimson? [(Crimson speaks:)] Because you married another, our young lady will marry Zheng Heng, as originally planned. (Student speaks:) Can such an absurd thing happen?

"Qing dongyuan" (Student sings:)
How can trees with intertwined branches grow on a dungheap
Or fish with paired eyes live in a mudpool?
In their ignorance they will defile the record of karmic unions—
O Oriole, you will marry a deep-fried monkey of a husband.

[(Student speaks:)] O Crimson,   155a

[(Student sings:)]
You'll wait on a smoked badger of a master.

[(Student speaks:)] O Student Zhang,

---

[6] It was a general custom as described in fiction and drama for young men to agree to marry women by accepting from them a silken whip. This is also an oblique reference to "The Tale of Li Wa," in which a young courtesan tempts and then fleeces a student en route to the examinations, leaving him a physical and mental wreck. She later takes him back, nurses him to health, and sends him to success in the examinations. In the end, she marries him and, like Oriole in the drama, is endowed with a patent of nobility. In the tale, and in the dramas based on it, the young student drops his whip several times when he first sees her so that he can tarry for a better look.

[7] This was a four-legged table topped with iron nails. The convicted was first strapped to the top, then paraded through the streets as a warning to would-be criminals. The punishment concluded with death by "slow slicing."

[(Student sings:)]
You've bumped into a water-soaked rat of a fuckmate.[8]
This lout destroys custom and injures mores.

"Qiaomu cha" (Crimson sings:)
This serving maid comes forth to bow;
Spare us the anger in your heart.
Have you enjoyed yourself since we parted?
Where is your new bride staying?
How does she match up against my sister?

(Male lead speaks:) Even you are all mixed up! No one knows the misery I've suffered because of your sister. I can't deceive you; how could I do such a thing when we were barely married?

"Jiao zhengpa" (Student sings:)
155b   May I drop dead on the spot
If I've looked for another wife!
Could I ever forget waiting for the moon in the winding corridor?
Impossible to dismiss, my companion in blowing the flute![9]
I suffered hell in life,
Spent my energies to the death,
And yet we barely became man and wife!
Here I bring a lady's patent,
The title of countess.[10]
More than anything else I wanted in all happiness
To present them to her with both my hands—
But out of the blue you concoct accusations!

(Crimson, addressing old lady, speaks:) I would say that Student Zhang is not that kind of person. Let's call missy out and have her question him herself. (She acts out calling female lead and [speaks]:) Sister, come quickly and question Student Zhang and find out what the facts really are. I don't believe he's one to betray love. When I was called out to greet him, his rage stormed against the heavens—but with just cause. (Female lead acts out greeting male lead. Male lead speaks:) I hope you've been well, missy, since our separation. (Female lead speaks:) Myriad blessings, sir. (Crimson speaks:) Tell him what you want to say! (Female lead, having heaved a long sigh, [speaks]:) What can I say

"Chenzui dongfeng" (Female lead sings:)
Before seeing him, I had ready a thousand words and myriad phrases;
But upon meeting him, they've all turned to short sighs and long moans.

---

[8] This a word we have coined in English for the Chinese term *yifu* (two men who share one woman).

[9] See the story of Xiao Shi and Nongyu, play III, act 2, n. 8.

[10] In Chinese, *xianjun*—a title given to the wives of prefects.

He, with all deliberate haste, has just returned;
I, flustered with embarrassment, don't know where to look.
Of the sorrows in my belly I had wanted to lay plaint;
But as we meet, I have but a single line,
Which is simply to say, "Myriad blessings, sir."

(Female lead speaks:) Student Zhang, how did my family betray you, sir, that you have rejected me, your serving maid, to become a son-in-law to the house of Minister Wei? Where is the principle in this? (Male lead speaks:) Who told you this? (Female lead speaks:) Zheng Heng told the madam. (Male lead speaks:) Missy, how can you listen to that scoundrel? Only heaven can be witness to Zhang Gong's heart!

"Luomei feng" (Student sings:)
Once I left the commandery East of Pu
And reached the capital prefecture,
If I saw a beauty, I never turned my head to look.
Yet you stubbornly dream up some marriage to a daughter from the house of
    Minister Wei.
If ever I saw even a shadow of her,
Let my family be extinguished and all my posterity annihilated!

(Student speaks:) This all devolves on Crimson. I'll outflank her with words and see what she says. Crimson, I asked around and someone told me that you took a note to summon Zheng Heng for missy. (Crimson speaks:) You simpleton! I never should have helped you out! You see me just the same, as if I hadn't.

"Tianshui ling" (Crimson, explaining to student, [sings]:)
Mister Junrui,
You shouldn't be indecisive.
What need is there to be anxious or to worry?
That lout has always been a mess;
Our household, pure and spotless.
Our ancestors were the wise and the good;
The chancellor had fame and name.
Would I, in their presence,
Deliver a note or transmit a letter?

"Zhegui ling" (Crimson, cursing Heng, [sings]:)
Either that fit-for-beating scoundrel is chewing maggots in his mouth,
Or that lout is talking black into yellow
Or hates purple snatching vermilion.[11]
Even though my sister bends too easily and puts up no fight,

[11] *Analects*, 17.18: "I hate purple for taking the place of vermilion. I detest the sound of Zheng's corruption of classical music. I detest those with keen mouths' overturning of state and family."

How could she marry a not-worth-a-penny, human-shaped boar pig?
You, Lord of the East, have to be responsible for Oriole.[12]
How could you let such a supple sprig be plucked by this woodcutter?
That lout, all empty bluster,
Is scheming to harm you.
I can find no words for it:
The swelling rage breaks my chest!

(Crimson speaks:) Student Zhang, if you really didn't get married, I will use all my power to protect you in front of the madam. When that scoundrel comes, you argue it out with him. (Crimson greets old lady and speaks:) Student Zhang never married anyone else. It's all Zheng Heng's lies. Let the two of them argue it out. (Old lady speaks:) Since he never   we'll wait for that scoundrel Zheng Heng to get here, let them argue it out, and then see what to do. (Bald one enters and speaks:) Who would have thought that Student Zhang would pass the examinations on his first try and then get the position of prefect of Hezhong? I'll go straight to the madam's place to offer congratulations. When will this wedding be completed? I was in on it at the beginning, but the madam lacks all determination and wants to give Oriole to Zheng Heng. What if she gives her up and Student Zhang comes today? (Bald one and male lead act out exchanging polite conversation. [Bald one] speaks to old lady:) Madam, today I am proven right. Student Zhang is definitely not that kind of unprincipled budding talent. Would he have dared forget you, madam? General Du was also a witness, so how could he have backed out of this wedding? (Female lead speaks:) Student Zhang, for this affair we need General Du here.

"Yan'er luo" (Female lead sings:)
He scoffs at Sun and Pang for being utterly stupid;[13]
And when it comes to a discussion of Jia and Ma—they are no flowering talents.[14]
He has been appointed Grand Generalissimo for the Subjugation of the West
And is concurrently in charge of Hezhong Circuit in Shaanxi.

"Desheng ling" (Female lead sings:)
He was our former life-protecting amulet;
Today he has authority and power;
And in the future he will help you.
He is certain to execute that villain,

---

[12] Dong Jun (Lord of the East) is the god of spring. The oriole is a bird of spring and therefore under his control.

[13] Sun Bin and Pang Juan, legendary paragons of military wisdom of the Warring States period.

[14] The Han scholars and poets Jia Yi (201–169 B.C.) and Sima Xiangru. Roughly paraphrased, these lines mean that Du's own skills outstrip the legendary figures of the military and civil worlds.

Who can't tell who's related and who's not
And who tries to steal away a good man's wife.
You can't distinguish the wise and stupid—
If you have no poison, you're not a real man.

(Madam speaks:) Tell missy to go to her bedroom. *why*

[(Crimson and female lead leave.)]

([Extra as] General Du enters and speaks:) I have departed Pu Pass and come to the Monastery of Universal Salvation to congratulate my brother. I will also conclude his wedding for him. (Male lead speaks to extra:) Thanks to your tigerlike might, I, your brother, succeeded in my first attempt at the examinations. When I got back, I had wanted to marry, but Zheng Heng, the madam's nephew, had already arrived and told her that I was the live-in son-in-law of the family of Minister Wei. The madam was angry and wanted to back out of the marriage and give Oriole to Zheng Heng as originally planned. Isn't that unprincipled? Isn't it said, "A chaste woman doesn't take a second husband"? (Extra speaks:) Madam, you are mistaken in this affair. Junrui is the son of a minister of the Board of Rites. Moreover, he succeeded in his first attempt. At first, madam, you did not want to accept a budding scholar clad in white, yet you still run counter and want to cancel the marriage. Isn't that against all principle? (Old lady speaks:) Originally, when my husband was alive, he promised Oriole to that lout. No one thought that we'd run into this disaster that fortunately Student Zhang rescued us from by summoning you, General, to slay and beat back the rebellious troops. I did not go back on my word, and wanted to accept him as my son-in-law. But who could have expected that Zheng Heng would say that Zhang had become a son-in-law to the house of Minister Wei? In my anger I promised Oriole to Zheng Heng as originally planned. (Extra speaks:) He's a villain at heart. You should have known he was slandering Zhang. How could you believe him, madam?(Clown enters and speaks:) I'm all dressed up spick-and-span, ready to be the bridegroom. Today is an auspicious day. Leading a goat and carrying wine, I'm on my way to cross the gate. (Student speaks:) Zheng Heng, what are you doing here? (Clown speaks:) Aw, shit! When I heard that you had made head of the list, I came especially to congratulate you. (Extra speaks:) You scoundrel. How dare you steal by deceit another man's wife and commit such an inhumane deed? What do you have to say in front of me? I will memorialize the court to execute such a villain!

158b

not Really

"Luomei feng" (Student sings:)
You've forced your way onto the Peach Spring Road,[15]
Without noting who is the host.
By the Lord of the East you, you honeybee, have been barred.

159a

[15] In the original story, Ruan Zhao and Liu Chen take up with two transcendent maidens who have long been destined to become their quite willing lovers. Here Zheng Heng is trying to take to wife someone who is not willing. See play I, act 1, n. 27.

If you don't believe it,
Go to the shade of the green willows and listen to the cuckoo
That says in every note, "Better go home."[16]

(Extra speaks:) If that lout doesn't leave, my guards, arrest him! (Clown speaks:) You don't have to arrest me—I withdraw myself from this marriage! Give her to Student Zhang! (Old lady speaks:) Your Excellency, still your rage! Let it be enough to drive him away (Clown speaks:) What of this life? I'm better off dying by butting a tree.

159b
> In vain did I contest for a wife, but couldn't carry it off;
> As of old, the romantic love the romantic.
> These three inches of breath I've used in a thousand ways—
> A single day's mishap and all things come to an end!

he died?! how?

(Clown acts out falling down. Old lady speaks:) We did not drive him to his death! Since I am his aunt and he has no parents, I will take responsibility for burying him. Call Oriole out. Today we will have a congratulatory banquet and have the two of them united.

[(Female lead and Crimson enter.)]

"Gu meijiu" (Student sings:)
At the gate we welcome the four-horse chariot;[17]
At the door are displayed eight pepperwood pictures.[18]
A fourfold virtuous, threefold obedient chancellor's daughter[19]—
My life's desire is fulfilled!
Thanks to all you relatives and friends!

160a
"Taiping ling" ([Male lead and female lead] sing in unison:)
If our great benefactor had not drawn his blade to help us,
How could this fine couple be like fish in water?
Achieved it is, the original inscription on the pillar;[20]
Rightly paired are husband and wife in this life.
As of old, the girl has been physiognomized as a husband's fit mate—
A new head of the list, flowers fill the road!

---

[16] See play I, act 1, n. 5.

[17] On his departure from the city of Chengdu, Sima Xiangru wrote on the pillar of a bridge, "If I am not riding a tall four-horse carriage, I will not cross this bridge", that is, if there is no success, there is no return.

[18] These were pictures of animals engraved in the door lintel. Traditionally, only high officials were entitled to display them.

[19] The seven wonders of a good wife: the four virtues are good character, pleasant speech, fine handiwork, and good looks; the three obediences are obedience to the father before marriage, to the husband during marriage, and to the son after the death of the husband.

[20] See above, n. 17.

"Jinshang hua" (Student sings:)
Nothing untoward in the wide world:
Each calls himself a loyal minister or subject;
All nations come to pay court,
Wishing our emperor myriad years.
His deeds surpass Xi and Xuan,[21]
His virtue exceeds that of Shun and Yu:[22]
Sage plans and divine tactics,
Humane culture and righteous might!
At court the prime minister is wise;
Throughout the realm citizens are prosperous.
For ten thousand miles the Yellow River runs clear;[23]
All five grains mature at harvest.
Door after door lives in peace,
From place to place stretches a happy land.
Phoenix couples come to preen;
The unicorn repeatedly appears.[24]

"Qingjiang yin" ([In unison male and female lead] sing:)   160b
We thank the present sagely and enlightened sage ruler of Tang,
Who bestowed on us a decree making us man and wife:
For all eternity without separation,
For all infinity forever united.
May lovers of the whole world all be thus united in wedlock!   161a

"Coda" [(Male and female lead sing in unison:)]
Because they matched couplets by the light of the moon,
A frustrated girl and unmarried man have been brought together.
It displays well the abilities of that ambitious head of the list
And the misery of that unfeeling Zheng Heng!

Title: (Student:) Many thanks, General, for bringing it all to an end.

(Female lead:) I am grateful, Mother, for your management as head of the house.

(Old lady:) The husband is glorious, the wife is noble, this day brings satisfaction.

(Extra [female lead]:) May you be together in the mandarin-duck bed-curtains for a hundred years!

---

[21] Fu Xi and Xuan Yuan, two mythic rulers who governed in times of perfect peace and harmony.

[22] The great sage kings of antiquity, culture heroes of the Confucian tradition.

[23] The river runs clear only during reigns of perfect virtue.

[24] These creatures are also signs of a virtuous reign.

(A poem is recited:)

The monastery in East of Pu: the scene is desolate and cold;
Upon his arrival a traveler will secretly break his heart.
Willows still catch up the vexation of those days;
Lotus blossoms still wear the makeup of years gone by.
Where is he now, who questioned Crimson on that moonlit night?
Forgotten now is their common tryst in the eastern wind.
Only the eternal moon of passion
In dead of night, as of old, sets over the western wing.

Volume V of the Deluxe, Completely Illustrated, and Annotated Story of the Western Wing

[Publisher's Advertisement]

It was once said that the classical poetry (*shi*) of the ancients is the aria (*qu*) of 161b modern men. Although arias can sing and chant of the passions and nature of men and can cleanse the minds and ambitions of men, there is also much in them that relates to the way of the world.[1] Many are those who have labored over arias through the years, but it is *The Western Wing* that is best of all of the poetry of arias; and so, it is sung by people and passed along, even among those families who live in the small alleys of local districts.

To make a play or to perform one, it is absolutely necessary that the words and phrases be true and exact; only after the songs match the prints[2] will a text do. Now the editions [of *The Western Wing*] that are cut and circulated in the city are full of errors and are in terrible condition. The intent is certainly to have the work in circulation, but the texts become unsuitable for reading and the earlier format of the texts is completely lost. Our bookstore, relying on a classic [i.e., an excellent] edition, has had the text rewritten and new pictures drawn for the woodblock prints. Precise in our collation, we have arranged pictures and text into a custom edition in large type.

Now the songs and the pictures match, so people lodged in inns or traveling on boats—whether they be roaming for pleasure or sitting in some distant place—can get a copy of this text, look it over, and sing it correctly from beginning to end and thereby refresh their hearts.

We have commissioned the cutting of the blocks and a printing of the play so that it will be available for reading everywhere.

Recut and printed by the Yue family of Jintai in late winter 1498, the year *wuwu* of the reign period of Encompassing Order.

---

[1] These are the traditionally held beliefs of the effects and function of poetry.

[2] *Tu* below clearly refers to the woodblock prints that have been placed in the top register of the text, but it is possible that here it could refer to musical charts as well.

APPENDICES

APPENDIX I

A Pair of Battling Quacks

This scene of two physicians raising cain is taken from act 2 of the anonymous fifteenth-century *zaju* entitled *Calling Down Mulberry Fruit: Cai Shun Takes Care of His Mother (Jiang sangzhen Cai Shun fengmu).*[1] The dramatis personae include: Cai Shun, a scholar and a gentleman; his wife; someone offstage (the stage manager?); Cai's mother, who is ill; his father, Squire Cai; and two physicians who have been summoned to treat Cai Shun's mother. Although this play is of later date than *The Story of the Western Wing*, we consider this version of the battling quacks skit a representative write-up of the traditional stage routine.[2] In what follows we have not attempted a scientific translation of the names of the diseases mentioned for two reasons. First, the meaning of some terms has changed over time. The disease to which the modern term refers may be an illness identified only during the nineteenth or twentieth centuries and not at all related to that described in this fifteenth-century text. Second, although the illness denoted may be vaguely related to the modern term, the modern term may describe symptoms far more specific than those described by its fifteenth-century counterpart. Furthermore, we desire to keep the context of usage in the translation as close as possible to its intended effect in the original, in which grammatical, phonological, or other linguistic features such as alliteration or parallelism rather than any specific disease have dictated word choice.

A Pair of Battling Quacks

(Female lead speaks:) Cai Shun, how come that physician you summoned hasn't come yet?

(Male lead speaks:) My wife, prepare some tea. That doctor will be here any moment.

(Main clown, dressed as a physician, enters and speaks:)

---

[1] We are basing our translation on the text as found in *Mowangguan chaojiaoben gujin zaju*. Punctuated editions of the play are found in Wang Jilie, *Guben Yuan Ming zaju*, 1:10b–13a; and in Sui Shusen, *Yuanqu xuan waibian*, 1:428–31. Another recension, with some notes, is found in Hu Ji, *Song Jing zaju kao*, 82–88. Earlier translations are found in West, *Vaudeville and Narrative*, 33–43; in Dolby, *Eight Chinese Plays*, 21–29; and in Crump, *Chinese Theater*, 152–67.

[2] See Idema, "Yüan-pen as a Minor Form of Dramatic Literature," 62–63.

As a grand physician, I'm quite high falutin',
I know my texts, my pressure points, and all the right prescriptions.
When people summon me to treat their kin,
I have them prepare a coffin to carry 'em away in.

I'm known as Song Liaoren—that is, my surname is Send and my given name is 'Emtotheirdeath. My skills aren't of the common kind. I was born to a family of medical men and trained by meticulous regimen. I can play the lute, I can sing up high. I drink fine wine and stuff down fat ducks. If anyone ill calls me to prescribe some medicine, I only make them sicker: some live, but a lot more die.

(Offstage interjects:) Isn't his a perfect name?

(Grand physician speaks:) I've a colleague called Hu Tuchong—Old Chucklehead. His father was called Hu Luobo—Old Turniphead. Our skills are about equal, so we've formed a sworn brotherhood. When someone calls a doctor, neither of us will go without the other. When I check the symptoms, he prescribes the doses; and when brother checks the symptoms, I prescribe the medicine. We've sworn an oath together: if one of us goes by himself to see a patient, he'll grow ugly chancres on his lips! Today the scholar Cai of this place summoned me. He told me that his mother was really sick and asked if I would go treat her. I sent someone off to tell my brother to come along too. I'm waiting here on Prefecture Bridge[3] for my brother. He ought to be here soon.

([Second] clown, dressed as Chucklehead, enters and speaks:)

As a physician, I've got great bedside manner;
I'm the king of the mountain of medicine.
Brewing up potions and prescribing herbs,
I'm as effective as a god!

The ancient physician Bian Que of Lu could be my great-grandson for all he knew. Those who summon me for treatment lose consciousness after the first dose.

(Offstage interjects:) Isn't that just so!

(Chucklehead speaks:) I'm a physician, and my name is Chucklehead. As a child, I was known as Dimwit. My ancestors have practiced medicine for three generations. If it comes to my skills, well—

I can't read any pulse
Or understand any medical text.
When I treat a patient,
I first polish off three flagons, two cups, and one bottle of wine,
And top them off with five baked buns.
When I've stuffed it all down,
I go crazy.

---

[3] Zhouqiao, a major bridge in the Song capital of Kaifeng; it would have made a well-known spot to meet.

> I may not be able to cure anyone,
> But I'm no slouch at eating.

(Offstage interjects:) What a fine pair!

(Chucklehead speaks:) In the medical profession I have a colleague who's called Send 'Emtotheirdeath. When you put our skills together, it's all a fine mess, so we've become sworn brothers. He's the elder and I'm the younger. When someone calls a doctor, neither of us will go without the other. There's no Dr. Crazy without Dr. Death and no Dr. Death without Dr. Crazy Death and Crazy are quite a pair! This is dreath and cazy and dazy and creath!

(Offstage interjects:) Now he's into tongue twisters!

(Chucklehead speaks:) This morning Dr. Send sent someone to tell me that the scholar Cai's mother was quite ill; he asked me to come prescribe the doses. Since my brother is waiting at Prefecture Bridge, I'd better go see him. Here I am already (They act out seeing each other. [Chucklehead] speaks:) Don't blame me for being late—if you take offense at it, you're a son-of-a-bitch!

(Offstage interjects:) Quite to the point!

(Grand physician speaks:) You're still flapping your lips! You're a good-for-nothing scoundrel! On such a freezing day you've made me wait so long that my legs have nearly frozen off!

(Chucklehead speaks:) Brother, don't blame me for being late. I'm suffering from humors of the heart. I got up a bit early and caught some kind of chill. The pain nearly killed me! My wife was in a panic and called a doctor; he dosed me until the pain finally stopped.

(Offstage interjects:) You're a doctor! Why take anyone else's medicine?

(Chucklehead speaks:) If my medicine was fit to take, I'd take it.

(Offstage interjects:) How come your medicine isn't fit to take?

(Chucklehead speaks:) I'd have been dead two hours already if I'd taken my own medicine!

(Offstage interjects:) Why canst thou not "heal thyself, physician"?

(Grand physician speaks:) Business has been stinking since that last court case.

(Offstage interjects:) What was that court case about?

(Grand physician speaks:) The two of us doctored someone to death.

(Offstage interjects:) What a pair of oily mouths! Quite right!

(Grand physician speaks:) Younger brother, today Squire Cai's wife has taken ill and has called me to treat her. He's a rich man. When we get there, if she's 10 percent sick, we'll say it's 100; if she's 100 percent sick, we'll say 1,000. Once we arrive, we'll stick her here with acupuncture and burn her there with moxa and make her take her medicine.

If she recovers,
The two of us will demand lots and lots of goods and money;
If she should suddenly die,
We'll pack our medicine sacks
And make tracks to safety.

(Offstage interjects:) Isn't that right! These rascals!

(Chucklehead speaks:) Brother, your words are wise! Because of our good hearts, heaven should vouchsafe us half a bowl of rice.

(Offstage interjects:) Isn't that right!

(Grand physician speaks:) Brother, let's go. Here we are. Announce us and say that the two top physicians are here.

(Household servant speaks:) You wait here while I announce you.

([Household servant] acts out greeting and announcing and speaks:) Squire, you should know that the grand physicians have arrived.

(Squire Cai speaks:) Tell them to come in.

(Household servant speaks:) Yes, sir. [Addressing clowns:] You're early.

(Chucklehead speaks:) Careful, brother, you might slip!

(Offstage interjects:) Why?

(Chucklehead speaks:) [He just said,] "It's oily! It's oily!"

(Offstage interjects:) Boy, is he panicky!

(Grand physician speaks:) We are gentlemen of the five senses.[4] If we come to his house to treat someone, he must come out and greet us himself—and he tells us to go on in!

(Offstage interjects:) Don't criticize him. There's someone sick here. Just go on in!

(Grand physician speaks:) My good boy, out of consideration for you, your father will go on in.

(Offstage interjects:) This bastard's really puffed up!

(Grand physician acts out giving way and speaks:) Younger brother, please—

(Chucklehead speaks:) Oh, no. Elder brother, please—

(Grand physician speaks:) My esteemed younger brother, please—

(Chucklehead speaks:) You're wrong, brother. I may never have read the books of Confucius and Mencius, but I do know a bit about the rituals of the Former Kings. Haven't you heard that the sage said,

---

[4] The text here reads *wuguan* (a high official, an official with five perspicacious senses), which does not make sense. Other editors have emended *wu* to *ge* (an indefinite measure word). We choose to emend it to *wuguan* (five sense organs) to retain the pun on high official and five senses that seems clearly indicated in the *Mowangguan* text.

He who walks slowly and puts his elders first is called younger-brotherly. He who walks quickly and gets in front of his elders is called unyounger-brotherly. The plowman yields the field, the pedestrian yields the road; the older one is the elder brother; the next in line, the younger. You're my elder, hence I am my older brother's younger brother. Once there is an elder and a younger, then one has to distinguish superior and inferior.

Such is a ritual of the Former Kings, and it ain't wrong. If I went first, I'd be a donkey's offspring—a real ass—and an oily mouth to boot.

(Offstage interjects:) What pedantic gibberish!

(Chucklehead speaks:) Oh, no. My elder brother, please—

(Grand physician speaks:) Oh, no. You, my esteemed younger brother, are a fine and noble gentleman. I, on the other hand, am just a stupid and uncouth lout without the slightest, smallest chaff-width of ability, whereas you, my esteemed younger brother, have the power of the nine rivers. Judging by the way you, my esteemed younger brother, treat illnesses, you must have spiritual power of great efficacy In the doctoring of illnesses, you have many fine prescriptions. You are a man of grand accomplishments and I'm just the skin of a maggot. If I went first, then I, your humble student, would be just a bag of dog bones.

(Offstage interjects:) That's enough of this bullshit! Go on in!

(Two clowns act out greeting old lady Grand physician speaks:) Ah, there, the mother, feeling poorly and ill affected.

(Chucklehead speaks:) To banish the illness, the physician a medicine has selected.

(Grand physician acts out taking her left pulse. Chucklehead acts out taking the right pulse. Physician speaks:) Just watch the pair of us take your pulse!

(Grand physician, while taking the left pulse, sings:)

[Southern: "Qing ge'er"]
To this house we've come, the eight pulses to interpret.

(Chucklehead takes the left pulse of the old lady and sings:)
I feel a thready tapping, hemp-stalk delicate.

(Grand physician sings:)
My drug pouch I must quickly open and manipulate.

(Chucklehead speaks:) Oh, what a pity, a very poor pulse action.

(Sings:) Quickly, go out and buy—

(Male lead speaks:) Physician, buy what?

(Grand physician sings:)
Go buy a coffin.

(Chucklehead sings:)
Buy a coffin and lie her in state.

(Offstage interjects:) How long will this go on?

(Grand physician knocks old lady down with his medicine pouch. Old lady speaks:) He's beating me to death!

(Offstage interjects:) She's the patient. How come you're beating her?

(Grand physician speaks:) It's no matter, it's no matter. She's still all right. She can feel pain!

(Offstage interjects:) Wouldn't she be dead for sure, if she didn't know pain?

(Grand physician speaks:) Dr. Crazy, what ails her?

(Chucklehead speaks:) My brother, I'm not bragging—I've just examined her expression and checked her pulse. Just feel this side of her body—burning like fire. She's suffering from a caloric disease.

(Grand physician speaks:) You're crazy! This pulse is leaping an inch high. How can you say it's a caloric disease? Just look at this side of her body—as cold as ice. She's suffering from a disease of gelidity!

(Chucklehead speaks:) Dear brother, that's no problem. We'll wind a twine around the tip of her nose and let it fall straight to the ground, where we'll peg it in. You treat your disease of gelidity on the left-hand side, and I'll take care of my caloric disease on the right. What do you think about that, brother?

(Grand physician speaks:) Yeah, yeah. We've settled that clearly. Suppose, though, that as soon as she takes the medicine you dose her with, you kill off this right side?

(Chucklehead speaks:) It won't interfere with the matter of your gelid left.

(Grand physician speaks:) Well, that makes sense.

(Chucklehead speaks:) Suppose that as soon as she takes the medicine you dose her with, you kill off the left side?

(Grand physician speaks:) That won't interfere with the matter of your caloric right.

(Chucklehead speaks:) But, I say—suppose we mess up and doctor both halves to death?

(Grand physician speaks:) That's no problem for anyone.

(Offstage interjects:) What awful bastards!

(Squire Cai speaks:) What kind of medicine are you going to dose her with?

(Grand physician speaks:) Well, the first dose will be the pill that snatches life from death and the second, the pellet that hastens immediate death.

(Squire Cai speaks:) Why are you giving her two kinds of medicine?

(Grand physician speaks:) You don't understand. I've got my methods. If she takes both at the same time—well, if you wanted the old lady to die, she couldn't; and if you wanted her to live, she couldn't do that either!

(Offstage interjects:) How right, you bastards.

(Chucklehead speaks:) Now old man Cai, do you want your old lady to get better?

(Squire Cai speaks:) Of course I want her to recover.

(Chucklehead speaks:) I have a prescription of otherworldly power, but it calls for an ingredient that you may not want to part with.

(Squire Cai speaks:) I want my wife better—I'll part with anything.

(Chucklehead speaks:) With a sharp scalpel we'll gouge out your eyes, and she can take them with a flagon of hot wine. Your wife'll be better then!

(Squire Cai speaks:) She may be better, but what about me?

(Chucklehead speaks:) You'll have to use a blind man's cane.

(Offstage interjects:) Quite right, you bastards. Bullshit!

(Squire Cai speaks:) Enough, enough. Stop your shouting match. Which one of you is really better? Let one of you treat her.

(Two clowns, alternately hitting each other with their medicine pouches, recite. Grand physician, hitting Chucklehead, speaks:) I can regulate the rheums of all four seasons;

(Chucklehead, hitting Grand physician, speaks:) I am skilled at curing diverse and sundry symptoms.

(Grand physician speaks:) I cure children's rickets and infant diarrhea;

(Chucklehead speaks:) I treat ladies pre- and post-natally.

(Grand physician speaks:) I have physicked the four limbs and the eight pulses;

(Chucklehead speaks:) I have physicked the five lassitudes and the seven kinds of wounds.

(Grand physician speaks:) I can physic left-hand palsy and right-hand paralysis;[5]

(Chucklehead speaks:) I can physic sudden exhaustion and chronic lassitude.

(Grand physician speaks:) I can physic painful numbness in both the legs;

(Chucklehead speaks:) I can physic utter exhaustion in the four limbs.

(Grand physician speaks:) I can cure bitter mouth and sour tongue;

(Chucklehead speaks:) I can cure belly bloats and abdominal distention.

(Grand physician speaks:) I can physic crippled legs and lamed thighs;

(Chucklehead speaks:) I can physic lack of speech and impaired hearing.

(Grand physician speaks:) I can physic bouts of chills and bouts of fever;

(Chucklehead speaks:) I can physic bouts of seizures and bouts of madness.

---

[5] We are reading *huan* (paralysis) for *huan* (suffering).

(Grand physician speaks:) I can cure bugs of the water and those of ether too;

(Chucklehead speaks:) I can cure aches of the head and those of the temples too.

(Grand physician speaks:) I can cure papillomas growing on the chest;

(Chucklehead speaks:) I can cure ulcers destroying the shoulders.

(Grand physician speaks:) The squire wants me to give the dose

(Chucklehead speaks:) And make the old lady lose what little life's left!

(Grand physician speaks:) Use a cup of cold water filled to the brim

(Chucklehead speaks:) And a full half-pint of castor beans.

(Grand physician speaks:) Have the old lady drink it down,

(Chucklehead speaks:) And it will make her stomach ache right away!

(Grand physician speaks:) It will immediately straighten out stomach and bowels;

(Chucklehead, acting out beating old lady with his medicine pouch, speaks:) We'll give this old mama the shits, and everything will come out clean in the end!

(Offstage interjects:) You fucking bastards, beat it!

(Two clowns are beaten off the stage.)

APPENDIX II

A Noontime Dream in the Garden Grove

This farce was written by Li Kaixian (1502–68), the famous scholar and dramatist of the Ming period.[1] The skit involves a dispute between Oriole, female lead of *The Story of the Western Wing,* and Li Wa, heroine of the Tang "Tale of Li Wa" by Bo Xingjian and of later dramas based on that story.[2] Li Wa is a courtesan in the Tang capital of Chang'an with whom a certain student, called Zheng Yuanhe in the plays, becomes infatuated. He is supposed to be studying for the imperial examinations but instead spends his bankroll on the young prostitute. After his funds are depleted, he is tricked by Li Wa and her madam and is left out in the cold to fend for himself. Eventually he is reduced to begging and is disowned by his father. Traveling the streets of the capital in a snowstorm, singing his beggar's song, he is recognized by the young woman. She takes him in, nurtures him back to health, helps him study for the examinations, and effects a reconciliation between him and his father. Despite Li Wa's desire to give him up, Zheng Yuanhe remains faithful to Li Wa after his success in the examinations and finally marries her. The farce introduces Autumn Cassia (Qiugui) as Li Wa's maid and refers to Squire Liu as one of the prostitute's earlier patrons. The other characters in the farce are already familiar from *The Story of the Western Wing.* One notable feature of the farce is that one of its songs (the one to the tune "Jisheng cao") interlards the text with titles of *qu* commonly found in drama.

A Noontime Dream in the Garden Grove

[Opening announcement:]

> May your heart remain unmoved in each cycle of rebirth;
> What can be the use of strife and competition?
> Brush away the idle worries of the dusty world
> And listen now to *A Noontime Dream in the Garden Grove.*

(Male lead, dressed as an old fisherman, enters and sings:)

---

[1] The text used in translation is that reproduced in Li Kaixian, *Li Kaixian ji,* 857–61. An earlier translation, upon which this is based, appears in Idema, "Yüan-pen as a Minor Form of Dramatic Literature," 70–73.

[2] On Li Wa, see Dudbridge, *The Tale of Li Wa;* on the plays, see Idema, "Shih Chün-pao's and Chu Yu-tun's *Ch'ü-chiang-ch'ih.*"

["Qingjiang yin"]
A fishing jetty is hard to buy, even if you have the money:
No fisherman will sell it lightly
My fishing boat lies athwart within the willow trees,
The fishing nets dry in the sun along the river's edge:
A fishing village has no room for any who scheme for fame and profit.

[Again:]
Last night the storm-swept billows on the Long River
Startled the old fisherman from his sleep.
When even one's angling platform is unsteady,
One should know to retire from official service.
Many times have I sighed long before my bed.

[He declaims:]

> I drop my line and vow not to heed the imperial summons;
>   Drifting over lake and sea, I seek my safety here.
> Swallowing and vomiting, fish and dragon frighten me not;
>   Rising and falling, gulls and egrets seek me out as friends.

I am a fisherman on the river: my name is unknown by my neighbors, my sense of time has no fixed point in season or year. I make my livelihood by fishing and spend my leisure time reading. I found the two tales of Oriole and Li Wa on my table, and when I read them carefully, the two seemed roughly the same. If it's impossible to tell who's the more noble, then how can one determine who's the lower of the two? One caused Zheng Yuanhe to sing his beggar's songs loudly in the market so that he did not clamber up the cassia tree at heaven's edge.[3] The other made Zhang Junrui send notes and deliver messages, hoping for a rendezvous, so that he pounded his bed and turned his pillow, suffering from love's longing. Well, it's noon and I'm worn out. I'll just take a short nap here in the garden grove.

(Oriole enters his dream and sings:)

["Jisheng cao"]
I have a mind to "welcome the transcendent traveler"
But have no intention of "dotting my crimson lips."
"The ground-scraping wind" has scraped so much that spring's blossoms
    disappear;
"The balcony-leaning person" has leaned so much that spring's light has ended.
"Trimming the silver lamp," she has trimmed so often that spring's finery is
    worn out;
"The powdered butterflies" all in vain busy themselves on spring's behalf.
"The yellow oriole" does not know how to transmit spring's messages.[4]

---

[3] I.e., he did not go to take the examinations.
[4] The phrases in quotation marks are in flact tune titles.

([Oriole] declaims:)

> My compassionate mother lodges temporarily at a Buddhist monastery;
> My stern father's coffin is housed for the time beneath the western wing.
>   Better to plot at the present to perch now on a single branch
> And not even talk about the thousand-room mansion of years gone by.

I hail from Boling and am Oriole Cui, daughter of Chancellor Cui. That fisherman said that I was just the same as Li Wa, so I came here to argue it out with her.

(Li Wa enters and sings:)

> ["Yan'er luo," carrying over into "Desheng ling"]
> Fine clothes were my fur and feather;
> Clever words were my snare and trap.
> How could he know about that hole into which men stumble?
> There's no defense against that net that covers heaven!

[(She speaks:)] Oh

> [(She sings:)]
> They wind up at a bridge downwind
> And bump up against a rule that offends heaven.
> Heartlessly I stir up floss in the wind
> And deceptively hide away the sword in the smile.
> It truly is all just an empty ruse
> And a pit of love-longing that can never be filled.
> With false feeling I weep sadly,
> But it cannot break apart their undying love.

([Li Wa] declaims:)

> My dancing waist is as supple as a willow's branch;
> My dancing garments are as light as a spider's web:
> Winds and strings in a moonlit night at a place where we sing and smile;
> Flowers and willows in the spring wind at the Serpentine Pond.

I hail from Chang'an and am Li Wa, daughter of Bandleader Li. That fisherman said that I was just the same as Oriole, so I came here to argue it out with her.

(Oriole speaks:) What makes you so much better than me?

(Li Wa speaks:) What makes me less than you?

(Oriole speaks:) You flirted with passing strangers at the Serpentine Pond.

(Li Wa speaks:) At Universal Salvation you set your eyes on roving monks.

(Oriole speaks:) In front of the grotto chamber you stroked your lover with glances.

(Li Wa speaks:) In the winding corridors your footprints relayed your heart's secrets.

(Oriole speaks:) You tricked Zheng Yuanhe into dropping his riding crop from his horse.

(Li Wa speaks:) You enticed Zhang Junrui to strum his zither under the moon.

(Oriole speaks:) You sent off the old and welcomed the new just for food and clothing.

(Li Wa speaks:) You forgot to sleep and gave up eating just because of love-longing.

(Oriole speaks:) You invited those good-for-nothing spongers to eat up all his wine and meat.

(Li Wa speaks:) You begged that winsome little matchmaker Crimson, promising her innumerable jewels and pins.

(Oriole speaks:) Zheng Yuanhe sang his beggar's song on the main street, panting for breath with a voice ever waning.

(Li Wa speaks:) Zhang Junrui suffered a devastating illness in his study, hovering between life and death.

(Oriole speaks:) My Zhang Junrui plucked the blossom and passed the examination.

(Li Wa speaks:) My Zheng Yuanhe also inscribed his name on the golden plaque.

(Oriole speaks:) How can you compare with me, who received the five-colored patent of nobility?

(Li Wa speaks:) I was also enfeoffed as a lady of the first rank!

(Oriole speaks:) You purchased good girls and made them base; by precedent you should have been divorced!

(Li Wa speaks:) You fucked first and married later; according to what's right, you two should have been whipped apart!

(Oriole speaks:) When your old madam found out Zheng Yuanhe was broke, you hid away in Frog Alley.

(Li Wa speaks:) When you asked Zhang Junrui to defeat the rebels, you jilted Zheng Heng.

(Oriole speaks:) In the poorhouse you can still see where Zheng Yuanhe was laid to sleep.

(Li Wa speaks:) In the western wing you can still see the scratches where Zhang Junrui jumped down.

(Oriole speaks:) For Magnate Liu, in the flash of an eye, you had not a drop of love left.

(Li Wa speaks:) For Yamen-rat Zheng, in the lowering of your head, you had a thousand plans.

(Oriole speaks:) For generations your family have been crackers of doors and priers of windows.

(Li Wa speaks:) For all three of you, it was just your nature to work your way through the monks.

(Oriole speaks:) I won't argue with you anymore; I'll call out Crimson to join in the fray!

(Li Wa speaks:) I've got my Autumn Cassia to repel the enemy!

(Crimson enters and speaks:) Just a maid who sets out the pisspot—what insolence.

(Autumn Cassia [enters and] speaks:) Just a lackey who watches the door—what impudence.

(Crimson speaks:) You'll never change your face as a double-dyed lackey who begs for wine and seeks money

(Autumn Cassia speaks:) You'll never alter your innards as an adulterous bitch who delivers letters and sends notes.

(Crimson speaks:) You've sewn a whole lifetime of rotten shoes.

(Autumn Cassia speaks:) You've worn half-a-life of tattered jacket.

(Crimson speaks:) You were Zheng Yuanhe's conspirator.

(Autumn Cassia speaks:) You were Zhang Junrui's accomplice.

(Crimson speaks:) You caught an occasional whiff of the aroma of powder and rouge.

(Autumn Cassia speaks:) Your whole body stinks of oil, salt, sauce, and vinegar.

(Crimson speaks:) You're a prop in the market of wind and moon.

(Autumn Cassia speaks:) You're the manager of the guild of flesh and skin!

(Crimson speaks:) If Zheng Yuanhe hadn't become an official, Li Wa would still be a whore and you, an apprentice slut!

(Autumn Cassia speaks:) If General Du had not repulsed the troops, Oriole Cui would have become a bandit's wife and you, a bandit's slave!

(They act out fighting. The fisherman wakes up and declaims:) How strange, how strange. I had just closed my eyes in this garden grove, when in a dream I saw two female immortals who each vaunted their skill and two girl servants who each defended their mistresses. It must be because I still have a mind so easily moved that my dreams are troubled. From now on I'm going to cut off any link to the vulgar world and strive to reach the dreamless state of the perfected man.

([He] declaims:)

The yellow millet that steamed so long is still not cooked;
A single sound of the village drum startles one awake.
All affairs in the end are but a dream,
So what is the use of floating fame vexing the poet's thoughts?

GLOSSARY

An Lushan 安祿山
Bai Pu 白樸
"Baitou yin" 白頭吟
Bai Wujiu 白無咎
Bao (judge) 包
"Beici chuanshou" 北詞傳授
beiqu 北曲
Bian Que 扁鵲
bianwen 變文
bimuyu 比目魚
Bo Juyi 白居易
Boling 博陵
Bowang 博望
Bo Xingjian 白行簡
Bu'erhan 布爾罕
buru gui 不如歸
Bu Xixiang yiqi 補西廂突棋
Buyi 不易
Cai Yong 蔡邕
caizi 才子
caizi jiaren 才子佳人
can 參
canhong 殘紅
Cao Cao 曹操
Cao Zhi 曹植
chaibai daozi 折白道字
Chang'an 長安
Chang'e 嫦娥
"Changhen ge" 長恨歌
Chao Fu 巢父
chengda 撐達
Cheng Hao 程顥

Cheng Yi 程頤
Chen Hong 陳鴻
Chen Hongshou 陳洪綬
Chen Xuanyou 陳玄佑
Chen Yinke 陳寅恪
chou 愁
choumou 綢繆
chu 齣
Chuaizhe qieyu xin touxiang xing 揣著
    竊玉心偷香性
chuanqi 傳奇
chuixiao 吹簫
chujia 出家
chujiazhe 出家者
chunfeng 春風
Chunqiu 春秋
"Chunye" 春夜
Chunyu Kun 淳于髡
ci 詞
congliang 從良
Cui Jue 崔珏
"Cuiniang yizhao" 崔娘遺照
Cui Peng 崔鵬
Cui Shipei 崔時佩
Cui Yingying 崔鶯鶯
Cui Zhang shiliu shi 崔張十六事
cun (inch) 寸
cun (rustic) 村
daban 打扮
Dade 大德
Dadu 大都
daiyue 待月

305

dan 旦

daofeng dianluan 倒鳳顛鸞

"Dengtu Zi haose fu" 登徒子好色賦

Dexin 德信

Dezong 德宗

dianbula 顛不剌

diandao 顛倒

diao 屌

"Dielianhua" 蝶戀花

Ding Wenya 丁文雅

diyi zhe 第一折

Dong Jieyuan 董解元

Dong Jun 東君

Dongqiang ji 東牆記

"Dou anchun" 鬥鵪鶉

Dou Tao 竇滔

"Duanzheng hao" 端正好

dudie 度牒

dujuan 杜鵑

Du Mu 都穆

Du Que 杜確

Du Weiniang 杜韋娘

Ehuang 娥皇

erben 二本

ermo 二末

Facong (Dharma Wit) 法聰

fan'an 反案

Fancha chuan 販茶船

Fan Li 范蠡

Fan Ye 范曄

Feihong 飛紅

fen 分

fengdie 蜂蝶

fenghua 風花

Feng Kui 馮魁

Fengliu 風流

fengyue 風月

fenxiang niyu 粉香泥玉

Fu Chai 夫差

Fuchun tang 富春堂

Furong ting 芙蓉亭

Fu Xi 伏羲

gan 干

"Gaotang fu" 高唐賦

Gaozong 高宗

geguan 個官

Gegu yaolun 格古要論

"Gejia zongping" 各家總評

Gongsun Hong 公孫弘

Gongyang zhuan 公羊傳

Gou Jian 勾踐

Guan Hanqing 關漢卿

Guanyin 觀音

guben 古本

guci 鼓詞

"Gufeng" 谷風

Guiyuan changgong 閨怨蠻宮

"Gu junzi xing" 古君子行

Gu Kaizhi 顧愷之

Guliang zhuan 穀梁傳

gun 棍

Guo Pu 郭璞

guzi ci 鼓子詞

Han (lady) 韓

Han Peng shiyi ji 韓朋十義記

Han Shou 韓壽

Han Wudi 漢武帝

Han Xin 韓信

haosha ren wu ganjing 好煞人無乾淨

Henei 河內

He Wenxiu Yuchai ji 何文秀玉釵記

He Yan 何晏

Hezhong 河中

Honglou meng 紅樓夢

Hongniang 紅娘

Hongzhi 弘治

"Hou Chibi fu" 後赤壁賦

Houqing lu 侯鯖錄

Hou Yi 后羿

hu 戶

huadan 花旦

Hua Guansuo chushen zhuan 花關索出
身傳

hualiu 花柳

Huai'an 槐安

huan (paralysis) 瘓

huan (suffering) 患

Huang'er 黃耳

Huang he nali zui xiong? Wuguo Hezhong
fu. 黃河那裡最雄無過河中府

Huang Yingguang 黃應光

Huanlang 歡郎

Huaqing 華清

Huashan 華山

huaxin 花心

Huilan ji 灰闌記

Huiming 惠明

huiyin zhi shu 誨淫之書

"Huizhen ji" 會真記

Hu Luobo 糊蘿蔔

Hu Tuchong 糊突蟲

Jia Baoyu 賈寶玉

Jia Chong 賈充

jiachu 假處

Jia Dao 賈島

Jiajing 嘉靖

jiamen 家門

jian 奸

jiangjun 將軍

jiangpan 將叛

Jiang sangzhen Cai Shun fengmu 降桑椹
蔡順奉母

Jiang Yan 江淹

Jiangzhou 江州

jiao 嬌

Jiao Hong ji 嬌紅記

"Jiao Hong zhuan" 嬌紅傳

Jiaoniang 嬌娘

jiaose 腳色

jiaren 佳人

jiayi 假意

Jia Yi 賈誼

jie 潔

jiehua 界畫

jieyuan 解元

Ji Junxiang 紀君祥

Jimu daxian 繼母大賢

Jin (dynasty) 金

jin (kerchief) 巾

jing 淨

Jing Chu suishi ji 荊楚歲時記

"Jingdi yin yinping" 井底引銀瓶

jinlian 金蓮

Jin Ping Mei 金瓶梅

Jin shi 金史

jinshi 進士

Jin shu 晉書

Jintai 金台

"Jiubian" (Nine Mutations) 九變

Jiubian (Nine Disputations) 九辯

jiuzhou 九州

"Ji zaju ming yongqing" 集雜劇名詠
情

juan 卷

Junrui 君瑞

Junshi 君實

junzi 君子

kezeng cai 可憎才

kong (empty) 空

kong (hole) 孔

"Kongque dongnan fei" 孔雀東南飛

Kong Sanzhuan (Professor Kong) 孔
三傳

kouhao 口號

kuaguan youjie 誇官遊街

kulong 窟窿

kun 坤

Kunqu 崑曲

lai 倈

Lanqiao yuchu ji 藍橋玉杵記

Laozi 老子

li (Chinese mile) 里

li (vulgar) 俚

Liang 梁

Liang Hong 梁鴻

Liangyuan 梁園

lianhuan tuhua 連環圖畫

lianli zhi 連理枝

"Liao'e" 蓼莪

Li Bo 李白

Lichun tang 麗春堂

Lienü zhuan 列女傳

Li Fang 李昉

Li Gonglin 李公麟

Li Gongzuo 李公左

Li He 李賀

"Lihun ji" 離魂記

Liji 禮記

Lin Daiyu 林黛玉

Ling Chucheng 淩初成

Ling Mengchu 淩濛初

Linqiong 臨邛

"Lisao" 離騷

Li Shen 李紳

Liu Bang 劉邦

Liu Bei 劉備

Liu Chen 劉晨

Liu Dui 劉兌

Liu Gongquan 柳公權

Liu Longtian 劉龍田

"Liushi zhuan" 柳氏傳

liusi (intent to keep one behind) 留思

liusi (willow threads) 柳絲

Liu Yu 劉裕

Liu Yue'e 劉月娥

Liu Zhiyuan 劉知遠

Liu Zongyuan 柳宗元

Li Wa 李娃

"Li Wa zhuan" 李娃傳

Li Xingdao 李行道

Li Yannian 李延年

Longcheng lu 龍城錄

Lu (mountain) 廬

Lu Cai 陸采

Lu Ji 陸機

Lu Jia 陸賈

Lu Kai 陸凱

"Luoshen fu" 洛神賦

"Luosiniang shawei" 絡絲娘煞尾

Luoyang 洛陽

Luoyang hua 洛陽花

Lu Yang 魯陽

lü 敂

Lü Mengzheng 呂蒙正

"Lü xing" 呂刑

Lüzhu 綠珠

ma 馬

Ma Shaopo 馬少波

Ma Siniang 馬四娘

Meng Guang 孟光

mian 面

Mingdi 明帝

minghe 鳴合

Minghuang 明皇

Min Qiji 閔齊伋

mo 末

Mouling 茂陵

mu 木

mudan 牡丹

Mudan ting 牡丹亭

Mudanting huanhun ji 牡丹亭還魂記

mugua 木瓜

muyu shu 木魚書

naitang 乃堂

Nanchang 南昌

Nanhao shihua 南濠詩話

"Nanke taishou zhuan" 南柯太守傳

Nanlü 南呂

nianhua 年畫

niao (nao) 嬲

ni xiuyao daili sajian 你休要呆裡撒奸

Nongyu 弄玉

nou 耨

nü 女

Nüying 女英

ousi (lotus root) 藕絲

ousi (loving thoughts of a happy couple)
偶思

pai 拍

Pan An 潘安

Pang Juan 龐涓

Panke Shuoren zengai dingben Xixiang ji
槃薖碩人增改定本西廂記

Pan Yue 潘岳

Pei Hang 裴航

peng 鵬

pianma 騙馬

pinghua 平話

pinxiao 品簫

Pipa ji 琵琶記

"Pipa xing" 琵琶行

poti 破題

Poyao ji 破窯記

Pudong 蒲東

Puzhou 蒲州

Qi 齊

qian 乾

Qiannü 倩女

Qiantang meng 錢塘夢

qiao (crafty) 喬

qiao (handsome) 俏

qiao moyang 喬模樣

Qiaosun 巧孫

Qiao Zhongchang 喬仲敞

qieyu touxiang 竊玉偷香

Qifeng guan 起鳳館

qima 騎馬

Qin 秦

Qinfeng Lou tishi 寢鳳樓題識

"Qinfu yin" 秦婦吟

"Qingdaifu zhang" 卿大夫章

qingguo 傾國

qinxuan 琴絃

qiu 秋

Qiugui 秋桂

Qiu Rucheng 丘汝乘

Qiu Ying 仇英

qu 曲

Quanxiang pinghua 全相評話

Quanxiang Sanguo zhi pinghua 全相三
國志評話

"Quanxue pian" 勸學篇

Qu Yuan 屈原

ren 人

ren qi ren 人其人

Ruan Zhao 阮肇

sang 喪

sangeng (third watch) 三更

sangeng (three kernels of rice) 三粳

sangeng zao 三更棗

Sang Weihan 桑維翰

sanqu 散曲

Sanyuan ji 三元記

Sengjia 僧伽

shajiao 傻角

Shangdiao 商調

"Shanghua shi" 賞花時

shang tu xia wen 上圖下文

shen 參

Shen Chun 申純

sheng 生

shenxian zhi tu 神仙之徒

Shen Yue 沈約
shi (corpse) 尸
shi (poetry) 詩
Shi Chong 石崇
shifen (ten grams) 十分
shifen (ten parts) 十分
Shiji 史記
Shijing 詩經
Shishuang 石霜
shixin 失信
Shu 蜀
Shuangdiao 雙調
Shuang Jian 雙漸
shuangtou hua 雙頭花
shuangwen 雙文
"Shuangwen xiaoxiang" 雙文小像
Shuihu zhuan 水滸傳
Shujing 書經
shuli 殊俚
Shun 舜
Shunzhi 順治
shuochang wenxue 說唱文學
Sima Xiangru 司馬相如
sinou 厮耨
Si of Bao 褒姒
Sizhou 泗州
Song Liaoren 宋了人
Song Meidong 宋梅洞
Song Yu 宋玉
suan 酸
suanji weng 酸虀甕
Su Hui 蘇蕙
Sui He 隋何
Sun Biao 孫彪
Sun Bin 孫臏
Sun Feihu (Flying Tiger) 孫飛虎
Sun Jichang 孫季昌
Sun Jing 孫敬
Sunzi bingfa 孫子兵法
Su Qin 蘇秦
Su Shi 蘇軾
Su Xiaoqing 蘇小卿
Taihang 太行
taiyang 太陽
tanci 彈詞
tang 燙
tanhua lang 探花郎
taoshu 套數
Tao Yuanming 陶淵明
Tian Han 田漢
tianlai da 天來大
"Tianshui ling" 甜水令
Tiantai 天台
tidu 剃度
timu 題目
tong 同
tongxin lou 同心縷
tu 圖
tuanyuan 團圓
waimo 外末
Wang Bocheng 王伯成
Wang Jiaoniang 王嬌娘
Wang Jie 王結
"Wang Lushan, qi'er" 望廬山，其二
Wang Xianzhi 王獻之
Wang Xizhi 王羲之
Wang Yizhong 王以中
Wang Zhi 王銍
Wanli 萬曆
Wei Sheng 尾生
Wenjun 文君
Wu 吳
Wu Changling 吳昌齡
Wu Daozi 吳道子
wuguan (five sensory organs) 五管
wuguan (high official) 五官
wuhe 烏合
Wuling 武陵

Wushan 巫山
"Wuti" 無題
wutong 梧桐
wuwu 戊午
Wu Zetian 武則天
Xiahou Dun 夏侯惇
Xiang (king) 襄
Xiang (river) 湘
Xiangfei 湘妃
Xiangjun 湘君
Xiang Nanzhou 項南洲
Xiang Yu 項羽
xianjun 縣君
Xianlü 仙呂
xiansheng 先生
Xianyang 咸陽
xianzhuang 線裝
xiao 肖
Xiao He 蕭何
Xiaojing 孝經
xiaoren 小人
Xiao Shi 蕭史
xiezi 楔子
Xihe 羲和
xing 星
xinyuan yima 心猿意馬
Xiong Longfeng 熊龍峰
Xi Shi 西施
Xiwangmu 西王母
xiwen 戲文
Xixiang tu 西廂圖
Xiyou ji 西遊記
xizi (daddy longlegs) 蟢子
xizi (happy one) 喜子
Xuande 宣德
Xuan Yuan 軒轅
Xuanzang 玄奘
Xuanzong 玄宗
Xue Baochai 薛寶釵

Xu Fenpeng 徐奮鵬
Xu Shifan 徐士範
Xu Wei 徐渭
Xu Yaozuo 許堯佐
Xu You 許由
ya (childish) 丫
ya (raven) 鴉
Yan 燕
yang 陽
Yang Guifei 楊貴妃
Yang Guozhong 楊國忠
Yang Ne 楊訥
Yang Xiong 揚雄
Yan Hui 顏回
Yan Junping 嚴君平
yanlü yingchou 燕侶鶯儔
Yan Zhenqing 顏真卿
Yao 堯
yaoying 搖影
yao yinzi 藥引子
yeyuan 業冤
yicui weihong 倚翠偎紅
yifu 姨夫
Yijing 易經
Yiyang 嶧陽
yin (natural force) 陰
yin (to hide) 窨
Yingbu 英布
Yingwu ji 鸚鵡記
"Yingwu qu" 鸚鵡曲
yingxin songjiu 迎新送舊
Yingying 鶯鶯
"Yingying benzhuan ge" 鶯鶯本傳歌
"Yingying yixiang" 鶯鶯遺像
"Yingying zhuan" 鶯鶯傳
Yinshan zhengyao 飲膳正要
Yongxi yuefu 雍熙樂府
You 幽
youwu 尤物

yuanben 院本

"Yuandao" 原道

yuanjia 冤家

Yuanlin wumeng 園林午夢

yu bao shen'en 欲報紳恩

yu bao zhi de 欲報之德

Yue (family) 岳

Yue (state) 越

Yuediao 越調

Yuefu qunzhu 樂府群珠

Yuhuan 玉環

yuhuan 玉環

yujing 玉莖

Yunying 雲英

yunyu 雲雨

yushui 魚水

yuti (jade body) 玉體

yuti (jade stem) 玉莖

Yu Tianxi 庾天錫

"Yu Xu Mian shu" 與徐勉書

Yu You 于祐

zaju 雜劇

zao (early) 早

zao (jujube) 棗

Zetian Huanghou 則天皇后

Zhang Chang 張敞

Zhang Dian 張顛

Zhang Gong 張珙

Zhang Qian 張騫

Zhang sheng 張生

Zhang Shenzhi 張紳之

Zhang Wo 張渥

Zhang Xu 張旭

Zhang Yu 張羽

Zhangzong 章宗

Zhan Shiyu 詹時兩

"Zhanyang" 瞻卬

Zhao Lingzhi 趙令時

Zhaoshi gu'er 趙氏孤兒

Zhao Tuo 趙佗

"Zhegui ling" 折桂令

Zheng 鄭

zhengdan 正旦

Zheng Dehui 鄭德輝

Zhenggong 正宮

Zheng Heng 鄭恆

zhengming 正名

zhengmo 正末

Zheng Yuanhe 鄭元和

"Zhengyue" 正月

zhenren 真人

Zhenzong 真宗

Zhonglü 中呂

Zhou Fang 周昉

Zhouqiao 州橋

zhuang 妝

zhuangyuan 狀元

Zhuangzi 莊子

Zhuge Liang 諸葛亮

zhugongdiao 諸宮調

Zhuo Wangsun 卓王孫

Zhuo Wenjun 卓文君

Zhu Xi 朱熹

zidi shu 子弟書

Zixia 子夏

Zou Meixiang 搊梅香

Zuozhuan 左傳

SELECTED BIBLIOGRAPHY

A Ying 阿英 [Qian Xingcun 錢杏邨]. *Zhongguo lianhuan tuhua shihua* 中國連環 圖畫史話 Beijing: Zhongguo gudian yishu chubanshe, 1957

Ban Gu 班固 *Hanshu* 漢書 20 vols. Beijing: Zhonghua shuju, 1962.

Bo Songnian 薄松年 "Tan Ming kanben *Xixiang ji* chatu" 談明刊本西廂記 插圖 *Meishu yanjiu* 美術研究, 1958, no. 4: 45–47

Cao Xueqin 曹雪芹 *Honglou meng bashihui jiaoben* 紅樓夢八十回校本 Collated by Yu Pingbo 俞平伯 and Wang Xishi 王熙時. Beijing: Renmin wenxue chubanshe, 1958.

———— *The Story of the Stone.* Vols. 1–3. Translated by David Hawkes. Harmondsworth: Penguin Books, 1973–80.

Carlitz, Katherine. *The Rhetoric of Chin p'ing mei.* Bloomington: Indiana University Press, 1986.

Ch'en, Li-li. "Outer and Inner Forms of *Chu-kung-tiao,* with Reference to *Pien-wen, Tz'u* and Vernacular Fiction." *Harvard Journal of Asiatic Studies* 32 (1972): 124–49.

———— "Some Background Information on the Development of *Chu-kung-tiao.*" *Harvard Journal of Asiatic Studies* 33 (1973): 224–37

Chen Shunlie 陳順烈 and Xu Dianxi 許佃璽, eds. *Wudai shixuan* 五代詩選 Shanghai: Shanghai guji chubanshe, 1988.

Chen Zhongfan 陳中凡. "Guanyu *Xixiang ji* de chuangzuo niandai ji qi zuozhe" 關於西廂記創作年代及其作者 *Jianghai xuekan* 江海學刊 2 (1960).

Clunas, Craig. "The West Chamber: A Literary Theme in Chinese Porcelain Decoration." *Transactions of the Oriental Ceramic Society* 46 (1981–82): 69–86.

Cong Jingwen 叢靜文 *Nanbei Xixiang ji bijiao* 南北西廂記比較 Taipei: Commercial Press, 1976.

Crump, J. I. *Chinese Theater in the Days of Kublai Khan.* Tucson: University of Arizona Press, 1980.

———— "The Conventions and Craft of Yüan Drama." *Journal of the American Oriental Society* 91 (1971): 14–29.

———— "The Elements of Yüan Opera." *Journal of Asian Studies* 17 (1958): 417–34.

———— *Songs from Xanadu.* Michigan Monographs in Chinese Studies. Ann Arbor: University of Michigan Center for Chinese Studies, 1983

———— "Yüan-pen, Yüan Drama's Rowdy Ancestor." *Literature East and West* 14 (1970): 473–90.

Dai Bufan 戴不凡 *Dai Bufan xiqu yanjiu lunwen ji* 戴不凡戲曲研究論文集
Hangzhou: Zhejiang renmin chubanshe, 1982.

——— *Lun Cui Yingying* 論崔鶯鶯 Shanghai: Shanghai wenyi chubanshe,
1963.

——— "Wang Shifu niandai xintan" 王實甫年代新探 In *Dai Bufan xiqu
yanjiu lunwen ji*, 62–81.

Delbanco, Dawn Ho. "*The Romance of the Western Chamber.* Min Qiji's Album in
Cologne." *Orientations* 14, no. 6(June 1983): 12–23.

Denda Akira 傳田章 "Manreki ban *Seishōki* no keitō to sono seikaku" 萬曆版
西廂記の系統とその性格 *Tōhōgaku* 東方學 31(1965): 93–106.

——— *Min kan Gen zatsugeki Seishōki mokuroku* 明刊元雜刻西廂記目錄.
Rev ed. Tokyo: Kyûko shoin, 1979.

Ding Ruming 丁如明, coll. *Kaiyuan Tianbao yishi shizhong* 開元天寶遺事十
種 Shanghai: Shanghai guji chubanshe, 1985.

Dittrich, Edith. *Hsi-hsiang chi, Chinesische Farbholzschnitte von Min Ch'i-chi, 1640*
Cologne: Museum für Ostasiatische Kunst der Stadt Köln, 1977

Dolby, William. *Eight Chinese Plays.* New York: Columbia University Press, 1978.

——— *A History of Chinese Drama.* London: Paul Elek, 1976.

Dong [Jieyuan] 董解元. *Dong Jieyuan Xixiang ji zhugongdiao* 董解元西廂記諸
宮調 Annotated by Ling Jingyan 凌景埏. Beijing: Renmin wenxue chubanshe, 1962.

——— *Master Tung's Western Chamber Romance (Tung Hsi-hsiang chu-kung-tiao).*
Translated by Li-li Ch'en. Cambridge: Cambridge University Press, 1976.

——— *Ming Jiajing ben Dong Jieyuan Xixiang ji* 明嘉靖本董解元西廂記
Shanghai: Zhonghua shuju, 1963.

——— *Het verhaal van de westerkamers in alle toonaarden* Translated by W L.
Idema. Amsterdam: Meulenhoff, 1984.

——— *Xixiang ji zhugongdiao zhuyi* 西廂記諸宮調注譯 Annotated by Zhu
Pingchu 朱平楚 Lanzhou: Gansu renmin chubanshe. 1982.

Dong, Lorraine. "The Creation and Life of Cui Yingying (c.803–1967)." Ph. D
diss., University of Washington, 1978.

——— "The Many Faces of Cui Yingying." *Historical Reflections* 8, no. 3(1981):
75–98.

Duan Miheng 段洣恆 "Xinbian jiaozheng Xixiang ji canye de faxian" 新編校正
西廂記殘頁的發現 *Xiqu yanjiu* 戲曲研究 7(1982): 261–68.

Duan Qiming 段啓明. *Xixiang lungao* 西廂論稿 Chengdu: Sichuan renmin
chubanshe, 1982.

Dudbridge, Glen. *The Hsi-yu chi: A Study of Antecedents to the Sixteenth-Century
Chinese Novel.* London: Cambridge University Press, 1970.

——— *The Tale of Li Wa: Study and Critical Edition of a Chinese Story from the
Ninth Century.* London: Ithaca Press, 1983.

Fitzgerald, Charles. *The Empress Wu.* Vancouver: University of British Columbia, 1968.

Fu Xihua 傅惜華, ed. *Xixiang ji shuochang ji* 西廂記說唱集 Shanghai: Shanghai chuban gongsi, 1955.

———— *Yuandai zaju quanmu* 元代雜劇全目. Beijing: Zuojia chubanshe, 1957

———— *Zhongguo gudian wenxue banhua xuanji* 中國古典文學版畫選集 2 vols. Shanghai: Renmin meishu chubanshe, 1981

Gao Ming 高明. *The Lute: Kao Ming's P'i-p'a chi.* Translated by Jean Mulligan. New York: Columbia University Press, 1980.

Goldblatt, Howard. "The *Hsi-yu-chi* Play· A Critical Look at Its Discovery, Authorship, and Content." *Asian Pacific Quarterly of Cultural and Social Affairs* 5, no. 1(1973): 31–46.

Guanzhong congshu 關中叢書 Compiled by Song Liankui 宋聯奎. N. p., 1934?–1936?

Guben xiqu congkan 古本戲曲叢刊. Ser. 1 and 4. Shanghai: Shangwu yinshuguan, 1954, 1958.

Guo Moruo 郭沫若 *Xixiang ji* 西廂記. Shanghai: Taidong tushuju, 1922.

Guo Xun 郭薰, comp. *Yongxi yuefu* 雍熙樂府 Reprint of 1617 woodblock ed. *Sibu congkan* ed.

Haenisch, Erich. "Review of Vincenz Hundhausen, *Das Westzimmer, Ein chinesisches Singspiel in deutscher Sprache.*" *Asia Major* 8(1932): 278–82.

Han Yu 韓愈. *Changli xiansheng wenji* 昌黎先生文集. *Sibu beiyao* ed.

Hanan, Patrick. *The Chinese Short Story, Studies in Dating, Authorship, and Composition.* Cambridge: Harvard University Press, 1973.

He Guichu 何貴初 *Yuandai xiqu lunzhu suoyin* 元代戲曲論著索引 Hong Kong: Privately printed, 1983.

Hervouet, Yves. *Le chapitre 117 du Cheki.* Paris: Presses universitaires de France, 1972.

———— *Un poète de cour sous les Han: Sseu-ma Siang-jou* Paris: Presses universitaires de France, 1964.

Hightower, James R. "Yüan Chen and 'The Story of Ying-ying.'" *Harvard Journal of Asiatic Studies* 33(1973): 90–123.

Hong Zengling 洪曾玲 *Xixiang ji* 西廂記 Illustrated by Wang Shuhui 王叔暉 Beijing: Renmin meishu chubanshe, 1958.

Hsia, C. T "A Critical Introduction." In Wang Shifu, *The Romance of the Western Chamber,* translated by S. I. Hsiung, xxi–xxxii.

Hsu Wen-chin. "Fictional Scenes on Chinese Transitional Porcelain (1620–ca. 1683) and Their Sources of Decoration." *Bulletin of the Museum of Far Eastern Antiquities* 58(1986): 1–146.

Hu Ji 胡忌. *Song Jin zaju kao* 宋金雜劇考 Beijing: Zhonghua shuju, 1958.

Hu Wenhuan 胡文煥, comp. *Qunyin leixuan* 群音類選. Reprint of 1595 woodblock ed. Beijing: Zhonghua shuju, 1980.

Huo Songlin 霍松林 *Xixiang ji jianshuo* 西廂記簡說. Beijing: Zuojia chubanshe, 1957.

——— *Xixiangshuping* 西廂述評 Xi'an: Shaanxi renmin wenxue chubanshe, 1982.

Idema, W. L. *The Dramatic Oeuvre of Chu Yu-tun (1379–1439)* Leiden: E. J. Brill, 1985.

——— "Performance and Construction of the *Chu-kung-tiao*" *Journal of Oriental Studies* 16(1978): 63–78.

——— "Satire in All-Keys-and-Modes." In Tillman, Hoyt C., and Stephen H. West, ed. *China Under Jurchen Rule*, 238–80

——— "Shih Chün-pao's and Chu Yu-tun's *Ch'ü-chiang-ch'ih* The Variety of Mode within Form." *T'oung Pao* 66(1980): 217–65.

——— "The Story of Ssu-ma Hsiang-ju and Cho Wen-chün in Vernacular Literature of the Yüan and Early Ming Dynasties." *T'oung Pao* 70(1984): 60–109.

——— "The *Wen-ching yüan-yang hui* and the *chia-men* of Yüan Ming ch'uan-ch'i" *T'oung Pao* 67(1981): 91–106.

——— "Yüan-pen as a Minor Form of Dramatic Literature in the Fifteenth and Sixteenth Centuries." *Chinese Literature, Essays, Articles, and Reviews* 6(1984): 53–75.

Idema, W. L., and Stephen H. West. *Chinese Theater 1100–1450: A Source Book.* Münchener ostasiatische Studien, no. 27. Wiesbaden: Franz Steiner Verlag, 1983.

Irwin, Vera Rushforth, ed. *Four Classical Asian Plays in Modern Translation* Baltimore: Penguin Books, 1972.

Itô Sôhei. "Formation of the *Chiao-hung chi*: Its Change and Dissemination." *Acta Asiatica* 32(1977): 73–95.

Jia Zhongming 賈仲明. *Tianyige lange xieben zhengxu Lugui bu* 天一閣藍格寫本正續錄鬼簿 Shanghai: Zhonghua shuju, 1960.

Jiang Xingyu 蔣星煜 "Cao Xueqin yong xiaoshuo xingshi xie de *Xixiang ji* pipingshi" 曹雪芹用小說形式寫的西廂記批評史. In his *Zhongguo xiqushi tanwei*, 124–261.

——— "'Dianbula' wei meiyu meinü kao" 顛不剌為美玉美女考 In his *Xixiang ji kaozheng*, 173–80.

——— "Guanyu Baoyu Daiyu suo du de shiliuchu ben *Xixiang ji*" 關於寶玉黛玉所讀的十六出本西廂記. In his *Ming kanben Xixiang ji yanjiu*, 210–14.

——— "He Bi yu *Ming He Bi jiaoben Bei Xixiang ji*" 何壁與明何壁校本北西廂記. In his *Mingkanben Xixiangji yanjiu* 163–83.

——— "Hongzhi ben *Xixiang ji* de tili yu 'Yue ke' wenti" 弘治本西廂記的體例與岳刻問題 In his *Mingkanben Xixiangji yanjiu* 26–37.

———— *Ming kanben Xixiang ji yanjiu* 明刊本西廂記研究. Beijing: Zhongguo xiju chubanshe, 1982.

———— "Ming kan *Xixiang ji* chatu yu zuozhe zalu" 明刊西廂記插圖與作者雜錄. *Xiqu yanjiu* 19(1985): 168–76.

———— "Wang Shifu *Xixiang ji* wancheng yu Jin dai shuo pouxi" 王實甫西廂記完成于金代說剖析. In his *Xixiang ji kaozheng*, 24–36.

———— "Xin faxian de zuizao de *Xixiang ji* canye" 新發現的最早的西廂記殘葉 In his *Ming kanben Xixiang ji yanjiu*, 20–25.

———— "*Xixiang ji* de riwen yiben" 西廂記的日文譯本 *Wenxue yichan* 文學遺產, 1982, no. 3: 32.

———— "*Xixiang ji* de zhuangtai kuijian yu *Honglou meng* di ershisan hui" 西廂記的妝台窺簡與紅樓夢第二十三回. In his *Ming kanben Xixiang ji yanjiu*, 293–96.

———— *Xixiang ji kaozheng* 西廂記考證 Shanghai: Shanghai guji chubanshe, 1988.

———— "Xu Fenpeng ji qi jiaoke zhi pingzhu ben *Xixiang ji* yu yanchu ben *Xixiang ji*" 徐奮鵬及其校刻之評注本西廂記與演出本西廂記. In his *Ming kanben Xixiang ji yanjiu*, 225–26.

———— *Zhongguo xiqushi gouchen* 中國戲曲史鉤沈   Henan Province: Zhongzhou shuhuashe, 1982.

———— *Zhongguo xiqushi tanwei* 中國戲曲史探微 Jinan: Qi Lu she, 1985.

Jin Shengtan 金聖嘆 *Guanhuatang diliu caizishu Xixiang ji* 貫華堂第六才子書西廂記. Annotated by Cao Fangren 曹方人 Nanjing: Jiangsu guji chubanshe, 1986.

———— *Guanhuatang diliu caizishu Xixiang ji*. Annotated by Fu Xiaohang 傅曉航. Lanzhou: Gansu renmin chubanshe, 1985.

———— *Jin Shengtan piben Xixiang ji* 金聖嘆批本西廂記 Collated by Zhang Guoguang 張國光. Shanghai: Shanghai guji chubanshe, 1986.

Johnson, Dale R. *Yuarn Music Dramas: Studies in Prosody and Structure and a Complete Catalogue of Northern Arias in the Dramatic Style* Michigan Papers in Chinese Studies, no. 40. Ann Arbor: University of Michigan Center for Chinese Studies, 1980.

Kao, Karl S. Y., ed. *Classical Chinese Tales of the Supernatural and Fantastic: Selections from the Third to the Tenth Century.* Bloomington: Indiana University Press, 1985.

Lau, Joseph, and Y W Ma, eds. *Traditional Chinese Stories: Themes and Variations* New York: Columbia University Press, 1978.

Legge, James. *Confucian Analects.* Hong Kong: Chinese University Press, 1960.

———— *The She King, or the Book of Poetry.* Hong Kong: Chinese University Press, 1960.

Lévy, André. "Un document unique sur un genre disparu de la littérature populaire: 'Le rendez-vous d'amour où les cous sont coupés.'" In his *Etudes* sur le conte et le roman chinois, 187–210.

———— Etudes sur le conte et le roman chinois. Paris: Ecole Française d'Extrême-Orient, 1971.

Levy, Howard. *Harem Favorites of an Illustrious Celestial.* Taipei: Zhongtai chubanshe, 1958.

Li Hanqiu 李漢秋 and Yuan Youfen 袁有芬, comps. *Guan Hanqing yanjiu ziliao* 關漢卿研究資料 Shanghai: Shanghai guji chubanshe, 1988.

Li Kaixian 李開先. *Li Kaixian ji* 李開先集. Edited by Lu Gong 路功 Beijing: Zhonghua shuju, 1959.

Li Rihua 李日華 *Xinke chuxiang yinzhu Li Rihua Nan Xixiang ji* 新刻出象音注李日華南西廂記 In *Guben xiqu congkan*, 1st ser., vol. 33.

Li Shangyin 李商隱 *Li Shangyin xuanji* 李商隱選集 Annotated by Zhou Zhenfu 周振甫 Shanghai: Shanghai guji chubanshe, 1985.

Li Xiusheng 李修生 "Jianguo yilai Yuan zaju yanjiu zhi huigu" 建國以來元雜劇研究之回顧 In his *Yuan zaju lunji*, 374–75.

———— *Yuan zaju lunji* 元雜劇論集 Tianjin: Baihua wenyi chubanshe, 1985.

Liang Tingnan 梁廷枏 *Quhua* 曲話 In *Zhongguo gudian xiqu lunzhu jicheng* 8:232–95.

Liu, James J. Y "*The Feng-yüeh chin-nang*, A Ming Collection of Yüan and Ming Plays and Lyrics Preserved in the Royal Library of San Lorenzo, Escorial, Spain." *Journal of Oriental Studies* 4(1957–58): 79–107.

———— *The Poetry of Li Shang-yin, Ninth-Century Baroque Chinese Poet* Chicago: University of Chicago Press, 1969.

Liu Shiheng 劉世珩, ed. *Nuanhongshi huike Xixiang ji* 暖紅室彙刻西廂記 Yangzhou: Guangling guji keyinshe, 1973

Liu Xin 劉歆. *Xijing zaji* 西京雜記. *Guanzhong congshu* ed.

Liu Yongji 劉永濟 *Songdai gewu juqu luyao* 宋代歌舞劇曲錄要 Shanghai: Gudian wenxue chubanshe, 1957

Liu Zhiyuan zhugongdiao 劉知遠諸宮調 Reprint of 14th-century woodblock ed. Beijing: Wenwu chubanshe, 1958.

[————.] *Ballad of the Hidden Dragon (Liu Chih-yüan chu-kung-tiao).* Translated by J. I. Crump and M. Doleželová-Velingerová. Oxford: Clarendon Press, 1971

[————.] "*Kôchû Ryu Chi-en shokyûchô*" 校注劉知遠諸宮調 Annotated by Uchida Michio 內田道夫 *Tôhoku Daigaku bungakubu kenkyû nempô* 道北大學文學部研究年報 14(1974): 240–319.

Lu Gong 路功 *Fangshu jianwen lu* 訪書見聞錄 Shanghai: Shanghai guji chubanshe, 1985.

———— "Mingchu kanben *Xixiang ji* canye" 明初刊本西廂記殘葉 In his *Fangshu jianwen lu*, 232–35.

Lugui bu xubian 錄鬼簿續編. In *Zhongguo gudian xiqu lunzhu jicheng*, 2:277–300.

McMahon, Keith. "Eroticism in Late Ming, Early Qing Fiction: The Beauteous

Realm and the Sexual Battlefield." *T'oung Pao* 73 (1987): 217–64.

Ming Chenghua shuochang cihua congkan 明成化說唱詞話叢刊   Shanghai: Shanghai guji chubanshe, 1967

Ming kan Xixiang ji quan tu 明刊本西廂記全圖. Illustrations reprinted from Wang Shifu, *Xinkan qimiao quanxiang zhushi Xixiang ji.* Shanghai: Renmin meishu chubanshe, 1983.

Mowangguan chaojiaoben gujin zaju 脈望館鈔校本古今雜劇   In *Guben xiqu congkan*, 4th ser., vols. 9–92.

Ning Zongyi 寧宗一, Lu Lin 陸林, and Tian Guimin 田桂民. *Yuan zaju yanjiu gaishu* 元雜劇研究概述. Tianjin: Tianjin jiaoyu chubanshe, Xinhua shudian, 1987.

Ouyang Xiu 歐陽修 "Luoyang mudanji" 洛陽牡丹記 In *Ouyang Wenzhong quanji* 歐陽文忠全集, 72.1a–7a. *Sibu beiyao* ed.

Palandri, Angela Jung. *Yüan Chen.* Twayne World Authors Series. Boston: Twayne Publishers, 1977.

Perng, Ching-Hsi. *Double Jeopardy· A Critique of Seven Yüan Courtroom Dramas* Michigan Papers in Chinese Studies, no. 35. Ann Arbor: University of Michigan Center for Chinese Studies, 1978.

Qian Nanyang 錢南揚. *Song Yuan xiwen jiyi* 宋元戲文輯佚 Shanghai: Gudian wenxue chubanshe, 1956.

Schafer, Edward H. *The Divine Woman: Dragon Ladies and Rain Maidens* Berkeley: University of California Press, 1973

Shen Defu 沈德符 *Guqu zayan* 顧曲雜言 In *Zhongguo gudian xiqu lunzhu jicheng*, 4:195–228.

Shih, Chung-wen. *The Golden Age of Chinese Drama: Yüan Tsa-chü* Princeton: Princeton University Press, 1976.

Sibu beiyao 四部備要 2405 vols. Shanghai: Zhonghua shuju, 1934–36.

Sibu congkan 四部叢刊 3025 vols. Shanghai: Shangwu yinshuguan, 1937–38.

Sima Qian 司馬遷 *Records of the Grand Historian of China* Translated by Burton Watson. 2 vols. New York: Columbia University Press, 1961

———— *Shiji* 史記 10 vols. Beijing: Zhonghua shuju, 1959.

Su Xing 蘇興 "Wang Shifu zaju*Xixiang ji* fanfengjian zhuti de fazhan de shenhua: zaju *Xixiang ji* yu zhugongdiao de bijiao yanjiu" 王實甫雜西廂記劇反封建主體的發展的深化雜劇西廂記與諸宮調的比較研究 *Shehui kexue zhanxian* 社會科學戰線 7(1980): 241–49.

Sui Shusen 隋樹森 *Yongxi yuefu quwen zuozhe kao* 雍熙樂府曲文作者考 Beijing: Shumu wenxian chubanshe, 1985.

————, ed. *Quan Yuan sanqu* 全元散曲. 2 vols. Beijing: Zhonghua shuju, 1964.

————, ed. *Yuanqu xuan waibian* 元曲選外編. 2 vols. Beijing: Zhonghua shuju, 1959.

Sun Kaidi 孫楷第 *Cangzhou ji* 滄州集 Beijing: Zhonghua shuju, 1965.

——— "Ji *Yongxi yuefu* ben *Xixiang ji* quwen xu" 輯雍熙樂府本西廂記曲文序 In his *Cangzhou ji*, 2:406–24.

——— *Yuanqu jia kaolüe* 元曲家考略 Shanghai: Shanghai guji chubanshe, 1981.

——— "Yuanqu xinkao" 元曲新考 In his *Cangzhouji*, 1:317–21.

Sun Xun 孫遜 *Dong Xixiang he Wang Xixiang* 董西廂和王西廂 Shanghai: Shanghai guji chubanshe, 1983

Taiping guangji 太平廣記 10 vols. Beijing: Zhonghua shuju, 1958.

Tan Zhengbi 譚正璧 *Yuanqu liudajia lüezhuan* 元曲六大家略傳 Shanghai: Shanghai wenyi chubanshe, 1955.

Tan Zhengbi and Tan Xun 譚尋 "Guan Hanqing zuo huo xuzuo *Xixiang ji* shuo suyuan" 關漢卿作或續作西廂記說溯源 In their *Quhai lice*, 1–7

——— "Wang Shifu yiwai ershiqi *Xixiang* kao" 王實甫以外二十七西廂考. In their *Quhai lice*, 8–30.

———, eds. *Quhai lice* 曲海蠡冊 Hangzhou: Zhejiang renmin chubanshe, 1983.

Tanaka Kenji 田中謙二 "Bungaku toshite no *Tô Seishô*" 文學としての董西廂 Parts 1–2. *Chûgoku bungakuhô* 中國文學報 1(1954): 93–112; 2(1955): 75–100.

——— "Imbun kô." *Nippon Chûgoku gakkaihô* 日本中國學會報 22(1968): 169–91.

——— "Gendai sankyoku no kenkyû" 元代散曲の研究. *Tôhôgakuhô* 東方學報 40(1969): 1–114.

——— "*Seishôki* shohon no shimbyôsei" 西廂記諸本の信憑性 *Nippon Chûgokugakkaihô* 日本中國學會報 2(1950): 89–104.

——— "Zatsugeki *Seishôki* ni okeru jimbutsu seikaku no kyôchô" 雜劇西廂記における人物性格の強調. *Tôhôgaku* 東方學 22(1961): 67–83.

——— "Zatsugeki *Seishôki* no nangekika" 雜劇西廂記の南戲化. *Tôhôgakuhô* 東方學報 36(1964): 543–75.

Tang Xianzu 湯顯祖 *The Peony Pavilion (Mudan Ting)*. Translated by Cyril Birch. Bloomington: Indiana University Press, 1980.

Tao Junqi 陶君起, comp. *Jingju jumu chutan* 京劇劇目初探. Beijing: Zhongguo xiqu chubanshe, 1963.

Tillman, Hoyt C. and Stephen H. West, ed. *China Under Jurchen Rule*. Albany: State University of New York Press, 1994.

Wang Bomin 王伯敏. *Zhongguo banhua shi* 中國版畫史 Shanghai: Renmin meishu chubanshe, 1961

Wang, Chiu-kuei. "Lü Meng-cheng in Yüan and Ming Drama." *Monumenta Serica* 26(1984–85): 303–408.

Wang, Elizabeth Te-chen. *Ladies of the Tang*. Taipei: Mei Ya Publications, 1973.

Wang Guowei 王國維 *Qulu* 曲錄. Taipei: Yiwen yinshuguan, 1964.

Wang Jilie 王季烈, ed. *Guben Yuan Ming zaju* 孤本元明雜劇. 14 vols. Beijing: Zhongguo xiju chubanshe, 1958.

Wang Jisi 王季思. "Cong *Fengqiuhuang* dao *Xixiang ji*" 從鳳求凰到西廂記. In his *Yulunxuan qulun xinbian*, 16–38.

——— *Cong "Yingying zhuan" dao Xixiang ji* 從鶯鶯傳到西廂記 Shanghai: Shanghai gudian wenxue chubanshe, 1955.

——— "Guanyu *Xixiang ji* zuozhe de wenti" 關於西廂記作者的問題. In his *Yulunxuan qulun*, 135–44.

——— "Guanyu *Xixiang ji* zuozhe wenti de jinyibu tantao" 關於西廂記作者問題的進一步探討 In his *Yulunxuan qulun*, 145–55.

——— "*Xixiang ji* xushuo" 西廂記續說 In his *Yulunxuan qulun*, 20–37

——— *Yulunxuan qulun* 玉輪軒曲論. Beijing: Zhongguo xiqu chubanshe, Xinhua shudian, 1980.

——— *Yulunxuan qulun xinbian* 玉輪軒曲論新編. Beijing: Zhonghua shuju, 1983.

Wang, John Ching-yu. *Chin Sheng-t'an*. Twayne World Authors Series. New York: Twayne, 1972.

Wang Lina 王麗娜. "*Xixiang ji* de waiwen yiben he Man Meng wen yiben" 西廂記的外文譯本和滿蒙文譯本 *Wenxue yichan* 文學遺產, 1981, no. 3: 148–54.

Wang Liqi 王利器, comp. *Yuan Ming Qing sandai jinhui xiaoshuo xiqu shiliao* 元明清三代禁燬小說戲曲史料 Rev ed. Shanghai: Shanghai guji chubanshe, 1981

Wang Mengou 王夢鷗. *Tangren xiaoshuo yanjiu* 唐人小說研究. Vol. 2. Taipei: Yiwen yinshuguan, 1973

Wang Renyu 王仁裕 *Kaiyuan Tianbao yishi* 開元天寶遺事 In *Kaiyuan Tianbao yishi shizhong*, edited by Ding Ruming, 45–117

Wang Shifu 王實甫. *Huitu xin jiaozhu guben Xixiang ji* 繪圖新校注古本西廂記. Annotated and collated by Wang Jide 王驥德 Reprint of 1614 woodblock ed. Beijing: Fujian shushe, Donglaige shudian, 1927

——— *Jiping jiaozhu Xixiang ji* 集評校注西廂記. Annotated by Wang Jisi 王季思 and compiled by Zhang Renhe 張人和 Shanghai: Shanghai guji chubanshe, 1987

——— *Ming He Bi jiaoben Bei Xixiang ji* 明何壁校本北西廂記. Collated by He Bi 何壁. Reprint of 1616 woodblock ed. Shanghai: Shanghai guji shudian, 1961.

——— *The Moon and the Zither. The Story of the Western Wing.* Translated by Stephen H. West and Wilt L. Idema. Berkeley and Los Angeles: University of California Press, 1991.

——— *The Romance of the Western Chamber.* Translated by S. I. Hsiung, with a critical introduction by C. T. Hsia. New York: Columbia University Press, 1968.

————— *Si-siang-ki: ou, L'histoire du pavillon d'occident, comédie en seize actes* Translated by Stanislas Julien. Geneva: H. Georg.–Th. Mueller, 1872–80.

————— *The West Chamber, A Medieval Drama* Translated by Henry H. Hart. Stanford: Stanford University Press, 1936.

————— *The West Chamber (Hsi-hsiang chi).* Rendered into English verse by Henry W Wells. In *Four Classical Asian Plays in Modern Translation,* edited by Vera Rushforth Irwin, 95–230.

————— *Das Westzimmer, Ein chinesisches Singspiel aus dem dreizehnten Jahrhundert* Translated by Vincenz Hundhausen. Eisenach: Erich Roth Verlag, 1926.

————— *Xinkan qimiao quanxiang zhushi Xixiang ji* 新刊奇妙全相註釋西廂記. Reprint of 1498 woodblock ed. In *Guben xiqu congkan,* 1st ser., vols. 1–2.

————— *Xinkan qimiao quanxiang zhushi Xixiang ji* 新刊奇妙全相註釋西廂記. Reprint of 1498 woodblock ed. Shanghai: Shangwu yinshuguan, 1955. (Title on inside leaf: *Xinkan dazi kuiben quanxiang canzeng qimiao zhushi Xixiang ji* 新刊大字魁本全相參增奇妙註釋西廂記.)

————— *Xixiang ji* 西廂記. Annotated by Wu Xiaoling 吳曉鈴 Beijing: Zuojia chubanshe, 1954.

————— *Xixiang ji tongsu zhushi* 西廂記通俗注釋 Kunming: Yunnan renmin chubanshe, 1983.

————— *Xixiang ji xinzhu* 西廂記新注 Annotated by Zhang Yanjin 張燕瑾 and Mi Songyi 彌松頤 Nanchang: Jiangxi renmin chubanshe, 1980.

————— *Yuanben tiping Xixiang ji* 元本題評西廂記. Compiled by Liu Longtian 劉龍田 In *Guben xiqu congkan,* 1st ser., vols. 3–4.

Wang Shizhen 王世貞　*Quzao* 曲藻 In *Zhongguo gudian xiqu lunzhu jicheng,* 4:15–42.

Wang Yisheng 王藝生. *Yuju chuantong jumu huishi* 豫劇傳統劇目匯釋 Zhengzhou: Huanghe wenyi chubanshe, 1986.

Wang Zhuo 王灼. *Biji manzhi* 碧雞漫志. In *Zhongguo gudian xiqu lunzhu jicheng,* 1:91–152.

Wei Zhuang 韋莊　*Wei Zhuang ji jiaozhu* 韋莊集校注 Annotated by Li Yi 李誼. [Chengdu]: Sichuansheng shehui kexueyuan, 1986.

West, Stephen H. "Jurchen Elements in the Northern Drama *Hu-t'ou-p'ai.*" *T'oung Pao* 63 (1977): 273–95.

————— *Vaudeville and Narrative: Aspects of Chin Theater (1115–1234).* Münchener ostasiatische Studien, no. 20. Wiesbaden: Franz Steiner Verlag, 1977

Wu Guoqin 吳國欽　*Xixiang ji yishu tan* 西廂記藝術談　Guangzhou: Guangdong renmin wenxue chubanshe, 1983.

Wu Mei 吳梅, comp. *Shemotashi qucong* 奢摩他室曲叢 Ser. 2. Shanghai: Shangwu yinshuguan, 1928.

Xu Fuming 徐扶明. *Yuandai zaju yishu* 元代雜劇藝術 Shanghai: Shanghai wenyi chubanshe, 1981

Xu Jian 徐堅 *Chuxue ji* 初學記. 2 vols. Beijing: Zhonghua shuju, 1962.

Xu Qinjun 徐沁君, ed. *Xinjiao Yuankan zaju sanshizhong* 新校元刊雜劇三十種 2 vols. Beijing: Zhonghua shuju, 1980.

Xu Wenzhao 徐文昭 *Fengyue jinnang* 風月錦囊 Reprint of 1553 woodblock. In *Shanben xiqu congkan* 善本戲曲叢刊, edited by Wang Qiugui 王秋桂. Taipei: Xuesheng shuju, 1987.

Yan Han 彦涵 "Tan *Xixiang ji* muke chatu" 談西廂記木刻插圖 *Meishu* 美術, 1954, no. 6: 12–15.

Yang Yinliu 楊蔭瀏 and Cao Anhe 曹安和, eds. *Xixiang ji sizhong yuepu xuanqu* 西廂記四種樂譜選曲 Beijing: Yinyue chubanshe, 1962.

Yang Zhenxiong 楊振雄 *Xixiang ji* 西廂記 Shanghai: Shanghai wenyi chubanshe, 1983.

Yannan Zhi'an 燕南芝菴 [pseud.]. *Changlun* 唱論 In *Zhongguo gudian xiqu lunzhu jicheng*, 1:153–66.

Yao Shuyi 么書儀. "Yuanqu jia cuotan" 元曲家脞談 *Xiqu yanjiu* 戲曲研究 18(1986): 254–58.

Yuan Zhen 元稹 "Yingying zhuan 鶯鶯傳 " In *Taiping guangji*, 10: 4012–17

Yunshui Daoren 雲水道人 [pseud.]. *Lan Qiao yuchu ji* 藍橋玉杵記 In *Guben xiqu congkan*, 1st ser., vol. 107.

Zang Jinshu 臧晉叔, comp. *Yuanqu xuan* 元曲選 4 vols. Beijing: Zhonghua shuju, 1959.

Zeng Yongyi 曾永義 *Shuo suwenxue* 說俗文學 Taipei: Lianjing chuban shiye gongsi, 1980.

——— *Shuo xiqu* 說戲曲 Taipei: Lianjing chuban shiye gongsi, 1976.

——— "Yuan zaju fen zhe de wenti" 元雜劇分折的問題 In his *Shuo xiqu*, 71–74.

——— "Zhongguo gudian xiju jiaose gaishuo" 中國古典戲劇角色概說 In his *Shuo suwenxue*, 233–96.

Zhang Dihua 張棣華 *Shanben juqu jingyan lu* 善本劇曲經眼錄 Taipei: Wenshizhe chubanshe, 1976.

Zhang Hua 張華, attributed author. *Bowu zhi* 博物志 *Sibu beiyao* ed.

Zhang Renhe 張人和 "*Xixiang ji* de banben yu tizhi" 西廂記的版本與體制. In Wang Shifu, *Jiping jiaozhu Xixiang ji*, 345–47

——— "*Xixiang ji* lunzha" 西廂記論札. In *Gudai xiqu luncong*, ed. Zhongshan daxue xuebao, 7–25.

Zhang Shibin 張世彬, ed. *Shen Yuan Bei Xixiang xiansuo pu jianpu* 沈遠北西廂絃索譜簡譜 Hong Kong: Zhongwen daxue, 1981

Zhang Yanjin 張燕瑾 *Xixiang ji jianshuo* 西廂記簡說 Tianjin: Baihua wenyi chubanshe, 1986.

Zhao Jingshen 趙景紳 "Yuanqu de erben" 元曲的二本 In his *Zhongguo xiqu chukao*, 87–88.

———— *Yuanren zaju gouchen* 元人雜劇鉤沈   Shanghai: Shanghai gudian wenxue chubanshe, 1956.

———— *Zhongguo xiqu chukao* 中國戲曲初考 Luoyang: Zhongzhou shuhuashe, 1983.

Zheng Qian 鄭騫 *Beiqu taoshi huilu xiangjie* 北曲套式彙錄詳解   Taipei: Yiwen yinshuguan, 1973.

———— *Beiqu xinpu* 北曲新譜 Taipei: Yiwen yinshuguan, 1973.

———— "*Xixiang ji* banben lu" 西廂記版本錄   *Youshi xuezhi* 幼獅學誌 11, no. 4(1973): 32–44.

———— "*Xixiang ji* banben lu buyi" 西廂記版本錄補遺. *Youshi yuekan* 幼獅月刊, 1977, no.5: 47–88.

———— "*Xixiang ji* zuozhe xinkao" 西廂記作者新考   *Youshi xuezhi* 11, no.4(1973): 1–44.

————, ed. *Jiaoding Yuankan zaju sanshizhong* 校訂元刊雜劇三十種 Taipei: Shijie shuju, 1962.

Zheng Zhenduo 鄭振鐸 "Lun Yuanren suoxie shangren, shizi, jinü jiande sanjiao lian'aiju" 元論元人所寫商人士子伎女間的三角戀愛劇. In his *Zhongguo wenxue yanjiu*, 2:535–58.

———— "Song Jin Yuan zhugongdiao kao" 宋金元諸宮調考 In his *Zhongguo wenxue yanjiu*, 3:843–970.

———— "*Xixiang ji* de benlai mianmu shi zenyangde" 西廂記的本來面目是怎樣的 In his *Zhongguo wenxue yanjiu*, 2:596–612.

———— *Zhongguo banhua shi tulu* 中國版畫史圖錄 20 vols. Shanghai: Zhongguo banhuashi she, 1940–42.

———— *Zhongguo wenxue yanjiu* 中國文學研究 3 vols. Beijing: Zuojia chubanshe, 1957.

Zhong Sicheng 鍾嗣成 *Lugui bu* 錄鬼簿 In *Zhongguo gudian xiqu lunzhu jicheng*, 2:85–274.

Zhongguo gudian xiqu lunzhu jicheng 中國戲曲論著集成   10 vols. Beijing: Zhongguo xiju chubanshe, 1959.

Zhongshan daxue xuebao 中山大學學報, ed. *Gudai xiqu luncong* 古代戲曲論叢. Zhongshan daxue xuebao zhexue shehui kexue luncong 中山大學學報哲學社會科學論叢 Guangzhou: Zhongshan daxue xuebao, 1983.

Zhou Deqing 周德清 *Zhongyuan yinyun* 中原音韻. In *Zhongguo gudian xiqu lunzhu jicheng*, 1:167–283.

Zhou Miaozhong 周妙中 "*Xixiang ji* zaju zuozhe zhiyi" 西廂記雜劇作者質疑. *Wenxue yichan zengkan* 文學遺產增刊, no. 5: 264–77 Beijing: Zuojia chubanshe, 1957

Zhou Tian 周天 *Xixiang ji fenxi* 西廂記分析   Shanghai: Shanghai gudian wenxue chubanshe, 1956.

Zhou Xugeng 周續賡 "Tan *Xinbian jiaozheng Xixiang ji* canye de jiazhi" 談新編校正西廂記殘葉的價值 *Wenxue yichan* 文學遺産, 1984, no. 1: 108–14.

Zhou Yibai 周貽白 *Zhongguo juchang shi* 中國劇場史 Shanghai: Shangwu yinshuguan, 1936.

———, ed. *Mingren zaju xuan* 明人雜劇選. Beijing: Renmin wenxue chubanshe, 1958.

Zhu Pingchu 朱平楚, comp. *Quan zhugongdiao* 全諸宮調. Lanzhou: Gansu renmin chubanshe, 1987.

Zhu Quan 朱勸 *Taihe zhengyin pu* 太和正音譜 In *Zhongguo gudian xiqu lunzhu jicheng*, 3:1–232.

Zhu Youdun 朱有燉 "Baihezi yong qiujing youyin" 白鶴子詠秋景有引. In his *Chengzhai yuefu*, 1.11b–13a.

——— *Chengzhai yuefu* 誠齋樂府 In *Yinhong yisuo kequ* 飲虹簃所刻曲, compiled by Lu Qian 盧前 Taipei: Yiwen shuju, 1961.

——— *Xinbian Liu Panchun shouzhi Xiangnang yuan* 新編劉盼春守志香囊怨 15th-century woodblock ed.

——— *Xinbian Qinghexian Jimu daxian* 新編清河縣繼母大賢 15th-century woodblock ed.

——— "Zuixiang ci ershipian" 醉鄉詞二十篇 In his *Chengzhai yuefu*, 1.1a–8b.

INDEX